THE
SUPERMAJORITY

How the
Supreme Court
Divided America

MICHAEL WALDMAN

SIMON & SCHUSTER

New York   London   Toronto   Sydney   New Delhi

Simon & Schuster
1230 Avenue of the Americas
New York, NY 10020

First Simon & Schuster hardcover edition June 2023

SIMON & SCHUSTER and colophon are registered
trademarks of Simon & Schuster, Inc.

For information about special discounts for bulk purchases,
please contact Simon & Schuster Special Sales at
1-866-506-1949 or business@simonandschuster.com.

The Simon & Schuster Speakers Bureau can bring authors
to your live event. For more information or to book an
event, contact the Simon & Schuster Speakers Bureau at
1-866-248-3049 or visit our website at www.simonspeakers.com.

Interior design by Lewelin Polanco

Manufactured in the United States of America

1   3   5   7   9   10   8   6   4   2

Library of Congress Cataloging-in-Publication Data is available.

ISBN 978-1-6680-0606-1
ISBN 978-1-6680-0608-5 (ebook)

For Ben, Susannah, and Josh

Contents

THE
SUPERMAJORITY

INTRODUCTION

T HE U.S. SUPREME COURT PLAYS A singular role. In no other
major country do judges—independent, esteemed, serving for
life—wield so much power. Nowhere else do people wait breathlessly
each June for new rulings from nine unelected individuals. It is an
anomaly in our democratic system. Its members have no innate authority. The Court has this power because we choose to believe in its status
as above and beyond politics.

Over three days in June 2022, the Supreme Court changed America.

It overturned *Roe v. Wade*, repealing the protection for abortion
rights in place for American women for a half century, and putting at
risk all other privacy rights. It radically loosened curbs on guns, amid
an epidemic of mass shootings. And it hobbled the ability of government agencies to protect public health and safety and stop climate
change when the topic is a "major question." The Court crammed decades of social change into three days.

This book tells the story of those cases, the year that built up to that
moment, and the decades of organized politics that led us to this point
of judicial extremism and overreach.

For years the Supreme Court tilted right, but barely, with a five-to-four
majority. Now a supermajority of six conservative justices is in control.
Numbers matter. For convenience we name eras of American law after
the chief justice: the Warren Court, or the Roberts Court, led by the canny
chief, with one eye always on institutional legitimacy as he steered it to
the right. John Roberts is still chief justice, but it is no longer his Court.

Clarence Thomas, for decades an outlier, now dominates. Roberts holds the gavel, but Thomas holds the power. Thomas derides the idea of following precedent as "a mantra when we don't want to think." He is joined by Samuel Alito, a voice of reaction, inexplicably angry, fulminating like a cable news pundit. Neil Gorsuch, an intellectual carrying on a family crusade for a sharply limited federal government. Brett Kavanaugh and Amy Coney Barrett, each stepping carefully, but usually marching with the other conservatives.

Then there were the three liberals. Stephen Breyer: deflated, a technocrat unable to stop or even respond to the shouting ideologues around him. Mid-term, he announced he would resign. Elena Kagan, a sharp-witted would-be dealmaker who found herself instead called on to defend democracy's first principles. Sonia Sotomayor, barely concealing her magisterial anger. After Ketanji Brown Jackson joined Kagan and Sotomayor, the country now saw a remarkable tableau: the three liberal justices, likely three repeat dissenters, are all women—one Black, one Latina, and one Jewish.

Those three days in June capped one of the most consequential terms in the country's history. It was also one of the noisiest. Usually the Supreme Court strives to wrap itself in majesty and mystery. Not this year. Instead, it careened toward the term's end amid raucous controversy. The *Dobbs* decision overturning *Roe v. Wade* leaked to the media. Ginni Thomas, the wife of Justice Thomas, was revealed to be enmeshed in the effort to block the peaceful presidential transfer of power, a drive that culminated in the insurrection at the Capitol. Protesters picketed the justices' homes, one of whom barely escaped assassination. And the members began to attack each other in public. An earlier observer once likened the Court to nine scorpions in a bottle. Now the scorpions were crawling all over the table.

The Supreme Court has always been an intensely political institution. At times we want it to protect rights against the impulses of the majority. But increasingly it represents entrenched power for a minority faction. Democrats won the popular vote in seven of the last eight presidential elections, the longest winning streak in American history. But Republican presidents chose six of the nine justices. Five of them were picked by a president who took office after losing the popular vote. Here's another fact: Over the past half century, party control of the

White House has changed hands seven times. But Republican appointees have controlled the U.S. Supreme Court since 1970. In fact, the last Democrat to be appointed chief justice took office in *1946*.

Today's hard right supermajority was installed by a fierce and effective political drive waged over decades. Senator Mitch McConnell called it his "judges project," and bragged that ensuring that President Barack Obama could not fill a Supreme Court seat for a year was one of his "proudest moments." The new Court's first big moves on abortion, guns, and the interests of fossil fuel companies precisely mirrored key goals of the Republican coalition.

The new supermajority has radically shifted the rationale for how rulings are made. The justices now claim to be guided by "originalism." The Constitution's meaning, they ruled, is "fixed." Their job is to go back in time to ask the Founders what Americans should do today. This grasp of history is as ritualized, and as unrealistic, as the costumed characters at a Medieval Times theme restaurant.

In *Bruen*, which ransacked the past searching for supportive evidence on the Second Amendment, the originalism was fake. In *Dobbs*, it was terrifying: a declaration that the Court would only recognize rights "deeply rooted in this Nation's history and tradition," thus only those recognized by the white men of the 1700s and 1800s. In other cases, the justices wield a hyper-literal "textualism," squinting at dictionaries rather than asking what the purpose and impact of a law would be. Readers of the children's book *Amelia Bedelia* would find it familiar.

Putting it mildly, this is not how the Supreme Court operated before. Ironically there is no "history and tradition" of originalism. At their best justices understood they had to interpret a broad and often vague charter for an ever-changing country. "It is a Constitution we are expounding," as the first great chief justice, John Marshall, declared. They knew better than to pretend otherwise.

———

I work on these issues every day. I lead the Brennan Center for Justice at NYU School of Law. It's a nonpartisan law and policy institute that works to strengthen the systems of democracy and justice so they work for all. I've written about the history of how constitutional change really happens. I believe we are in the middle of a great fight for the future of American democracy. This won't be waged or won primarily in the courts. It's a people's fight. This contest over the Constitution and the structure of our system will be waged above all in the court of public opinion.

Every day the Court's power grab pushes us closer to a crisis, a catastrophic loss of institutional legitimacy.

Throughout the country's history, most of the time the Court has reflected the public's consensus, or at least the approach of the governing political coalition. But sometimes it veers off this road. When the Court is extreme or ideological or partisan or activist, it provokes controversy and a fierce political response.

This has happened before. Three times in the country's history the Court divided America.

That happened after the *Dred Scott* ruling in 1857. Anger at the Court propelled the rise of Abraham Lincoln's Republican Party and helped to provoke the Civil War that ended slavery. (That, by the way, involved the first really big and controversial leak of a Supreme Court opinion.)

It happened again in the early twentieth century, when the Supreme Court tried to block the protection of workers, women, and public safety. That led to a fierce backlash from Progressives and liberals. It was a central issue in Theodore Roosevelt's third-party run for the presidency in 1912. Later, when the Court tried to block his cousin Franklin Roosevelt's New Deal, the conflict nearly wrecked FDR's presidency but led to a constitutional revolution.

And it happened in the wake of the Supreme Court's greatest era, the Warren Court. That period began when the Court struck a blow for equality with *Brown v. Board of Education* and issued sweeping rulings that reflected and spurred vast changes in American life. But the Court's leadership in the social transformation of the 1960s and 1970s led to its own backlash, a social counterrevolution. That long backlash is what brought us to today.

Each time, the Supreme Court provoked an explosive public reaction—protest, public organizing, even political realignment. This regular cycle of overreach and backlash has shaped American history. Likely it is happening again.

We saw this stirring in the 2022 elections. Running in defense of abortion rights, Democrats achieved the best result in a midterm for a party in power in decades. Ballot measures protecting reproductive freedom prevailed across the country. Young voters, especially women, were galvanized. Public support for the Supreme Court reflected in polls fell to its lowest level in decades. It's just the start.

Today the country is growing younger, more diverse, more open to governmental action to solve problems. The country is moving in one direction, yet the Supreme Court is moving in another. That clash will be a central fact of public life for years to come. Just as rulings on abortion, guns, and regulation were won by advocacy campaigns that began in the 1970s, today's activists will need to think for the long term.

We begin by asking how the Supreme Court came to play its role, how it came to amass so much power in the first place. The story starts in 1787 in Philadelphia.

PART ONE

COURT FIGHTS

CHAPTER ONE

AMERICAN ARISTOCRACY

I N MAY 1787, DELEGATES FROM TWELVE of the thirteen American states straggled into Philadelphia for a federal convention. They gathered ostensibly to revise the Articles of Confederation, which loosely bound the newly independent states. Most of those unpacking their bags at the city's boardinghouses and private homes hoped the conclave would do much more, even if they did not always say so out loud. One week into the meeting delegates voted to keep the proceedings entirely secret. Nobody was to be told what was going on. James Madison later insisted, "no Constitution would ever have been adopted if the debates had been public."

For three months, the doors were closed, with armed sentinels posted inside and outside the Statehouse. The windows were locked as well, while the temperature in Philadelphia hovered in the mid-80s. Delegates sweltered.

And they talked up a storm. At length they debated whether representation in Congress, which was to be the preeminent branch of a new national government, would be by population or by states. Just when it seemed the impasse might scuttle the whole project, a Great Compromise established a Senate of states and a House of Representatives elected by the people. Alexander Hamilton of New York was not impressed. "As states are a collection of individual men," he asked, "which ought we to respect most, the rights of the people composing them, or the artificial beings resulting from that composition?"

Then there was the executive. When James Wilson of Pennsylvania proposed that there be a single executive, a president, the delegates were struck dumb. George Washington, after all, was, well, *sitting right there.* James Madison's notes dryly record "a considerable pause ensuing," at which point it was suggested they just vote without a debate. (Only Ben Franklin's interjection led to an actual if desultory conversation about the presidency.) Outside the hall, newspapers speculated feverishly about what the delegates were up to. To quell one rumor, a leak informed a local printer that "tho' we cannot, affirmatively tell you what we are doing; we can negatively tell you what we are not doing—we never once thought of a king."

Even in private, though, the delegates barely discussed the courts. Article III of the Constitution, creating the judicial branch, is 377 words long, only one tenth the amount of text devoted to the other two branches. There was no model for what the federal courts were to become.

The Constitution established a Supreme Court as well as other "inferior courts," all to be set up by Congress. James Wilson was the leading legal thinker among the delegates. He repeatedly proposed that the Court serve as a "Council of Revision" and be able to veto laws just as the president could before they took effect, an idea Madison endorsed. "Laws may be unjust, may be unwise, may be dangerous, may be destructive; and yet may not be so unconstitutional as to justify the Judges in refusing to give them effect," Wilson argued. The delegates voted for that, then later in the summer thought better of it. One warned the judges would become "by degrees the lawgiver." Eventually they authorized a third branch, a Supreme Court and a chief justice (whose only formally assigned responsibility was to preside over impeachment trials). Beyond that, the Constitution itself has little to say.

But Madison's notes of the convention hint that the Supreme Court could declare laws unconstitutional. Whether the framers expected the new Supreme Court to become perhaps the most powerful part of the government, energetically striking down laws enacted by Congress and the states, protecting individual rights, and acting as a super-legislature governing much social policy, is harder to imagine.

Americans invented judicial review. In Great Britain, Parliament was supreme, and no court could override its actions. Before the Revolution, in the colonies there was no such thing as judicial review as we know it today. Colonial governors appointed judges to act as agents of the crown. They did the bidding of the far-off seat of empire. Whether people would obey a court ruling was, at best, iffy. Local juries had a big role, deciding which edicts to follow and which to ignore, often with little guidance from lawyers. As scholar Larry Kramer notes, before independence Americans believed they could decide whether a legislative enactment complied with "the higher law." The people themselves debated constitutional issues and made their voices heard. They could choose to help officials by joining in a "hue and cry" to catch wrongdoers, or resist authority through a carefully staged riot (known as "mobbing").

The idea that courts could scrutinize the actions of legislatures took hold as part of the backlash against the Articles of Confederation. Britain lacked a written constitution, then as now. The former colonists were done with that. In the first few months of revolution in the spring and summer of 1776, the rebels drafted new constitutions for most states as they cast aside the mother country. Sovereignty was held by the legislature, chosen by the people. Some of these new governments were markedly democratic in form. Benjamin Franklin led the drafting of Pennsylvania's constitution and wrote the world's most radical such document thus far. The state eliminated the property requirement for voting so that working-class and poor men had the franchise. Pennsylvania would have only one legislative house. Instead of a governor, a committee chosen by legislators served as the executive. Other states had two chambers and a governor, our familiar checks-and-balances in embryo.

Throughout the 1780s, these state governments earned a bad reputation among the well-to-do. Intermittent violence and armed resistance to foreclosures spread. The assemblies passed laws to protect debtors and issue paper money (which caused inflation and thus hurt creditors). Property owners were aghast. "Fundamental law" included the right to property, they reasoned. These legislative measures amounted to an assault on that fundamental law. Couldn't a court strike them down? One prominent Pennsylvania businessman, worrying about the usurpations by legislatures, said he did not believe in judicial review, but "was at the same time at a loss what expedient to substitute."

Madison looked for ways to rein in the irresponsible states. His preferred method—an idea he returned to again and again—was to give Congress the power to veto state laws. At first the delegates voted for that, but practical objections began to crop up. (What about the

distance between the capital and far-flung states—would Congress
need to stay in permanent session to pass judgment on state laws?) In
the end the Constitution did not grant Congress that general power.
Instead, it included a provision making clear that the Constitution and
federal statutes are the "supreme law of the land," binding state governments.

Today scholars divide over whether the framers intended there to
be judicial review in the U.S. Constitution. William Treanor, the dean
of Georgetown Law School, has surveyed cases and concluded that
some form of judicial review had become commonplace in the states
by the time of the Constitution. Kramer, on the other hand, points out
that while the men who wrote the Constitution likely wanted courts
to be able to block state laws, they were silent and probably unde-
cided about whether courts could review statutes passed by Congress.
Behind the closed doors of the Constitutional Convention, the delegates freely speculated that judges might have the power to strike
down statutes. Elbridge Gerry of Massachusetts, one of the noisiest
delegates, warned, "In some states, the judges actually set aside laws as
being against the Constitution. This was done too with general appro-
bation." Gerry was so alarmed by the U.S. Constitution that he refused
to sign it.

Such arcane academic inquiries, improbably, matter a lot. One of
the oddest aspects of American constitutional law is the fact that 235
years later, we still find it imperative to discern exactly what the Founders were thinking. The framers themselves were unenthusiastic about
establishing their original intent as a guide. They chose to keep their
deliberations secret, as we know. In writing the Constitution they often
deployed broad wording. When the Bill of Rights was added two years
later, it relied even more on vague language. It barred "cruel and unusual punishments," for example, rather than itemizing specific kinds
of prohibited torture. And members of the founding generation disagreed among themselves. Washington, Adams, Jefferson, and Madison all became president, and each interpreted the First Amendment
differently. Within two years after writing the *Federalist Papers* together,
Madison and Hamilton were waging fierce battles over the very nature
of government's structure and power.

The possibility that courts might have the power to strike down
laws—and especially that federal courts, as part of the new national

government, could override states and their rash legislators—might have been on the minds of the drafters of the Constitution. When it came to selling their controversial plan to the public, however, they kept mum. One problem with relentlessly looking backward at the "original public meaning" of the founding generation is that the arguments made in public were so often so clearly disingenuous. The Constitution was ratified by political spin.

We revere the *Federalist Papers* as the guide to the framers' thinking, for example. The *Papers* were a series of essays, what we would call op-eds, written by Madison, Hamilton, and John Jay under the pseudonym "Publius." They debated tendentiously with other op-ed writers, tossing out arguments to rebut other arguments, always with an eye to winning ratification votes in New York and other states. Frequently the *Federalist* authors underplay the impact of the new Constitution. Their assertions often amount to some version of "nothing to see here, move along."

The *Federalist* did not get around to explaining the judicial branch until the seventy-eighth article in the series. "Publius" jousted with "Brutus" (who as Julius Caesar could attest, was keenly alert to signs of tyranny). That was the pseudonym of Robert Yates, a New York judge who warned that newly established federal courts would "operate to a total subversion of the state judiciaries, if not to the legislative authority of the states," and that judges would be too hard to remove by impeachment. Alexander Hamilton insisted that the judicial branch would be the "least dangerous to the political rights of the Constitution; because it will be least in a capacity to annoy or injure them." The executive, Hamilton explained:

> not only dispenses the honors but holds the sword of the community. The legislature not only commands the purse but prescribes the rules by which the duties and rights of every citizen are to be regulated. The judiciary, on the contrary, has no influence over either the sword or the purse; no direction either of the strength or of the wealth of the society, and can take no active resolution whatever. It may truly be said to have neither FORCE NOR WILL but merely judgment; and must ultimately depend upon the aid of the executive arm even for the efficacy of its judgments.

Whether the public knew it or not, a structure had been put in place that would eventually lead to the modern era of judicial supremacy. That robust power for the Supreme Court would not emerge immediately, however.

As the infant institutions of the new national government were established, the Supreme Court was particularly feeble. In its first decade it had three chief justices. It had a hard time rustling up members. For a time it lacked a quorum. Justices were obliged to "ride circuit"— literally, to gallop from place to place hearing cases and supervising matters. (Hence today's "circuit courts.") Justices joined and quit with some frequency. James Wilson—who did so much to create the Court—served as a justice, but twice during his time on the bench he found himself in jail for failing to pay his debts. John Jay, coauthor of the *Federalist*, was confirmed by the Senate to be chief justice for a second time, but declined, complaining that the Court lacked "energy, weight, and dignity."

From the first days the federal courts, however weak, were entangled in politics.

All the high-minded warnings about partisanship quickly were forgotten. Washington's cabinet fractured into factions, and Thomas Jefferson and Madison organized a new political party, the Democratic-Republicans, to oppose the Federalists. Americans chose sides as war intensified between England and France. An ambassador sent by the French Revolution's Convention helped organize Jefferson's party. During John Adams's term, the United States slipped into a "quasi-war" as France harassed and seized American ships. The radical and violent revolution in Paris terrified the Federalists. Pressure mounted to form a standing army, nominally commanded by the now feeble former president but actually to be led by Hamilton, which could dominate the civilian government. In this fevered atmosphere the Federalists enacted the Alien and Sedition Acts, four laws that stifled dissent.

The federal courts became the instrument of the crackdown. Consider the case of Matthew Lyon of Vermont, a congressman who was pursued by Federalist prosecutors and judges. Lyon was an Irish immigrant who had come to the colonies as an indentured servant. While serving in the militia during the Revolution, he demanded the right to vote and a democratic constitution for his state, which was itself a break-away from New York. A bumptious force, the new democracy personi-fied, Lyon was elected to Congress in 1796. When called a "scoundrel" on the floor of the House he was unable to provoke a duel. So he spat tobacco juice into his tormentor's face, earning him a beating with a hickory stick and the nickname the "Spitting Lyon." When the Sedition Act passed, Lyon correctly predicted he would be one of its first targets. He had written that President Adams had "an unbounded thirst for ri-diculous pomp, foolish adulation, and selfish avarice." Adams decided to prosecute him. Since Supreme Court members doubled as trial judges, Justice William Paterson went to Vermont, where he told grand jurors to pay close attention "to the seditious attempts of disaffected persons to disturb the government." Lyon was convicted, and Paterson sentenced him to the harshest punishment he could—four months in jail. Before his conviction, Lyon's political career seemed to be fading. From prison, though, he became a national hero, and was reelected. Things were not off to a good start for the notion of impartial courts.

Then voters ousted the incumbent Federalists in the 1800 election, a sweeping electoral rebuke. This nonviolent transfer of power had few parallels in history. Jefferson called it "the Revolution of 1800." The election tested the new government's barely unwrapped constitutional machinery. One misfire came from the absentminded design of the Electoral College system, which led to weeks of deadlock in the House of Representatives as Aaron Burr, Jefferson's vice presidential candi-date, tried to elbow himself into the top job.

The judiciary, too, got caught up. In those days, four months stretched between the election and when a new administration would be sworn in. The Federalists viewed the new team as seditionist, pro-French, and dangerous. They used those months to burrow into the courts as a seat of remaining power. Nineteen days before Adams left office, the lame-duck Federalist Congress passed a Judiciary Act elim-inating a Supreme Court seat (so Jefferson could not make a pick) and creating sixteen federal judgeships, lifetime jobs to which party loyalists could quickly be appointed. In a raucous scramble Federalist politicians pressed to get new judges named and confirmed.

This first frenetic politicization of the federal courts led to the first or-ganized political backlash. Jefferson's supporters decried the "midnight judges" appointed by Adams. The Federalists, Jefferson complained, "have retired into the judiciary as a stronghold. There the remains of Federalism are to be preserved & fed from the treasury, and from that battery all the works of republicanism are to be beaten down & erased." Congress quickly repealed the law that had allowed the appointment of all those judges, who suddenly lost their jobs. Unpacking the courts, so to speak.

A quirky case arising from the chaotic transfer of power quickly tested the Supreme Court's authority. William Marbury had been named a justice of the peace, but in the confusion of the administration's final hours, he did not receive his certificate from outgoing secretary of state John Marshall. Marbury filed a suit in the U.S. Supreme Court to compel the government to give him his lucrative commission. By the time the Court heard the case, Marshall was chief justice. (For a time he served in both roles.) He was Jefferson's cousin and his political rival, and he wanted to establish the authority of the national government, and within it, of the Court itself.

Marshall's opinion was political wizardry. The justices stayed in Stelle's Hotel across the street from the Capitol, on a spot where the Library of Congress now stands. When one of the justices was stricken with a painful case of gout, Marshall relocated operations there from a first-floor room in the still unfinished Capitol building. Marshall read the ruling to listeners packed into the hotel lobby. The case presented a political dilemma with few good solutions. If the Court simply ruled Marbury was owed his commission, it would reveal its powerlessness. "Marshall knew that such a decision would prompt a national crisis," as Cliff Sloan and David McKean write in their book on the case, since Jefferson would just shrug. Or Marshall could rule for the Jefferson administration and deny the job to Marbury, but that, too, would neuter the Court, revealing weakness despite a rather clear-cut legal case. As Marshall read the opinion page by page to the expectant onlookers, the facts were on Marbury's side. Sloan and McKean note, "One hundred seventeen paragraphs into the opinion, everything had gone Marbury's way." Then, in what must have been a head-snapping surprise for those crammed into the hotel, the justices ruled that the statute granting the Supreme Court the power to rule in the case was itself unconstitutional, so it could not help Marbury. Jefferson lost by winning. The Court refused to act, in a way that enhanced its own power.

Law professors, high school history teachers, and generations of judges reverently quote Marshall: "It is emphatically the province and duty of the judicial department to say what the law is." He added, "an act of the legislature, repugnant to the constitution, is void." Later generations of justices would treat it as a talisman when they were trying to work up the nerve to make a courageous stand, as when the Supreme Court cited it in ruling unanimously against school segregation in Little Rock. When the Court ordered Richard Nixon to turn over his incriminating tapes to the Watergate special prosecutor, the rhetorical high point of the opinion quoted the case.

It was, indeed, a great decision. But for a long while it was not a particularly important one. Having announced its primacy, for decades after *Marbury* the Supreme Court was a nonfactor in American politics. Every so often it would confirm federal power, such as in the *McCulloch v. Maryland* case that recognized Congress's self-proclaimed authority to establish a national bank. Doing much more would have revealed its political weakness. In 1832 President Andrew Jackson was busy pursuing a genocidal policy that sought to drive Native American tribes away from the Atlantic coast, pushing them inland. The Supreme Court ruled unconstitutional a Georgia law under which two Protestant missionaries were arrested for trespassing on sovereign Cherokee land. Jackson backed Georgia in its efforts to crush the Native Americans. He was reputed to have responded, "Well, John Marshall has made his decision, now let him enforce it."

But the country evolved quickly away from the tight-knit hierarchy of colonial times. The American political system was set off on a course that would continue to elevate law and lawyers to a preeminent place, a role that has not really been relinquished since.

There was one more factor that boosted the role of lawyers and especially judges. The writers of the Constitution assumed it would be amended frequently. After all, they amended it ten times within the first two years of its operation. They were wrong, however. It turns out to be very hard to pass a constitutional amendment. As a result, over the years much constitutional change was effected through judicial reinterpretation of the document.

Alexis de Tocqueville, the sharp-eyed observer writing in the 1830s, was both thrilled and unnerved by the country's emerging and unruly democratic culture. He saw the country driving inexorably toward greater equality. He was endlessly amazed by the outward signs of the emerging democratic culture: boosterism, people forming clubs, people shaking hands rather than bowing to their betters. But he worried about the potential for tyranny—not of a king, or a minority claque, but of the majority. Things could get out of hand. We had no inherited aristocracy to keep democracy in check, he wrote. From these early days the legal system was more central to American life than in most other countries. "The American aristocracy is on the lawyers' benches and in the judges' seats," he wrote. Lawyers were nobility, or at least fancied themselves that way. "The lawyer belongs to the people by his interest and his birth and to aristocracy by his habits and his tastes; he is, so to speak, the natural link between these two things, as it were the band that unites them."

Tocqueville added, "There is almost no political question, in the United States, that does not sooner or later resolve itself into a judicial question."

CHAPTER TWO

"NO RIGHTS"

T HE NEXT TIME THE SUPREME COURT thrust itself into the center
of a public controversy, it nearly broke the country apart. It was the
first great court fight after the nation's founding. It also marked the
start of the Court's half-century campaign to bolster the racial caste system in the South. The fight began with the leak of a major decision—
the advance disclosure of *Dred Scott*, with huge consequences, to none
other than the president-elect.

The decades before the Civil War had been a time of constitutional
conflict and compromise, even if the Supreme Court played little part.
Legislative maneuvers among Daniel Webster, John C. Calhoun, and
Henry Clay—each greater in stature than most presidents—tamped
down slavery as an issue. The Missouri Compromise in 1820 had set the
terms: it drew a straight line west to the Pacific. Below the 36th parallel,
Black people would be enslaved; north of the line, slavery would be
barred. It affirmed the compromise over slavery that was made to reach
agreement on the Constitution in 1787, and the approach seemed so
settled it was unofficially considered a part of the constitutional system,
as scholar Noah Feldman has observed.

Instead of somehow fading away, as some naively (or disingenuously) hoped, slavery became more entrenched. Over time, two economic and social systems competed and jostled for land, power, and
lucrative railroad routes. That equilibrium was greatly disrupted in
1848 when a war with Mexico waged by pro-slavery Democrats brought
the Southwest into the Union. How would the new states affect the balance? And how would they be governed?

Senator Stephen Douglas of Illinois proposed a new doctrine of "popular sovereignty," meaning any new state in any part of the country could choose whether to be slave or free. Douglas's Kansas-Nebraska Act let the white residents of those two new northern states choose for themselves. The vain "Little Giant" seems to have been scheming to gain southern support for a lucrative railroad route to the West, but he underestimated the tumult that would follow. Suddenly northern white voters, who did not want to compete with slave labor, had a stake in the outcome. Democrats defended slavery. The Whigs flew apart under the strain of the issue. Former Whigs formed a new Republican Party, which immediately made huge electoral gains. Its platform above all else called for limiting slavery so it would not spread outside the South. Abolitionist sentiment and agitation spread. Thousands of escaped enslaved people fled north via the Underground Railroad. Meanwhile, popular sovereignty led to chaos, as thousands of settlers poured into "Bloody Kansas," violently struggling for control of the new state. Things were getting tense.

The U.S. Supreme Court evidently thought that it had the credibility to solve the problem once and for all. Seven of its nine members had been appointed either by southerners who owned slaves or northern presidents tolerant of slavery. Roger Taney was in his third decade as chief justice. As a young man Taney had freed his own slaves and called the institution a "blot on our national character," but by 1857 he was labeling abolitionism "northern aggression." The first Catholic on the high court and a close colleague of Andrew Jackson, he was held in such esteem that antislavery senator William Seward recently had proposed placing a bust of Taney in the Capitol. Whether the justices should try to stop debates over slavery was another matter. "For one, I may say, with every respect for those judicial dignitaries, that I would rather trust a dog with my dinner," warned *New-York Daily Tribune* editor Horace Greeley.

The Supreme Court made its move in ruling on *Dred Scott v. Sandford*. The case involved one enslaved man's eleven-year struggle for his freedom. Dred Scott had traveled with his master, an army doctor, from Missouri, a slave state, into Illinois, a free state, and a territory that included Minnesota and Wisconsin, both free. After five years they returned to Missouri. His master died and Scott sued, arguing that he had become a free man while living in the North, and should not be forced back into bondage. Years of precedent in Missouri backed up Scott's claim. But the case wended its way to the high court, and the justices plainly wanted to make a statement of some sort. "Seldom, if ever, has there been a case before this high tribunal of greater importance, or one in which such a general and deep interest is felt," wrote one newspaper. It was argued over four days, then again for another four days later in the year. "Slavery promises to exist through all time, so far as human vision can discover," a former U.S. senator, representing the slaveowner in the case, told the justices. "The extension of slavery on this continent is the only thing which will preserve the constitutional freedom we now enjoy."

It all came together in a season of political intrigue during the four months between Election Day and the inaugural in early March 1857.

Newly elected James Buchanan was a pro-slavery Pennsylvania Democrat, a northern man with southern sympathies. He grew increasingly agitated as his swearing in approached, hoping that the justices would relieve him of the pressures of the issue. Buchanan's machinations inspired contemporary theories of a Slave Power conspiracy. Spectators saw him huddle with Taney on the inaugural platform at the Capitol. The reality was worse: historians later discovered extensive secret efforts by the incoming president to pressure the justices to decide, to go big, and to overturn the Missouri Compromise. Buchanan's finagling was successful, and the justices leaked the result to him. One wrote to the president-elect thanking him for his intervention, explaining, "We have thought it due to you to state to you in candor and confidence the real state of the matter."

Sure of the outcome, Buchanan declared disingenuously in his Inaugural Address that the Supreme Court would soon dispose of the problem of slavery in the territories. "To their decision, in common with all good citizens, I shall cheerfully submit, whatever this may be," he purred. Listeners caught his broad hints. "We said, when the Kansas-Nebraska bill passed, 'The revolution is accomplished, and Slavery is king,'" the *New-York Daily Tribune* wrote. "We point to Mr. Buchanan's inaugural and the coming decision of the Supreme Court as the coronation of that power." Two days later came the jolt from the bench.

For the first time since *Marbury v. Madison*, the Supreme Court invalidated a law enacted by Congress. *Dred Scott v. Sandford* announced that the Missouri Compromise, which already had been repealed, was unconstitutional in the first place. The Constitution denied Congress the power to ban slavery in any territories, North or South. Moreover, Scott could not sue in federal court for his freedom anyway, because neither slaves nor free Black people could be citizens. Men of African descent were "so far inferior," Taney wrote, "that they had no rights which the white man was bound to respect; . . . the negro might justly and lawfully be reduced to slavery for his benefit." Slavery, the Supreme Court now ruled, was constitutionally protected nationwide.

Dred Scott relied on what would later be called "originalism." It was in fact the first major originalist opinion. A member of the founding generation had written *Marbury v. Madison*, after all, and it reflected the debates among them. *Dred Scott* came a generation later. To buttress his intervention, Taney picked through founding era documents, laws passed in the early republic, and views of the framers to claim they intended the United States to grant rights only to white people throughout the country. "If any of [the Constitution's] provisions are deemed unjust, there is a mode prescribed in the instrument itself by which it may be amended; but while it remains unaltered, it must be construed now as it was understood at the time of its adoption." One scholar called the opinion "a riot of originalism."

At the same time, it introduced a new notion into American law: that the Fifth Amendment with its requirement of "due process" protected the slaveowner's right to bring his "property" when he traveled. This was the birth of "substantive due process," the idea that the Constitution concerns itself not just with fair procedure but with underlying rights, albeit, in this case, in a twisted form.

The reaction to *Dred Scott* also marked the start of another major strain of American political thought: the progressive insistence on judicial restraint. Critics of the opinion did not focus on its originalism (in part because the use of that method was so transparently done in service to a political, even a partisan end). They focused instead on its usurpation of power, the draining of authority from the democratically elected parts of the government, state and federal. Foes insisted that its heinous provisions on citizenship, and its overruling of the Missouri Compromise, was not even binding law—they were dicta, merely an expression of Taney's point of view. That way Americans still in thrall to the Court could attack the ruling without denying the rule of law.

⸻

The Supreme Court's decision instantly fractured public opinion. The justices and the president seemed to be colluding to expand slavery. The ruling took direct aim at the Republican Party's central political project, which was to keep the institution from spreading outside the South. Contemporaries understood this was the most important, and to many the worst, ruling the Court had made up to this point. Readers across the country were astounded that the Court claimed it could strike down a key congressionally enacted law. The *New-York Daily Tribune* wrote that it was "entitled to just so much moral weight as would the judgment of a majority of those congregated in any Washington bar-room." Other Republican newspapers issued daily denunciations. The *Chicago Tribune* declared, "We scarcely know how to express our detestation of its inhuman dicta, or to fathom the wicked consequences which may flow from it." Another Chicago paper expressed "a feeling of shame and loathing" for "this once illustrious tribunal, toiling meekly and patiently through this dirty job." Democrats hailed the Court. The New Orleans *Picayune* lauded that "august and incorruptible body, which, elevated above the turmoils of party, has so adjudged the vexed question of the times." "Southern opinion upon the subject of southern slavery," exulted the Augusta, Georgia, *Constitutionalist*, "is now the supreme law of the land."

Frederick Douglass, speaking for abolitionists, poured fury. The escaped slave turned author denounced the ruling. The "infamous decision of the slaveholding wing of the Supreme Court" had performed a service by revealing the truth. "I have no fear that the National Conscience will be put to sleep by such an open, glaring, and scandalous tissue of lies," he said. "The Supreme Court of the United States is not the only power in this world. It is very great, but the Supreme Court of the Almighty is greater. Judge Taney can do many things, but he cannot perform impossibilities," he declared, adding, "He cannot change the essential nature of things—making evil good, and good, evil."

⸻

Abraham Lincoln was one person galvanized by the ruling. Lincoln was practicing law in Springfield, Illinois, and giving speeches for the new

Republican Party in the mid-1850s, and he had thrown himself into agitation against the Kansas-Nebraska Act. Lincoln was convinced *Dred Scott* was the product of a conspiracy between the Court, the new president, and the slaveholding South. He called it "an astonisher in legal history" and made his opposition to it a central issue in his campaign for U.S. Senate in 1858.

In his speech to the Republican convention in Springfield, Lincoln sought to polarize the election between himself and Stephen Douglas, originator of popular sovereignty, who he charged was merely posing as a moderate on slavery. " 'A house divided against itself cannot stand,' " Lincoln said, quoting scripture to make a shocking prediction. "I believe this government cannot endure, permanently half slave and half free." But the bulk of the speech was devoted to sketching out the mechanics of what he said was a plot involving Douglas, the new president, and the Supreme Court, all aiming toward a second ruling, one that would require slavery nationwide. "We shall lie down pleasantly dreaming that the people of Missouri are on the verge of making their State free; and we shall awake to the reality, instead, that the Supreme Court has made Illinois a slave State." Throughout their seven debates, he pressed Douglas, who finally declared that despite what the Supreme Court might say, the people of a territory in fact could bar slavery. Lincoln lost the election but had turned the Court's ruling into a political albatross.

Lincoln now contended for the Republican presidential nomination. "The taste is in my mouth a little," he would soon admit. But as a largely unknown and uncouth westerner, he needed to prove himself to a national political audience, and his solution was to accept a speaking invitation in New York City to display his erudition. Lincoln hit the books. "He searched through the dusty volumes of congressional proceedings in the State library, and dug deeply into political history," recalled Lincoln's law partner. "He was painstaking and thorough in the study of his subject." Arriving in New York, he discovered that his speech had been moved from an antislavery church in Brooklyn Heights to the Cooper Union in Manhattan, closer to the business center.

In his hourlong address, Lincoln picked apart the Supreme Court's ruling. It was a lengthy dissent. If *Dred Scott* was an early example of originalism, of pretending to divine the thoughts of the framers to buttress a conclusion, Lincoln's speech was an early example of counter-originalism—of a critic also relying on carefully curated evidence from the founding period.

Systematically he ticked through the roster of the Founders, showing that each had voted in one way or another to limit or prohibit slavery. Most of them had voted in 1787 for the Northwest Ordinance, for example, which organized areas that became Ohio, Michigan, Indiana, Illinois, and Wisconsin. It declared, "There shall be neither Slavery nor involuntary Servitude in the said territory otherwise than in the punishment of crimes," in language that found its way into the Thirteenth Amendment decades later. Lincoln aimed to show that the framers in fact intended to put slavery on the road to extinction, and that the Constitution did not bar Congress from regulating or even prohibiting it in federal territory.

A year later, improbably, Lincoln won the presidency in a four-way race. Seven states in the deep South seceded by inauguration day. Lincoln took the oath before an anxious crowd in the east front of the half-built Capitol, ringed by troops, nestled in between two slave states still in the union, Virginia and Maryland.

Lincoln's inaugural was partly an anguished plea to keep the country from breaking apart. He pledged not to disturb the existing constitutional arrangements, which included slavery. But he repudiated the Supreme Court and its handiwork. He archly noted "the position assumed by some that constitutional questions are to be decided by the Supreme Court." Those decisions, he insisted, should only bind the parties to a legal dispute. "At the same time, the candid citizen must confess" that if government policy is to be "irrevocably fixed by decisions of the Supreme Court . . . the people will have ceased to be their own rulers, having to that extent practically resigned their Government into the hands of that eminent tribunal." Southerners heard a threat of war: "In your hands, my dissatisfied fellow countrymen, and not in mine, is the momentous issue of civil war." Abolitionists criticized the speech as avoiding the glaring issue of slavery, ending as it did with a plea for reconciliation, "touched by the better angels of our nature."

After Lincoln spoke, Roger Taney swore him into office, no doubt through gritted teeth.

The two men—and the branches of government they embodied—contended until the chief justice's death in 1864. Mostly they fought over Lincoln's use of emergency powers, such as his suspension of the writ of habeas corpus. A conflict with even longer-term ramifications came in Lincoln's repudiation of the Taney Court's constitutional vision.

They clashed not just about the Constitution but about the place of the Declaration of Independence as a constitutional text. The 1776 document had done more than break with Great Britain. In its preamble, it set out a revolutionary creed derived from Enlightenment ideas about natural rights. It began by asserting it to be "self-evident" that "all men are created equal," that they are endowed by their Creator with the "unalienable rights" of "life, liberty, and the pursuit of happiness." As scholar Danielle Allen's sleuthing and careful examination of the parchment has pointed out, the sentence keeps going, pointing above all to the idea of government resting on the "consent of the governed." These egalitarian principles powerfully propelled the Revolution. The U.S. Constitution, written eleven years later, shed many of those ideals. It was a careful compromise, balancing the interests of big states and small states, debtors and creditors. The Constitution reflected, too, the fight already emerging between slavery and opposition to it. During and just after the Revolution five northern states had begun to end slavery. The final Constitution never mentions slavery, and gave Congress the power to end the slave trade. But it counted enslaved Americans as three-fifths of a person. It let the practice continue, in what all recognized was a contravention of the principles of the Declaration of Independence.

In *Dred Scott* Taney acknowledged that the Declaration had proclaimed a vision of equality. But that language, no matter how ringing, could not have included Black people, he explained. The drafters could not have meant that, because if they had, it "would have been utterly and flagrantly inconsistent with the principles they asserted." Well, yes.

Lincoln had long embraced that same preamble as the "sheet anchor of our liberty." But at the start of the war, he had not yet dedicated himself to using the opportunity to end slavery. The war changed that. At the dedication of the cemetery at Gettysburg in 1863, Lincoln alchemized the Declaration into a new founding creed for the country. Like his Cooper Union speech, the Gettysburg Address responded to *Dred Scott*. At his inaugural he had pledged to uphold the Constitution. Now he changed the founding date to "four score and seven years ago"—1776, not 1787—and asserted the "new nation" was "dedicated to the proposition" as proclaimed in the Declaration's preamble. At Gettysburg, Lincoln did not cite or even hint at the Constitution. From now on the Constitution would be read to embody the aspirations of the Declaration. That would be its "new birth of freedom."

⸻

After the war the Republicans amended the U.S. Constitution three times. The amendments were the instrument of that new birth, designed to write the ideals of the Declaration into the sometimes cynical and heavily compromised machinery of the nation's charter. The Thirteenth Amendment prohibited slavery. The Fifteenth Amendment guaranteed Black men the right to vote. The Fourteenth Amendment had a broader purpose. It established equality for Black Americans, guaranteeing equal protection of the law and due process, and the "privileges and immunities" of citizens. It overturned *Dred Scott*, the second amendment spurred by a Court ruling. Anyone born in the United States was a citizen, it declared. Its authors were Radical Republicans, and it offered a truly radical vision of a strong national government that could enforce civil and racial equality. All together these amendments represented a "Second Founding," a founding in repudiation of the Court.

Ratified just a decade after Taney's disastrous ruling, the amendments pointedly gave Congress power to enforce them.

But the Supreme Court had tasted its own power. As the war receded it set about narrowing the reach and impact of the Civil War amendments. After the founding the Court led by John Marshall had stood for a strong national government, surmounting the sovereignty of contentious states. After the Second Founding, the Court instead undermined that national government, standing for states' rights.

And painful as it is to acknowledge, in all this the Supreme Court followed political opinion rather than leading it. This time the justices' aggressive moves were not met with wide outcry, or town hall meetings, or congressional resolutions. In its retreat on equal rights the Court reflected the political consensus. White Americans in the North were exhausted by two decades of conflict and had lost their interest in ensuring the rights of Black Americans. In a deal to keep the White House after the 1876 election, Republicans agreed to withdraw troops from the South. At that same moment, the Court—by narrowing and neutering the Fourteenth and Fifteenth Amendments—essentially also withdrew the federal courts and federal law enforcement. In 1875 Congress passed the Civil Rights Act, which banned segregation in public accommodations such as railroad cars and inns. The Supreme Court struck it down: the Fourteenth Amendment, it claimed, did not cover private conduct. Frederick Douglass called the Court's ruling in the *Civil Rights Cases* "an act of surrender." Indeed, in one key voting case, the justices explained that the Jim Crow voting law in Alabama did in fact discriminate, but that federal courts could do little about it since military force would be needed to enforce the Constitution—and, well, they weren't going to impose *that*. Congress did not enact the protections for nearly another century.

In all, the Supreme Court heard over 150 cases interpreting the Fourteenth Amendment in the last quarter of the nineteenth century, but only around twenty of them dealt with the rights of Black people. W. E. B. Du Bois called it a "counter-revolution of property."

The notorious low point of the Court's abdication was *Plessy v. Ferguson.* Homer Plessy was a mixed-race man who lived in clamorous multiethnic New Orleans. Seeking a test case, he deliberately refused to move from the "whites only" section of a streetcar and was arrested. Black leaders including Frederick Douglass opposed bringing the case, because they knew the Supreme Court might enshrine segregation. The Court indeed ruled that New Orleans's law requiring "equal, but separate" railway cars did not violate the Fourteenth Amendment. The amendment protected formal legal equality for Black people, the justices ruled, but nothing more; it did not seek to introduce social equality. The opinion dripped condescension. Henry Billings Brown rejected the idea "that the enforced separation of the two races stamps the colored race with a badge of inferiority. If this be so, it is not by reason of anything found in the act, but solely because the colored race chooses to put that construction on it."

John Marshall Harlan wrote a furious dissent. *Plessy*, he warned, would "in time, prove to be quite as pernicious as the decision made by this tribunal in the *Dred Scott Case*." Harlan had owned slaves in his youth. "But in view of the Constitution, in the eye of the law, there is in this country no superior, dominant, ruling class of citizens. There is no caste here. Our Constitution is color-blind, and neither knows nor tolerates classes among citizens." At the time Harlan's prophetic insistence on a color-blind Constitution rebuked the existing system of racial preferences—one that benefited white Americans.

———

The nineteenth century ended with the Court fully entrenched as a tribune for privilege and the status quo. It was part of a government increasingly unable to address the challenges of rapid change: demographic, economic, political. Once again the Court's increasing activism sparked a fierce and unrelenting backlash. This time the political fight lasted three decades.

CHAPTER THREE

"NINE OLD MEN"

A MERICA IN THE EARLY TWENTIETH CENTURY faced challenges that feel very familiar: widening inequality, reckless business leaders, ineffective government. The response came in a remarkable burst of civic activity and policy creativity, first in the Progressive Era and then in the New Deal. Again, the Supreme Court thrust itself into the fray, seeking to stop the legislative response to massive social change. And again, the justices provoked a political backlash and an assault on the Court's legitimacy that outlasted the original judicial move.

Between 1860 and 1900, the population of the United States more than doubled. Immigrants surged in, no longer from Northern Europe but Catholics and Jews from Italy, Poland, and Russia. The economy industrialized with power and resources concentrated into fewer hands. For the first time, major national corporations, known as trusts, came to dominate and monopolize industry. Steel, oil, sugar, and other sectors once saw jostling competition among small companies. Now they were controlled by men as famous then as Bezos or Musk today: Rockefeller, Carnegie, Morgan, Mellon. Wealth inequality soared. In 1860, the national wealth was $16 billion; by 1900, it was $88.5 billion. But average wages barely kept pace, and for many they fell. The wealthiest one percent owned nearly half the property, while a third to a half of industrial workers lived in poverty. Mark Twain dubbed it the "Gilded Age," a time when a thin cover of gold paint could barely cover the rot underneath.

Amid these economic upheavals, government was corrupt and outmatched. There were new national corporations but no effective national government. Businesses and their defenders embraced notions of Social Darwinism, a twisted version of the latest scientific development. Accumulated wealth simply was proof of survival of the fittest, applied to the human species.

The first response came from the Populists, whose far-reaching radical program was crushed in the 1896 presidential election. But the reform impulse continued. Long before "progressive" was a euphemism favored by people trying to avoid the word "liberal," the Progressive Movement defined an era of economic and social turmoil. Progressives campaigned for health and safety protections, banking reforms, and environmental conservation. Modern American government took shape: Food safety laws. Wage and hours laws to protect vulnerable workers, who were working six or seven days a week in putrid conditions. Antitrust and other regulatory laws to curb corporate consolidation and power. Expanded voting rights, as women won the right to vote and the Constitution was changed to have U.S. senators chosen by "the people," not legislators. It was a time of creative ferment, involving millions from all political parties. These rudiments of a modern regulatory and social welfare state were not unique to the United States; Germany, for example, under conservative governments, had instituted national health insurance, accident insurance, and old age pensions.

Only in the United States did the Supreme Court step forward to try to stop the progress, in its greatest wave of activist decisions—rulings that tried to limit or stop government from reining in the market.

The rulings came as quickly as legislators could pass new laws. One scholar reports that although the Court had invalidated federal laws only twice before 1860 (in *Marbury* and *Dred Scott*), it held twenty-one unconstitutional between 1865 and 1898. It struck down state laws at an even faster clip, at three times the rate it did before the Civil War. Corporations learned to remove lawsuits from sometimes populist state courts to more reliable federal courts.

The Republican presidents serenely installed railroad lawyers and corporate counselors on the Court. Ethical standards were notably relaxed. In one case before the justices former senator Roscoe Conkling, arguing for a railroad, claimed that secret records from the drafting of the Fourteenth Amendment showed it had intended to treat corporations as "persons" under the law. Inconveniently, that never had been mentioned during the ratification debates. "The American people builded better than they knew," he told the justices. Shortly after, hearing another railroad case, the chief justice simply announced that the Court did not want to hear arguments about whether the Constitution treats corporations as people. "We are all of opinion that it does."

In one year, 1895, the Court led by Chief Justice Melville Fuller issued three major rulings addressing the new economic order. Each relied on arguments that were formally clever and substantively appalling, all to protect the wealthy and restrict government's ability to do much of anything in the economy.

First the Court gutted the new antitrust laws. With charming brevity, the Sherman Antitrust Act had proclaimed that people who "monopolize, or attempt to monopolize, or combine or conspire" with others are guilty of a crime. (Today we would expect such a sweeping notion to require hundreds of pages.) When the federal government brought its first antitrust prosecution, the Court blocked it. One firm, the American Sugar Refinery Company, had cornered 98 percent of the market by taking over smaller producers. It had the cozy name of the "Sugar Trust." The Justice Department sued to stop the Sugar Trust. But the Supreme Court ruled the federal government could not apply antitrust law to manufacturing, since the law only intended to govern "interstate commerce" (even if the resulting product was sold across state lines). This was tendentious hairsplitting even at the time.

Then it upheld the use of an injunction by a federal court against a railroad workers strike led by Eugene V. Debs, the socialist labor leader. The Court's authorization led to decades where labor unions were blocked by the federal courts, a policy that endured until the 1930s.

Also in 1895 the Court declared that a federal income tax was unconstitutional. The levy had first been tried during the Civil War, and in 1894 Congress enacted it again. One of the lawyers arguing against the tax told the justices that "class legislation and attempts of the majority to spoliate private property would ultimately wreck the American republic." Another, Joseph Choate, represented Standard Oil and the tobacco trust. He thundered to the Court that the income tax was based on "principles as communistic, socialistic—what shall I call them—populistic as ever has been addressed to any political assembly in the world."

Outraged attacks on the Supreme Court and its retrograde rulings became part of the political turmoil of the time. Thirty-six-year-old congressman William Jennings Bryan focused on the tax decision in his

1896 campaign for president. His "Cross of Gold" speech upended the Democratic convention, caused a near riot, and unexpectedly won him the nomination. Bryan declared, "They say that we passed an unconstitutional law; we deny it." The "boy orator" set off on an unheard-of speaking tour of the country, giving 250 speeches to five million listeners. But when he traveled to East Coast cities such as New York and Boston, Democratic strongholds, Bryan found resistance to his prairie politics. Attacks on "money lenders" and the Gold Standard puzzled factory workers and political machine foot-soldiers. Bryan found that urban audiences thrilled instead to the assault on the Court. "Our criticism of the Supreme Court is not one bit stronger than that contained in the platform upon which Abraham Lincoln was elected in 1860," he told supporters at New York's Tammany Hall, a crowd so large it spilled out into Union Square. Bryan and the Populists lost, and anger at the Court never cohered. But the critique began to form part of the catechism of a nationwide reform movement.

Since it was cities and states rather than Congress that were more open to protective laws, so it was state high courts that mostly struck them down. Those cases rarely made it to Washington. When one did, in the era's most controversial decision, the U.S. Supreme Court showed it would twist traditional legal notions into a well-baked pretzel.

Think of a "bakery" and you might imagine sweet smells, bright lights, colorful frosting. At the turn of the century, though, bakeries were dangerous and fetid, mostly jammed into the windowless basements of urban tenements, infested with vermin. Bakery workers frequently fell sick with tuberculosis (which did not keep them from preparing and handling massive quantities of food). Hours were punishing. One strike protested the requirement that bakers work twelve hours a day. The Bakeshop Act in New York State prohibited bakeries from employing people for more than ten hours a day, or to work more than sixty hours in a week.

In 1905, the Supreme Court struck down that law in *Lochner v. New York*, a case so notorious that the entire period of judicial activism became known as the "Lochner Era." The Court said that the right of a private business to make contracts was a fundamental liberty protected by the Fourteenth Amendment and its Due Process Clause, and the law interfered "with the right of contract between the employer and employees." The "right of the individual to labor for such time as he may choose"—in other words, of a worker to toil nearly unlimited hours in order to cling to a job—also must be protected. "There is no reasonable ground . . . for interfering with the liberty of person or the right of free contract, by determining the hours of labor, in the occupation of a baker." At the very moment of industrialization and spreading class conflict, the five justices barred the government from setting and enforcing labor rules.

Lochner was noteworthy in another way. One part of the Fourteenth Amendment declared that the "privileges and immunities" of citizenship could not be denied. The Supreme Court had neutered this provision in its rulings on Reconstruction. The amendment also requires "due process of law." That, the justices ruled with greater frequency in the late nineteenth century, did not just refer to fair proceedings. It covered areas of human conduct with which laws could not interfere. "Substantive due process" was a self-contradictory phrase at the very least, combining notions of fair means and hoped-for ends. Substantive due process lives on today and is the basis for many of the Supreme Court's most controversial and important rulings in the past half century. In any case, at the turn of the twentieth century, the evisceration of the Fourteenth Amendment was now complete: it did not protect the rights of people, but it did protect the rights of businesses to exploit those people.

As the justices embarked on pro-business judicial activism, progressives called for judicial restraint—to insist that the unelected federal courts, insulated from public opinion and social change, were the last people to be making social policy. Justice Oliver Wendell Holmes dissented in *Lochner*. "This case is decided upon an economic theory which a large part of the country does not entertain," he wrote. Holmes was firing the first shots in what became a sustained assault on overreaching judges, a stance that united liberals on the Court for decades. *Lochner*, he said, sought to write libertarian economic philosophy and Social Darwinism—the "survival of the fittest"—into the Constitution. "The Fourteenth Amendment does not enact Mr. Herbert Spencer's Social Statics." Holmes spoke for the view, common among progressives, that judges should allow democracy to work through the electoral process. As he wrote to a friend, "If my fellow citizens want to go to Hell I will help them. It's my job."

Conservatives in turn lauded the Court's rulings. *The New York Times*—then a predictable voice for the sensible business-minded establishment—hailed *Lochner*. "The tendency of State Legislatures," it wrote, "under the pressure of labor leaders and professional agitators, to enact laws which interfere with 'the ordinary trades and occupations of the people' is sharply checked by this decision."

Reformers grew almost frantic trying to navigate the obstacles strewn by the courts. For the first time, women led the push for legislation and the increasingly militant response to the judiciary. Socialist attorney Florence Kelley led the National Consumers League, one of the profusion of civic groups founded during this time, which pressed states to address the problem of "sweated labor," where work was parceled out to people working in their own crowded apartments, often sixteen hours a day.

Unions, consumer groups, and middle-class women's clubs eager to learn about social issues (from a distance) all demanded the ten-hour workday. For them it had become a crusade. An Oregon law banned child labor and limited working hours for women. It was Labor Day in 1905 when an overseer at the Grand Laundry in Portland, Oregon, ordered a young worker named Emma Gotcher to work more than ten hours in violation of state law. Bad move: a labor activist, Gotcher refused and had the laundry's owner, Curt Muller, arrested. Muller sued Oregon to overturn its law, and eventually the case reached the Supreme Court. The *Lochner* obstacle loomed.

The National Consumers League scrambled to find legal help. Florence Kelley first met with Joseph Choate, the same aristocratic partner at a top New York firm who had argued against the income tax. Choate demurred, explaining he could not understand why "a great husky Irish woman should not work in a laundry more than ten hours a day." Next she turned to a lawyer who spent his career fighting the clients of lawyers like Choate, Louis Brandeis.

Brandeis invented public interest law. A successful private attorney, he had made his name in Boston as the "People's Lawyer," taking on electric power companies and railroads. He was brilliant: his 1890 law review article proposed there be something he called "the right to privacy," what he called "the right to be let alone," launching an idea that has only grown in American life and law. (He was complaining about that era's version of paparazzi who stalked his fashionable law partner.) At times Brandeis said he was not representing a client, just the public interest, a stance so baffling that some people saw it as an ethical breach. This time he took over the case, representing Oregon, and insisted on controlling all the filings.

Brandeis produced a brief for the Supreme Court only two pages of which made a legal argument. The rest, 111 densely printed pages, was an overwhelming compendium of research, social science, medical analysis, and more, showing the need for Oregon's law. To modern eyes the arguments grate, since they focus on ways women were weaker than men and thus needed extra protection. For example, Brandeis cited a source which claimed "there is more water" in women's than in men's blood. The argument spoke to the justices' old-fashioned, sentimental notion of womanhood and morality. There was a meta message as well: concrete consequences in the lives of women and men must matter, and are legitimately a source of decision making, not just abstract theories. If you rule for workers' "freedom of contract" you crush the health and aspirations of those actual workers. Brandeis's brief so impressed the justices that just three years after *Lochner*, they unanimously upheld Oregon's law.

Brandeis and Kelley's Supreme Court success was a rarity. Judges at all levels ruled as if they were still representing their corporate clients. The drive for labor protections, for women's rights, and for the first stirrings of the regulatory state were the topics of countless rallies, articles, strikes, and election campaigns. Reformers proposed constitutional amendments and laws to restrict the justices. Chief Justice Walter Clark of North Carolina's high court proposed that U.S. Supreme Court justices be elected. (Clark was appalled by the federal courts' rulings for business, and urged the courts to protect workers and consumers. He also called for the repeal of the Fourteenth Amendment.) Others called for mandatory retirement. Scholars excavated constitutional history to show that the framers did not intend the high court to be able to overturn statutes. Charles Beard, the leading progressive historian, published a bestseller, *An Economic Interpretation of the Constitution of the United States*, which argued that the framers were mostly interested in protecting their own property interests. Richard

Hofstadter later observed that Beard's book confronted "a nation of Constitution-worshipers and ancestor-worshipers . . . with a scholarly muckraking of the Founding Fathers and the Constitution itself."

The simmering anger—what one historian calls a "muted fury"— finally took the form of a full and threatening backlash when the most dynamic, revered, and controversial figure of the age made the issue of the courts his own.

On June 18, 1910, a steamship pulled up to the Battery at the foot of Manhattan, accompanied by six navy battleships, tooting tugboats, and a flotilla of yachts. Theodore Roosevelt bounded off the ship. The former president, only fifty-two years old, was returning from a sixteen-month world tour, where he had been entertained by heads of state and had hunted animals in Africa for the new Museum of Natural History. Thousands thronged the Battery, where Roosevelt was greeted by uniformed veterans of his old military unit, the Rough Riders, celebrities, and a giant teddy bear bobbing from a ninth-story window. Millions more cheered his slow parade through five miles of city streets. He told the crowd he wanted privacy—he would "close up like a native oyster"—and was then "ready and eager to do my part" to help solve the nation's problems. Very soon it was clear that he wanted above all to bag the Supreme Court.

Roosevelt had long shed the awe and reverence toward judges shared by many contemporaries. As a young state legislator, he led investigative trips into the tenements of New York's Lower East Side, peering into apartments jammed with adults and children who manufactured cigars into the night. Together with the cigarmakers union Roosevelt lobbied for a new state law to ban cigar manufacturing in tenements. But the New York Court of Appeals, the state's highest court, struck down the law as a violation of the manufacturers' rights of private property. "It was this case which first waked me to a dim and partial understanding of the fact that the courts were not necessarily the best judges of what should be done to better social and industrial conditions," he recalled. The judges "knew nothing whatever of tenement house conditions," he charged, "they knew nothing whatever of the needs, or of the life and labor, of three-fourths of their fellow-citizens in great cities." By the end of his nearly eight years as president, he had grown to embrace the need for a strong central government to stand up to the business titans, whom he called "malefactors of great wealth."

He began his 1910 speaking tour in Denver, Colorado, bellowing out five talks in one day. A local newspaper reported, "Everywhere he went he was greeted by cheering multitudes, which blocked the streets, interfered with traffic and packed to suffocation the various buildings in which he spoke." The visit culminated in an address to a joint session of the Colorado legislature. Roosevelt attacked the U.S. Supreme Court, citing the Sugar Trust case and *Lochner*. In print, the former president charged that the justices had "strained to the utmost (and, indeed, in my judgement, violated) the Constitution in order to sustain a do-nothing philosophy which has everywhere completely broken down when applied to the actual conditions of modern life."

In 1912, Roosevelt launched another campaign for president, challenging the incumbent of his own party, William Howard Taft. Speaking to the Constitutional Convention in Taft's home state of Ohio, Roosevelt made an audacious proposal: state court rulings that strike down laws under the federal or state constitutions should be subject to a "recall" vote by the public. "[W]hen a judge decides a constitutional question, when he decides what the people as a whole can or cannot do, the people should have the right to recall that decision if they think it wrong," Roosevelt argued. His idea was wildly controversial. *The New York Times* called a version of it "the craziest article ever published by a man of high standing." Roosevelt took pains to insist his proposal would only apply to state courts but confided to a journalist that it would likely eventually apply to the U.S. Supreme Court as well. Returning home from Columbus, Roosevelt told reporters, "My hat is in the ring," coining a new political cliché. He added, "the fight is on and I am stripped to the buff."

His attack on the courts became the defining issue of the 1912 campaign. Taft, sluggish and depressed about his former mentor's campaign, was incensed at the proposal. He told a New Hampshire audience he was confident the American people "will never give up on the Constitution and they are not going to be honey-fugled out of it by being told that they are fit to interpret nice questions of constitutional law just as well as or better than judges."

It was one of the country's most thrilling elections: a former president, challenging his handpicked successor. Roosevelt swept the Republican primaries, which showed public support but did not produce enough delegates to win the nomination. His insurgent campaign— and his attacks on the courts—won support from seven governors. But Taft and the "Old Guard" controlled the party convention. They engineered a platform that began with an attack on judicial recall and a defense of "an untrammeled and independent judiciary." Roosevelt and his supporters stormed out of the Chicago Coliseum. A mile away they met at Symphony Hall and formed the Progressive Party, committed to court reform (as well as to social regulation, campaign finance reform, voting rights for women, and environmental protection). Settlement house leader Jane Addams seconded his nomination. "We stand at Armageddon and we battle for the Lord," Roosevelt roared.

The Democrats nominated New Jersey governor Woodrow Wilson. He had been critical of the Constitution itself as being too restrictive to efficient government earlier in his career, but ducked the court issue and stayed far from challenging the Supreme Court itself. The Democrat won as the Republicans split, with Roosevelt taking 27 percent— the largest share ever won by a third-party candidate. When TR lost the court issue faded. Taft later became chief justice, where he led a Court that continued to blockade progressive laws.

The issues Theodore Roosevelt raised would not be resolved until the administration of his cousin, Franklin.

Franklin Roosevelt had gone to law school and even practiced a bit of law. But his reverence for the courts, too, was pro forma. He paid homage to the Supreme Court's progressive giants, the dissenters who had battled for judicial restraint. Only two days into his presidency, Roosevelt visited the recently retired Oliver Wendell Holmes, now ninety-two years old. After the gregarious new president stayed for a half hour, Holmes summed him up: "A second class mind, but a first class temperament." The Court's progressives had close ties to the new administration: Louis Brandeis—now on the Supreme Court—even quietly paid Roosevelt's gossipy advisor, Harvard professor Felix Frankfurter, for off-the-books political work. But Roosevelt relished wielding power. Historian Jeff Shesol, in his definitive look at the court fights of the 1930s, uncovered a plan by the president to simply ignore the Court if it had ruled against him on monetary policy in 1933.

The day FDR took office, one third of the workforce was idle and the nation was in the middle of a month-long banking crisis, with panicked depositors trying to withdraw their money. Within days he closed the banks. Within weeks he had persuaded Congress to establish an "alphabet soup" of new government agencies to boost wages and farm prices, regulate the economy, enlist business, police the stock market, and more. Fifteen major laws passed in the First Hundred Days. Many were improvised, a product of Roosevelt's call for "bold, persistent experimentation." Political scientist V. O. Key observed that before Roosevelt took office, the federal government "had been a remote authority with a limited range of activity. It operated the postal system, improved rivers and harbors, maintained armed forces on a scale fearsome only to banana republics, and performed other functions of which the average citizen was hardly aware."

Watching all this unfold, the Supreme Court seemed distant, unmoved, in a different century from the anguish and conflict of the Depression. Critics called the justices the "Nine Old Men." Four of the nine ardently opposed the New Deal. Known as the "Four Horsemen" (as in "of the Apocalypse"), they were not just cautious, they were reactionary. One of them refused to speak to Brandeis for years.

On "Black Monday" in May 1935, the Court struck against the New Deal. Chief Justice Charles Evans Hughes sported a pointy white beard and glowering eyebrows, and was said to look like Jehovah. He vehemently read the opinions, in increasing order of importance, to heighten the drama. All were unanimous. That day the justices declared a law designed to help farmers recover their foreclosed homes was an unconstitutional "taking" of property from the bank. They ruled that FDR lacked the power to remove a reactionary member of the Federal Trade Commission. (He had insisted on showing up for work until his fellow commissioners barred him.)

Most significant, in *Schechter Poultry v. U.S.* the Supreme Court struck down the National Recovery Administration: the centerpiece of the New Deal. The NRA, as it was known, set prices and wages, protected against "ruinous competition," and encouraged the right to organize a union for workers. At one point an estimated 85 percent of businesses had enlisted. Its Blue Eagle logo was embraced as a sign of patriotic participation. In September 1933, 250,000 workers and businesspeople marched in a great parade supporting the agency in New York City before one and a half million cheering spectators. Many of the newspapers that reported on the ruling themselves sported the Blue Eagle with its slogan: WE DO OUR PART.

In *Dred Scott* the Court had used originalism; the Progressive Era Court brandished "freedom of contract" nowhere found in the text of the Constitution. The anti–New Deal court grasped for whatever theoretical tools it had lying around. In *Schechter*, the justices cited the structure of the government itself. For the first time ever, they ruled that Congress had given over too much of its power to regulatory agencies, power that only elected lawmakers themselves could use. It was called the "nondelegation doctrine." The justices borrowed, too, from the strained semantics of the Sugar Trust case, claiming that the Schechter Poultry company did not engage in interstate commerce, since it had sold its sick chicken to a local butcher. The justices explained that mining, agriculture, and manufacturing—in other words, much of the national economy—were merely "intra-state commerce." It was a specious opinion, at a time when a national economy linked millions of local businesses and their decisions into a stream of commerce.

The NRA was the heart of the New Deal so far, what FDR had called "the most important and far-reaching legislation ever enacted by the American Congress," and now it lay in ruins. Brandeis warned two of Roosevelt's young aides, "This is the end of this business of centralization, and I want you to go back and tell the president that we're not going to let this government centralize everything."

On the last day of May, with reporters crammed around his desk scribbling notes, Roosevelt held a furious press conference to attack the Court, reading angry telegrams from constituents. He called the ruling "more important than any decision probably since the *Dred Scott* case." Roosevelt decried the Court's reading of the Constitution. "We have been relegated to the horse-and-buggy definition of interstate commerce." Seven months later, the justices demolished his farm program. Regulating agriculture, the justices ruled, did not fall within the Constitution's language allowing Congress to protect the "general welfare of the United States."

So as 1935 went on, with his agenda having been reduced to rubble, and facing populist pressure from Louisiana senator Huey Long and his "share the wealth" program, FDR moved to the left. The "Second New Deal" enacted a generation's worth of long-sought progressive goals. The National Labor Relations Act protected the right of unions to organize. Laws broke up power company monopolies and strengthened antitrust. Through the Works Progress Administration, the federal government launched its largest ever public works and public employment effort. And the Social Security Act created a nationwide system of old age support and unemployment insurance.

As the American welfare state was being created, it appeared once again that the justices were preparing to thwart it. In the last day of the 1935–36 term, the Supreme Court struck down a New York law requiring that employers pay women a minimum wage—showing it feared not only federal power, but social legislation at any level of government. "If this decision does not outrage the moral sense of the country," said Interior Secretary Harold Ickes, "then nothing will." Roosevelt told reporters that the Court had created a " 'no-man's-land' where no Government—State or Federal—can function."

Roosevelt tried to craft Social Security so it could evade a Court veto. He had some inside help. At an afternoon tea, Justice Harlan Fiske Stone ran into Labor Secretary Frances Perkins, the architect of Social Security. "He looked around to see if anyone was listening," she recalled. "Then he put his hand up like this, confidentially, and he said, 'The taxing power, my dear, the taxing power. You can do anything under the taxing power.' " But all expected a looming clash between the New Deal and the Court.

It became a big issue in the 1936 campaign. At Madison Square Garden, in the last speech of what he expected to be his final campaign for office, Roosevelt practically shouted, "Never before in all our history have these forces been so united against one candidate as they stand today. They are unanimous in their hate for me—and I welcome their hatred." His new electoral coalition included rising and radical industrial unions such as the United Steelworkers and the Amalgamated Clothing Workers, which organized all workers in an industry rather than their trades (such as plumbers). Catholic and Jewish immigrants in northern cities, an increasing number of Black voters, and anticorporate western progressives who once had backed the Republicans all combined with solid support from white voters in the South to create a new dominant political coalition. In November 1936, Roosevelt won 61 percent of the popular vote and the biggest Electoral College margin in history. Supporters from fifteen states assumed he would propose a constitutional amendment to undo the Court's rulings from *Lochner* forward, and began to organize a campaign in support.

At the very moment the Supreme Court was poised to strike at the New Deal again, the country faced rising, nearly revolutionary, social agitation.

On December 30, 1936, fifty assembly line workers at General Motors' Fisher Body plant in Flint, Michigan, workers who had struggled for months to win recognition of their union, laid down their tools and went on strike. They did not walk out to picket; they sat down. That protected them against company goons, against the frigid weather, and against the likelihood of being replaced by other workers. Sit-downs spread to nearby plants. The strike choked off supplies to other GM buildings, and soon thousands of workers were occupying the vast compound of auto factories. One evening women—wives, mothers, and girlfriends of the strikers—gathered at the gate to bring food. When guards refused entry, they broke open the fence and poured in. Flint police arrived and began firing bullets and tear gas into the factory. They were met with a hail of rocks, with tools raining down from the roof. Genora Johnson, the twenty-three-year-old wife of a striker, took the microphone in a sound car belonging to the union. "Cowards! Cowards!" she shouted at the police. "Shooting unarmed and defenseless men!" Firing continued all night.

A state judge issued an injunction to end the strike. Governor Frank Murphy—who in three years would become a U.S. Supreme Court justice—prepared to send in the National Guard to expel the strikers. Labor leader John Lewis of the Committee for Industrial Organizations met with Murphy. "Tomorrow morning, I shall personally enter Chevrolet No. 4. I shall order the men to disregard your order, to stand fast," he told the governor.

> I shall then walk up to the largest window in the plant, open it, divest myself of my outer raiment, remove my shirt, and bare my bosom. Then when you order your troops to fire, mine will be the first breast that those bullets will strike! And as my body

falls from that window to the ground, you listen to the voice of your grandfather [executed for rebellion in Ireland] as he whispers in your ear, "Frank, are you sure you are doing the right thing?"

Murphy, shaken, decided to send in the Guard only to restore peace, not to take sides and not to end the strike. Soon the company and the union were negotiating. Grinding talks led to the United Auto Workers being recognized with a handshake, the second week of February 1937.

That very same week, with the Wagner Act that protected union organizing coming before the Supreme Court and the entire New Deal on the line, Roosevelt acted.

The president relished his own deviousness. "Roosevelt's first instinct was always to lie," wrote *New York Times* reporter Turner Catledge, "but halfway through an answer, the president realized he could tell the truth and get away with it, so he would shift gears and something true would trickle out." On February 4, 1937, Roosevelt had the Supreme Court over for a traditional reception and dinner. Hovering in a corner, Attorney General Homer Cummings confided to speechwriter Samuel Rosenman, "I feel too much like a conspirator."

The next morning, Roosevelt summoned congressional leaders and handed out a proposal to expand the Supreme Court, then was wheeled to the Oval Office next door to read the message to the press. The president claimed he was worried about overwork for the aging justices. He proposed legislation that would add as many as five seats to the Court, one for each justice over seventy years old. Roosevelt read the message with comic asides, practically winking, and had the reporters in stitches. "Roosevelt's presentation—his mock earnestness and ironic asides—made it hard for reporters to take the text, or even the substance of the proposal, at face value," Shesol wrote. The confident New Dealers expected Congress, where sixty-nine Democrats outnumbered twenty-three Republicans in the Senate, to vote for the "court packing" plan.

But immediately lawmakers recoiled. For many, chafing at the president's dominance, it was a chance to push back—a "barons' revolt" against the king, as one White House aide put it. But it was more than that. In the car on the way back from the White House briefing, the House Judiciary Committee chairman told his colleagues, "Boys, here's where I cash in my chips." When the presidential message was read in the Senate, FDR's own vice president, John Nance Garner, held his nose and turned down his thumb. He then went back to Texas. The bill was opposed by progressive westerners and by conservative Democrats, along with Republicans. A new conservative coalition, in defense of property rights and the Constitution, was being born in opposition to Roosevelt's plan.

A roaring public debate erupted. Historian William Leuchtenburg recounts, "The question was debated at town meetings in New England, at crossroads country stores in North Carolina, at a large rally around the Tulsa courthouse, by the Chatterbox Club of Rochester, New York, the Thursday Study Club of La Crosse, Wisconsin, the Veteran Fire Fighters' Association of New Orleans, and the Baptist Young People's Union of Lime Rock, Rhode Island. In Beaumont, Texas, a movie audience broke out in applause for rival arguments on the plan when they were shown on the screen." With dictatorship rising in Europe a long-standing American fear of concentrated power motivated many who had previously backed Roosevelt's reforms. At the same time conservative business interests quietly funded new "nonpartisan" lobbying and organizing efforts, such as the National Committee to Uphold Constitutional Government. Bankrolled by publisher Frank Gannett, it aimed to "mobilize and coordinate individual and mass protest against the proposed undermining of an independent judiciary." Meanwhile southerners who had supported the New Deal out of party loyalty and a regional desire for investment realized a more liberal Supreme Court might strike down segregation.

Finally Roosevelt came out swinging for his plan—and at the Court. In a fireside chat radio broadcast, Roosevelt gave what Jeff Shesol calls "the most unsparing series of attacks any president had ever made—publicly, at least—against the judiciary." "The Court has been acting not as a judicial body, but as a policy-making body," he charged angrily, adding that the Court "has improperly set itself up as a third House of the Congress—a super-legislature, as one of the justices has called it—reading into the Constitution words and implications which are not there, and which were never intended to be there. We have, therefore, reached the point as a Nation where we must take action to save the Constitution from the Court and the Court from itself."

The fight had many twists and turns. The chief justice wrote a

bombshell letter to Congress. Then the Senate majority leader, to
whom Roosevelt had promised the first new seat, died of a heart attack
in his boardinghouse in the middle of the debate.

But the most unexpected surprise was this: the Court backed down.
It began to uphold the New Deal. Swing vote Owen Roberts suddenly
started to vote with the liberals. First, a month after Roosevelt's bill was
introduced, the Court overruled a 1923 case that had said minimum
wage laws were an affront to liberty and an attack on "freedom of contract." Then, in *West Coast Hotel v. Parrish*, Hughes wrote that the Constitution allowed "the protection of law against the evils which menace
the health, safety, morals, and welfare of the people," as long as the law
was reasonably related to its goal.

Two weeks later came an even bigger surprise. The Court upheld
the National Labor Relations Act, which protected the right of workers to form unions. For forty years manufacturing had been deemed
exempt from federal regulation because it was not "interstate commerce." Now the Court began to recognize the reality of a modern,
interconnected, national economy. Jones and Laughlin, in Pittsburgh,
was the country's largest steel manufacturer, sucking in raw materials
from Minnesota and Michigan, and selling its steel across the country.
That, it turns out, is interstate commerce. If a business has "a close and
substantial relation to interstate commerce," the justices now ruled,
the federal government can regulate it.

Two months later the Court upheld the Social Security Act. It decided in a hurry, as Congress was still debating Roosevelt's court packing plan, and ruled just two weeks after hearing arguments. The ruling
involved three cases. Two upheld the act's unemployment compensation and old age pensions. The third reached a more fundamental issue, one as old as the Constitution. The Founders had debated
whether the federal government had broad general power to act to
protect the public, or only powers specifically spelled out in the document. Now the Court settled the debate: "The conception of the
spending power advocated by [Alexander] Hamilton . . . has prevailed
over that of [James] Madison."

A newspaper humorist called it "the switch in time that saved nine."
Quickly the momentum drained from Roosevelt's bill. It never received
a floor vote. So—what just happened?

Most immediately, Roosevelt faced humiliating reversal. He appeared to be caught attempting a power grab, at a time when dictators were rolling across Europe. His clever evasions did not help. But Roosevelt also hit an invisible barrier. Polls never supported his plan. It turned out that, despite his overwhelming popularity, despite his record-setting electoral victory in 1936 and lopsided congressional margins, and despite ardent public support for the New Deal, there was a latent and powerful strain of reverence for the Supreme Court. His political slide worsened the next year. Roosevelt tried to reorder politics in the 1938 primaries, backing liberal challengers to incumbent Democrats, a "purge" that failed to oust any officeholders. The political coalition that triumphed in the court packing fight—southern Democrats and Republicans—became a new conservative coalition that dominated Congress for most of three decades, and which then became the nascent Republican majority that often controlled politics over the next eighty years.

Court packing lost, yet Roosevelt won the larger legal war. The Court backed off its project of stopping the creation of a regulatory state. It allowed the growth of a powerful government, one that could regulate the economy and erect nationwide social protections. The Court no longer would interfere with economic regulation, no longer impose its policy preference for smaller and weaker government under the guise of "freedom of contract." Some called it a refounding, a new constitutional order.

The Supreme Court was now out of the business of restricting government intervention in the economy. Cases would come before it relating to the procedures of regulation: for a decade business attorneys at the American Bar Association pushed for an Administrative Procedure Act, later so embedded as to seem practically part of the Constitution, as a way to curb Roosevelt's suspiciously pink agencies. There would be no new profusion of federal offices directing this or that segment of industry. But the Securities and Exchange Commission to police the stock market, the National Labor Relations Board to umpire labor disputes, and many others now stood as permanently as their granite buildings in Washington, D.C.

Later generations of conservatives would bemoan this. To them, 1937 was a dark turning in the country's constitutional history—when the justices shrank from their duty to protect private property and an unfettered market economy. They pined for the law as it stood before that moment, and called it the "Constitution in Exile." (Libertarian strategist Randy Barnett objects to the phrase. He prefers "the lost Constitution.")

What would the Court focus on now? Its future direction was mapped out in miniature precision in 1938, in an aside in an otherwise unremarkable case, *Carolene Products*. The company had been caught selling "filled milk," which mixed skim milk with oil, in violation of federal law. The offending milk producer argued that Congress allowed the sale of margarine, which also included oil, so the law was irrational and violated its Fifth Amendment rights. The Court took a clear step back from scrutinizing the basis for government's economic regulation. If Congress was rational, if it held hearings and had a reason for doing what it did, that was enough. The Supreme Court would not block such a regulation. Thus one more stronghold surrendered in the Court's retreat in the wake of the court packing fight. The case was decided only two weeks after it was argued, and the decision did not merit coverage in *The New York Times*.

Its significance over time came in footnote four, certainly the most famous in legal history. In it the justices spelled out what they would and would not scrutinize. Economic regulation would now be presumed to be constitutional. But then what would the Court do? It would likely direct "more exacting scrutiny" to laws where the political process was broken—the very system "which can ordinarily be expected to bring repeal of undesirable legislation"—laws such as "restrictions upon the right to vote," "restraints upon the dissemination of information," "interferences with political organizations," "prohibition of peaceable assembly."

And of perhaps greatest significance for the next eighty years, the Court might review "statutes directed at particular religious or racial minorities." After all, the footnote continued, "prejudice against discrete and insular minorities may be a special condition, which tends seriously to curtail the operation of those political processes ordinarily to be relied upon to protect minorities, and which may call for a correspondingly more searching judicial inquiry."

Protecting the rights of "discrete and insular minorities"—that would be a new vision for the Supreme Court, one at odds with the approach it had taken for the previous 149 years. No longer would it focus on protecting property rights and curbing regulation. It would now, to the extent it acted, focus on individual rights, human rights, and democracy.

This began the rights revolution that would elevate the role of the Supreme Court while transforming the country. Starting in the 1940s and continuing up until the 2010s—nearly three quarters of a century—national politicians and judges, prodded by social movements, built a system of national citizenship rights for the first time. Some of this came from the establishment of a truly continent-wide economy, through defense spending, public works, and highway programs under presidents of both parties. Some of it came from the enactment of civil rights statutes—especially the Civil Rights Act of 1964 and the Voting Rights Act of 1965, in which Congress imposed national oversight of the South and its mistreatment of Black citizens. And some of it, indeed more and more of it over time, came from the actions of the federal courts, which aggressively announced the protection of rights and imposed those protections on balky state and local officials.

At first, though, in the wake of its retreat before Roosevelt, most people expected the Court to step back. Within five years after the court packing plan failed, Roosevelt had appointed seven justices, New Dealers all, no doubt expecting them to share the long-standing liberal commitment to judicial restraint. World War II was a time of overwhelming assent to government power: the military draft, rationing, price controls, orders to major industries to produce tanks not cars. In the infamous *Korematsu* case, the Court allowed the federal government to intern Japanese Americans. (Former Michigan governor Frank Murphy, now a justice, dissented, calling it "legalization of racism.") It blocked wartime freedom of speech. It let school districts force children to recite the Pledge of Allegiance, though it quickly regretted the decision and soon reversed it. The national mood was consensus and again the Supreme Court bobbed along.

The Supreme Court never before had its own building. It heard cases and made its rulings in the old Senate chamber in the U.S. Capitol, a

physical manifestation of its secondary role in the system of government. The imposing "Marble Palace" across the street from the Capitol did not open until 1935. It gleamed and intimidated. With Greek
style columns and the slogan EQUAL JUSTICE UNDER LAW carved above
two giant brass doors, the building was, according to Justice Harlan
Fiske Stone when he saw it, "almost bombastically pretentious." The
new building coincided with the Court's year of hubris, when it struck
down the New Deal laws, and then its humiliation as it was forced to
retreat. But as the public got used to seeing the justices rule from what
seemed more than any other official building in Washington to be a
Greek temple, the Court's prestige soared.

CHAPTER FOUR

THE WARREN COURT

T HROUGHOUT HISTORY, THE SUPREME COURT TRACKED the country's consensus, at least as reflected in the ascendant political coalition of the time. Rarely did it venture beyond this unmarked spot. When it did, as we have seen, it often blundered or provoked a backlash. Only one time did the Supreme Court act boldly but not simply to protect property and uphold the social order. That came in the mid-twentieth century, under Chief Justice Earl Warren. The Warren Court was a brief anomaly. By its end, it, too, had veered far from the public consensus, with lasting political consequences.

Earl Warren had been a crusading prosecutor and then the Republican governor of California, and was the party's nominee for vice president in 1948. At the Republican convention in 1952, Richard Nixon delivered his state's delegation to Dwight Eisenhower, double-crossing Warren, but the governor won a promise of a court appointment. Warren loved campaigning, with a slap on the back, a grin, and a freakish memory for names. Bromides about patriotism and fellowship, he believed them all. He had overseen the internment of Japanese Americans during World War II as state attorney general, but as chief justice he led the Court to become the principal and for a time only organ of the federal government fighting for racial equality.

The Warren Court began with its most revered case: *Brown v. Board of Education.*

The NAACP Legal Defense and Educational Fund had pressed for a ruling on school segregation, waging a careful campaign over two decades. Charles Hamilton Houston and his protégé Thurgood Marshall first won rulings that desegregated law schools and required the admission of Black applicants to other graduate schools, rulings that proved that separate but underfunded schools were not equal. But public schools in the South (and in much of the rest of the country) loomed as the most daunting edifice in segregation and of the Jim Crow system that still dominated much of the country. *Brown* consolidated lawsuits that were brought across the country, including one from Topeka, Kansas.

Marshall first argued the case in 1952. Had the Court ruled then, it might have struck down school segregation, but would have issued a divided, dissonant opinion. Activists such as Hugo Black would have voted quickly to strike down separate-but-equal. Black was a surprising champion. He had been a liberal U.S. senator from Alabama—a zoological species hard to imagine today—and a backer of Roosevelt's reforms, including court packing. He was appointed the first new justice after the "switch in time." But Black also had once been a member of the Ku Klux Klan, a fact that emerged only after he was confirmed for the bench. Black was so humiliated by the scandal that he became a fierce adherent of the Bill of Rights. The other southern justices would likely have dissented in *Brown*. Felix Frankfurter, crony of Roosevelt and Brandeis, was torn: a refugee himself, he had been a civil rights activist, but he hesitated, still in the grip of the progressive commitment to judicial restraint.

As the Court wavered, Chief Justice Fred Vinson died. Frankfurter declared privately, "This is the first indication I have ever had that there is a God." The case was put off for another year, and the parties were asked to reargue it.

Soon after, Earl Warren arrived. Quickly he made clear he saw segregation as a moral issue, and he wanted the Court to speak unanimously. "I can't escape the feeling that no matter how much the Court wants to avoid it, it must now face the issue," he said in his first conference on the case, the private meeting where the justices tell each other their views. Warren waged a high-EQ campaign within the court, lunching with wavering segregationist justices five days in a row before the final vote. He drafted an opinion that was short so newspapers would print it in full. *Brown* declared in plain language that "separate but equal" in public schools is unconstitutional, a violation of the Fourteenth Amendment's requirement of "equal protection under the law." In the ruling, the justices declared the education systems of eight states to be unconstitutional. The justices wrestled with whether *Plessy* was wrong or just outdated, whether segregation was unconstitutional from the start or whether evidence now showed that separate could not be equal. The opinion did not formally overturn all of *Plessy*; that case had been about transportation, not education. But it aimed to upend the entire racial caste system of a large part of the country. Restrained, it was not.

Brown did not end school segregation. A decade after the ruling, less than 2 percent of Black children in the South attended integrated schools. Change can create a demand for more change, and *Brown* helped induce a revolution of rising expectations among young Black people in the South. Twenty-six-year-old Martin Luther King Jr. said in his first speech to a mass meeting on the bus boycott in Montgomery less than two years later, "If we are wrong, the Supreme Court of this nation is wrong," earning his first thunderous applause after a nervous start. "If we are wrong, the Constitution of the United States is wrong. If we are wrong, God Almighty is wrong."

But one thing *Brown* was not, at the time of the ruling, was deeply unpopular. The Truman administration had argued for it the first time the justices heard the case. (Already the Democratic Party platform had come out against racial discrimination.) The Justice Department noted that State Department files bulged with evidence that international focus on Jim Crow was "growing in alarming proportions." The new Eisenhower administration argued in 1953 that the fight against communism abroad compelled action. India had declared itself "nonaligned" in the Cold War, Africa was in play, and segregation was a blight. When the Court announced its ruling, the government's Voice of America radio network quickly broadcast the news around the world and bragged about this feat to journalists. At home, legally enforced segregation was seen as a regional quirk, with broad majorities in the rest of the country approving of the Court's ruling. Just days after the announcement, 58 percent of respondents and 80 percent of those outside the South told the Gallup Poll they supported *Brown*. According to a Gallup Poll two years later, when the Court struck down segregation in streetcars and buses in Montgomery, Alabama—formally overruling *Plessy*—70 percent of respondents outside the South supported the ruling. In the South, only 27 percent approved. (Of course, actual discrimination and segregation was hardly limited to one region.)

In the 1950s the Warren Court was just feeling its power and recognizing the magnitude of the task it had set out for itself. It was at war with
officialdom in much of the country. *Brown* was deliberately vague about
enforcement. The next year the Court reassured officials they could
act with "all deliberate speed."

At first, some southern white leaders acquiesced, but a new and
more virulently racist crop of politicians challenged them. Two years
after *Brown* was decided, southern members of Congress—almost all
of them Democrats—signed a brazen document. The Southern Manifesto decried a "clear abuse of judicial power" and vowed all "lawful
means" of defiance. Across the South, the Court's rulings were met
with "massive resistance," as school boards and governors simply refused to desegregate. Alabama's populist governor Jim Folsom vetoed
bills that had tried to preserve segregation. "When the Supreme Court
speaks, bud, that's the law," he explained. In the 1958 governor's race
to succeed Folsom, George Wallace ran as a populist and a racial moderate. He lost to a more extreme candidate. Four years later Wallace
routinely denounced the Court, sputtering, "Earl Warren does not
have enough brains to try a chicken thief in my home county!" He
would be elected in 1962 as a vicious segregationist. In parts of Virginia, officials shut down the public schools rather than integrate. In
Arkansas a court ordered the integration of Little Rock Central High
School, and as white mobs beset the seven Black students on their first
day of classes, local officials refused to enforce the law. Only federal
troops restored order.

Eight months later the state argued it did not have to follow a
federal court order. The Supreme Court responded with force. Each
justice signed *Cooper v. Aaron*. For the first time they announced two
principles. First, the Supreme Court of the United States was solely responsible for deciding what was constitutional. "[T]he interpretation
of the Fourteenth Amendment enunciated by this Court in the *Brown*
case is the supreme law of the land." And its rulings, and even more, its
precedents are binding on all cases in federal and state court. This, the
opinion claimed, was "long-settled doctrine."

In fact, the Supreme Court's declaration in *Cooper*—a sweeping
assertion of its own power—was something new. Judicial review had

been long established. But mostly that meant courts would not enforce unconstitutional laws. Other people in other parts of government had a duty to interpret the Constitution as well. Some said, as Lincoln did in his inaugural, that court rulings did not bind parties not before the Court. In its 1958 ruling the Court took a step beyond judicial review: judicial supremacy. When it interprets the Constitution, the whole country must follow its interpretation. The doctrine was established at the Court's high point, and at a moment when that assertion of national authority was necessary to break segregation. Without it the rulings of the federal judges throughout the South (often the only pro-integration official, and often the only Republican) would lack teeth. It set up the Supreme Court as the super-legislature, not doing battle with the other branches but presiding over them.

Outside the South, the Court's credibility, its aura of power and independence, all soared. Its prestige could be glimpsed beyond the courtroom. In November 1963, conspiracy theories already swirled in the grief-stricken days after the assassination of John F. Kennedy in Dallas. Lyndon Johnson frantically sought a way to investigate the shooting and the televised murder of the accused assassin, in a way that the public would accept. Earl Warren was his solution. Johnson's mentor, segregationist senator Richard Russell, balked at serving on a commission to investigate the assassination. "I couldn't serve there with Chief Justice Warren. I don't like that man," Russell told Johnson. It was too late, the president replied: he had already announced it.

As for Warren, he had long criticized judges who served in high-profile roles off the court, such as when Robert Jackson prosecuted Nazi war crimes at Nuremberg. He refused to chair the panel. In the Oval Office, Johnson turned on his treatment, citing Warren's service in World War I, warning that many people assumed the Soviet Union had ordered the assassination and that belief could lead to World War III, and leaving Warren in tears. Robert A. Caro writes, "It hadn't even taken that long—according to the White House log, twenty-two minutes at most. It's possible to make a sale quickly, even a very big sale, if the salesman is good enough."

In the early 1960s, Earl Warren finally won control of the Warren Court. When he had taken the chief justiceship, the New Deal acolytes installed after 1937 were at each other's throats. Frankfurter, still leery of right-wing judicial activism, demanded restraint, while Hugo Black and former Securities and Exchange Commission chairman William O. Douglas were eager for the Court to wade into things. Segregationists rounded out the roster. A key moment came in 1956, as Eisenhower ran for reelection in a country still dominated by Democrats. He had an opening to fill shortly before the election. Eisenhower wanted a Catholic Democrat, one on a state supreme court, and preferably someone young. William Brennan of New Jersey fit the bill, and he was appointed without so much as a job interview. Brennan had a recess appointment, which meant, impossible to imagine as it is today, that he took his seat temporarily without a Senate vote. When he did come up for confirmation, only red-baiter Joseph McCarthy voted against him.

In the 1950s and 1960s a cultural revolution transformed the United States. Social roles changed with astounding velocity. The civil rights movement and its victories for racial justice helped kindle other movements for change. The role of women began to shift. By decade's end, gay rights—once so taboo that homosexuality could get a person denied government employment as a blackmailable security risk—had its own movement, after riots following a police vice squad raid at the Stonewall Inn in Greenwich Village. The modern environmental movement began to question the impact of industrial progress on nature and public health. While it did not receive as much attention as the Civil Rights and Voting Rights Acts, the 1965 Immigration and Nationality Act reopened America's borders to immigrants, with an extraordinary long-term impact.

The Supreme Court, for the first time, and the only time, rode the wave of that cultural revolution. In fact, it became an instigator of it. To Warren *Carolene Products* was no footnote. His court relied on its approach to craft a nationwide regime of expanded individual rights.

In the early 1960s, most public schoolchildren in the United States recited a mandatory government-written prayer to start the school day. Many of these were nondenominational: in New York State, along with attendance and the Pledge of Allegiance, students were required to recite, "Almighty God, we acknowledge our dependence upon Thee, and we beg Thy blessings upon us, our parents, our teachers and our country. Amen." Other prayers were more explicitly Christian. In 1962, the Supreme Court banned them all. The next year the justices prohibited school-sponsored Bible reading.

The Warren Court did more. It barred the introduction in criminal trials of evidence illegally seized by police in cases all across the country. It ruled that criminal defendants had to be represented by a lawyer, that poor defendants would have one provided for them, and that police needed to warn suspects—resulting in lines now so familiar from television and movies that most could recite without thinking: "You have the right to remain silent. Anything you say can and will be used against you in a court of law." The justices ruled, in a case stemming from a newspaper ad in support of Dr. Martin Luther King Jr., that the First Amendment applied to libel law, previously a matter of state law. As a result, public figures could now be criticized without fear of legal sanction unless the attacks were knowingly false or made with "reckless" carelessness. The modern era of robust and rambunctious political speech began with this case.

The justices even began to rewrite the rules of politics. For a century the Court had largely stayed away from addressing antidemocratic practices or enforcing voting rights. It avoided what it called "political questions." In 1920, when the census showed cities outnumbering rural areas for the first time, Congress simply refused to reapportion congressional seats. The judiciary did nothing. Every so often there would be an exception, such as the case in 1944 where the Court struck down a "whites only" Democratic primary in Texas. But mostly justices shrank from involvement. Sometimes, it was because they were perfectly comfortable with the biased system that resulted. Sometimes, as with Frankfurter—a political liberal who had become a judicial conservative, endlessly railing against stumbling into the "political thicket"—it was a product of the long progressive devotion to judicial restraint. In any case, by its inaction over at least a century the Supreme Court had allowed an imbalanced and inequitable political system to evolve. In large stretches of the country, it could barely be described as a democracy. As cities grew, their power shrank compared to rural areas entrenched in legislatures. By 1960, according to legal historian J. Douglas Smith, "in nineteen states, the largest [congressional] district had more than twice the number of residents as the smallest. . . . The largest district in Texas contained four times the number of residents as the smallest district." State legislatures were even more lopsided. Nearly 40 percent of the population of California lived in Los Angeles County, but under California's constitution that county was entitled to just one of forty state senators.

In 1962 the Supreme Court waded into the thicket and revolutionized representation. In *Baker v. Carr*, the justices decided that courts would hear cases alleging political inequality due to apportionment. Two years later, in *Reynolds v. Sims*, the Court proclaimed the doctrine of "one person, one vote," decreeing roughly equal-sized legislative districts. "Legislators represent people, not trees or acres. Legislators are elected by voters, not farms or cities or economic interests. The right to vote freely for the candidate of one's choice is the essence of a democratic society, and any restrictions on that right strike at the heart of representative government." By 1968, ninety-three of ninety-nine state legislative chambers had their lines redrawn to comply with the Supreme Court's ruling.

The Warren Court by one key measure was not activist. While willing to override the states, an assertion of federal power, it was "conspicuously reluctant to strike down laws passed by Congress," one recent analysis concluded. This contrasted sharply with the attitude of later courts.

Much of the transformation came from how the Warren Court applied the Bill of Rights. The first ten amendments to the Constitution were always admired and quoted, but they had little impact on how most of the country was governed. That is because the Supreme Court, in 1833, had declared that the Bill of Rights curbed only the power of the federal government, not of states. The Fourteenth Amendment—enacted to create a national presumption of equal rights, after a war fought to eradicate the slavery protected by states' rights—might have been expected to change that. But in 1873, as they gutted the Fourteenth Amendment, the justices claimed that the "privileges and immunities" it protected only referred to those in the U.S. Constitution and associated with U.S. citizenship, not any rights that might be infringed by states.

The act of applying the protections of the Bill of Rights to actions by state and local governments is known as "incorporation." The justices began to do that in the 1920s, when the First Amendment's guarantee of freedom of speech first blocked action by a state government. A socialist politician named Benjamin Gitlow had been arrested during the Great War for distributing a newspaper, *The Revolutionary Age*, that included a "Left Wing Manifesto" calling for workers to strike. The justices ruled that the Bill of Rights protected speech against overreach by states as well as the federal government, and that First Amendment rights were "among the fundamental personal rights and 'liberties' protected by the due process clause of the Fourteenth Amendment from impairment by the States." (Gitlow had been a member of the New York State legislature. He later became the Communist Party's candidate for vice president, pledging to convert the White House into apartments for workers and poor farmers. After Joseph Stalin expelled him from the party, Gitlow became a conservative anticommunist crusader.) Bit by bit, at the same moment that the national government was extending its reach, the Court began to extend the Bill of Rights to states as well.

But by the 1950s most Bill of Rights protections still had not yet been applied to the states—which meant, with most infringements on rights taking place not in Washington, D.C., but in states and counties the Bill of Rights was largely unenforced. The Warren Court changed that, almost instantaneously in constitutional time. Suddenly the full array of safeguards was deployed and deployable against police officers, county courts, and government officials across the country. Suddenly we had a truly national constitution.

For readers today, it's important to understand the magnitude of this change. For the very first time, a national set of rights extended throughout the country. It now mattered much less where you lived. The right to vote, the right to speak, criminal rights, and more were now protected equally, at least in theory, in Oregon and in Mississippi, in Minnesota and in Texas. That was not reality, of course, especially when it came to race, but it became the national ideal and the national expectation. Nearly everyone reading these words grew up in this world. In some ways this was the extension of the New Deal moment to constitutional law and individual rights. Like the New Deal, it seemed a new permanent reality.

But the Warren Court got swept up in the excesses of the era. It is hard to know how much of the backlash was an inevitable response to racial and gender revolutions. But the Court at times seemed to become unmoored. Like much of the American establishment, straining to find its footing at a time of epochal change, it seemed like it was going through a midlife crisis.

William O. Douglas was one of its most controversial members. FDR had named him the crusading chairman of the Securities and Exchange Commission soon after the agency was created. He joined the Court in 1939. In 1944, when political party leaders told the distracted wartime leader that he had to jettison Vice President Henry Wallace, Roosevelt suggested he preferred Douglas to be the successor. "He plays an interesting game of poker," Roosevelt explained. Douglas never stopped hungering for higher office. His children from the first of four marriages claimed he spoke to them only when "press photographers wanted a picture." Scholar Jeffrey Rosen summarized, "he left his third wife for a high school student who had asked him to sponsor her senior thesis, and then divorced her after twenty-four months for a college student whom he had met while she was a waitress in a cocktail lounge."

Douglas, of all people, was chosen to write for the Court on its landmark 1965 opinion about the legality of contraception, *Griswold v. Connecticut.* It is hard to imagine it being issued at any other moment, at least not the way it was written.

Contraception was legally distributed in nearly all states. A few had some restrictions. It was illegal to sell contraception in Massachusetts, for example, but not to possess it. Connecticut, though, had an 1879 law passed during an anti-smut campaign that forbade the "use" and "abetting" of contraception. The law had been championed by state senator Phineas T. Barnum (yes, that P. T. Barnum). Barnum's law remained on the books though it was rarely enforced. Planned Parenthood clinics repeatedly sued to overturn the statute, but their efforts failed. Over the years the Catholic Church grew increasingly opposed to birth control, and it wielded enough power in the state legislature in Hartford to prevent repeal. Much of Connecticut's politics revolved around the fight, pitting Yankees against Irish and Italian voters. At the time, birth control was a Republican Party pastime. Prescott Bush lost a U.S. Senate election when it was revealed he had served as the national treasurer of Planned Parenthood, and his son George H. W. Bush, transplanted to Texas, earned himself the nickname "rubbers."

In 1959, a couple using pseudonyms of Pauline and Paul Poe sued, and their case reached the U.S. Supreme Court. Their lawyer made a novel argument: even though there is no explicit right to privacy in the

Constitution, "When the long arm of the law reaches into the bedroom and regulates the most sacred relations between a man and his wife, it is going too far." John Marshall Harlan II—the grandson of the great dissenter, now a justice himself—embraced the argument in his own dissent. "[T]he full scope of the liberty guaranteed by the Due Process Clause [of the Fourteenth Amendment] cannot be found in or limited by the precise terms of the specific guarantees elsewhere provided in the Constitution. This 'liberty' is not a series of isolated points. . . . It is a rational continuum which, broadly speaking, includes a freedom from all substantial arbitrary impositions and purposeless restraints."

That was sober enough. When Douglas wrote for a seven-to-two majority three years later, that buttoned-down reasoning had gotten rather groovy. "Specific guarantees in the Bill of Rights have penumbras," Douglas wrote, "formed by emanations from those guarantees that help give them life and substance." Penumbras and emanations, all to uphold a right that however intuitive and profound did not appear in the text of the Constitution. It made the ruling an easy mark. Douglas, immune to irony, waxed eloquent about marriage. "Would we allow the police to search the sacred precincts of marital bedrooms for telltale signs of the use of contraceptives? The very idea is repulsive to the notions of privacy surrounding the marriage relationship."

Other justices squirmed at the psychedelic language. A few (including Warren) said they thought the protection for contraception could be found in the explicit language of the Ninth Amendment, which makes clear that people retain rights even if they are not spelled out in the previous eight amendments. Harlan himself pointed to the Due Process Clause as a sturdier foundation. Another simply said Connecticut's law did not have a "rational basis."

Griswold was a constitutional landmark. The right to privacy, to be let alone, is deeply felt, widely recognized, and the foundation for many later rulings on abortion rights, marriage equality, and more. William Brennan summarized it in 1972: "If the right of privacy means anything, it is the right of the individual, married or single, to be free from unwarranted governmental intrusion into matters so fundamentally affecting a person as the decision whether to bear or beget a child." The next year privacy was the basis for *Roe v. Wade.* Yet if "privacy" was a foundation of American law it was one built on "penumbras." *Griswold's* arguments, and even more the sense that the justices were now just making up rights to fit their political predilections, became a compelling talking point for the judicial wars that would shortly begin—a time of polarized ideological combat about the Supreme Court that brings us up to today.

All of this had major consequences.

One was that American liberalism increasingly became a discourse about rights, not about social systems or even equality. Civil rights, women's rights, gay rights, all drew from the approach taken by the Supreme Court. Long-standing issues of economic power, about wealth and unionization, receded. Liberalism reoriented around cultural issues, with a focus on individual freedom. Soon business interests began to advance their goals using rights language, especially trying to harness the power of the First Amendment and its protection of freedom of speech to immunize corporate conduct. Consumer advocates won a First Amendment ruling that customers would benefit when pharmacists could advertise. Soon the major drug companies were spending hundreds of millions of dollars to sell prescription drugs under the same protected speech theory. When campaign finance laws, which previously had been deemed a way to enhance democracy, were treated as though the spending of billionaires was the same as a lonely protester distributing pamphlets on a street corner, it ushered in a wave of money in the name of rights. As rights advanced, notions of equality receded.

Another consequence was that the political left became enamored of litigation as a driver of social change and came to hold the Supreme Court itself in near-religious reverence. Legal groups proliferated even as grassroots organizing withered. "Legal Defense Funds" modeled after Thurgood Marshall's onetime organization drew millions of dollars in funding. Liberals lost muscle mass when it came to practicing politics. They relied on the courts. And they continued to venerate the Supreme Court even as its decisions for decades should have made it a target for activism, or as something to discredit.

The Court was now supreme. Its discourse was now firmly rights based. The conditions had been set and now they would be captured by the right.

CHAPTER FIVE

THE LONG BACKLASH

I T ONLY TOOK FOUR YEARS FOR *Dred Scott* to help provoke the Civil War. Roosevelt's court packing plan, too, came less than two years after the "Black Monday" rulings that invalidated much of the New Deal. Sometimes backlash comes in a sudden spasm.

The backlash to the Warren Court took longer to build, but its impact lasted longer as well. It was a response not solely to the court's rulings—many of which remained popular and became deeply in-grained in the society—but the social change they reflected and has-tened. The backlash to the 1960s lasted much longer than the 1960s did. Most of us have spent most of our lives living in it.

Throughout the backlash, notably, both left and right agreed on one unspoken thing: the dominant role of the Supreme Court, and the framing of public issues as revolving around rights, susceptible to action by the judiciary, with everything "sooner or later . . . a judicial question," as Tocqueville would recognize.

The backlash began regionally after the first rulings on desegrega-tion. Violence rose, as federal judges backed the budding civil rights movement and took on a supervisory role in much of the South. Even so they rarely bore the full brunt. Fury was vented at Dr. Martin Luther King Jr., or at the sit-ins and marches, rather than at the Supreme Court itself. The glow around the Court, as with so many governmental insti-tutions after World War II, meant there was not really an organized, coherent, cohesive opposition. "Impeach Earl Warren" billboards dot-ted the South and West, though it was never clear what exactly he was to be impeached for. On his way to landslide defeat, 1964 Republican presidential nominee Barry Goldwater charged the Court exercised "raw and naked power." Criticism of the Court was seen as a fringe obsession, akin to warnings about water fluoridation.

The political reaction intensified as the 1960s wore on. After *Baker v. Carr* and *Reynolds v. Sims* required that legislative districts be redrawn on an equal population basis, Senate Republican leader Everett Dirksen organized a nationwide campaign for a new constitutional convention to draft an article overturning the decisions. Dirksen won plaudits for helping pass the Civil Rights Act of 1964, but when it came to equal political representation, he organized massive resistance. The idea was that states could draw their lines on some basis other than population if a majority voted for it in a referendum. They organized a well-funded and cutting-edge communications campaign, the Committee for Government of the People. Instead of "One person, one vote," its slogan was "Let the people decide." Dirksen's effort failed.

The Court's rulings on criminal justice, especially those excluding the use of unlawful evidence, coincided with a sharp surge in crime and violence. Riots consumed Detroit, Newark, and other cities. Richard Nixon once allied with the civil rights movement, but now he ran for president pledging "law and order," a new attorney general, and "strict constitutionalist" Supreme Court justices. His Southern Strategy sought to attract to the party of Lincoln white voters angry about civil rights. A young campaign aide, Kevin Phillips, explained the plan to journalist Garry Wills: "the whole secret of politics" was "knowing who hates who." The third-party vote of disgruntled Democrats who supported George Wallace in 1968 kept migrating and was the basis of the new Republican coalition—reflected first in presidential races, then in Congress, and finally in the states.

Having run against the liberal Supreme Court, Nixon tried to put his stamp on it, not always successfully. In his first four years Nixon filled four seats. Earl Warren, a bitter rival from their days in California politics, left the Court shortly after swearing in the new president. As chief justice, Nixon chose Warren Burger, a silver-haired, deep-voiced conservative judge from Minnesota. Burger was mocked for his pomposity. According to Bob Woodward in his book about the Burger Court, *The Brethren,* Thurgood Marshall would scandalize the new leader by greeting him, "What's shakin', Chiefy baby?"

According to his aide John Ehrlichman, Nixon aimed to "stick it to the liberal, Ivy League clique who thought the Court was their own private playground." For a vacancy in 1970, Nixon first proposed Clement Haynsworth. Supporters and opponents agreed Haynsworth was not a stellar thinker. Nebraska senator Roman Hruska tried to defend him. "There are a lot of mediocre judges and people and lawyers," said the Nebraska Republican. "They are entitled to a little representation, aren't they?" The Senate rejected Haynsworth. "Find a good federal judge further South and further to the right," Nixon instructed an aide. They found G. Harrold Carswell, an appeals court judge from Florida. Three days after Carswell was nominated, he found himself having to disavow an earlier speech, in which he had declared, "I am Southern by ancestry, birth, training, inclination, belief and practice. And I believe that segregation of the races is proper and the only practical and correct way of life in our states." The Senate rejected Carswell, too.

Still, the Burger Court is typically seen as a holding action, a hesitation after the turmoil of the 1960s. That's not quite right; the Court continued to exert its authority over more and more of American law and life.

In July 1974, the Court ruled unanimously that Nixon had to honor a grand jury subpoena for tapes of his White House conversations on Watergate. Within two weeks Nixon resigned when one of the recordings showed him ordering a criminal cover-up soon after the burglars were arrested. ("Play it tough. That's the way they play it, and that's the way we are going to play it.")

Other cases reflected the hubris of the Court in its full flush of power. After the Watergate scandal a new campaign finance law sought to restrain both rising spending and big campaign contributions, which were often extorted from businessmen with business before government. *Buckley v. Valeo* blocked the law's spending limits but allowed contribution limits, leaving the system teetering as candidates now were forced to raise huge sums in relatively small amounts. For the first time, the First Amendment was used as the basis for a major campaign finance ruling. In a jumbled opinion with no named author, the justices decided that strengthening democracy was not a legitimate basis for regulation, that millionaires could spend whatever they wanted on their own races, and that committees could spend freely if they professed to be "independent." ("Money is speech and speech is money," as one justice pithily summarized at the argument.) It was an early example of how business and conservative interests began to wield the First Amendment to blunt regulation, a case that eventually led to *Citizens United* and our money-drenched system of campaign finance.

In 1972, the Court found for the first time that the death penalty could constitute "cruel and unusual punishment" prohibited under the Eighth Amendment. The application of that sanction was "freakishly" random, the justices ruled. "These death sentences are cruel and unusual in the same way that being struck by lightning is cruel and unusual," Douglas wrote. But the justices could not agree on the rationale for such a sweeping ruling. It imposed a moratorium, not a ban. The death penalty had been fading away—there had been no executions in the United States for six years—but the fact of a Supreme Court decree mobilized state lawmakers. Public opinion shifted for capital punishment. States began to pass new death penalty laws, and executions began to rise.

Both trends—brash assertion of judicial supremacy, and an expansive vision of rights and willingness to find them where they had not been articulated before—were visible in the Burger Court's most consequential case, *Roe v. Wade.*

It was not at first particularly controversial. The ruling was decided by a seven-to-two vote. States had begun to ease abortion laws and in some cases even to legalize the practice. Arizona, Alaska, New York, and California had ended the ban on abortion in the four years before *Roe.* But the procedure was still entirely illegal in thirty states, and the ruling struck down laws in most of the country. A national move to legalize abortion might have been in the works, but it had not yet happened, and it was immediately supplanted by the Court's ruling. Indeed, in many states, bans stayed untouched on the books, unused for decades.

The opinion grounded the constitutional protection of a woman's right to choose in the "right to privacy." *Roe* set up rules based on how long a woman had been pregnant. There could be no restrictions in the first trimester; limited regulation in the second trimester; and abortions could be banned in the third trimester except to protect the health of the mother. *Roe* was derided by many legal observers, including those friendly to abortion rights, but over time it became entrenched in constitutional law and people's expectations of their rights.

At the time of the ruling, it was the Catholic Church, ancestral home of big-city northern Democrats, that most ardently opposed abortion. Political conservatives and evangelical Christians were largely silent. They viewed it as a "Catholic issue." A March for Life on the first anniversary of the decision drew few protesters. That began to change. Baptists and evangelical churches mobilized, with Rev. Billy Graham's magazine calling abortion "manslaughter, if not murder." In 1977, two days after Jimmy Carter's inauguration, the now annual march drew forty thousand people. The 1972 Republican platform had not discussed the topic; the 1976 platform mentioned *Roe*, and noted there were two sides to the issue; the 1980 platform "reaffirmed" the party's support for a constitutional amendment to overturn the ruling. By the end of the 1970s, the backlash to the Court burned hot. As governor, Ronald Reagan had signed the California law legalizing abortion in 1967. Now, two days after his presidential inaugural in 1981, he met with the organizers of the antiabortion march. In later years he would speak to the growing crowds by loudspeaker. For the veteran actor, it was deft stagecraft: because he did not appear in person, there were no television images.

Reagan's election in 1980, and the surprise sweeping electoral victory of Republican lawmakers in his wake, realigned politics. He ran as an angry voice of backlash, an insurgent ideologue, not a chuckling grandfather. (Reagan's demeanor softened after he was shot in 1981.) The New Right united social conservatives appalled by the proposed Equal Rights Amendment and abortion, economic libertarians pushing back against consumer and environmental regulation, and "supply side" economics boosters urging massive tax cuts for the wealthy. After the Civil Rights Act of 1964, propelled by white backlash, the "Solid South" which anchored Democratic victories now shifted to the Republicans in presidential elections. To the surprise of many, the right became the "party of ideas" as the New Deal consensus crumbled.

Some lawyers and professors joined the crusade. They gathered at the Justice Department around the unlikely figure of Attorney General Edwin Meese. A former California official, Meese was the conservative ideologue among Reagan's "troika" of top aides, along with smooth James Baker III and loyal Michael Deaver. His confirmation dragged on for thirteen months until a special prosecutor cleared him of corruption charges. Meese was no intellectual but surrounded himself with legal activists. His team mapped an audacious strategy to overturn

laws and precedents of recent decades in fifteen separate topics, ranging from the "exclusionary rule" barring the use of criminal evidence
gathered in violation of the Fourth Amendment, to public initiatives to
fund private religious education, to challenging progressive taxation.
They assumed the strategy would take decades.

Soon after finally arriving at the Justice Department, in July
1985, Meese spoke to the American Bar Association, the stodgy trade
group. The attorney general accused the Supreme Court justices of
"roam[ing] at large in a veritable constitutional forest." Ideologically
polarized voting blocs "all reveal a greater allegiance to what the Court
thinks constitutes sound public policy, rather than deference to what
the Constitution—its text and intention—may demand," he said. Without "a coherent jurisprudential stance," the Court risked drifting back
toward "radical egalitarianism."

> What, then, should a constitutional jurisprudence actually
> be? It should be a jurisprudence of original intention. By seek-
> ing to judge policies in light of principles, rather than remold
> principles in light of policies, the Court could avoid both the
> charge of incoherence and the charge of being either too con-
> servative or too liberal. . . . Those who framed the Constitution
> chose their words carefully; they debated at great length the
> minutest points. The language they chose meant something.

Meese's brash assertion launched a jurisprudential movement.
Originalism was hardly the only or the obvious choice for conservatives
seeking a coherent philosophy as they took their places on the bench.
They could have focused on respect for tradition, a sense rooted in the
ideas of Edmund Burke that societies change best when they change
slowly. Another approach drew from libertarian economics and public
choice theory. Law and economics subjected governmental actions to
cost-benefit analysis, using economic tools to argue against regulation.
But originalism had the added value of appealing to the sentimental
veneration of the founding generation (coming after the Bicentennial
of 1976 and before the anniversary of the Constitution in 1987). It had
religious overtones. It also held out the promise of precision and certainty, since the text as written and intended to be read is (originalists
argued) frozen. The year after Meese's controversial speech, Antonin

Scalia—one of the leading conservative legal thinkers—was confirmed by the Senate 98–0. For years, Scalia would respond to students who asked if the Constitution is a living document, "It is not living. It is dead, dead, dead!"

Amid the overheated ideological politics of the Reagan administration, the modern era of rancorous confirmation battles began. Thirty-five years later, conservatives still bemoan the fate of Robert Bork in 1987.

Such fights were not unheard of before, but they were rare. Early on, the Senate voted down one of George Washington's choices for chief justice. Three times in the nineteenth century the Senate rejected nominees, and others withdrew before a vote. (One estimate is that one in three nominees back then never made it onto the Court.) But by the twentieth century all assumed a president got to make his choice, and that senators regardless of party would acquiesce. Dwight Eisenhower even installed his chief justice choice using a recess appointment, without a Senate vote.

Woodrow Wilson's choice of Louis Brandeis provoked the first public brawl over a nomination. After his populist battles with railroads and power companies, Brandeis advised Wilson on his 1912 campaign. Four years later, seeking reelection, Wilson needed to appeal to Theodore Roosevelt's progressive followers. He named Brandeis, the first Jew to be chosen for the Court. One surprised columnist professed to being "stunned as if by a bomb from an unseen Zeppelin."

The Senate Judiciary Committee held nineteen days of hearings over six months, though Brandeis himself never appeared. Former president William Howard Taft led the opposition. "He is a muckraker, an emotionalist for his own purposes, a socialist, prompted by jealousy, a hypocrite . . . a man of infinite cunning . . . of great tenacity of purpose, and in my judgment, of much power for evil," Taft wrote privately. *The Wall Street Journal* editorialized, "Where others were radical, [Brandeis] was rabid; where others were extreme he was super-extreme; where others would trim he would lay the ax to the root of the tree." By the end, seven past presidents of the American Bar Association opposed the nomination. Regardless, a Democratic Senate confirmed Brandeis.

Another exception came in 1930, when the Republican Senate by two votes rejected Herbert Hoover's nomination of John J. Parker.

The nominee had declared a decade before, "The participation of the Negro in politics is a source of evil and danger to both races and is not desired by the wise men in either race or by the Republican Party of North Carolina." The American Federation of Labor, which was angered by an antiworker ruling, and the NAACP, the leading civil rights group waging its first major federal fight, both lobbied against Parker. It was the only time the Senate rejected a nominee between 1894 and 1968.

Protocol frayed in the contentious 1960s. In 1967 Thurgood Marshall went before the Judiciary Committee as the first Black nominee at a time when the top three Democratic senators on the panel were all segregationists. Marshall had won twenty-eight of the thirty-two Supreme Court cases he argued as a civil rights lawyer, then had served as a federal appeals court judge and as solicitor general, who argues for the executive branch before the Court. Strom Thurmond, the onetime Dixiecrat presidential candidate, tried to trip him with obscure historical questions. (They resembled the unanswerable queries southern registrars posed to Black voters.) Another senator grilled Marshall on his belief that the Constitution is a "living document." Repeatedly the southerners implied he was soft on crime. One demanded to know why he did not think voluntary confessions could be admitted in court if a lawyer had not been present. "Well, Senator, the word 'voluntary' gets me in trouble," Marshall replied. "I tried a case in Oklahoma where the man 'voluntarily' confessed after he was beaten up for six days." In the end the Senate confirmed Marshall, 69 votes to 11. The next year the Senate rejected Johnson's choice for chief justice, and soon after that two of Nixon's nominees.

Then conflict over nominations subsided for nearly two decades—until the Bork choice, which entrenched partisan and ideological combat directly and permanently into the judicial confirmation process.

In Bork, Reagan chose a provocateur, a leading conservative intellectual, and sent him to the Senate just after Democrats had regained control of the chamber. Bork's academic mentor had instructed him, "wreak yourself upon the world!" As a Yale professor Bork had revolutionized antitrust, with polemics that steered it away from the law's original goals of protecting against concentration of corporate power and monopolization. Louis Brandeis had decried a "curse of bigness" in business. For Bork, the only measurable and thus legitimate test was "consumer welfare," a phrase that appears nowhere in the text of anti-trust statutes. Monopolies should be lauded if they led to lower prices, even if they gobbled up competitors. A half century of lax antitrust enforcement followed his book.

Bork denounced activist courts with the fervor of an earlier generation of progressives. He decried "judicial imperialism." He believed the First Amendment protected only political speech, nothing else (not pornography, on the one hand, but not literature either). In 1963 he had written that to require business owners to serve African Americans "is itself a principle of unsurpassed ugliness."

The public had briefly met Bork in October 1973 during his dramatic role in the Watergate scandal. Nixon had ordered Attorney General Elliot Richardson to dismiss special prosecutor Archibald Cox for his pursuit of the Oval Office tapes. When Richardson and his deputy resigned in protest, it fell to Bork to fire Cox. The former professor paced nervously around a Justice Department office that night. His theories on executive power persuaded him Nixon was within his rights, but he realized it would upend his smooth career ascent. "I don't want to be seen as an apparatchik," Bork fretted, but acted anyway. What instantly became known as the Saturday Night Massacre was so shocking it led to the start of impeachment proceedings and widespread demands that Nixon resign.

Minutes after Reagan announced Bork's nomination, Edward M. Kennedy of Massachusetts hurried to the Senate floor. "Robert Bork's America," he intoned in his broad Boston accent, "is a land in which women would be forced into back-alley abortions, Blacks would sit at segregated lunch counters, rogue police could break down citizens' doors in midnight raids, schoolchildren could not be taught about evolution, writers and artists could be censored at the whim of the Government, and the doors of the Federal courts would be shut on the fingers of millions of citizens." Kennedy's oratory froze other Democrats, who might otherwise have signaled routine support for a president's nominee.

Liberal activists ran a sophisticated lobbying campaign. People for the American Way, founded by the sitcom producer Norman Lear, ran a television ad with sonorous narration by Gregory Peck, Atticus Finch himself from *To Kill a Mockingbird*. The National Abortion Rights Action League (NARAL) published full-page advertisements in newspapers across the country. "You wouldn't vote for a politician who threatened to wipe out every advance women have made in the twentieth century. Yet your senators are poised to cast a vote that could do just that." Ads by Planned Parenthood were even more alarming. "If your senators vote to confirm the administration's latest Supreme Court nominee, you'll need more than a prescription to get birth control. It might take a constitutional amendment." All this language—so familiar now—was brand-new.

In September 1987, the Senate Judiciary Committee opened its confirmation hearings, broadcast for the first time live on television. The panel's chair, Joe Biden, had just dropped out of the 1988 presidential race in a cloud of embarrassment. *New York Times* reporter Maureen Dowd had revealed that the glib senator borrowed language and even biographical details from British Labour Party leader Neil Kinnock in his closing statement at a debate. Breathless television reports proliferated at a time when such gotcha video clips were rare. It was an absurd scandal, but just enough to snuff a presidential candidacy. For Biden a high-caliber intellectual joust could provide redemption. Previously he had praised Bork. But he set out a new standard: the Supreme Court had attained such a central role in American life, lawmakers should undertake a searching review of a would-be-justice's views. "In passing on this nomination to the Supreme Court, we must also pass judgment on whether or not your particular philosophy is an appropriate one at this time in history," Biden told Bork.

Bork's testimony was a disaster. With his bristly red beard he looked like a character actor playing a mad scientist, an oddball look later copied by *The Simpsons* for the ponderous Judge Roy Snyder in two dozen episodes. (Lecherous Mayor Quimby, in turn, looks and sounds suspiciously like Bork's pursuer Ted Kennedy.) Bork airily told the senators he wanted to be on the Court because it would be an "intellectual feast." Most damaging, he allowed himself to be dragged into debates about the Constitution. Supporters and foes shadow-boxed about *Roe v. Wade*, decided only fourteen years before. But neither side spoke much about abortion. Instead they debated privacy, and *Griswold v. Connecticut*. That case, Bork charged, had been dreamed up by his colleagues on the Yale faculty. And the Supreme Court had erred gravely: there was no limit to the right to privacy as the Court articulated it. Bork testified for five days.

The hearings lasted more than two weeks. Viewed now, they offer an intellectual yet accessible debate over how the Constitution should be interpreted, far from today's sessions where senators mug for the cameras while nominees robotically refuse to comment on substance. Bork's nomination went to the Senate floor, where it was defeated 58 to 42. Six Republicans voted no. A book celebrating the campaign against Bork listed ninety activist leaders in the fight, and another ninety-six groups opposed to the nomination.

For Republicans and conservatives, whose hero had fallen, it was all egregiously unfair. They blamed the sophisticated pressure campaign and called it being "Borked." The judge himself curdled into bitterness. One of his books, entitled *Slouching Towards Gomorrah*, denounced liberal "rot and decadence." He reserved much of his ire for Yale—the school where he had taught but which did not support him. Near the end of his life the longtime advocate for curbing tort lawsuits sued the university for one million dollars for injuries after he slipped and fell while giving a speech at the Yale Club in Manhattan. In the end he seemed close to the crank his opponents had portrayed.

The Bork brawl did not instantly change confirmation politics. Reagan's next nominee, Douglas Ginsburg, withdrew upon news he had smoked marijuana as a law professor years before (inconvenient for an administration whose drug policy was "Just Say No"). But the Democratic Senate easily confirmed Reagan's next pick, Anthony Kennedy, and George H. W. Bush's choice of David Souter. The Senate smoothly confirmed moderate liberals Ruth Bader Ginsburg and Stephen Breyer, too, when Bill Clinton nominated them.

But Bork's backers smoldered. They vowed to focus not just on the Court's rulings, on school prayer or abortion, but on the Court itself—its approach, its power, and above all its membership. Conservatives were more unhappy with the Court than liberals, and more focused on it as a campaign issue. In the past jurists had surprised their patrons once they were safely ensconced on the bench. Eisenhower called his choice of Warren and Brennan his biggest mistakes. Souter was touted as a reliable conservative based on his record as a judge in New Hampshire, but as a justice he drifted left, becoming a liberal mainstay. Conservative activists vowed "no more Souters." One judge claimed there was a "Greenhouse effect"—the supposed desire of conservative justices to earn the praise of *New York Times* Supreme Court correspondent Linda Greenhouse. Others explained these evolutions by noting that justices are exposed to the human facts of individual cases, which overcomes theory.

Legal conservatives began to muster steely discipline. In 2005 they killed a nomination made by their own president, George W. Bush. Harriet Miers admittedly was a strange choice. She had been Bush's personal lawyer in Texas and followed him to the White House, where she served as staff secretary in charge of paper flow, and then as White House counsel. Bush already faced criticism for cronyism after his chummy praise—"heck of a job, Brownie!"—of the director of the Federal Emergency Management Agency during Hurricane Katrina. David Frum, a former Bush speechwriter who worked with the nominee, wrote, "Miers was best known, not as a conservative, not as a legal thinker, but as a petty bureaucrat." He helped organize three thousand conservative activists to oppose the choice of their own president. She was done in not by competence but ideology: an unnerving lack of fealty to conservatism. Senator Sam Brownback of Kansas, a top critic of the nomination, warned she could be a "Souter-type candidate." "The circumstances seem to be very similar," said Brownback. "Not much track record, people vouching for her, yet indications of a different thought pattern earlier in life." After three weeks and three days, Miers withdrew.

For many Republicans, remaking the courts and hastening their conservative tilt became a central political project. Two highly effective institutions made a huge difference.

Three conservative law students formed the Federalist Society a few years before the Bork nomination. They felt marooned at largely liberal law schools. (Today the schools have moved even further left. One later study found that only 15 percent of law professors are politically conservative.) University of Chicago professor Antonin Scalia was their first faculty advisor. A conference at Yale heard from Bork and others. As Noah Feldman argues, a group that started as a student club over time "grew to become the most influential legal organization in U.S. history."

Eventually the Federalist Society had two hundred chapters and seventy thousand members. Much of the time, as its members insisted, it has been a debating society. It honed and advanced the arguments for originalism. But over time it evolved into something unheard of in the American legal system: a party within a party, a necessary credential for upward mobility. In a country long obsessed with supposed conspiracies and cells such as the Masons, this was the real deal. All six members of the conservative supermajority are current or former members of the Federalist Society. So were 80 percent of Donald Trump's appointees to the courts of appeals. Many more became Supreme Court clerks, a prime establishment credential which yields a hefty six-figure signing bonus at law firms. (Federalist Society students even have been known to jump ahead of the official system for clerkship hiring, sometimes landing their job after just a few months at law school, an ironic bit of affirmative action.)

The organization insists it does not take positions on issues, and that it merely offers a forum for varying views. Indeed, its panel discussions can be lively. At its gatherings and galas, though, the real action happens in the hallways and bars. Libertarians hatched the lawsuit to challenge the Affordable Care Act in a Mayflower Hotel corridor at a Federalist Society conference.

Potential judges are cheered and judged like aspiring presidents at a political convention. Amy Coney Barrett was a little-known law professor when a White House lawyer whom she knew through the Federalist Society arranged for her to be named to the bench. Trump's aides soon told a meeting of the group that she was on the short list for the Supreme Court. In 2018 at the society's annual convention, Barrett—who had been a judge for little over a year—received raucous applause.

That night Senator Mitch McConnell and the organization's leader chatted onstage at a black-tie gala in the grand hall of Washington's Union Station. McConnell talked with pride of his "judges project."

To put muscle behind the ideas, conservatives developed a political machine to support nominees for the bench. Leonard Leo of the Federalist Society was the sachem. He would take a leave of absence to work in the Trump White House. "We're going to have to understand that judicial confirmations these days are more like political campaigns," he told a group of activists. "We're going to have to be smart as a movement." Leo claimed to be uninterested in the effort's financial operations. "I'm not particularly knowledgeable about a lot of it," he told journalists. "I don't waste my time on stories that involve money

and politics because what I care about is ideas." Journalist Ruth Marcus
called that "beyond disingenuous." Over three years he raised more
than $250 million from mostly secret donors for ads and organizing.

The most effective operation was that of the Judicial Crisis Network, led by a Leo protégé and former Thomas clerk, Carrie Severino.
She wielded not footnotes but funds. The group's principal financial
support for a decade came from a political committee financed by
Charles and David Koch, oil company owners active in libertarian politics. "Since 2012," a report by U.S. Senate Democrats reported, "JCN
has made more than 14,000 ad buys, most of them so-called 'issue
ads' that don't require the disclosure of donors." It spent $10 million
against Obama's nomination of Merrick Garland, including television
spots thanking senators for holding firm against filling the seat, and
matched that spending to support Trump's choice of Neil Gorsuch. It
spent $15 million to back Brett Kavanaugh's nomination, using funds
from an intermediary, the Wellspring Committee, cash that was publicly untraceable. Republican nominees knew they could float in on a
well-funded, professionalized, effective media machine. Wavering senators knew they would face pressure to toe the party line, and advertis-
ing backup if they did.

Over the decades the confirmation process has become not only more
contentious, but much more partisan. Aren't those the same thing?
No: in past eras, both parties were comprised of disparate blocs. Inside
the Republican tent were Northeast liberal Rockefeller Republicans,
western libertarians, and Midwest small-town isolationists. The GOP
always cohered as the party of white Protestants, but it was still more
varied than would be recognizable today. Democrats were a less stable compound of northern ethnic political machines, southern segregationists, university-educated liberals, and eventually Black voters
who shed their Republican identity. ("Boston and Austin," as in the
Kennedy-Johnson ticket in 1960, or "Grits and Fritz," Georgian Jimmy
Carter and Minnesotan Walter (Fritz) Mondale in 1976.) Now, both
parties have sorted: the most conservative Democrat in Congress is still
to the left of the most progressive Republican.

Not only did the parties sort, they grew increasingly polarized, as
well. No longer was it assumed that presidents would get their pick; no

longer was it assumed that lawmakers would vote without only assessing partisan considerations. The intense divisions within Congress spread to judicial nominations and came to be the central fact in how American courts were comprised.

Numbers tell the story. President Biden appointed a Commission on the Supreme Court of the United States in 2021. It summarized the trend of escalating partisanship:

> Justice Sonia Sotomayor received 68 votes (all Democrats and nine Republicans voting to confirm); Justice Elena Kagan, 63 (all but one Democrat and only five Republicans voting to confirm); Justice Gorsuch, 54 (all Republicans and only three Democrats voting to confirm); Justice Kavanaugh, 50 (all Republicans and just one Democrat voting to confirm); and Justice Barrett, 52 (all but one Republican and no Democrat voting to confirm).
>
> To be sure, over the last fifty years, some nominees have received significant bipartisan support. Some of those nominations—including Justice [Antonin] Scalia (confirmed in 1986 with 98 votes), Justice [Ruth Bader] Ginsburg (confirmed in 1993 with 96 votes), and Justice Stephen Breyer (confirmed in 1994 with 87 votes)—occurred when the Senate was controlled by the President's party. Others—including Justice [Anthony] Kennedy (confirmed unanimously in 1988, an election year, after Judge Bork's nomination was rejected) and Justice David Souter (confirmed in 1990 with 90 votes)—occurred when the Senate majority was not aligned with the President. Unmistakably, however, the trend over the last three decades has been toward more partisan conflict, which has affected nominations to the lower courts as well as to the Supreme Court.

The fierce confirmation fights affected the Court in another way, one less visible to the naked eye. Presidents of both parties learned to choose justices whose future rulings could be predicted by past actions.

Far more than at any other time, the justices now are technocrats, elite-trained lawyers, rather than leading public figures. For most of the country's history, the Supreme Court justices were people at the peak of their careers, leaders in government or law. John Marshall had been secretary of state, Roger Taney the attorney general. William Howard Taft had been president. Charles Evans Hughes was secretary of state, the Republican presidential nominee, and governor of New York, and Earl Warren was the governor of California. The Court that decided *Brown v. Board of Education* included one governor, three U.S. senators, two attorneys general, the top securities regulator, and a Harvard law professor. Members of the Court brought a political sense to the work, in ways good (a humane notion of right and wrong) and bad (a blithe willingness to legislate from the bench).

Today the Court is comprised of lawyers who are highly skilled but narrow in their professional background. Starting with Nixon and for the next fifty years, all but three of the seventeen appointees served as federal appeals court judges. On today's Supreme Court, eight of nine justices were appeals court judges who earned a promotion. Eight of nine attended Yale or Harvard law school. Eight had served as Supreme Court clerks. None ever ran for office. There are no graduates of public universities, but two graduates of one tony Catholic prep school in the Washington, D.C., suburbs.

Most significant, few had leadership roles in other parts of government. None ran a cabinet agency. Only Elena Kagan had a prominent political role in the executive branch—as solicitor general, and before that, as one of Bill Clinton's top policy aides in the White House. Clarence Thomas chaired the Equal Employment Opportunity Commission, an important body, but far from the center of the political action. They were two of three with experience managing an institution (Samuel Alito served as chief federal prosecutor in New Jersey). The formalism of the opinions, the parsing of dictionaries and fixation on "text," the growing volume of footnotes and word count, all suggested that the methods of the Court could only be understood by the most elevated intellects.

Presidents sometimes yearned for something different. Indeed, Bill Clinton—the schmoozing politician who had also gone to Yale Law School—was determined to break the mold. He ardently wanted to pick an elected official, a proven leader who could charm, cajole, assemble majorities, and orate from the bench. He told reporters he wanted someone "with a big heart." On several occasions he offered a seat to New York's eloquent Governor Mario M. Cuomo, who true to his nickname as the "Hamlet on the Hudson" froze with indecision and eventually said no. Clinton wooed Majority Leader George Mitchell, a former judge, who turned him down. Clinton tried to appoint Interior Secretary Bruce Babbitt, former governor of Arizona, but backed off when environmentalists began to fight with western senators over who would take his spot. Finally, Clinton gave up and chose two appellate judges.

There was one more way the Court resembled the country less and less. For most of the past decade, there were six Catholic justices, and three Jewish justices—and no Protestants in a nation long dominated, culturally and politically, by its biggest religious group. (There have been forty-three Protestant presidents, for example, and only two Catholics.) Protestants Clinton, George W. Bush, and Obama installed exclusively Catholic and Jewish justices. Today six Catholics, one Jew, one Episcopalian raised Catholic, and one Protestant sit on the Court. Consider this progress: a remarkable sign of growing tolerance and religious diversity in a country becoming less homogeneous. But an awkward silence surrounded this fact. For years, it was taboo to dwell on the religion of the justices.

The modern Supreme Court was taking shape: cloaked in expertise, technically skilled, more diverse than before, and increasingly embedded in larger political movements.

CHAPTER SIX

THE TRUMP COURT

IN 2005 JOHN ROBERTS BECAME CHIEF justice. The Court began
to issue a series of five-to-four decisions on high-profile issues. But
it held its ambitions in check, guided by the chief's canny instincts—
whether out of a concern for the institution's legitimacy or an eye on
poll results.

Chief justices, as we've noted, have little formal power. They cast
one of nine votes. But some can steer the Court. Roberts seemed
acutely aware of the risks to the Court's credibility if it went too far, or
if it too aggressively injected itself in politics. His path suggested he was
exquisitely attuned to backlash. At a time when many American institutions seemed decrepit, at times led with garish incompetence, Roberts
appeared above all to be savvy, deft, and effective.

In only one area during the first fifteen years of his chief justiceship did Roberts shed that caution: the law of democracy. On voting
rights, on campaign finance, on redistricting, and more—on all the
ways the rules can bolster or undermine a fair and equal political
system—the court led by Roberts was aggressive and destructive. Much
of today's toxic and polarized politics flows from the rulings and dicta
of the Court.

Citizens knew little of Roberts until just before he took office. During
his confirmation hearing he insisted judges should only call "balls and
strikes, not pitch or bat." A memorable, sticky phrase, it conjured mid-
western ballfields. As a description of what Supreme Court justices
do, it was also transparently inadequate. Yankees fan Sonia Sotomayor
later observed, "Figuring out where the strike zone is requires a value

judgment. That's why different umpires have different strike zones but they all try to stay within the parameters of what their eyes give them."

The aw-shucks metaphor daubed a nostalgic sheen on a career marked by hard-edged ideological ambition. John Roberts grew up in the Midwest in the middle of the century. He was quickly swept up in the Republican Party's political lawyering operation.

Roberts clerked at the Supreme Court. His boss, William Rehnquist, had nearly been blocked from confirmation as chief justice when his own memos as a clerk opposing *Brown v. Board of Education* emerged. Roberts burned with conservative passion, but left behind no incriminating memos. He worked first in the White House counsel's office and then at the Justice Department's Office of Legal Policy, intense locales for movement lawyers during the "Reagan Revolution." He became the principal deputy solicitor general. The political deputy must be a talented lawyer, but is also akin to a commissar, there to ensure that arguments made before the Court align with the administration's political goals.

In Washington, D.C., when a party loses executive branch power, its army of lawyers does not leave town, but decamps a few blocks away to major law firms. Roberts became a partner at Hogan & Hartson. His clientele was an unremarkable roster of major corporations, and he became known as one of the most skilled Supreme Court advocates of his generation.

His partisan bona fides were burnished in the presidential election of 2000, especially after the riveting and unprecedented election night. Vice President Al Gore won the popular vote and seemed to have won the presidency when television networks called Florida with its twenty-five electoral votes for him. Then the networks pulled their projections, and called the state for George W. Bush. Gore was on his way to a rally to concede when his campaign realized that the state would go to a recount. "Circumstances have changed dramatically since I first called you," Gore told Bush. "The state of Florida is too close to call." "Are you saying what I think you're saying? Let me make sure I understand. You're calling back to retract that concession?" "Don't get snippy about it," Gore replied. Bush gave a response that revealed much: "My little brother says it's over." Jeb Bush was serving his first term as Florida's governor. "With all due respect to your little brother," Gore replied, "he is not the final arbiter of who wins Florida."

Within days hundreds of lawyers poured into Florida, snowbirds with briefcases. Roberts joined the throng, working on the state court litigation and shuttling between Tallahassee and his Washington, D.C., legal practice, where he was preparing for an argument before the Supreme Court. (Brett Kavanaugh and Amy Coney Barrett also worked in Florida that month for Bush on the recount.) The Republican effort was legendarily tough, mixing arcane legal arguments with street brawling, as the HBO movie *Recount* vividly captured. Unlike other future senior officials, Roberts did not participate in the "Brooks Brothers riot" or other dramatic scenes. In the end, as cases pinballed around state and federal courts, the U.S. Supreme Court in a five-to-four ruling stopped the counting of ballots that had been ordered by the Florida Supreme Court. George W. Bush became president by a margin of 537 votes in Florida, out of nearly six million cast in that state, and 105 million cast nationwide.

Bush nominated Roberts for the D.C. Circuit Court of Appeals, and he was serving there in 2005 when the president chose him for an open Supreme Court seat, the one vacated by Sandra Day O'Connor. Her decision to retire, when she was in the prime of her power, was prompted by agonizing personal tragedy: her husband was succumbing to Alzheimer's disease. (Within a year, he would barely recognize her.) Roberts was midway through his confirmation process when Chief Justice Rehnquist unexpectedly died.

Roberts's elevation together with the nomination of the man chosen for O'Connor's seat, Samuel Alito, combined to pull the Court to the right. Quickly the court majority began to issue five-to-four rulings on predictable ideological grounds. "It is not often in the law that so few have so quickly changed so much," quipped Stephen Breyer from the bench. The notion began to harden that the Court's blocs were political, often partisan, not calling balls and strikes but moving the strike zone. Roberts especially became known for surprisingly strident views on race. "It is a sordid business, this divvying us up by race," he wrote in one early case. "The way to stop discrimination on the basis of race is to stop discriminating on the basis of race," he said in another.

Roberts focused on conserving the Court's institutional legitimacy in the public eye. He was ready to cast strategic votes to pull it back from controversy. But when it came to the law of democracy, cautious, prudent John Roberts was missing. There he led an activist bench of judges who seemed every bit as willing to strike down laws as a *Lochner* era jurist in a starched collar. Journalist Jeffrey Toobin observed astutely, "Every Chief Justice takes on a project. Earl Warren wanted to desegregate the South. Warren Burger wanted to limit the rights of criminal suspects. William Rehnquist wanted to revive the powers of the states. It increasingly appears likely that, for John Roberts, the project will be removing the limits that burden wealthy campaign contributors—the 'whole point' of the First Amendment, as he sees it." This jurisprudence was increasingly radical and ultimately partisan—backed by, and benefiting, the Republican Party. It was fully "activist," abandoning the critique made by generations of conservative Court critics.

The push started with *Citizens United v. Federal Election Commission* in 2010, a five-to-four ruling that undid a century of campaign finance law. Corporations were long barred from directly spending in federal elections. The rule dated to 1907 when Theodore Roosevelt signed the Tillman Act after he was embarrassed by a scandal. In 1946 Congress again prohibited direct spending, this time by labor unions. *Citizens United* involved a misguided enforcement action against an obscure pay-per-view film criticizing Hillary Clinton. Nobody in the case had asked for a big ruling, and under the tradition of "constitutional avoidance," the majority should have found a way to decide without ever reaching major constitutional issues. Instead the justices seized the chance for epic change.

Conservatives often mocked Anthony Kennedy for his flowery homages to human liberty and sexuality; here he rhapsodized about the rights of corporations. "The censorship we now confront is vast in its reach," he warned. "The Government has muffled the voices that best represent the most significant segments of the economy." John Paul Stevens, also a Republican but now a reliable liberal, had been appointed by President Gerald Ford, the more moderate Republican whom Reagan had challenged in the primaries. "While American democracy is imperfect, few outside the majority of this Court would have thought its flaws included a dearth of corporate money in politics," he wrote.

Citizens United held that corporations and unions could spend unlimited sums in federal elections if they do so "independent" of the candidates they backed. That gave birth to "super PACs," which could raise those funds in unlimited amounts from the wealthy. Quickly that independence proved illusory, as presidential contenders and other federal candidates raised hundreds of millions of dollars for their campaigns, all of it supposedly independent.

The Roberts majority now regularly brandished the First Amendment: free speech used to undermine democracy, a constitutional contradiction. The next year another campaign finance decision, again five to four, again matching the preferences of the political parties, ruled against Arizona's system of voluntary public financing of campaigns, on the grounds that parts of it had chilled the speech of nonparticipating candidates. The year after that, the Court struck down a long-standing cap on the amount of money individuals could give to federal candidates.

Just a few days after the Supreme Court ruled in *Citizens United*, President Obama stood before Congress to deliver his 2010 State of the Union Address. Six justices sat berobed in the front row. "With all due deference to separation of powers," he scolded, the decision "will open the floodgates for special interests—including foreign corporations—to spend without limit in our elections." As lawmakers applauded, Samuel Alito irritably shook his head. Able lip readers noted he was saying, "Not true."

The Roberts Court's rulings on campaign finance law remade American politics. Wealthy individuals rather than brand-name businesses began to fund election candidates. In the new Gilded Age of fantastically concentrated wealth, billionaires again dominated the electoral system.

In the first five years after *Citizens United*, campaign spending exploded. Some came from small donations given by millions of individuals. But the small donor triumph was an illusion. Big money's role grew even faster. It pulled Republican candidates, especially, far to the right. Over a decade super PACs spent $3 billion on federal races. Incumbents learned to fear a well-funded primary challenge more than general election swing voters. Before *Citizens United*, a big faction of Republican lawmakers supported action to address climate change. But the ruling let the Koch brothers and other fossil fuel interests dominate Republican primaries. After, the political network established by Charles and David Koch grew to rival the Republican Party in funding and sophistication. Its libertarian interests were more than ideological. According to the EPA, in 2012 Koch Industries was the number two producer of toxic waste in the United States.

The shift in the country's political economy was dramatic and largely unremarked. According to one analysis, in 2010 billionaires spent around $31 million in federal races. A decade later they spent $1.2 billion, a forty-fold increase. Soon the pretense of independent expenditures melted away altogether. Billionaires sponsored candidates like prize racehorses. In 2022 two of Silicon Valley investor Peter Thiel's employees ran for the U.S. Senate. He provided nearly $30 million in "independent" funds to bankroll J. D. Vance in Ohio and Blake Masters in Arizona. (Thiel "functionally underwrote" Vance's primary campaign, the Cleveland *Plain Dealer* reported. Vance is now the junior senator from Ohio. Masters lost.)

Citizens United also shifted the politics of cultural issues. Religious conservatives embraced the drive to deregulate money in politics, as scholar Mary Ziegler has documented. The National Rifle Association had long sought to strike down campaign finance rules. More recently it was antiabortion groups who took the lead. Once they had pushed for a constitutional amendment, but from the mid-1980s on focused instead on changing the courts. In a telling sign, it was James Bopp, general counsel of the National Right to Life Committee, who argued *Citizens United.*

The Roberts Court mostly moved cautiously, tacking here, tacking there. It found a right for an individual to own a gun under the Second Amendment, but said that safety regulations were also constitutional. It declared that privacy and equal protection require recognition of same sex marriage. That night crowds celebrated and the rainbow colors of the pride flag were projected on the White House. (Roberts dissented from that ruling.)

Barack Obama appointed two justices, Sonia Sotomayor and Elena Kagan. But overall, as before, Democrats focused less on the judiciary than Republicans did. Obama's lower court nominees were more diverse than those of previous presidents. Forty-two percent were women, and 36 percent were nonwhite. But they were overwhelmingly

corporate law firm attorneys or prosecutors, ethnically varied but ideologically muted. Of the leading intellectual lights or issue advocates
among progressives, none became federal judges.

The pace of judicial confirmations slowed to a crawl. Republican
leader Mitch McConnell was savvy, patient, and seemingly impervious
to criticism. A onetime liberal Republican (who authored an op-ed
article calling for public financing of campaigns and named his cat
Rocky after New York governor Nelson Rockefeller), he had turned
his focus almost obsessively to ensuring Republican control of the institutions of government. He fought against John McCain's bipartisan
campaign finance reform bill all the way to the Supreme Court, which
ruled against him in the *McConnell v. Federal Election Commission* case in
2003. And he focused on judges. McConnell would come to exercise as
much control over the judiciary as any president.

Either party can paralyze the Senate. When in the minority,
McConnell filibustered dozens of federal judge nominations, meaning
that each of them was required to achieve "cloture" with sixty votes or
overcome myriad other procedural hurdles.

The filibuster has so come to define the modern Senate that it
is easy to forget its origins and novelty. It is not in the Constitution.
In effect, it relies on the tradition of unlimited debate in the Senate.
For much of the country's history it was used only sparingly, usually
by southern senators seeking to kill civil rights and voting rights bills
that would otherwise gain a majority. In 1938 senators filibustered for
thirty days to block legislation that would have made lynching a federal crime. (The bill finally passed in 2022.) Lengthy filibusters stymied
civil rights bills in the 1950s. The 1964 Civil Rights Act passed only
after sixty working days, including seven Saturday Senate sessions. At
that time, before senators changed the rules in 1974, sixty-seven votes
were needed to choke off debate. But in practice, most legislation only
required a simple majority. At the LBJ Library in Austin, a 1964 strategy memo outlined the vote tally needed to win enactment of Medi-
care, for example; the master vote counter was looking only to get to
fifty-one votes. In recent years, as politics polarized, the filibuster was
used more and more. Senators need not actually stand on the floor
and orate as before—they merely had to phone in a threat. Sixty votes
became the assumed threshold for all legislation, and for the first time,
for the lifetime positions on the federal bench.

There were always tussles around judicial nominations, especially those that might point a superstar toward higher office someday. Judgeship bids by both John Roberts and Elena Kagan expired earlier in their careers. In 2003 Democrats blocked Miguel Estrada, a well-regarded forty-one-year-old Honduran immigrant, on the grounds that he was ideologically extreme (but with the unspoken understanding that he was being groomed for the Supreme Court). Two years later, Republicans threatened to eliminate the filibuster for judicial nominees—a move dubbed the "nuclear option." At the last minute, a group of senators from both parties struck a deal to confirm some of the judges and avoid the mushroom cloud.

McConnell's judicial blockade against Obama's judges was especially effective when it came to the court of appeals for the District of Columbia Circuit, perhaps the most prestigious lower court. It hears many cases involving government policy and is often the first place that new laws and regulations are tested. Conservatives came to see it as their redoubt. Five years into his presidency, Obama still had not successfully named anyone to that eleven-person court. Three times he nominated Manhattan prosecutor Caitlin Halligan. Each time the National Rifle Association accused her of being against gun ownership, and while a majority of the Senate backed her confirmation, she fell short.

Finally, in June 2013, with Democrats still in control of the Senate, a newly reelected Obama appointed nominees to fill the three vacancies on the court. McConnell likened the move to Roosevelt's court packing plan. After the third would-be-judge won a Senate majority, but not votes enough to break a filibuster, the president complained, "Four of my predecessor's six nominees to the D.C. Circuit were confirmed. Four of my five nominees to this court have been obstructed." Democratic leader Harry Reid of Nevada engineered a change in Senate rules so a majority could approve lower court federal judges. "You will regret this," McConnell objected on the Senate floor, "and you may regret this a lot sooner than you think." It was an imperfect status quo—after all, isn't there a better argument to require sixty votes for a lifetime judicial appointment than a routine piece of legislation?—but it opened the chance to fill the courts.

Yet despite all the contention, a seemingly unbreakable norm governed Supreme Court appointments. The president could make nominations, and the Senate would consider the president's choice.

Then on February 13, 2016, Antonin Scalia unexpectedly died at a hunting lodge in West Texas. The flamboyant jurist had become something of an anachronism: his dissents increasingly seemed to be written to be quoted on conservative news networks and in social media accounts rather than to influence the law. Cases involving LGBTQ Americans seemed to attract his most sputtering language. The ruling that overturned the federal Defense of Marriage Act, he harrumphed, was "legalistic argle-bargle." If he ever found himself supporting an opinion written like the historic *Obergefell* case that protected same sex marriage, "I would hide my head in a bag." Four justices had been appointed by Democratic presidents (Ginsburg, Breyer, Kagan, and Sotomayor). Scalia's successor would be the fifth, making a majority appointed by a Democratic president on the Supreme Court for the first time since 1970. It would tip the ideological balance on the Court as well.

The Constitution says the president "shall nominate, and by and with the Advice and Consent of the Senate, shall appoint . . . Judges of the supreme Court." It has been assumed since then that senators must respond to a president's choice. Every nominee sent up by a president had been considered by the Senate since the mid-nineteenth century. In early 2016 nearly a full year would have elapsed before a new president took office, leaving plenty of time to confirm a choice. Nominations took an average of sixty-seven days to process. Indeed, presidents had chosen justices in an election year eleven times since the Civil War. All received Senate votes (and all but one were confirmed). That pattern held when the Senate was controlled by the opposition party as well as the president's. When Scalia died, all expected a fight, as Republicans would try to slow or reject Obama's choice. Few expected what happened next.

An hour after Scalia's death was confirmed, McConnell issued a startling statement. "The American people should have a voice in the selection of their next Supreme Court Justice. Therefore, this vacancy should not be filled until we have a new president." This came as other senators were still churning out condolences to the justice's family, which included forty grandchildren.

Obama quickly announced his choice of Merrick Garland, the centrist, silver-haired, sixty-four-year-old chief judge of the D.C. Circuit Court of Appeals. Obama faced a choice: pick a liberal nominee, perhaps a pathbreaker, someone to stir partisan juices and draw attention to McConnell's blockade; or tap a safer candidate with a better chance.

Garland was widely respected and had led the prosecution of the Oklahoma City terrorist bombing. Conservative Utah senator Orrin Hatch had all but dared Obama. "The president told me several times he's going to name a moderate, but I don't believe him," Hatch said. "He could easily name Merrick Garland, who is a fine man. He probably won't do that because this appointment is about the election. So I'm pretty sure he'll name someone the [liberal Democratic base] wants."

Bland caution did Garland little good. McConnell ensured that the Judiciary Committee held no hearings on the nomination, and it was never debated or brought to a vote in the committee or the full Senate. Only a handful of Republican senators would even meet with the chief judge as he traipsed to Capitol Hill. "One of my proudest moments," McConnell bragged in a campaign speech that summer, "was when I looked at Barack Obama in the eye and I said, 'Mr. President, you will not fill this Supreme Court vacancy.'" For the full year the Supreme Court was short one justice.

The Senate's refusal to consider Garland's nomination—not to vote it down, but even to take it up at all—was unprecedented in modern times. An expectation of Senate action was as settled as the idea that presidents only seek to serve two terms, a norm so sacrosanct that the one time a president breached it, a constitutional amendment made sure it would not happen again. The first Black president was blocked from doing what others before him had the right to do. Republicans claimed they were merely following a previously unknown "Biden rule," and pointed to a speech Biden had given a quarter century before urging that any confirmation be put off until after the election. Mostly, they did it because they could, exercising raw power.

To Democrats, the unprecedented blockade meant something different: a stolen Supreme Court seat. That seat would now be filled by the next president.

Donald Trump trailed in the popular vote, losing by 2.9 million votes, but eked out victories in industrial states that long had backed Democrats, and thus won the Electoral College to become the forty-fifth president on November 8, 2016. His election was one of the most extraordinary, wrenching moments in American history. The former reality television show host and real estate developer had ditched policies on which Republicans had run since Reagan: he pledged to expand Social Security, opposed immigration, and criticized assertive American foreign policy. To that he added explicit racism and xenophobia, declaring as he announced that Mexican immigrants were "rapists." His rallies combined hints of violence, lengthy and often hilarious speeches, professional-wrestling-style pageantry, and chants of "lock her up" aimed at his opponent, former secretary of state Hillary Clinton.

One thing he did not run on at first was a pledge to remake the courts. Conservative activists still distrusted him as his nomination approached. Trump seemed to care little about their long-term project. On abortion rights, for example, he had once said on NBC's *Meet the Press,* "I am very pro-choice." As part of his effort to woo activists, Trump announced a list of jurists from which he would pick a Supreme Court justice. The Federalist Society provided the names, along with the Heritage Foundation, another conservative nonprofit. All were white; three had clerked for Clarence Thomas. The first list included none of the justices Trump would later appoint. But the point had been made: on judicial nominations, Trump would not be heterodox, he would govern as an orthodox conservative Republican, guided by the Federalist Society. It was a campaign pledge not to be independent.

Trump had declared in his Republican convention acceptance speech that American government was corrupt and broken, announcing that "I alone can fix it," a boast more typical of an authoritarian strongman than an American presidential aspirant. On January 20, 2017, Roberts swore Trump in wearing a look of pained good cheer. Memorable inaugural addresses come during crisis; Trump brought his own crisis with him. Rather than calm the waters, he stirred them further. He delivered an address stripped of the typically reverent homages to the democratic civic religion: it did not mention "the Constitution," "democracy," or "liberty." Instead, Trump painted a dystopian portrait of "American carnage." (George W. Bush's verdict as he left the inaugural platform: "That was some weird shit.")

Within days Trump began to implement some of his more ferocious campaign pledges. He had vowed a "total and complete shutdown of Muslims entering the United States," and a week after his inauguration he announced an executive order blocking visitors or immigrants from seven Muslim majority countries. Volunteer lawyers rushed to airports, where attorneys from the law firm Paul, Weiss and other major white-shoe firms worked in twenty-four-hour shifts along with immigrant rights activists, sitting cross-legged on Terminal 4's floor at John F. Kennedy International Airport, laptops open, advising distraught family members. The next day trial judges began to block the order. Perhaps they were emboldened by the beginnings of the "resistance" to Trump's rule—especially, the half a million attendees at the "Women's March" in Washington, D.C., the day after the inaugural, a crowd that dwarfed the attendance at Trump's ceremony. Federal courts fully or partly blocked the first versions of the White House's slapdash order before the Supreme Court eventually allowed it a year later. Soon it became clear that the Court would at times stand up to the new administration, but especially to insist that it follow the rules and procedures that shape how government is supposed to function. Its jurisprudence on Trump's presidential abuse of power reflected, again, Roberts's institutionalism, now elevated to a judicial philosophy.

McConnell's refusal to fill Scalia's seat for a year meant there was a nomination to make. Two weeks after taking office, Trump chose Neil Gorsuch, a conservative federal court of appeals judge from Colorado. At a confirmation hearing and on the Senate floor, Democrats objected to Gorsuch and to the fact of the nomination. There was no way that Gorsuch could be confirmed under rules requiring sixty votes to break a filibuster in a Senate with only fifty-one Republicans. So McConnell did what Democrats had done for appeals court judges: he triggered the "nuclear option" so the nominee could be approved with a majority vote. To Democrats, Trump had filled the "stolen seat" only after breaching the Senate's rules.

A few weeks later, Gorsuch joined McConnell for a speaking tour in Kentucky. Charles Pierce wrote in *Esquire* that the two did not appear to "even consider the propriety of a Supreme Court Justice being paraded around a state like a prize trout."

Trump's White House counsel, Don McGahn, had been the campaign aide who hit on the idea of releasing an ideologically vetted list. In a White House that would have four chiefs of staff and four national security advisors in four years, McGahn was a rare example of sharp competence. Despite the tweets, feuds, and bombast that drew attention, Trump's presidency may have its longest-lasting impact by filling the courts with conservatives. That extended beyond the Supreme Court. Trump would go on to appoint fifty-four federal appeals court judges, nearly as many in one term as Obama had managed in two.

Justice Anthony Kennedy still sat on the Court. Reagan had nominated him in 1987 but now he was a swing vote, a leader on issues protecting the rights of gay and lesbian Americans. Trump, with his visceral if unschooled sense of people's weakness, mounted a quiet campaign to encourage him to step down to open a seat.

This kind of thing happens more than one might expect.

Lyndon Johnson created two vacancies that way. In 1965, on an Air Force One ride to the funeral of U.N. ambassador Adlai Stevenson, Johnson persuaded Justice Arthur Goldberg to resign and take the diplomatic job after only three years on the bench. LBJ told the self-regarding justice that only he could end the war in Vietnam. Then he could run for higher office, the first Jew on a national ticket. "You never know what can happen, Arthur. You're over there on the Court, isolated from the action, and you can't get to the Vice Presidency from the Court." At Stevenson's gravesite, the justice's appalled friends tried to talk him out of the move. Goldberg took the job. Within weeks, Johnson decided to escalate the Vietnam War, and cut Goldberg out of policymaking. To replace him in the "Jewish seat" he chose his personal lawyer and close friend, Abe Fortas, the brilliant attorney who had represented the Texan in the 1948 election, which Johnson won by 87 votes.

Then in 1967 Johnson wanted to appoint Thurgood Marshall. Again, no seat was available. Johnson had an intermediary call Justice Tom Clark to confide a dilemma: he wanted to name Clark's son Ramsey as attorney general, but of course, could not while his father served on the Court. What a shame. The justice promptly retired and swore in his son, who would turn out to be unabashedly left-wing, to lead the Justice Department. In gratitude Johnson sent Justice Clark and his wife on a round-the-world trip, supposedly to exchange views on the judiciary with other leaders.

Trump was no LBJ but he knew his mark. Gorsuch had been a Kennedy clerk, and news reports made clear the two leading candidates for any opening were also Kennedy clerks. The president schmoozed the justice, with microphones picking up their conversation as he greeted

Kennedy on the House floor after delivering a State of the Union Address. "Say hello to your boy," Trump told the justice. "Special guy." Kennedy's son, as an executive at Deutsche Bank, had worked on a $640 million loan to the often bankrupt real estate developer at a time when other banks would not finance his projects.

Kennedy stepped down, and on July 9, 2018, Trump announced his second appointee, federal appeals court judge Brett Kavanaugh. He was a familiar figure in Washington, in Republican Party politics, and in the intersection of law and conspiracy mongering. He seemed less an ideologue than a fierce partisan.

At a young age Kavanaugh had been a top deputy to special prosecutor Kenneth Starr during their four-year-long pursuit of Bill and Hillary Clinton. Kavanaugh drove the focus on the suicide of White House lawyer Vincent Foster. Four previous investigations had confirmed Foster was depressed and took his own life. But radio talk show hosts and conspiracy theorists including Christopher Ruddy (later a Trump confidant) demanded a new probe. Kavanaugh sought authority to open a "full-fledged" new investigation into whether Bill and Hillary Clinton had their friend Foster murdered. Quickly he concluded the earlier findings had been correct, but kept the probe going for two more years.

Indeed, Starr's office was exquisitely attuned to pressure from right-wing activists. In 1997 the prosecutor announced he would resign, his work seemingly done, but faced harsh criticism. William Safire in *The New York Times* accused Starr of "the big flinch." He sheepishly announced he would stay on. Originally he had been tasked with looking into a land deal in Arkansas. Finally, still in operation years after he started, Starr began to investigate whether Clinton had lied under oath about an affair with former White House intern Monica Lewinsky. Kavanaugh demanded that prosecutors ask the president lurid sexual questions. The goal seemed to be to sandblast Clinton from office through public shaming. The young attorney wrote much of the Starr Report detailing the intimate details of encounters between Clinton and Lewinsky. Kavanaugh's defenders insisted he wrote only the legal sections, not those that read like pornography with footnotes.

Kavanaugh then worked for George W. Bush, growing close enough to the Texan that he even cleared brush with him at his ranch. Bush named Kavanaugh a federal judge, but Democrats held up the

confirmation for three years. Kavanaugh had long been seen as a potential Supreme Court nominee, one with unusual views on executive
power and accountability. After his years pursuing Clinton, Kavanaugh
now argued that presidents should be exempt from investigation, not
just indictment, a view that may have appealed to Trump. Inspector
Javert now empathized with Jean Valjean. As *Slate* journalist Dahlia
Lithwick noted, of all the possible nominees, Trump chose the one
most likely to say he could not be charged with a crime.

Kavanaugh glided through his confirmation hearings until Dr.
Christine Blasey Ford, a Palo Alto University professor, accused him of
sexually assaulting her while in high school. She testified that a drunk
Kavanaugh had pinned her to a bed and put his hand over her mouth
so she would not scream. "I am here today not because I want to be,"
she testified. "I am terrified. I am here because I believe it is my civic
duty to tell you what happened to me while Brett Kavanaugh and I
were in high school."

Kavanaugh returned to the hearing room to respond to the accusation. It was a "calculated political hit," he testified with red-faced anger,
"revenge on behalf of the Clintons." He turned to look at the Democratic senators. "You sowed the wind," he said, and "the country will
reap the whirlwind." He warned, "What goes around comes around."
The Senate confirmed Kavanaugh 50 to 48.

The Court still teetered, with a conservative majority, producing
five-to-four votes on major issues. But most rulings reflected far more
consensus. John Roberts kept one eye on the Court's legitimacy, and it
seemed to observers and Supreme Court Kremlinologists that he was
able to pull enough of his more conservative colleagues along with him.

Ruth Bader Ginsburg was now the Court's senior liberal. Her judicial career had an unexpected arc. She had been the country's pi-
oneering women's rights lawyer, a Thurgood Marshall for gender
equality. As a federal judge appointed by Jimmy Carter she had been
cautious, however, hewing to the center. When Byron White retired in
1993, a Democratic president could at last appoint a justice for the first
time in twenty-four years. Bill Clinton took three months to decide.
Feminist activists were leery of Ginsburg. She had sharply criticized
Roe v. Wade—not the fact that it protected abortion rights, but the approach taken by what she called a "breathtaking decision." "Doctrinal

limbs too swiftly shaped, experience teaches, may prove unstable."
The Supreme Court should have ruled more narrowly and relied on
the Fourteenth Amendment's Equal Protection Clause (since control
over reproduction is a critical part of gender equity). Former law professor Stephen Breyer, now a Boston federal appeals judge, was the
front-runner, but did poorly in his interview (he was suffering after a
bicycle accident). Ginsburg charmed and impressed Clinton, and he
announced her nomination the next day.

In her first two decades on the Supreme Court, Ginsburg was a
reliable but unremarkable liberal vote. She wrote important rulings
including one that opened up the Virginia Military Institute to women.
Ginsburg also faced extraordinary personal strains, surviving cancer
and nursing her husband through a lengthy illness that took his life. It
seemed she might retire. Then something unexpected happened: Ruth
Bader Ginsburg went viral. Law students, especially women, began to
spread the meme created by NYU first-year Shana Knizhnik calling her
"The Notorious R.B.G.," evoking the rapper Biggie Smalls, who had
been murdered in 1997. Her exercise regimen became famous, and at
age eighty-five she did push-ups with comedian Stephen Colbert on his
nightly show. Admirers jammed her speeches, even though she talked
so quietly that she could barely be heard. Audiences celebrated her
bond with ideological opposite Antonin Scalia. A cutesy opera, *Scalia/
Ginsburg*, purported to portray their friendship. Her daughter-in-law
performed a song cycle that set her dissents to music.

She seemed to enjoy the attention enormously. Supreme Court
justices operate under a set of perverse incentives. They gain their
greatest power (and in her case, acclaim) just when it might be time
to retire. The chief justice decides who writes an opinion. If the chief
is not in the majority, however, the senior justice who agrees with the
ruling makes the assignment. It was not until 2018 that Ginsburg was
the senior justice assigning a majority opinion.

All of this meant that Ginsburg should have retired, indeed got
many hints to retire, but never did. Barack Obama met with her in
2013 and noted that the Democrats were about to lose the Senate. But
he did not press, or ask her to step down, and unlike Lyndon Johnson,
he found no creative ways to induce her to make the decision on her
own. Ginsburg dismissed the idea of resigning anyway. "Anybody who

thinks that if I step down, Obama could appoint someone like me, they're misguided." Like others no doubt she expected Hillary Clinton to choose her successor.

On September 18, 2020, Ginsburg died. To replace her, Trump quickly named Amy Coney Barrett. If the refusal to consider the Garland nomination was a shocking breach of political norms, the Barrett choice, rushed through after early voting had started in nine states, was not too far behind. McConnell brought her nomination to the floor just twenty-seven days after her name was sent to the Senate. It came to a vote just eight days before Election Day. Republicans who had argued the Garland pick came too close to an election had a challenging rhetorical task. "I want you to use my words against me," Judiciary Committee chair Lindsey Graham had said four years earlier. "If there's a Republican president [elected] in 2016 and a vacancy occurs in the last year of the first term, you can say Lindsey Graham said let's let the next president, whoever it might be, make that nomination." In 2020 he explained, "There's nothing unconstitutional about this process." A president already in the midst of being voted out of office would send the nomination to a Senate whose Republicans were about to lose their majority. The night she was confirmed, Barrett appeared with Trump on the Truman Balcony at a White House celebration, a maskless fete so crowded that Trump contracted Covid and had to be rushed to Walter Reed National Military Medical Center.

As Trump hurried Barrett onto the bench, he explained his motives: he expected the Court to hand him the election. "I think this [election] will end up in the Supreme Court, and I think it's very important that we have nine Justices." He added, "This scam that the Democrats are pulling—it's a scam—the scam will be before the United States Supreme Court." Yet to Trump's sulfurous frustration, the Court did not overturn the election for him. The justices repeatedly refused to get involved in cases as Election Day approached, rejecting appeals from Democrats as well as Republicans.

On Election Day, despite the pandemic, the country saw the highest turnout since 1900. The Department of Homeland Security confirmed that it was "the most secure election in history." It was a remarkable civic achievement. Instead, Trump responded with his Big Lie of a stolen election and a barrage of lawsuits aiming to overturn the results. Sixty-three courts ruled on the cases, and rejected them using words such as "flimsy," "incorrect and not credible," and "strained legal arguments without merit and speculative accusations . . . unsupported by evidence."

Trump kept predicting an imminent high court showdown. The justices kept declining to hear his appeals. The most constitutionally outlandish case was filed at the Supreme Court itself, where one state can sue another: Texas sued Pennsylvania charging that the Keystone State had not properly enforced its own election laws. The Court quickly batted that one away. "The U.S. Supreme Court has been totally incompetent and weak on the massive Election Fraud that took place in the 2020 Presidential Election," Trump tweeted. "We have absolute PROOF, but they don't want to see it—No 'standing,' they say. If we have corrupt elections, we have no country!"

On January 6 Trump loosed his mob on the U.S. Capitol in a bid to stop the transfer of power. One week later, the House of Representatives voted to impeach him for a second time. One week after that, John Roberts again swore in a new president. This time it was an inaugural as odd and tense as any since the Civil War, held on a Capitol Hill ringed by fifteen thousand troops, required rather astoundingly to defend against the chance of an assault by the outgoing president's supporters.

Biden was president. Democrats controlled both houses of Congress, if barely. But the supermajority controlled the Court. It was shocking and swift: in constitutional time, lightning fast. The Court had been dominated by Republicans since 1970. Since 2000 it had been uneasily conservative, with five-to-four rulings on a string of issues. But with such a narrow margin there was always the possibility for a surprising result, and in some of the key decisions of the past decade—on marriage equality, Obamacare, and presidential power—the five votes were on the other hand. Now Trump, a president who never won the popular vote, defeated after his one term, had chosen three members of the Supreme Court. The supermajority was largely impervious to defection or persuasion.

The import of all this was not apparent in its first months. Barrett had joined halfway through the term. She held back from participating in some cases. Still it was something of a surprise in June 2021 when the new alignment—in place for six months—finished its first partial term. There were many unanimous or near-unanimous rulings. At a time when the Court was still meeting remotely, with its "Marble Palace" still protected by troops on a Capitol Hill ready to withstand assault by MAGA mobs, the justices seemed to strain for the return to normalcy promised by the new Biden administration. As the liberal *New Yorker* magazine put it admiringly, at a time when the country was torn by the pandemic, by the election and the defeated president's false claims of fraud, by the insurrection and more, the Supreme Court managed unanimity on many key points—or at least to avoid big bold rulings on a narrow majority. "Instead, the Justices repeatedly defied expectations, with conservatives and liberals together forming majorities in high-profile cases in order to avoid or defer the fighting of deeper wars," Harvard professor Jeannie Suk Gersen wrote. The legal director of the ACLU expressed relief about a "surprising consensus at the Supreme Court." Of the sixty-eight rulings, only ten were decided by the six most conservative justices. (Most of those involved ruling against prisoners and immigrants.)

But abundant clues suggested the next term would be different. After rebuffing cases on abortion, the justices agreed to assess a Mississippi law that plainly and explicitly flouted *Roe v. Wade.* It had been twelve years since the Court ruled on a major Second Amendment case; it took one of those, too. It also took a major case on climate change regulation. And in July 2021, the "phony war" ended. In the last case on the docket for the year, the Court's new radicalism was first felt on the law of democracy. It was in some ways the last ruling of the Roberts Court and the first flexing of the supermajority court on the eve of its big year.

PART TWO

SIX WHO RULED

CHAPTER SEVEN

MARCHING BACKWARD

Every March, thousands of people from across the country make a pilgrimage to Selma, Alabama, to re-create the 1965 march across the Edmund Pettus Bridge. Americans remember Selma as a landmark in the struggle for racial equality, a story retold in films, books, popular songs, graphic novels, and documentaries. They honor the courage of twenty-five-year-old John Lewis as he led nonviolent marchers into the clubs and whips of racist state troopers. They recount Lyndon Johnson's great address proposing the Voting Rights Act to Congress, declaring, "We shall overcome." And they repeat Dr. Martin Luther King Jr.'s hopeful words at the end of the march in Montgomery: "The arc of the moral universe is long, but it bends toward justice."

The pandemic shut down the annual in-person gathering in Selma, but on Sunday, March 7, 2021, celebrants staged a virtual march for voting rights. Days before, the Supreme Court had already heard arguments in a case that would eventually eviscerate much of what was left of the landmark law—*Brnovich v. DNC*, the first major case to be decided by the six-vote supermajority.

⸺

The Voting Rights Act of 1965 was perhaps the nation's most effective civil rights law. Nearly as many Black people registered to vote in southern states in its first five years as in the entire previous century combined. In Mississippi, African American registration jumped from 7 percent in 1964, to 59 percent four years later, and 71 percent by

1998. The law changed the South, and for the first time opened the way for a truly multiracial democracy in the United States. It relied on the Constitution's Fifteenth Amendment, which pointedly gave Congress (not just the courts) authority to protect voting rights.

Under its key provision, Section 5, states with a history of discrimination in voting had to get permission from the Justice Department or a federal court before changing voting practices. All told the act stopped nearly 1,200 discriminatory state voting changes between 1965 and 2013. Many more were not contemplated because of the fact of federal oversight. (H. L. Mencken's definition of conscience: the idea that someone, somewhere, might be watching you.)

Congress had to reauthorize the law periodically, invariably with bipartisan support. In 1982, the smooth path hit an obstacle. It had to do with the less-known part of the law, Section 2, which authorized lawsuits against discriminatory voting practices. In *Mobile v. Bolden*, the Supreme Court had held that Section 2 prohibited only intentional discrimination—a notoriously difficult standard to meet. Two years later, the House of Representatives responded and passed a change to the law making clear it aimed to prohibit laws with discriminatory "results," not just when there is proof of racist intent.

For young John Roberts, this was galling. At age twenty-six, he worked as a special assistant to Attorney General William French Smith, a patrician Republican. Roberts worried that Senate Republicans might join House Democrats to restore the voting law's strength. He fired off memos to his supervisors and ghostwrote letters to Congress raising the alarm. In one note to the attorney general he implored, "something must be done to educate the Senators on the seriousness of this problem." Another time he argued, "Such an effort is not only constitutionally suspect, but also contrary to the most fundamental tenants [*sic*] of the legislative process on which the laws of the country are based."

Older conservatives saw things differently. Kansas senator Bob Dole urged Republicans to make "the extra effort to erase the lingering image of our party as the cadre of the elite, the wealthy, the insensitive. . . . Our job now is to demonstrate concern to Blacks and others who doubt our sincerity." Dole drafted a version of the "results test" which was included in the law. President Reagan signed the measure, to Roberts's chagrin.

For years the Voting Rights Act was a topic for history textbooks and public television documentaries, not news coverage and urgent political activism. But the 2000 presidential election woke both parties to the power of the vote. It turned out that elections could turn on restricting the franchise, or on boosting turnout.

Surging demographic change began to shape politics, too, along with a rising white backlash. Republicans began to fling spurious claims of voter fraud. In a little remembered scandal, for example, George W. Bush's administration ordered prosecutors to bring charges against nonexistent election misconduct. Several U.S. attorneys refused and were fired. After months of controversy Attorney General Alberto Gonzales resigned, and White House aides narrowly escaped prosecution.

Still, in 2006 the Voting Rights Act had passed the Senate with ninety-eight votes. Bush proudly signed it with John Lewis, now a congressman, standing by his side. The revised statute had been the subject of extensive hearings, with dozens of witnesses, and hours of debate. In the end the law did not differ markedly from the version that bore Reagan's signature.

Now the Supreme Court readied its own assault on the act. It nearly gutted the law in 2009, soon after Barack Obama took office. After a very hostile public session, Roberts and the others surprised by letting the act live. "Whether conditions continue to justify such legislation is a difficult constitutional question we do not answer today." We will gut the Voting Rights Act soon, Roberts implied, but "not . . . today."

That moment came in June 2013, months into Obama's second term.

Shelby County v. Holder effectively ended preclearance, the Voting Rights Act's most effective provision. At the argument, Antonin Scalia groused that the law was little more than a "racial entitlement." Spectators gasped. But Scalia did not write the opinion; Roberts did, and he was more decorous. The South had evolved, he explained. In Alabama Black voting rates matched white voter participation, and were higher than in northern states. Obama, he did not need to say, sat in the White House. That was then, this is now. "Our country has changed, and while any racial discrimination in voting is too much, Congress must ensure that the legislation it passes to remedy that problem speaks to current conditions."

The majority paid little heed to Congress, which the Fifteenth

Amendment to the Constitution had charged with protecting equal access to the franchise. "Even the name of it is wonderful: *The Voting Rights Act*," Scalia had mocked at the argument. "Who is going to vote against *that* in the future?" A generation of conservatives had denounced "judicial activism" and paid tribute to the wisdom of legislators. For new conservatives that was beginning to change.

Ruth Bader Ginsburg published her memorable dissent. "Throwing out preclearance when it has worked and is continuing to work to stop discriminatory changes is like throwing away your umbrella in a rainstorm because you are not getting wet," she wrote sternly. Political equality in the South had advanced precisely because it had been shielded by federal protection.

Within hours, Ginsburg's warning proved prescient. Texas announced it would implement its new voter identification law, widely viewed as the nation's most restrictive. A federal judge found that 608,000 registered voters lacked the necessary paperwork, disproportionately Black and Latino citizens. After a lengthy trial, she blocked Texas's rule using the part of the Voting Rights Act that had been left intact: Section 2.

In fact, all over the country rights groups used Section 2 with surprising success. In 2016, for example, an appeals court struck down a restrictive voting law enacted in North Carolina. The state's plans, the judges ruled, "target African Americans with almost surgical precision."

Previously Section 2 was only used to challenge racial gerrymanders and laws that reduced minority representation. But for nearly a decade after *Shelby County*, the provision—imperfect and expensive to enforce—served as the principal legal protection against discriminatory voting laws themselves. That would change.

Bad cases make bad law, they say, and the *Brnovich* case represented a misjudgment by the Democratic Party and its lawyers. Amid a flurry of lawsuits by both sides, Democrats challenged some long-standing voting laws in Arizona. They claimed two technical provisions violated the Voting Rights Act. For years civil rights activists scrambled to keep such cases away from the conservative justices. Now partisan lawyers pushed the case up toward the high court. Legal scholar Rick Hasen, voicing misgivings privately shared by others, warned the case was an "overreach" and that the Arizona rules were "far from the most egregious voting rights violations."

By the time the case was argued in the spring of 2021, less than two months after Donald Trump's mob stormed the Capitol on January 6, the stakes had risen sharply.

American democracy seemed more fragile than ever. State legislators galvanized by Trump's false claims were rushing to pass restrictive voting laws. That same month in Georgia, for example, lawmakers prepared to end vote-by-mail for younger voters, repeal automatic voter registration, and cancel early voting on the day used by Black churches, all moves with an unmistakable racial and partisan impact. Republicans pulled back at the last minute after an outcry from critics that included Atlanta-headquartered Delta Air Lines and Coca-Cola. They enacted a law less draconian but still racially targeted. Governor Brian Kemp signed it in front of an oil painting of a slave plantation, flanked by white men in suits. Beefy state police dragged a Black state legislator from the scene.

Thus *Brnovich* took on new significance. The fate of the arcane Arizona laws mattered less than how the Supreme Court would treat the Voting Rights Act. Must voters or prosecutors prove that a legislature deliberately intended to discriminate? Or is it enough to show that a law in a state with a history of discrimination hurts minority voters (or hurts them more than white voters)?

On March 2, 2021, one year into the pandemic, lawyers for the Democrats, the Republicans, and the Arizona government jousted by phone before the Supreme Court.

The pandemic continued to upend normal patterns. The Supreme Court building remained shut to the public. The parties made their arguments on conference calls. In contrast to the chaotic barking of questions and quips when the justices met in person, Roberts imposed some order on these telephone sessions. Lawyers could make their case for two minutes before being interrupted. Justices would decorously ask questions in order of seniority. Among other things, that meant Clarence Thomas went first. For years, he had refused to talk in the Court's public sessions, never joining his colleagues in their questioning. Now he began to keynote the sessions in his booming baritone. Some analysts think the conference call arguments hurt the liberals since they could not pepper advocates with challenging questions one after another. There was one upside: the justices interrupted each other less, and in particular, the men were less prone to speaking over the women. Even so, in the telephonic age, "nine of the eleven instances in which the Chief Justice interrupted a justice, he interrupted a female justice."

These conference calls were not perfect. Questions were more stilted than when asked in person, with justices less able to test each other in what typically is the first time they air and hash out their views. Other problems were more prosaic. During one May 2020 argument someone, evidently a justice, could be heard flushing a toilet.

Elena Kagan led the Arizona Republican Party's lawyer, Michael Carvin, through barely disguised hypotheticals. "A state has long had two weeks of early voting, and then the state decides that it's going to get rid of Sunday voting on those two weeks, leave everything else in place," she surmised, even though "Black voters vote on Sunday 10 times more than white voters." That would not violate the Voting Rights Act, the lawyer argued.

"These are all hypotheticals that have never existed in the real world," he complained. "You know, this doesn't seem so fanciful to me," Kagan replied.

The new justice, Amy Coney Barrett, asked a question that (perhaps inadvertently) exposed motives. "What's the interest of the Arizona [Republican Party committee] here in keeping, say, the out-of-precinct voter ballot disqualification rules on the books?"

"Because it puts us at a competitive disadvantage relative to Democrats," Carvin replied. "Politics is a zero-sum game, and every extra vote they get through unlawful interpretations of Section Two hurts us. It's the difference between winning an election fifty to forty-nine and losing an election fifty-one to fifty."

The ruling came in July 2021, at a time when justices typically would be finished and headed for the beach. Samuel Alito wrote it. After sixteen years as a justice, Alito often seemed consumed by anger. Rarely did a witticism or a smile leaven his stern public visage. "He treats lawyers like children caught in a lie, grilling them on every minor point of their argument while dismissing their logic as idiotic," Mark Joseph Stern wrote after observing him on the bench. "He handles fellow justices like hecklers who have thoughtlessly interrupted his train of thought."

Observers struggled to figure out why Alito, with a nice upbringing and a golden career, seemed so dyspeptic. Perhaps family history explained some of his intensity. Alito had written in a Justice Department job application that he opposed the Warren Court's landmark "one person, one vote" rulings. That was, he later explained, because of his father's experience as chief researcher for the New Jersey legislature. After the Court had ruled, Alito would later recall hearing his father struggling late at night to redraw the maps. What others might have spun into a tale of how he learned the value of hard work from dear old dad, Alito seemed to view as punishment that had been inflicted on his father by the liberals.

He attended Princeton, still dominated by tony eating clubs. His roommate said that as Catholics they were painfully aware of being surrounded by people whose ancestors went back to the *Mayflower*. Alito joined ROTC after drawing a low number in the Selective Service draft lottery (which made him more likely to be sent to Vietnam) hoping to become an officer if drafted. But the university ended the program after students firebombed the ROTC building. Worse, professors canceled classes to protest the war. Alito continued to attend drills and classes off-campus and joined a conservative campus group out of frustration. He came to see himself as an outsider in a sea of privileged radicals.

As a junior Justice Department lawyer, Alito ran into a superior at a Federalist Society lunch at a restaurant. "This is like meeting a friend at a bordello," the fellow traveler confided. Soon Alito was handed assignments, including Supreme Court arguments, that more liberal colleagues shunned. He quietly pitched articles to the *National Review* and other conservative publications. He was swept into the flow of movement lawyering. He became United States attorney for New Jersey, then sat on a federal appeals court for sixteen years.

When his time came in the full glare of national attention after years of obscurity, Alito found it agonizing. His wife, sitting behind him as he testified at his Supreme Court confirmation hearing, burst into tears from the stress. Press photographers unnerved him. He remained furious that reporters had called his ninety-year-old mother to try to find out his views on abortion. "I hope what I experienced will not happen again," he told a reporter a decade later. Yet by modern standards his confirmation was far from acrimonious, indeed was largely glitch-free. The Senate backed him with a comfortable 16-vote margin.

Over time Alito hardened into perhaps the most partisan justice. Scholars could not point to a single five-to-four ruling where he joined the liberals. His *Hobby Lobby* opinion gave private companies owned by religious Christians the right to exclude contraception from employee health insurance. Alito regularly gave defiant speeches to the Federalist Society and other conservative audiences. Law professor Aziz Huq, after studying the justice's writing, wrote, "To read his opinions is to inhabit a world in which it is white Christian men who are the principal targets of invidious discrimination, and where a traditional way of life marked by firm and clear gender rules is under attack."

In *Brnovich* Alito growled at the Voting Rights Act, and little was left of it by the end. Years before, when the Supreme Court had first interpreted Section 2 with its "results test," it looked at what Congress had intended the law to mean. A Senate committee report had spelled out an expansive understanding of the provision's wording. Alito explained that this was no longer how the Supreme Court did things. It no longer paid much attention to legislative history. The opinion spends little time on what the law was for or what its sponsors hoped it would do, but much energy parsing what the words in the text meant. In a move common today but which would have seemed bafflingly odd in 1982, Alito pulled out dictionaries to construe each phrase. Having deconstructed the text and having left the pieces all over the table, Alito then felt free to explain how he thought judges should limit use of Section 2. Deference to the legislature did not seem front of mind.

He wrote a checklist, essentially a numbered set of excuses states could use to evade the law. Most surprising, it asked judges to assess "the degree to which a voting rule departs from what was standard practice when Section Two was amended in 1982." That year, Congress had rewritten the law precisely to cover unforeseen voting practices. That was always the story of the fight for equal rights in voting: in the Jim Crow era, if courts struck down one law, something new popped up to take its place. Elena Kagan wrote in her dissent, "Combating those efforts was like 'battling the Hydra,'" quoting opera-loving Ruth Bader

Ginsburg, "or to use a less cultured reference, like playing a game of whack-a-mole." In any case, voting practices had changed greatly since 1982. Back then, few voted early or by mail, and there were no out-of-precinct drop boxes. Why should practices then—when voter turnout was considerably lower than it is today—be the standard?

Alito charged that the dissenters and their vision of how to apply the law was "radical." Kagan, writing for Sotomayor and Breyer, pointed out that Alito actually aimed at the Voting Rights Act itself and the Congress that strengthened it. "The majority fears that the statute Congress wrote is too 'radical'—that it will invalidate too many state voting laws. So the majority writes its own set of rules. . . .What is tragic here is that the court has (yet again) rewritten—in order to weaken—a statute that stands as a monument to America's greatness, and protects against its basest impulses."

Elena Kagan had become a predictably passionate voice on the democracy law cases before the Court, almost always in dissent, on matters including campaign finance reform, redistricting, and election administration. That was not a given. She joined the Court with the potential to forge a center-left, center-right bloc. Instead she found herself obliged to be a fervent defender of first principles.

Kagan was born in 1960 in New York City to an attorney and a public school teacher. At her 2010 Supreme Court confirmation hearing, Lindsey Graham—with stagey dramatic flair, seeking to score points about a foiled terrorist attack the previous December—asked her where she had been on Christmas. "Like all Jews, I was probably at a Chinese restaurant," she answered deadpan. The audience applauded. One lawmaker cracked, "Senator [Chuck] Schumer explained that to me earlier."

Political pros spotted her early as a leading attorney of her generation, someone possibly pointed to the Supreme Court. Bill Clinton's chief of staff Erskine Bowles would routinely introduce her as "the smartest person in the White House." Rare among the justices, she had moved easily in and out of the Oval Office. Formally she was deputy director of domestic policy, but her supervisor elevated her to something akin to a codirector. Kagan was a "New Democrat," one of the centrists who steered policy in the Clinton era. She was responsible for the federal government's initiatives on issues including tobacco and gun safety, and wrote John McCain's bill regulating tobacco. One job involved mediating between New York attorney general Eliot Spitzer and Housing Secretary Andrew Cuomo, already elbowing each other as opponents of the National Rifle Association long before either of them either won or resigned the New York governorship.

After leaving government Kagan wrote a long law review article as a bid to win tenure at Harvard. It lauded how presidents could induce agencies to advance policy at a time of divided government. Other Democrats had decried the willingness of the courts during Reagan's terms to hand administrative power to the executive; she showed how a progressive president could wield the levers of power as well. She became the university's first woman law school dean after deftly handling both the central university administration, which wanted to move the school across the river from its Cambridge home, and the faculty, who opposed the idea with lie-down-in-front-of-the-bulldozers fervor. Conflicts divided conservative and leftist faculty and students. As dean she bolstered student happiness, installing an ice rink, offering hot chocolate, and hiring conservative professors. Obama was an old friend from the University of Chicago faculty. He named her solicitor general in 2009. The first case she ever argued in any courtroom was *Citizens United* before the Supreme Court. When the court vacancy opened, she was a natural choice.

Kagan's wit, sharp mind, and personal gregariousness made her a natural member of a possible bloc in the Court's center. Her horse-trading skills were evident in cases such as the Affordable Care Act, where she pulled Roberts away from striking down the whole law but herself agreed to limit Medicaid expansion in the process. (Ironically, Medicaid expansion would do nearly all the work of getting people health insurance; the individual mandate, subject of so much constitutional agita, turned out to be much less relevant. However, the limits the Court set let states refuse federal funds and exclude their citizens from medical coverage.) She embraced some conservative approaches to judging. "We are all textualists now," she said, referring to the approach to interpreting statutes that does not ask what Congress's intent was, just what the words on the page mean. This was itself a witty paraphrase of "We are all Keynesians now," something reputedly said by Richard Nixon as he took the country off the gold standard.

But as the supermajority veered right, opportunities for droll compromise were few. Kagan frequently found herself dissenting. She became particularly fervent as the Court hammered away at the scaffolding that protected democratic institutions and election reforms. Kagan wrote with sharp, conversational punchiness, a modern take on the style of Oliver Wendell Holmes.

She read her dissents from the bench only three times in her first decade as justice. The first was on a case about Arizona's voluntary public financing system for political campaigns. Another dealt with political speech by union members.

The third time came in the 2019 case where the Court announced it would not police partisan gerrymandering. Both parties manipulated legislative lines, of course, and always have. But digital data tools and aggressive operatives produced increasingly imbalanced maps. Pennsylvania offered an extreme example. It was an evenly divided state (parties split the vote in elections for president, governor, and senator). But the legislature created a congressional map in 2011 with thirteen solidly Republican and only three solidly Democratic districts. For years the justices had written prolifically about the danger of unrepresentative redistricting, but despaired about finding a workable standard. Finally in *Rucho v. Common Cause*, a five-to-four majority led by Roberts declared there was no precise way to find partisan gerrymanders unconstitutional; even more, federal courts were barred from hearing those claims again. "For the first time ever," she declared in dissent, "this court refuses to remedy a constitutional violation because it thinks the task beyond judicial capabilities." Mark Joseph Stern of *Slate* described the scene as she spoke from the bench. "At first, her voice is filled with righteous fury, but it soon shifts into profound sorrow as she nears the end. . . . Her voice wavers as she delivers the final line: 'With respect, but deep sadness, Justices Ginsburg, Breyer, Sotomayor, and I dissent.'"

In her growing focus on preserving American democracy, Kagan reflected a generational impulse. She had entered politics at a time when liberals sought to curb the excesses of the left that had drained popular support from the Democratic Party. She was a dealmaker at a time when deals could be made. Now she found herself charged with defending core institutions of self-government.

The *Brnovich* case had big political implications, on and off the Court.

It was the first time the new supermajority wielded its power—the first major six-to-three ruling, with Amy Coney Barrett joining her longer-serving colleagues.

It also came in the middle of the first great congressional fight over voting rules in decades. A year after the 2020 election, 70 percent of Republican voters believed that President Biden stole the election. Trump's Big Lie inspired legislators across the country to propose a wave of restrictive laws. By the end of 2021, according to the Brennan Center's assessment, eighteen states had passed thirty-four new laws that made it harder to vote. Some were worse than others, but frequently they hit Black, Latino, Asian, Native, and young voters the hardest. Had the Voting Rights Act been at full strength, it would have stopped the harshest laws from taking effect in states such as Georgia, Texas, Arizona, and Florida.

In response, the Democratic Congress moved to pass national legislation to protect voting rights and modernize election law. For years John Lewis and others had pushed to restore preclearance after *Shelby County*. After he died, the measure was renamed in his honor: the John Lewis Voting Rights Advancement Act. The legislation, like all previous versions of the Voting Rights Act, had bipartisan support. By 2021, though, Republicans pulled back amid Trump's screams about rigged elections. Legislation quickly was drafted to undo *Brnovich* as well.

The measure was combined with other reforms into one bill, the Freedom to Vote: John Lewis Voting Rights Act. It passed the House and won support of a Senate majority. At the National Constitution Center in Philadelphia Biden decried "the most significant test of our democracy since the Civil War," and promised to sign the legislation. But the measure lacked sixty votes to overcome a Senate filibuster. Only one Republican, Lisa Murkowski of Alaska, indicated she would restore the Voting Rights Act, and none would do even that for the other proposed provisions. Democrats Joe Manchin of West Virginia and Kyrsten Sinema of Arizona refused to change rules so the voting rights bill could pass, and on January 19, 2022, it failed after days of debate. (Their behavior baffled. Manchin, a former state election official, had spent months crafting the legislation. But he came from a state Trump had won by 39 points. Sinema hailed from a state with two Democratic senators, where Biden won, and where Latinos, often targeted by voting rules, made up a third of the electorate and much of her support base.)

The Supreme Court's rulings on democracy law had the makings of a highly partisan perpetual motion machine. In *Citizens United* and other campaign finance cases the Court deregulated campaign finance and empowered corporations and wealthy individuals. That helped Republicans. *Shelby County* and *Brnovich* gutted the Voting Rights Act. That, too, helped Republicans. It had been over a decade, in fact, since the Court struck down a restrictive state voting law at all. Because the Court refused to police partisan gerrymandering, in four states in 2022 elections used maps already declared illegal or discriminatory by lower courts, adding about five to seven Republican seats, enough to control the House of Representatives. Republican senators in turn engineered Trump's three appointments to the Supreme Court—which now was prepared to make more rulings desired by the Republicans to further tilt power their way.

The Court's rulings on democracy had another implication—one that became increasingly clear throughout the 2021–22 term. At times only strong national standards can stop states from abusing the rights of their people. Indeed, that dynamic shaped much of the country's history. As noted above, in the past three quarters of a century the federal government—through congressional action, through enforcement by the Justice Department, and through the rulings of federal courts—established a more or less uniform set of rights when it comes to voting and many other constitutionally protected aspects of civic life. The events of 2021 rattled that system. If Congress cannot protect voting rights because of the filibuster, despite the support of a majority, and the federal courts will not protect voting rights, then states have free rein to do their worst. There is no reason to think that the current state of voting rights will not get worse, far worse.

CHAPTER EIGHT

THE SHADOW DOCKET

A LL KNEW THAT ONCE THE SUPREME Court term began in October 2021, it would hear major cases and likely make big, disruptive rulings. The future of *Roe v. Wade* and abortion rights teetered. Briefs were readied, with the argument scheduled for December.

But over the summer of 2021, with growing nonchalance, the justices made significant decisions before the term even began. These moved the law sharply while drawing less attention than in the usual end-of-June blockbusters. At summer's end, the Supreme Court allowed the second biggest state to overturn *Roe v. Wade*. It used what is called the "shadow docket."

A conservative scholar coined the catchy phrase in 2015. William Baude identified "a range of orders and summary decisions that defy normal procedural regularity." These emergency orders differ from the Court's usual "merits" cases, the familiar rulings—roughly sixty to seventy a year—with full briefing and a carefully written decision that takes months. Instead of "opinions," shadow docket actions are "orders" to lower courts. Often they come in the summer, between the end of a term in June and the start of a new one in October, when justices receive urgent requests for immediate action.

Such orders announce everything from deciding not to hear a case to delaying an execution. Parties do not file extensive briefs; there are no oral arguments; frequently there are no friend of the court manifestos from outside groups and experts. Usually we do not know how individual justices voted. The shadow docket cases, reports University of Texas scholar Stephen Vladeck, the leading expert on the topic, are not even found in one place on the Supreme Court website.

In some ways this was not new. The Supreme Court has always found ways to act in a hurry. Robert Caro described how future justice Abe Fortas, then a young but very well-connected lawyer, persuaded a single Supreme Court justice, Hugo Black, to stop a recount in the 1948 Texas Senate election, thus sealing Lyndon Johnson's win by 87 votes. From the execution of the Soviet spies Julius and Ethel Rosenberg to the halt of Florida's recount in the battle between George W. Bush and Al Gore, newsworthy rulings have been made without a public argument or briefings. Most were less epic, routine in fact.

Then something changed. Starting in 2017, Vladeck reports, the use of the shadow docket skyrocketed. Divided opinions (where some justices dissented) rose sevenfold. That was when Donald Trump took office. The federal government rarely had asked for emergency relief before, but under Trump it asked the justices to intervene early on forty-one occasions. The Court sided with the administration three quarters of the time.

The Court acted on matters ranging from Trump's ban on travel from several Muslim-majority countries to his effort to redirect funds to build a border wall. Sonia Sotomayor described "a now-familiar pattern" as she objected to one such ruling. "The Government seeks emergency relief from this Court, asking it to grant a stay where two lower courts have not. The Government insists—even though review in a court of appeals is imminent—that it will suffer irreparable harm if this Court does not grant a stay. And the Court yields."

Then in 2021 Joe Biden became president. Suddenly, the shadow docket was being used to block progressive policies, not to expedite MAGA goals.

In August 2021, for example, the Court effectively ordered Biden to restart his predecessor's harsh immigration rules. Refugees long could claim asylum if they have a "well-founded fear of persecution" in their home country. These refugees legally work and live in the United States while courts hear their claims. Trump had required them to leave the country after they apply for asylum, stranding tens of thousands just over the border. Officials suspended the "Remain in Mexico" rule during Covid, and Biden had pledged to end it altogether. Then a trial judge in Amarillo, Texas, a newly appointed Federalist Society activist, ordered the federal government to restart the dormant policy. That would require the United States to open negotiations with the Mexican government, among other things. An aggressive move with foreign policy implications by one judge in one courtroom was the kind of thing a Supreme Court once would have stopped. Instead, in a single unsigned paragraph, six of nine Supreme Court justices kept the trial judge's order in place. The three liberal justices dissented. (Nearly a year later, the Court let the Biden administration end the policy after all. A year after that, in late 2022, the same judge overturned the policy again.)

The next week the Court blocked an extension of the federal government's ban on evictions, which the Centers for Disease Control had imposed at the start of the pandemic. Again the liberals dissented. The Court also threw thunderbolts from up high, intervening in litigation in its very earliest stages. From the time Amy Coney Barrett joined the Court, days before Biden's election, Vladeck reported, "the justices have issued seven emergency injunctions to block state coronavirus restrictions, compared with a total of four injunctions directly blocking state laws issued by the court during the first fifteen years" of Roberts's tenure.

So what is wrong with all this?

When a big case is decided in the shadows, it short-circuits public arguments. Rulings can be rushed and unsigned (unless a justice pens an indignant dissent). An example: early in the Covid-19 pandemic, a federal court had ordered California to make hand sanitizer available to prisoners. The Court blocked that ruling, five to four. "I have no idea why the Supreme Court would do such a thing," journalist Ian Millhiser wrote, "and neither does anyone else who isn't a justice or one of their closest advisers." All anyone had to go on was a single paragraph of legal boilerplate.

Frequently the rulings are released at odd hours—what one reporter dubbed the "night court." In 2020, by a five-to-four vote, the justices allowed federal executions for the first time in nearly two decades, with one order announced at 2:10 a.m. and another two nights later at 2:46 a.m.

Judges around the country, puzzling over how to interpret the Sphinx-like rulings, have begun to treat them as if they were precedent. The shadow docket may be the only time the Court speaks (if gruffly) about an issue. One trial judge, a longtime Federalist Society member, explained, "whenever a lower court can say with confidence that a majority of the Supreme Court has expressed a view on the merits of a stay applicant's case, the lower court should accord that view significant deference."

And then on September 1, 2021, the Supreme Court took one of its most significant actions in decades—without explanation and without argument, a major constitutional ruling whispered on the shadow docket.

Whole Woman's Health is a chain of clinics throughout Texas. It had been enmeshed in a case that typified the grinding fights over abortion restrictions. A 2015 state law purported to protect pregnant women. It required doctors to be admitted at a hospital within thirty miles of their clinic and required the facilities to have all the equipment of a surgical center, even regulating the size of hallways and tables. All but two clinics in Texas would have been forced to close. The rules were a pretext: abortion is safer for women than many other outpatient procedures and much safer than pregnancy or childbirth. The U.S. Supreme Court with an almost audible sigh ruled in 2016 that yes, this would impose an "undue burden" on women's reproductive rights.

As the decade wore on, Republican states grew increasingly emboldened, taunting the Supreme Court, enacting laws flatly at odds with what decades of precedent said the Constitution meant. In 2019, with Ruth Bader Ginsburg still on the bench, Louisiana passed a law nearly identical to the one already invalidated in Texas. John Roberts had voted to allow Texas's strict law. Now he joined the liberals to block the copycat statute. Stare decisis, he wrote, "requires us, absent special circumstances, to treat like cases alike. The Louisiana law imposes a burden on access to abortion just as severe as that imposed by the Texas law, for the same reasons."

Republicans were surprised and angry. "Chief Justice Roberts is at it again with his political gamesmanship," tweeted Senator Ted Cruz of

Texas, who had argued nine cases himself at the Court. Representative
Jim Jordan of Ohio demanded, with less logic, "What's next, Chief Justice Roberts? Our Second Amendment rights?"

Other states strained to test the Court. One of them, Mississippi,
enacted its new antiabortion law in 2018. The statute was flatly unconstitutional; that was its entire point. It didn't just "burden" abortion
rights, it banned abortions after fifteen weeks. The proposed barrier
was a legal tripwire: the law did not affect many women. Over 90 percent of abortions in Mississippi were performed before fourteen weeks
(and three quarters of them before ten weeks). But upholding the
measure would require undoing *Roe* and *Planned Parenthood of Southeastern Pennsylvania v. Casey*, the 1992 case that protected the right up
to about twenty-three weeks. The law openly challenged not just *Roe*
but the Supreme Court's authority. A federal appeals court blocked it.
Mississippi appealed in the summer of 2020, just weeks after the Louisiana ruling and in the middle of the presidential election. The Supreme Court stalled. Normally it would simply refuse to hear the case
but it never gave an answer.

Mississippi was an awkward showcase. It was the poorest state in the
nation. Sixty-three percent of pregnancies there were unplanned, and
the state barred teachers from demonstrating contraceptive use. It had
the nation's worst record on women's health, and the highest rate of
women who died in childbirth. The state refused to accept $900 million
in federal money to expand Medicaid. (Mississippi would have had to
chip in $100 million.) Lawmakers even balked at giving new mothers a
year of health care. Mississippi made clear the stark racial dimensions
of the issue. Black women are five times more likely to terminate a pregnancy than white women. Without health insurance, without access to
sometimes expensive contraception such as IUDs, poorer women are
more likely to have an unintended pregnancy, and more likely to decide to terminate it. In a place like Mississippi, generations of poverty,
racism, isolation, poor health care, and more combined to make the
protection of the right to abortion even more fraught.

Then Ginsburg died and was replaced by Barrett. Three Trump-
appointed justices now formed the core of the new supermajority. Suddenly a new justice would likely vote with the four who had wanted to
strike down *Roe* already. In May 2021, the Supreme Court announced
it would consider the appeal in *Dobbs v. Jackson Women's Health*, the

Mississippi case. It was ten months after the state had petitioned, and even then the case would not be heard until December.

The Court signaled a big and direct challenge to *Roe v. Wade.*

The justices asked a single question: "Whether all pre-viability prohibitions on elective abortions are unconstitutional." One hundred forty friend of the court briefs tumbled in. The Bioethics Defense Fund, the Billy Graham Evangelistic Association, thirteen governors, and 228 members of Congress demanded that the Court overturn *Roe* and *Casey.* The American Medical Association, the American Bar Association, and the ACLU urged the Court to uphold its precedent, often arguing that millions had relied on that constitutionally protected right. The machinery of an epic Supreme Court showdown was whirring into action in the glare of public debate and attention.

Would the justices go all the way? Would they say the politically explosive words, "we hereby overrule *Roe v. Wade*"—knowing that could set off a backlash as the original case had in 1973, this time faster and fiercer? Or would they try to find a way to avoid the contention? After decades where the conservative legal movement had fallen one vote short, losing out in a series of five-to-four rulings, now it had victory within its grasp—did it really want to win?

All of which made what happened in Texas all the more shocking.

Jonathan Mitchell was a former law professor comfortable in elite legal circles, a Thomas clerk who was a sought-after panelist at Federalist Society gatherings. Rather than joining a big white-shoe firm, he set up a solo shop in Texas. In 2018 he wrote an article with a devious proposal. States could pass laws that were unconstitutional, or revive old laws long deemed improper, even if those laws were explicitly barred by the Supreme Court. If the state government did not enforce them, but instead let private citizens do so instead, that would not count as "state action" under the law. It was a brazen challenge to the notion of judicial supremacy set out by the Supreme Court since the 1950s.

This made no sense. State courts are part of the government. If a law is set up to achieve a result that is otherwise illegal, it should also be found unconstitutional. The Supreme Court had ruled decades ago, for example, that when courts enforce a racially discriminatory contract, it is an action by the government. It was hard to know if the idea should even be taken seriously. The Texas legislature, casting about for new ways to defy the Supreme Court, took it seriously indeed. In May 2021, it passed S.B. 8, the Texas Heartbeat Act. It banned all abortions after a fetal heartbeat was detected, about six weeks of pregnancy. (That is not six weeks after a woman learns she is pregnant—it's six weeks after her most recent period, which means about two weeks after a *late* period. In other words, it banned abortion before many women even know they are pregnant.)

The law authorized members of the public to act as bounty hunters to enforce an otherwise unconstitutional law. Citizens could sue abortion providers, doctors, women, even an Uber driver who takes a patient to a medical appointment. These vigilantes could win $10,000 per procedure, plus attorney's fees and court costs. No more equivocation about admitting privileges or protecting women: Texas effectively had banned abortion. It was the nation's strictest law governing reproductive health in nearly fifty years.

The scheme was enacted in May 2021. The federal court in Austin quickly let the Center for Reproductive Rights and others sue to stop it, only to be blocked from further action by the Fifth Circuit Court of Appeals, perhaps the most conservative such body in the federal judicial system. The law's September 1 date approached rapidly. Clinics rushed to the Supreme Court, seeking an emergency ruling. If ever there were grounds for such an order, this would be it: an unconstitutional law, with massive consequences if it went into effect. Hours ticked by. The Court was silent.

At clinics throughout Texas, panicked women realized they had only hours to act. Reporters described the waiting room at the Whole Woman's Health clinic in Fort Worth, two hours before midnight, where "twenty-seven patients were still huddled in the waiting room." Doctors, some in tears, finished the last procedure at 11:56 p.m. Outside the clinic in the parking lot, antiabortion protesters jeered, flooded the scene with bright lights, and took photographs of who came and went while jotting down license plate numbers. At midnight tweets went out, as a Bloomberg reporter noted, praising God and the Republican Party. The law had gone into effect.

A day later the Supreme Court announced it would not block the statute. The unsigned order was just a paragraph long. The clinics had raised "serious questions" about the law's constitutionality, it said with dry understatement. But there were "complex and novel" procedural issues, so the Court would not stop the law or make a ruling. Texans could certainly sue to stop the law. Meanwhile, it remained in effect— and the network of public health clinics providing abortions simply stopped functioning. The "order is not based on any conclusion about the constitutionality of Texas's law," the opinion reassured.

John Roberts joined the liberal justices in dissenting with a note of despair. "The statutory scheme before the Court is not only unusual, but unprecedented," he wrote. Sotomayor called the action "stunning." Kagan charged the judicial shrug "illustrates just how far the court's 'shadow docket' decisions may depart from the usual principles of appellate process. Without full briefing or argument, and after less than seventy-two hours' thought, this court greenlights the operation of Texas' patently unconstitutional law banning most abortions."

Suddenly, in the second largest state, a state with four of the nation's biggest cities and a population of 28 million, abortion was illegal. In Texas *Roe* was not at risk, it was history. Over the weeks the story played out in thousands of individual lives. Women who could afford the trip slipped off to clinics in Colorado or New Mexico. The parking lot of a clinic in Shreveport, Louisiana, was filled with cars with Texas license plates. "I drove six hours and 58 minutes," one woman from Corpus Christi told a radio reporter. Nervous about her privacy, she would only give her name as "M." "I got here at 8:55 a.m. this morning. So I have not ate, we can't bring in anything to drink. My boyfriend's in the car asleep."

Eventually a few months later the Supreme Court heard the case. The justices seemed skeptical of the Texas law. Elizabeth Prelogar made her first argument as the Biden administration's solicitor general. If private parties could sue to enforce a law that so plainly flouts *Roe v. Wade*, she argued, "no constitutional right is safe." Why couldn't states use the same strategy to ban guns, or take on other constitutional rights proclaimed by the justices?

But the decision when finally published the next month was technical and convoluted, far from a ringing defense of the Supreme Court's authority. Gorsuch wrote for five conservatives. He still would not rule on whether the law violated *Roe v. Wade*. Instead he focused on the question of whom the abortion clinics could sue. They could not sue judges, or the clerks of the court, or the licensing authorities in state government, all of whom enforce the law. They could sue some officials who issue licenses for health providers down the road. Meanwhile, the Texas law would remain in effect. On the shadow docket, the majority of justices had let the law stand because it involved such major issues; now they let it stand by ducking those issues.

The chief justice dissented, irate. The Texas law was now in effect for three months. "It has had the effect of denying the exercise of what we have held is a right protected under the Federal Constitution." That was the law's goal, Roberts wrote, to "nullify this Court's rulings." He quoted *Marbury v. Madison,* as chief justices had before him. This time it was in angry dissent, not as a magisterial pronouncement about judicial supremacy. "Indeed," he said, quoting another early case, " '[i]f the legislatures of the several states may, at will, annul the judgments of the courts of the United States, and destroy the rights acquired under those judgments, the constitution itself becomes a solemn mockery.' . . . The nature of the federal right infringed does not matter; it is the role of the Supreme Court in our constitutional system that is at stake." It was an extraordinary rebuke by a chief justice to a Court that colloquially bears his name.

In any case, the December ruling was less important than the nonruling on the shadow docket months before. That had been a monumental constitutional decision, its impact coupled with a silent, almost nonexistent rationale.

And there was no mass reaction, no explosion of public protest.

The travails of women in Texas got a few days of media attention, but soon were overcome by other issues. Texas voters registered mild approval of the law in polls. Businesses spoke up—Uber and Lyft, the ride sharing apps ubiquitous on smartphones, vowed to pay the legal cost of any of their drivers who were sued for taking a woman to a medical appointment, for example, and database giant Salesforce pledged to pay for any employees who wanted to relocate. But there was no mass threat of business or tourism boycotts, as had occurred after laws passed in North Carolina seen as hostile to gay and transgender people. Austin had been America's boomtown, swelling to over a million people drawn by its supposedly "weird" lifestyle, vibrant music scene, and technology hubs. Would firms really want to relocate there now? In October, Elon Musk announced he would move his headquarters for Tesla and many of his other businesses to the Texas capital. There were few protests, no nationwide marches. Abortion rights ended for one out of ten American women without fuss.

Because it finishes its work in an end-of-semester frenzy of paper-writing in June, the Supreme Court is quiet in the summer. The justices scatter, some to vacation homes, others to teaching gigs around the world. There is a predictable rhythm.

The new Court term begins the first Monday in October. Some of the justices attend a Catholic religious service to bless the legal profession. In previous years many would pray at the Red Mass at the Cathedral of St. Matthew the Apostle. In 2010 Vice President Biden joined Roberts, Scalia, Thomas, Alito, and Breyer (who is Jewish). In 2018, Breyer, Thomas, and Roberts attended. In 2021, only John Roberts showed up. He heard a warning from Archbishop Gabriele Caccia, the permanent observer of the Holy See to the United Nations, "Today," he preached, "like at the time of Jesus, there is the risk to exploit justice instead of deliver it . . . if we do not place ourselves before God in this way, there is the risk to 'use' even God for our own ends instead of serving Him." Was he warning against hubris? Or urging action on abortion?

In the weeks before the new term began, something else interrupted the Court's sojourn. Its approval in the Gallup Poll already had dropped to 40 percent, the lowest level since 2000. The supermajority justices began, rather implausibly, a preemptive public relations campaign to defend the Court against charges it had veered to the right. This was not normal; it was a sign of thunderous things to come.

One defense of the Court was issued at the Seelbach Hotel, built in 1905 and recently renovated, in downtown Louisville, Kentucky. On September 12, 2021, one hundred guests filled a ballroom to hear the new Supreme Court justice, Amy Coney Barrett. Hosts had flown her to the event and presented her with a personalized Louisville Slugger baseball bat. She glowed in front of the crowd in a burgundy dress. Barrett refused to let her speech be livestreamed or videotaped, but a reporter from the Louisville *Courier-Journal* was there.

"My goal today is to convince you that this court is not comprised of a bunch of partisan hacks," she told the audience.

"Judicial philosophies are not the same as political parties," she continued, pointing to unanimous decisions over the previous year. "The media, along with hot takes on Twitter, report the results and decisions. . . . That makes the decision seem results-oriented. It leaves the reader to judge whether the court was right or wrong, based on whether she liked the results of the decision."

Stirring words at an odd location: the event was a celebration of the thirtieth anniversary of the founding of the McConnell Center at the University of Louisville, named after the one person who did more to forge the Court and its image, the person responsible for Merrick Garland not being on the bench, and Justice Barrett being on it. Donors to the institute and McConnell supporters from Kentucky's Republican aristocracy filled the audience. The senator himself sat serenely smiling as Barrett denounced the notion that the Court had become more partisan.

The next week Clarence Thomas spoke at Notre Dame, the school where Barrett had taught for eighteen years. Students asked him about the autonomy of the Court.

"I think the media makes it sound as though you are just always going right to your personal preference," Thomas said. "So, if they think you are anti-abortion or something personally, they think that's the way you always will come out." He compared Notre Dame football fans disagreeing with "bad calls" made against their team. "If a referee makes a call and it favors Notre Dame and Notre Dame wins, people would say, 'Well, that was a fine referee,'" Thomas said. "But, if the referee makes that very same call and it works against Notre Dame, 'Oh my goodness, this guy can't even see.'" He also laid blame at the confirmation process, and described his own path to the Court as "craziness." "It was absolutely about abortion, a matter I had not thought deeply about."

Samuel Alito made the surliest speech. He took on not only public critics but arguments made by other justices as well. He, too, spoke in South Bend to Notre Dame students, just days before the new term. "The catchy and sinister term 'shadow docket' has been used to portray the Court as having been captured by a dangerous cabal that resorts to sneaky and improper methods to get its ways. This portrayal feeds unprecedented efforts to intimidate the court and to damage it as an independent institution," he charged.

A better term, he said, would be "emergency docket." He rejected the "false and inflammatory claim that we nullified *Roe v. Wade*" in the

Texas case, the very assertion made by the dissenting justices including John Roberts. "We did no such thing, and we said that expressly in our order." Major rulings without arguments or briefing? "You can't expect the E.M.T.s and the emergency rooms to do the same thing that a team of physicians and nurses will do when they are handling a matter when time is not of the essence in the same way," he said.

The justices, one after another, spent September doth protesting too much. The whole public relations offensive had a tinny ring. It was all somewhat halfhearted, seemingly designed more to gird for what was coming than a serious effort to articulate a theory of judicial independence. As the supermajority prepared for rulings, its legitimacy depended more than usual on public acquiescence. The term was off to a contentious start.

CHAPTER NINE

ARGUMENTS

T HE SUPREME COURT PARTLY REOPENED ON October 4, 2021.
Since March of the previous year, it had heard arguments by conference call because of the pandemic. Chambers were often empty,
with the justices working at home or at vacation retreats. No lines of
tourists snaked into the building. The Court had been deprived of its
atmosphere of slightly kitschy formality. Now once again the courtroom hushed, the sergeant at arms called "Oyez, oyez," the justices
stepped out from behind the curtains.

The justices were back in their grand courtroom. But citizens still
were absent. The justices asked their questions and made their speeches
in front of an audience of reporters and clerks. Arguments were livestreamed as they happened, an innovation that began the previous year.

It was clear early that this term would be different from before.
By tradition the justices do not usually talk beforehand about their
views on a case. Questions from the bench often aimed to persuade
the other members of the court. At times the lawyers could find themselves numbed into silence, an afterthought, as the justices interrupted
each other, bantered, and bickered. When the court was more closely
divided, prone to five-to-four rulings on big cases, lawyers would invariably direct their arguments at one, maybe two of the jurists. The swing
justice, whoever she or he was, would be scrutinized for facial twitches,
slight head shakes, or other clues.

Those days were gone, it appeared. With a supermajority of six,
there was little point in directing arguments at one wavering Hamlet
or another. The questions took on a more aggressive tone. The Court's

factions began to rumble from the bench. The conservatives practically strutted. National Public Radio's Nina Totenberg had covered the Court for decades. She reported:

> At oral argument, Justice Elena Kagan, one of the court's best questioners, sometimes takes a different approach. She just shuts down, rather than alienate her colleagues. Still, her anger is often palpable, the color literally draining from her face. And Justice Stephen Breyer on occasion just holds his head.

Visibly, the Court was slipping away from John Roberts. When a nine-person bench is divided five to four, someone becomes the swing vote and gains inordinate power. Justice Abe Fortas once explained the difference between a five-to-four court and a six-to-three court on a taped phone call with Lyndon Johnson. "It will alter the balance of power."

Even though someone else's name may provide the shorthand for the Court, the law often bears the stamp of the person in the middle. William Brennan was revered as the "playmaker" of the Warren Court, the strategist for many of its most far-reaching opinions; he was also the fifth vote. Four justices voted to his right, and four to his left. Then that role was played by Lewis Powell, a Virginian who would now be considered a moderate. Then Sandra Day O'Connor, on cases such as *Casey*, at a time when feminist attorneys described writing their briefs "for an audience of one." Then Anthony Kennedy, whose apostasy guaranteed victory for LGBTQ equality and other rights-based arguments. Then, at last, John Roberts. Now, improbably, that "swing vote," if there is one, would be Brett Kavanaugh. The path from Brennan to Kavanaugh is one way to trace the Court's ideological march to the right over half a century.

Roberts still probed for common ground, still cast about for ways to soften the impact of harsh conservative rulings. But now he seemed to find no takers. The dynamic was on full display in the most anticipated argument of the year, in *Dobbs v. Jackson Women's Health* on the first morning in December.

Throughout the 1980s the backlash to *Roe v. Wade* drove the legal conservative movement and had become the fulcrum for both sides in

confirmation fights. By 1992, it seemed highly likely *Roe* would be reversed or dramatically cut back. A Democratic governor signed a state
law curbing abortion, and it came before the Court. There seemed to
be the votes to overturn abortion rights. *Roe* was less than twenty years
old. It stood on shaky ground.

But millions had come to rely on the right to reproductive choice.
When *Planned Parenthood of Southeastern Pennsylvania v. Casey* was announced in June 1992, in a fractured three-way decision, three Republican justices wrote the controlling opinion. Four others voted to
overturn *Roe*. But Sandra Day O'Connor—the last practicing politician to serve as a justice, having been majority leader in the Arizona
legislature—joined with David Souter and Anthony Kennedy to write
an opinion that dictated the result, when their votes were combined
with the two who simply would uphold *Roe*. The decision reaffirmed
Roe's "essential holding" that the Fourteenth Amendment protected
the individual right to end a pregnancy. At the same time, *Casey* made
it easier for states to impose restrictions. Its new standard would invalidate laws that posed an "undue burden" on the right, rather than
applying the "strict scrutiny" that *Roe* had used. Instead of setting the
rules based on three-month trimesters, as *Roe* had done, it limited the
right to a time before the fetus is viable.

Above all *Casey* was a political decision, a wisely political decision.
"An entire generation," the authors noted, had "come of age free to
assume *Roe*'s concept of liberty in defining the capacity of women to act
in society and to make reproductive decisions." The *Casey* compromise
steered abortion policy toward where the vast majority of the public
was: supportive of abortion rights, with some limitations.

Antonin Scalia was the widely lionized theorist for the Court's conservatives. He had expected O'Connor to join the solidifying conservative bloc. But his fulminating mockery had pushed her away. Three
years earlier, when she ruled that it was not time to reconsider *Roe*,
he had sneered her opinion was "irrational" and "cannot be taken seriously." Scalia was reduced to complaining, "The Imperial Judiciary
lives." He compared *Casey* to *Dred Scott* and *Lochner*, examples where justices used substantive due process to impose their own political views.

Casey established the pattern, the interplay between the courts and
the way tens of millions of Americans navigated their health care and

their own choices over the next three decades. With *Roe* it showed the strengths and also the distortions that could come from a judicially enforced regime. By framing the issue as an individualized constitutional right, resting on the right to privacy, *Roe* forced the subject into a binary debate about rights. You were for them or against; you had them or you didn't. The stark and specific choices that come from litigation affected the political fight as well. We shape our rights, and then our rights shape us. *Casey*, in turn, applied an approach that seemed to mirror the public consensus of support for abortion rights but recognition of the government's ability to impose some limits. But the "undue burden" test, precisely because it was so malleable, sentenced women's health advocates to three decades of attrition warfare, as antiabortion politicians pressed for ever more creative, ever more intrusive ways to restrict women's health choices. They would push, the women would push back, and ultimately courts would decide, often reaching inconsistent conclusions. The political energy still came from the electoral force of the anti-*Roe* backlash, which had become a central Republican tenet.

But after *Roe* and after *Casey*, in the lives of Americans (as opposed to the halls of legislatures or pages of law reviews), abortion rights had settled into a status quo. Five months after *Casey*, Bill Clinton was elected president. As with so many things, Clinton sought to sell progressive policies to a conservative electorate. Abortion, he declared repeatedly, should be "safe, legal, and rare." The previous Democratic nominees since *Roe*, Jimmy Carter, Walter Mondale, and Michael Dukakis, had backed abortion rights but felt it necessary to declare their personal distaste. Clinton had called himself antiabortion before, but now saw himself as the first pro-choice president. His framing, like that of *Casey*, made it possible to assemble a political majority of those who supported abortion and those who were queasy but could be persuaded to oppose antiabortion laws. Between 1969 and 1973 the number of legal abortions had grown to 800,000 per year, as states liberalized their laws. Numbers rose further after *Roe*, topping 1.6 million in 1981. But starting in the 1990s, the abortion rate started to fall steeply. In 2019, for example, there were 630,000 reported abortions in the country. The reason, above all, was the availability of new and better contraception. Conservative politicians continued to agitate, to raise funds, to declare loyalty to the cause. But somehow, they always fell just one vote short of victory, of the big moment where the ruling they hated could be vanquished. It was quite a coincidence, and suggested that the most sophisticated activists were not exactly eager to get that fifth vote.

Then somewhat unexpectedly, the foundations of abortion rights had started to crumble. Republicans swept state legislative elections in 2010, amid public disquiet over the Great Recession and opposition to President Obama's health care plan. Victory gave Republicans the chance to gerrymander and lock in gains for the rest of the decade. Immediately legislatures began to pass a slew of conservative laws— on voting rights, on gun regulation, and on abortion. More abortion restrictions were passed in 2011–13 than in the previous ten years, according to one analysis. In Missouri, state curbs led to all the clinics but one shutting down by the end of 2021, with only 167 abortions performed in the entire state; many women had to travel to neighboring Kansas. Five other states now also had only one clinic. These restrictions, in turn, were increasingly blessed by conservative federal appeals courts, especially the one covering Texas, Louisiana, and Mississippi. Twenty-four states, nearly a majority, filed a brief urging the Supreme Court to act in *Dobbs* and overturn *Roe v. Wade*.

There was no real reason for the justices to take the *Dobbs* case— nothing had happened in the country or in medical science. No meaningful "circuit split" divided appeals courts, the kind of thing that can prompt the Supreme Court to step in and set a nationwide rule. All that had changed was who sat on the Court. That seemed likely to be enough.

The Latin phrase *stare decisis* is the heart of legal reasoning: you base your arguments in precedent, rulings in previous cases. As Roberts wrote, treating like cases alike. Long-standing norms govern when the Supreme Court will overrule itself. Justices ask how long a ruling has been on the books. They ask if people have come to rely on the existing rule. They ask whether circumstances have changed, or if there is new and deeper factual understanding—an analysis that was the basis for the Warren Court's willingness to overrule *Plessy*. They ask if the existing rule is unworkable. Few of these factors seemed present.

The justices sitting in 2021 all had undergone confirmation hearings where a principal topic invariably was *Roe v. Wade*—no longer euphemistically called "the right to privacy." Donald Trump at a debate had said the overturning of *Roe* would "happen automatically" if he became president, just as Hillary Clinton said the opposite, so the hearings for Trump's three picks focused even more than before on the topic. Each implied that their minds were open on *Roe*, and indeed that they regarded it with the appropriate reverence due to precedents.

As a young law professor Elena Kagan had called confirmation hearings a stylized, ritualized "farce." At their hearings, she wrote, Ginsburg and Breyer "stonewalled the Judiciary Committee to great effect, as senators greeted their 'nonanswer' answers with equanimity and resigned good humor." Now "nonanswers" drew sighs and eye-rolling outrage from lawmakers—but the nominees still found ways to squirm out of responding to tough questions.

At his hearings in 2017, Gorsuch testified of *Roe*: it is "a precedent of the U.S. Supreme Court. It was reaffirmed in *Casey* in 1992 and in several other cases." He praised precedents and lauded the idea of respecting them. "So a good judge will consider it as precedent of the U.S. Supreme Court worthy as treatment of precedent like any other." A deft evasion, and a casual listener would think Gorsuch was pledging not to overturn that precedent. But he was not. "For a judge to start tipping his or her hand about whether they like or dislike this or that precedent would send the wrong signal. It would send the signal to the American people that the judge's personal views have something to do with the judge's job."

Kavanaugh's hearing one year later was more intense. He would replace Kennedy, one of the authors of *Casey*. Kavanaugh, too, called *Roe* an "important precedent of the Supreme Court that has been reaffirmed many times." He made sure to include quiet caveats. He would be willing at times to overturn "settled law," and noted that the Court had turned away from *Lochner* and other despised old cases. *Roe*, Kavanaugh said, is "settled as a precedent of the Supreme Court, entitled the respect under principles of stare decisis."

"It is not as if *[Roe]* is just a run-of-the-mill case that was decided and never reconsidered, but *Casey* specifically reconsidered it, applied the stare decisis factors, and decided to reaffirm it," Kavanaugh said. He called *Casey* "precedent on precedent."

At this point let us pull out the tool favored by Supreme Court originalists—a dictionary. According to the Merriam-Webster dictionary,

the first definition of "settle" is "to place so as to stay." The fifth definition is: "to fix or resolve conclusively," and the example used is "settle the
question." On dictionary.com, the first definition of "settled" is "fixed or
established; unlikely to change."

The senators also asked Gorsuch and Kavanaugh about whether
Roe was a "super precedent." Republican senator Arlen Specter had
first used this phrase in 2005, asking John Roberts whether he would
uphold *Roe*. (Specter also called some cases "super duper precedent.")
His question was influenced by conservative judge J. Michael Luttig,
who had written in 2000 that *Roe* was "super-stare decisis" because it
had been upheld so many times. Was *Roe v. Wade* a super precedent?
Gorsuch refused to bite. The ruling "has been reaffirmed many times,
I can say that."

The pretense dropped a bit at Amy Coney Barrett's hearing. She
had been a part of Notre Dame University's "Faculty for Life" group,
and had signed a full-page newspaper ad declaring she "oppose[d]
abortion on demand and support[ed] the right to life from fertiliza-
tion to natural death." The ad ran as an insert in a local newspaper
alongside a declaration that called *Roe* "barbaric." It would have been
hard for her to entirely deny having views on the subject. She confined
herself to committing to obeying "all the rules of stare decisis" such as
"reliance, workability, being undermined by later facts in law, just all
the standard factors."

On close reading, these highly skilled lawyers gave highly lawyerly
answers. They never quite got around to pledging to follow the precedent, merely acknowledging its existence. (*"Do you plan to burn down
that house?" "Yes, that is a house." "Do you plan to preserve the house?" "It is
most certainly a house, and has been for a long time."*) All, true, especially
when one only reads the words on the page. But a listener to the hearings would draw a different conclusion. The noise emitting from the
committee room was all about precedent, respect for stare decisis, and
more. One would be hard-pressed to discern an immediate intent to
knock down *Roe v. Wade*.

There was one exception, one justice who almost certainly lied
to the Judiciary Committee on the topic, albeit years ago. Clarence
Thomas testified under oath that he had never discussed *Roe v. Wade*
with anyone ever, and never had expressed a view on it. He made that
claim even though he was a second-year student at Yale Law School

when *Roe* was decided in January 1973. One prominent government coworker later confirmed that of course he had discussed it. (Also, at his hearing, he testified he believed the Fourteenth Amendment does protect a right to privacy, a view he would quickly repudiate on the bench.)

Crowds of demonstrators on all sides materialized in front of the Court building the morning of the argument. Some held signs reading ABORTION IS HEALTH CARE, others reading JESUS SAVES FROM HELL. Health care workers in white doctor's coats bowed heads in prayer. Cable networks broadcast the audio live. This was the case that directly confronted the question of how hard, how fast the new supermajority would push.

When state lawyers first appealed, they did not ask for a reversal of *Roe v. Wade*, even though that was plainly the whole idea of the statute. Then Barrett replaced Ginsburg. Mississippi now went all the way, not bothering to explain how to uphold the law under existing principles, demanding instead that the precedent be overturned. (To make sure nobody missed the point, Mississippi passed another law banning abortion after *six* weeks.)

Six votes changed the atmosphere in the Supreme Court chamber. The argument was intense, historic—and triumphalist. Mississippi's lawyer conceded nothing to questioning. He made little effort to ease concerns of nervous justices, because there weren't many. He did not woo Roberts. When lawyers appear before the Court, they usually bend themselves into unnatural shapes to argue that their position follows precedent, whatever the reality. Mississippi's lawyer was state Solicitor General Scott Stewart, a former clerk for Clarence Thomas. He spoke with chipper assurance, a bounce in his step.

Alito, Barrett, Gorsuch, and Kavanaugh minced no words. They were hostile to *Roe*. Alito told the attorney for the Center for Reproductive Rights, Julie Rikelman, that "the fetus has an interest in having a life." Barrett made clear that only respect for precedent might prevent a swift action. Earlier abortion cases "explicitly took into account public reaction. Is that a factor that you accept," she asked Mississippi's lawyer. In those cases, he confirmed, the Court had eyed public opinion and judicial legitimacy, but "I think it was a mistake." He urged the

Court to say: "It was wrong the day it was decided. We know it's wrong today. And it's led to all these terrible consequences. We should get rid of it."

Roberts seemed intent on finding a middle path. The Court had created the standard of fetal viability in *Casey*; couldn't it discard that standard, uphold Mississippi's law prohibiting abortions after fifteen weeks, but still allow some federal protection for abortion rights? Roberts quoted the late Justice Blackmun's papers calling the "viability line" dicta, meaning an aside in an opinion that lacks the force of law. Kavanaugh, as well, seemed intrigued by the question. Typically Mississippi's lawyer would tell a wavering justice he could rule for the client without going all the way. Not this time.

Barrett was still new to the Court, holding back as the more experienced judges fired away. When discussing the Texas abortion ban, she had seemed leery, with Roberts and Kavanaugh, of the impact on the Court's legitimacy should it suddenly undo abortion rights. In the *Dobbs* argument she implied that women can avoid the need for an abortion by simply carrying the child, giving birth, and giving the baby away. "In all fifty states, you can terminate parental rights by relinquishing a child," she challenged the reproductive rights lawyer. Unwanted parenting can impose a huge burden on women, but "why don't the safe haven laws take care of that problem?" Rikelman noted that states allowed adoption in 1973, and ever since. The notion that carrying a pregnancy to term and giving birth, and then the wrenching act of giving away the child, somehow avoided the pain and complexity of the issue seemed implausible. Barrett herself was the mother of seven children, two of whom were adopted and one of whom has Down syndrome. Roberts and Thomas had adopted children as well—a striking ratio in a country where around 2 percent of families adopt children.

There was one heart-stopping moment. Eleven minutes into the nearly two-hour argument, Sonia Sotomayor spoke: slowly, working hard to control her emotions. "[T]he right of a woman to choose, the right to control her own body, has been clearly set since *Casey* and never challenged. You want us to reject that line of viability and adopt something different." Fifteen justices over the past thirty years, she continued, "have reaffirmed that basic viability line. Four have said no, two of them members of this Court." The sponsors of the law before the Court "said we're doing it because we have new justices."

Sotomayor paused. "Will this institution survive the stench that this creates in the public perception that the Constitution and its reading are just political acts? I just don't see how it is possible."

The Court in *Casey*, she noted, had talked about watershed decisions, rulings such as *Roe* or *Brown v. Board of Education*, that create "entrenched expectations in our society—that this is what the Court has decided, this is what we will follow." She pointed to the Court's great libel decision in *New York Times v. Sullivan*, which set the rules for political speech, or even *D.C. v. Heller*, which recognized an individual right to gun ownership.

"If people actually believe that it's all political, how will we survive? How will the Court survive?"

Amy Coney Barrett embodied the religious intensity behind much of the work of the supermajority. She had not earned prominence as a regulatory scholar, as Scalia had, or as a confidant of presidents. She was the only member of the Court never to have worked as a prosecutor or for the federal government. When Barrett was nominated for the Court of Appeals, California senator Dianne Feinstein, who many colleagues found increasingly erratic each year she stayed in office, told her she feared "the dogma lives loudly within you." Feinstein rightly was condemned for what seemed an expression of religious bigotry. But Barrett's faith is central to her work. As one law professor enthused, "Amy Coney Barrett's confirmation would be a major victory for the Christian legal movement."

Indeed, the conservative legal movement now has grown so powerful that cracks within its coalition have become visible. After Gorsuch wrote a pro-LGBTQ-rights ruling in 2020 relying on textual analysis, Senator Josh Hawley angrily announced on the Senate floor that it signaled the end of "the conservative legal project as we know it." Now, he said, was the moment for "religious conservatives to take the lead." A Harvard professor, Adrian Vermeule, argued for a "common good constitutionalism" to supplant originalism with a "more moral framework," drawing attacks from liberals and conservatives that his views are incipiently authoritarian, an expression of illiberal democracy in the legal realm.

All of which makes Barrett's swift rise both significant and slightly mystifying. She was born in Louisiana and spent most of her life in South Bend, Indiana. She grew up in an intense faith community, the People of Praise. It is not the "Handmaid's Tale" cult some feared when Barrett was first nominated for the bench. But it is an immersive, close-knit faith community of mostly Catholics, advocating traditional gender roles, and embracing untraditional practices such as speaking in tongues. Its 1,800 adult members call it Charismatic Catholicism, and it borrows from Bible Belt Pentecostalism. Margaret Talbot in *The New Yorker* pointed out that it reflects the alliance between conservative Protestants and Catholics, long deeply hostile camps, that began to form with the antiabortion movement in the 1970s. (This alliance has led fundamentalists to strongly support a Supreme Court mostly comprised of people they once would have decried as "papists.")

Barrett by all accounts is intelligent, an excellent teacher, and an esteemed colleague. Her law review articles were typical Federalist Society panegyrics to originalism. In her brief time on the appeals court, she was busy. She wrote a dissent that would have struck down Wisconsin's law that prohibited all people with felony convictions from owning guns, since there was no "history and tradition" of such laws in the founding era. Yet outside of South Bend, few knew of her. What merited her elevation to the Supreme Court of the United States?

Barrett trod carefully her first year on the high court bench. She wrote little, and her questions were less cantankerously rhetorical than those of some colleagues. She was predictably conservative on most things. She had not yet cut her own path.

Meanwhile, as Carrie Severino of the Judicial Crisis Network put it, "She seems like she was tailor made for this moment."

By year's end the most significant arguments were over. The justices heard cases on the Second Amendment, climate change regulation, and religious rights, as well as abortion. The long season of writing opinions commenced, interspersed with occasional public sessions. It was the second gloomy winter of Covid, months when the Omicron variant swept through the Northeast. Offices and courthouses that had reopened scrambled, with some shutting down again as the year before, and others adopting protocols such as requiring masks. By the beginning of the year, nerves were frayed everywhere, with governors who had mobilized at the beginning of the pandemic now showily defying public health guidance. Anthony Fauci, the physician who had led the nation's response to AIDS in the 1980s and Ebola in the new century, and now Covid, became a maligned target, the bearer of bad news. Florida governor Ron DeSantis sold "Don't Fauci My Florida" merchandise even as the state neared the highest case load in the country. Tens of millions of Americans continued to refuse the vaccines that had been developed in near-miraculous time. They died at twelve times the rate of those who were fully vaccinated. The pandemic appeared to fracture not just society but reality.

The polarization seemed to have reached the courtroom on First Street. One day in January, at the first return to in-person arguments after Omicron, only eight justices arrived. All but Neil Gorsuch wore masks. Sonia Sotomayor was absent. Nina Totenberg, who for decades nursed uncanny access to the Court, reported that the sixty-seven-year-old Sotomayor, who suffers from diabetes and had worn a mask in previous sessions, did not feel safe sitting near people who were unmasked. According to Totenberg, Roberts had "in some form" asked the other justices to mask up. Gorsuch, who sits next to Sotomayor, had refused, she reported. The next day Gorsuch and Sotomayor issued a statement insisting she had not asked him to wear a mask. Roberts announced "he did not request" that the justices mask up. (The previous story had said only that he conveyed that request "in some form.") Totenberg did not back down. "NPR stands by its reporting," the radio network replied.

CHAPTER TEN

KBJ MEETS Q

O N JANUARY 27, 2022, A LETTER from eighty-three-year-old Stephen Breyer arrived at the White House. "I am writing to tell you I
have decided to retire from regular active judicial service as an Associate Justice of the Supreme Court of the United States." The resignation
would take effect after the term ended—so long as his successor had
been confirmed.

White House officials welcomed Breyer's letter. Indeed, it came
after a not-so-quiet outside campaign to persuade the justice to quit.
Liberals were chastened after Barrett replaced Ginsburg. Demand Justice, a group led by Brian Fallon, a former aide to Senate Majority
Leader Chuck Schumer, aimed to wage hardball political fights just
as the Judicial Crisis Network had for conservatives. On the morning
in January 2021 that Democrats won control of the Senate, the group
called on Breyer to retire. The group became unsubtly visible. It paid
for a truck to drive around the Court building flashing an electronic
sign: "BREYER, RETIRE—It's time for a Black woman Supreme Court justice. There's no time to waste." A ghostly black-and-white photo of the
justice, looking half retired already, accompanied the blaring words.

Breyer responded to the pressure campaign by insisting ever-
more-doggedly he would do no such thing. In speeches, articles, and a
book, he claimed that the Supreme Court was an apolitical institution.
The less plausible that assertion seemed, the more effusively he insisted
it was so. The month the Court allowed Texas to ban abortion without a
hearing, Breyer published a book, *The Authority of the Court and the Peril
of Politics*. "Political groups may favor a particular appointment," he

wrote, "but once appointed a judge naturally decides a case in the way that he or she believes the law demands. It is a judge's sworn duty to be impartial, and all of us take that oath seriously." Did he actually believe that? Or was it, as his former faculty colleague Laurence Tribe suggests, a Noble Lie? In any case, Breyer did admit he was aware of the pressure from progressive activists. "I don't live on Pluto," he remarked.

Breyer had been a Harvard Law professor and a staff member on the Senate Judiciary Committee, where he worked with Joe Biden, among others. A technocrat and a gentle liberal, he had engineered the deregulation of the airline industry on behalf of Ted Kennedy, an approach that led to lower prices and soaring travel, as well as frequent bankruptcies and labor tension. Bill Clinton had passed him over for the first open Court seat in part because he was put off by Breyer's cool demeanor.

Now Breyer's pragmatism showed in his decision to retire. Months before, he had let the White House staff know he would likely go. Still, his delay gambled with fate. Over the course of 2022, one Democratic senator would have a stroke, and another broke his hip. The death or incapacitation of one elderly lawmaker would shift control of the chamber to Republicans.

At last Breyer stood with Biden at the White House, thanking his family and brandishing a pocket Constitution. With evident relief the President praised the jurist and pledged to choose a successor soon. "The person I will nominate will be someone of extraordinary qualifications, character, experience and integrity, and that person will be the first Black woman ever nominated to the United States Supreme Court," Biden said. "I made that commitment during the campaign for president, and I will keep that commitment. It's long overdue in my opinion."

Biden made that pledge days before the South Carolina Democratic primary in 2020. The former vice president had finished fourth in the Iowa caucus (what he called a "gut punch"), fifth in the New Hampshire primary, and far behind Vermont's socialist senator Bernie Sanders in the Nevada caucus. South Carolina's voters were predominantly older African Americans. If they did not back Biden, his third try for the presidency would be over.

The key to that constituency was the support of Representative James Clyburn, the highest-ranking Black member of Congress. All

candidates coveted Clyburn's support, and they trooped to his "fish
fry" to try to win his favor. As Biden's candidacy reeled, he pulled Clyburn aside for a meeting on the USS *Yorktown*, now docked as a tourist
attraction in Charleston Harbor. After chiding the candidate for giving
meandering speeches and vague answers, Clyburn added a demand:
promise to put a Black woman on the Supreme Court. Biden agreed
instantly. Biden was so nervous during the next multi-candidate debate that he forgot to make the promise. Clyburn slipped backstage
during a commercial break to remind him. Biden made the pledge the
next time he was asked a question, even though it was on an unrelated
topic. The next day, Clyburn delivered his endorsement. "I know Joe.
We know Joe. But most importantly, Joe knows us." Biden triumphed
in South Carolina, winning thirty-eight of fifty-four delegates, and
then swept ten of fourteen primaries within days as most of his opponents dropped out and endorsed him. The promise to appoint a
Black woman drew little notice at the time. But the events it triggered
suddenly and dramatically shifted the race.

When a vacancy opened nearly two years later, Biden's campaign
pledge gave critics the vapors, or at least offered the chance to act
upset. Senator Roger Wicker of Mississippi called it "affirmative racial
discrimination." Senator Ted Cruz labeled it "offensive," telling podcast listeners, "Black women are, what, six percent of the U.S. population? He's saying to ninety-four percent of Americans: 'I don't give a
damn about you. You are ineligible.'" A Georgetown lecturer tweeted
that the pledge meant a "lesser black woman" would be chosen and
"will always have an asterisk attached."

The puffed-up outrage was for show. Presidents have always considered representation on the Court. Their opponents have always pre-
tended to be infuriated by such a thought.

For most of the country's history, geographic and religious diversity served as a key factor in nominations. Starting with Grover Cleveland, who appointed a former Confederate as a sign of national unity,
there was a "Southern seat." When Brandeis was nominated in 1916,
partly to appeal to Jewish voters who were then a swing constituency,
Senator Henry Cabot Lodge privately complained, "If it were not that
Brandeis is a Jew, and a German Jew, he would never have been appointed." For decades there was one "Jewish seat" (held sequentially
by Brandeis, Cardozo, Frankfurter, Goldberg, and Fortas). As noted

before, William J. Brennan Jr. was chosen because he was a young Catholic from a swing state. Presidents made sure to pick jurists from states with big electoral vote counts, such as Massachusetts and Pennsylvania. Not everywhere has equal representation: At one point recently a justice hailed from every New York City borough except Staten Island, but none from Texas. Rather amazingly, the last white Christian man appointed by a Democratic president joined the Court in 1962.

More recent presidents made even more explicit pledges. In 1980, candidate Ronald Reagan faced the first emergence of a gender gap with men and women voting differently, as he moved the Republican Party away from its prior support for the Equal Rights Amendment and abortion rights. Reagan held a press conference to rebut a "number of false and misleading accusations"—including the charge "that I am somehow opposed to full and equal opportunities for women in America." With that he pledged to pick a woman for "one of the first Supreme Court vacancies in my administration." Reading a prepared statement, he declared, "It is time for a woman to sit among our highest jurists." At the first opportunity he appointed Sandra Day O'Connor. When Trump announced his first short list of possible nominees during the 2016 campaign, all the people on it were white. When Ginsburg died, though, in the heat of the 2020 campaign, Trump made a different promise. "It will be a woman—a very talented, very brilliant woman. We haven't chosen yet, but we have numerous women on the list."

And all that leaves out the most blatant "quota" of all: 108 of the 115 justices were white men. Only two African American men had served, and no Black women. Most Americans are women, of course, yet they had made up less than 5 percent of the justices, and three of the five women ever to serve were sitting on the Court when Biden made his pledge. With a woman replacing Breyer, four of the nine justices would be women—44 percent of the Court, edging closer to parity (and more representative than Congress).

It matters when a judiciary looks like the country it serves. That is visible in state courts, too, which are little better than federal courts. In twenty states no supreme court justice identifies as a person of color, according to a 2022 analysis by the Brennan Center for Justice. Twenty-eight states have no Black justices; in thirty-nine states, no Latino justices; in forty-three states, no Asian American justices. Research confirms common sense: people bring different experiences to their service on the bench, just as in any other job. In one study, if even one woman sits on an appeals court panel the men are more likely to support sex discrimination claims, for example, though other issues showed no such change. Diversity of race or gender leads to more careful decision making, and fewer leaps to assumptions, according to numerous studies.

All that said, the president reiterated his pledge, then made no announcement. Joe Biden was fully immersed in the politics of judicial confirmations for a half century. Having waited for this moment, he would not be rushed.

Meanwhile, backers of possible nominees jostled. Clyburn and Lindsey Graham pushed for Michelle Childs of South Carolina, a trial judge awaiting confirmation to the appeals bench. Labor unions attacked her for her time as an attorney at a private law firm. Graham in turn accused critics of being backed by financier George Soros, a frequent target of conservatives. Leondra Kruger, a justice on the California Supreme Court, drew scrutiny for an argument she had made when working for the Justice Department on a religious freedom case. Sometimes presidents dangle names in public to see what opposition they draw. Colbert King, a longtime *Washington Post* columnist, made an uncomfortable but savvy point: Biden should have been ready to announce his pick right away. By keeping the media guessing, it trained focus solely on the race and gender of a faceless nominee. (Trump, by contrast, was ready to go with Amy Coney Barrett just eight days after Ginsburg's death.)

Finally on February 25, Biden announced his choice—and it was the longtime front-runner, the one he likely would have chosen all along, indeed someone long eyed for the role: Ketanji Brown Jackson.

Jackson had a dazzling rise through the meritocracy. She was a champion debater at a Miami high school, then studied at Harvard College and Law School. She clerked for three judges including Breyer.

In significant ways, though, she wandered off the path often followed by ambitious lawyers. She did not become a prosecutor (as Sotomayor had) or a partner at a major law firm (as Roberts had). She worked as a staff attorney at the U.S. Sentencing Commission, then became a public defender, and then was confirmed by the Senate to be vice chair of the Sentencing Commission, where she worked with experts to set penalties for a range of crimes. The Senate confirmed her unanimously to be a trial judge, and she served for a decade. She presided over 1,278 cases. Finally in 2021 she was nominated for the federal court of appeals, filling the seat vacated by Merrick Garland when he became Biden's attorney general. Hers was a career of quiet public service.

Jackson had an intimate knowledge of the justice system as it pulled and pushed men, especially Black men. One uncle was the police chief of Miami. Another was sentenced to life in prison on drug charges. Her brother was a police officer. Her college thesis was entitled, "The Hand of Oppression: Plea Bargaining Processes and the Coercion of Criminal Defendants." The Fraternal Order of Police, the national police union, endorsed her nomination.

No public defender ever previously sat on the U.S. Supreme Court. These attorneys, often beleaguered, represent indigent defendants. It can be grueling work. The Sixth Amendment to the Constitution guarantees criminal defendants the right to have "the Assistance of Counsel." It was the Supreme Court itself, in *Gideon v. Wainwright,* that applied that right to states in felony cases. Another case required effective counsel for those charged with misdemeanors as well. A half a century later, over one million Americans are in prison, and millions more churn through the criminal justice system every year. One in three Black men can expect to be jailed at some point. Public defender offices, funded mostly by state governments, are underresourced and overwhelmed. Many are fortunate if they can give clients a few hours of attention, far less than needed to offer effective assistance. Partly as a result, over 90 percent of criminal convictions result from a guilty plea before trial. The Supreme Court routinely hears hundreds of appeals from criminal convictions a year, and rules on matters ranging from the admissibility of evidence to what kind of legal defense is required. Lately it has rarely been sympathetic to defendants. In late 2022, for example, it ruled that defendants could not introduce new evidence in federal court to show they had ineffective counsel in their trial, even when they face execution.

Biden had told senators before he took office that he wanted to break the mold of who would join the federal bench. His incoming White House counsel wrote senators asking for the names of civil rights lawyers and public defenders. Compared with Republican presidents,

Clinton and Obama had chosen diverse nominees—but typically they had been prosecutors, big-firm lawyers working for businesses, or both. Biden had been a public defender himself in Delaware before winning a Senate seat at age twenty-nine. His shift in approach also was greased by the end of the Senate filibuster for confirmation of judicial appointments. Intense partisan polarization meant that there was little point in seeking to win over many opposition senators. Squeaking by on a party-line vote was not a dark mark; it was now the norm. Biden moved quickly to fill the bench with new types of judges. In the Second Circuit, for example, the appeals court including New York, Connecticut, and Vermont, he chose federal public defender Eunice Lee to fill the first available seat and voting rights lawyer Myrna Pérez for the next.

Jackson had not worked in a storefront office. She had clients in the federal system—which typically revolved around more significant crimes and conspiracies. In her case, drawing on her Supreme Court clerkship experience, she was assigned to help defendants file appeals. Among her clients were detainees at the U.S. military base at Guantánamo Bay in Cuba, men held on terrorism charges and in the wake of the war in Afghanistan. (In 2004 the Supreme Court had ruled that detainees could sue to challenge their detention.)

For years, enthusiasts boomed Jackson for the Supreme Court. Obama interviewed her in 2016 before he chose Garland. That one of Breyer's clerks might fill his seat was long hoped to be something that could encourage the wavering justice to retire. Kavanaugh replaced Kennedy, the judge for whom he had clerked; now Jackson would replace Breyer. It was part of a trend toward growing insularity in the Court and among those who worked there and argued before it. Days were long gone when senators and governors jousted for a judgeship. The notion that the Court is a place for technical expertise and formal credentialing seemed ever-more entrenched, despite the breakthrough reflected in Jackson's appointment.

Jackson was so impeccably qualified that her confirmation seemed assured from the minute Biden announced his choice, as she stood by his side beaming a broad smile. The Judicial Crisis Network did not spend significant sums to defeat her. It ran an ad tweaking her for mildly criticizing Clarence Thomas—hardly the incendiary assault nominees had come to expect. The group seemed to step carefully in criticizing the first Black woman nominated for the Court. Another reason for all this unexpected decorousness: why bother? As one of only three liberals on the Court, Jackson would not challenge the domination of the conservative supermajority.

Then came the confirmation hearings in late March, and the Republican senators could not help themselves.

Jackson was a calm presence. Her multiracial family sat behind her. A heart-tugging photograph of her teenage daughter, looking on proudly, circulated widely. The judge spoke about the sacrifices her career had imposed on her family. "It's a lot of early mornings and late nights. And what that means is there will be hearings during your daughters' recitals. There'll be emergencies on birthdays that you have to handle. And I know so many young women in this country, especially who have small kids who have these momentous events, and have to make a choice. I didn't always get the balance right." Her confident affect contrasted with the Republican senators and their increasingly dyspeptic interjections.

Jackson's backers braced for attacks on her record as a criminal defense lawyer. In other nomination hearings, senators sneered at the notion of representing accused defendants. In February the Republicans roasted one nominee from Philadelphia, Arianna Freeman, a federal public defender. Josh Hawley of Missouri demanded with theatrical indignance, "Do you regret trying to prevent this individual who committed these heinous crimes from having justice served upon him?" Ted Cruz told Freeman she had devoted her "entire professional career to representing murderers, to representing rapists, representing child molesters." The committee went on to deadlock on party lines on Freeman's nomination, 11 to 11. The full Senate confirmed her months later.

Such charges were not really a surprise: political campaigns long ago found ways to focus on lurid crimes to stoke the fears of white voters. Violent crime had fallen by nearly three quarters since the early 1990s. Wide perception of safety had created room for a growing reform movement to end mass incarceration, one that had united liberals and conservatives including the Koch brothers. Donald Trump had signed a federal sentencing reform bill and featured former prisoners as guests at his State of the Union Address. But crime had begun to rise again starting in 2020. Antipolice protests and riots in the wake of the murder of George Floyd in Minneapolis had also begun to consume the attention of cable news viewers. Hawley, Cruz, and Arkansan Tom Cotton, Ivy League graduates who decried elites, all opposed criminal justice changes and aimed to revive crime as a discordant issue. Mitch McConnell previewed the charge to the Senate, warning that "the soft-on-crime brigade is squarely in Judge Jackson's corner."

Still, despite all that, Judiciary Committee Republican senators did not focus on her record as a public defender as expected. Instead, they obsessed about her rulings as a trial judge. Oddly they insisted she was soft on a particular kind of crime: child abuse and child pornography.

Like most federal judges, Jackson had imposed sentences that differed from those recommended by federal guidelines. Hawley focused on a three-month prison sentence she had given an eighteen-year-old who possessed pornographic images. "I'm having a hard time wrapping my head around it," Hawley intoned. "We're talking about eight-year-olds, nine-year-olds, eleven-year-olds and twelve-year-olds." Repeatedly Hawley and Cruz returned to the charge that Jackson somehow was soft on child pornography. Andrew McCarthy, a legal analyst for the conservative *National Review*, called the claim "meritless to the point of demagoguery."

Why child pornography of all seemingly random possible topics? Did senators really think she had a soft spot for pedophiles?

The smear showed the rising influence among Republicans of the conspiracy theory known as QAnon, a shifting set of beliefs that can only be described as bonkers. QAnon adherents are convinced they are being fed inside information by a government official known as "Q." They believe the Democratic Party is run by a satanic child sex ring, and that its leaders such as Hillary Clinton eat children. The theory drew on the wild notion that children were imprisoned in the basement of a Washington, D.C., pizza parlor, which led a man carrying an assault weapon to raid the restaurant to "rescue" the nonexistent victims in 2016. From jail the gunman later admitted, "The intel on this wasn't one hundred percent." QAnon draws on classic anti-Semitic imagery and claims. Followers insisted that there would be a violent reckoning, a "storm" led by Donald Trump in combat with "pedophiles," with mass arrests of Democratic leaders, who would be executed or sent to Guantánamo.

It was all lunacy, spreading quickly during the mass psychological crisis brought on by the lockdowns of the Covid pandemic. Soon people holding signs reading "Q" were visible at Trump rallies and co-opted the hashtag #savethechildren from the venerable charity. The incessant questions about Jackson and child pornography seemed designed, if little else, to wink at QAnon believers. Supreme Court confirmation hearings had been forums for ideological debate or examination of nominees' personal conduct. This was the first such hearing where the subtext, at least, was a demented conspiracy theory.

One other line of questioning, seemingly obscure, portended significant constitutional change. Nominees are schooled to avoid polemical debate about constitutional theory, as Robert Bork had done to such ill effect. Repeatedly Republicans interrogated Jackson on her view of "unenumerated rights." "For more than two decades, confirmation hearings for Supreme Court justices have revolved around a single question: whether the nominee would uphold or overrule *Roe v. Wade*," wrote NYU professor Melissa Murray. Now the questioners assumed *Roe* would soon be overturned. They pointed to other rulings likely to face threat. John Cornyn of Texas repeatedly asked about *Obergefell v. Hodges*, the 2015 case that protected same sex marriage. Marsha Blackburn of Tennessee grilled Jackson on *Griswold* and contraception. "All this underscores that abortion was never the conservatives' endgame," Murray warned after watching the hearing. "It is merely a way station on the path to rolling back a wide range of rights—the rights that scaffold the most intimate aspects of our lives and protect the liberty and equality of marginalized groups."

Republican Ben Sasse of Nebraska focused on substantive due process, which he said "allows courts to create new fundamental rights." Jackson repeatedly pointed to *Washington v. Glucksberg*, a case in which the Court found no right to assisted suicide. In that case, she said, "the fundamental rights that are recognized or that are included in substantive due process are those that are deeply rooted in the nation's history and tradition." It was a safe answer, relying as it did on the Court's precedent. But the ferocity of the questions and her tactical retreat suggested the range of targets for the conservatives: the Court's long string of rulings defending rights for gay Americans, contraception, and more.

Over and over Republican senators pressed her on judicial philosophy. Would she adhere to originalism? Did she believe in the dreaded "living constitution"? Like other Democratic nominees, Jackson demurred. "I believe that the Constitution is fixed in its meaning. I believe that it's appropriate to look at the original intent, original public meaning, of the words when one is trying to assess because, again, that's a limitation on my authority to import my own policy." The conservative *National Review* cheered a "thoroughgoing rout for progressive theories of law."

By the hearing's third day, the scowling questions seemed designed purely for retweeting or replay on Fox News that evening. Cruz grilled the nominee about children's books in the library of a school on whose board she sat. Blackburn asked her to define "the word 'woman.'" (Jackson's reply: "I'm not a biologist.") The rants had little effect. But it was unnerving and painful to watch a procession of white men in identical blue suits berating a Black woman, who was compelled by circumstance to sit mostly silently. When Brett Kavanaugh objected to questions at his hearing, he noisily defended himself, red-faced. Jackson had no choice but to take the abuse, lest she reveal herself an "angry Black woman."

As her testimony ended, Jackson's unruffled demeanor barely betrayed her exhaustion. Cory Booker of New Jersey addressed the nominee. "Sit back for a second, 'cause I don't have questions right away." Instead he spoke of "some of the things that've been said in this hearing." "The way you have dealt with some of these things, that's why you are a judge, and I am a politician," he continued, "because you have sat with grit and grace and have shown us just extraordinary demeanor during the times where people were saying things to you that are actually out of the norm." He added:

> I'm telling you right now, I'm not letting anybody in the Senate steal my joy. . . . I want to tell you, when I look at you, this is why I get emotional. I'm sorry, you're a person that is so much more than your race and gender. You're a Christian, you're a mom, you're an intellect, you love books. But for me,

I'm sorry, it's hard for me not to look at you and not see my mom, not to see my cousins, one of them who had to come here and sit behind you. She had to have your back. I see my ancestors and yours. Nobody's going to steal the joy of that woman in the street, or the calls that I'm getting, or the texts. Nobody's going to steal that joy. You have earned this spot. You are worthy. You are a great American.

As Booker spoke Jackson wiped away tears.

By the time the hearings were over Jackson's nomination had become the most popular in years, with the support of 66 percent of the public. The evenly divided committee deadlocked on party lines, but the debate moved to the full Senate. It confirmed her with a 53-to-47 vote in April.

The next day a crowd gathered on the South Lawn of the White House to celebrate. Civil rights leaders and voting activists filled the seats. Jackson spoke after Biden and Vice President Kamala Harris. "It has taken 232 years and 115 prior appointments for a Black woman to be selected to serve on the Supreme Court of the United States," Jackson said. "But we've made it. We've made it. All of us."

She quoted the poet Maya Angelou, "bringing the gifts that my ancestors gave, / I am the dream and the hope of the slave." "So as I take on this new role, I strongly believe that this is a moment in which all Americans can take great pride. We have come a long way toward perfecting our union. In my family, it took just one generation to go from segregation to the Supreme Court of the United States."

CHAPTER ELEVEN

INSURRECTIONISTS

T HE SILENT MONTHS, WHEN JUSTICES RETREATED and wrote their opinions, in 2022 coincided with growing evidence that the country had barely escaped a coup d'état a year before. What had looked like a crazed mob egged on by a flailing defeated president in fact was part of an intricate plot to undo the peaceful transfer of power.

On November 4, 2020, at 2:30 in the morning after he had lost the presidential election to Joe Biden, with votes still being counted in a half dozen states, Donald Trump spoke to a crowd in the East Room of the White House. "Frankly, we did win this election." To puzzled cheers, he said, "This is a major fraud on our nation. We want the law to be used in a proper manner. So we'll be going to the U.S. Supreme Court."

The next day, White House chief of staff Mark Meadows received an incendiary text, urging him to fight on, to get busy overturning the election. It relayed astounding news. "Biden crime family & ballot fraud co-conspirators (elected officials, bureaucrats, social media censorship mongers, fake stream media reporters, etc) are being arrested & detained for ballot fraud right now & over coming days, & will be living in barges off GITMO to face military tribunals for sedition." The text added, "I hope this is true."

The text came from Ginni Thomas, wife of Justice Clarence Thomas. She sent Meadows twenty-nine in all. Like the one insisting that Democrats would be "living in barges off GITMO," many echoed the most delusional conspiracy theories on the dark reaches of the internet—with

QAnon adherents, especially, endlessly fantasizing about sending opponents to the prison camp in Cuba that holds accused terrorists.

Some were imploring, some shared fictional conspiracy theories, and some were fervent. "Help This Great President stand firm, Mark!!!. . .You are the leader, with him, who is standing for America's constitutional governance at the precipice. The majority knows Biden and the Left is attempting the greatest Heist of our History." Another: "Watermarked ballots in over 12 states have been part of a huge Trump & military white hat sting operation in 12 key battleground states." (More QAnon. The convoluted claim was that Trump stole the election *for Biden,* to ferret out the real perpetrators.)

Thomas urged Meadows to make Sidney Powell, the attorney whose increasingly absurd claims caused the campaign to back away from her, its lead attorney. (Later, when a voting machine company sued Powell for defamation, her defense argued that no reasonable person would have believed her charges.) "Make a plan," Ginni Thomas urged the White House. "Release the Kraken and save us from the left taking America down." The Kraken was the lawsuit, supposedly monstrous and inevitably headed to the Supreme Court, that Powell frequently promised to file.

Meadows egged Thomas on. "This is a fight of good versus evil. Evil always looks like the victor until the King of Kings triumphs. Do not grow weary in well doing. The fight continues. I have staked my career on it. Well at least my time in DC on it," he wrote to her. She replied, "Thank you!! Needed that! This plus a conversation with my best friend just now." That, she later confirmed, was her husband. He certainly had been clear about who *his* was. "My wife is my best friend. I can rant with her," he told students at Stetson University in 2010.

On January 6, Ginni Thomas was at the Ellipse for the "Stop the Steal" rally. As the crowd gathered, wearing red hats and carrying Trump flags, many of them armed, Thomas enthusiastically posted on her Facebook page. "LOVE MAGA people!!!! . . . GOD BLESS EACH OF YOU STANDING UP or PRAYING!" She arrived as Rudy Giuliani vowed a "trial by combat." She heard John Eastman, the former Clarence Thomas clerk who had devised the illegal scheme to have Vice President Mike Pence reject Biden electors from several states. Ginni Thomas left the rally before the violence at the Capitol. She later claimed she did so because she was cold.

When the House voted to create a select committee to investigate the attack on the Capitol, Republican leaders boycotted the panel, leaving it free to work with two prominent conservatives—Liz Cheney, recently ousted as GOP caucus chair, and Adam Kinzinger. Ginni Thomas joined other activists to write to party leaders urging them to expel Cheney and Kinzinger for their participation. Trump challenged the committee in federal court, trying to claim "executive privilege" to prevent documents from being shared with investigators. He lost in a unanimous appeals court ruling (with Ketanji Brown Jackson voting against him).

The former president appealed to the Supreme Court. By a vote of eight to one, the justices swatted down Trump's bid, and ruled that his administration's relevant documents should be turned over to the committee. Only Clarence Thomas voted to shield the records. At no point did he publicly disclose that evidence involving his own wife—including her incendiary texts—might be the subject of the lawsuit. Nor did he explain why he did not recuse himself.

Two months later Ginni Thomas's texts to Mark Meadows became public. Meadows had turned over 2,320 text messages to the committee after the Court rebuffed Trump. The explosive news came during the pause between arguments in the term's big cases and decisions, at the worst possible time. As the Court raced toward the end of its term, it became increasingly clear that Clarence Thomas—long the silent justice, the odd man out, with stubborn adherence to his own idiosyncratic vision of originalism—now was the dominant force.

For three decades Thomas was an outlier, the most conservative justice by far. His jurisprudence verged on eccentric. He had no reverence for precedent. If he concluded that an earlier ruling was wrong he did not hesitate to declare it a misreading of the Constitution. Mostly he voted with the Court's conservative wing. Even then he would file separate concurrences setting out his views. Over the years those became a roadmap for conservative legal activists and other judges, eventually pointing where the Court would go.

Thomas's life story is well known, marketed by him first as the "Pin Point strategy" during his stormy nomination, then in his memoir. He was born poor and isolated amid rice paddies and plantations in the

coastal region where Georgia and South Carolina meet. In the 1950s
Pin Point was barely connected to the rest of the South let alone the
rest of the United States. He spoke Geechee at home, a long-suppressed
amalgam of West African languages, slave dialect, and English. "When
I was sixteen, I was sitting as the only black kid in my class, and I had
grown up speaking a kind of a dialect . . . called Geechee. Some people
call it Gullah, and people praise it now. But they used to make fun of
us back then. It's not standard English," Thomas later recalled. One of
the few times he spoke from the bench in 2002, he transfixed the other
justices as he described what cross burning meant to Black people in
the South. "There was no other purpose to the cross. There was no
communication of a particular message. It was intended to cause fear
and to terrorize a population."

At age five he moved to Savannah, where he was raised by his grand-
parents. (He titled his memoir *My Grandfather's Son.*) Barely literate yet
proud and exacting, his grandfather stressed, as Thomas said when
he was put forward to the Court, "God . . . school, discipline, hard
work and 'right from wrong.'" Only when Thomas was sent to Catholic
boarding school did he sit in a classroom with white students. Growing
up under state-enforced segregation "is as close to totalitarianism as I
would like to get," he told a conservative audience.

Talented and driven he attended College of the Holy Cross in
Worcester, Massachusetts, and then Yale Law School. In trying to un-
ravel the mystery of Clarence Thomas, a compelling recent book by
Corey Robin noted that he was, during this time, a Black nationalist. He
memorized the speeches of Malcolm X, not Martin Luther King Jr. His
was the consciousness of Stokely Carmichael, not John Lewis, whom
Carmichael drove out of the Student Nonviolent Coordinating Committee. Thomas was convinced that American society was profoundly
racist, irredeemably so, and that efforts to undo that were fake or for
the benefit of the benevolent majority, not the aspiring minority. He
called affirmative action "racial paternalism."

He came to unexpected national attention at age thirty-two. At a
conference of Black conservatives, he talked openly with a tablemate,
who turned out to be Juan Williams of *The Washington Post.* "I marched.
I protested. I asked the government to help Black people," Thomas
told Williams. "I did all those things. But it hasn't worked. It isn't working. And someone needs to say that." He opined on his sister and her

children still living in Georgia. "She gets mad when the mailman is late with her welfare check," he told Williams. "That is how dependent she is. What's worse is that now her kids feel entitled to the check too. They have no motivation for doing better or getting out of that situation." (She had been on relief after her husband left her as she cared for an ill relative, as journalists were to report, but rejoined the workforce later.)

He had benefited from affirmative action, but that fact stung and shamed him. "A new media fad is to constantly harp on the plight of black college students on predominantly white campuses. Believe it or not, the problems are the same as they were twenty years ago," he wrote in a letter to *The Wall Street Journal* in 1987. He added, "The major difference is that the media paid little attention to them then." What was the solution? "Racial quotas and other race-conscious legal devices only further and deepen the original problem," he wrote. "Today . . . color conscious means something favorable to us. We have set-asides, we have affirmative action," he told a journalist. He added, "I firmly believe that just as we can use it for us it's going to be used against us again." That skepticism alchemized into a rigid conservatism.

But his white mentors and patrons never really noticed the severity of his approach. First he worked for Senator John Danforth of Missouri, an Episcopal priest and heir to the Ralston Purina fortune. Thomas was one of the few Black conservative attorneys available for service in the Reagan administration. He joined the Department of Education and then was named chair of the Equal Employment Opportunity Commission, where he served for eight years.

In 1990 George H. W. Bush named him to the D.C. Circuit Court of Appeals. When Thurgood Marshall retired in 1991 the president brought Thomas to the family compound in Kennebunkport, Maine, and announced his nomination. In their one backstage conversation Bush urged Thomas to rule "as an umpire would." He had chosen someone with ardently held views, a combatant within the Black community in ways invisible at the seaside home at Walker's Point. Reporters asked Bush the obvious question about Marshall's replacement, a touchy subject given Thomas's fierce opposition to racial preferences.

Q. Was race a factor whatsoever, sir, in the selection?
A. I don't see it at all.

Thomas's confirmation hearing went smoothly at first. Democrats had asked few tough questions of David Souter and were reluctant to grill the next nominee. Thomas backed off from some stances. He told senators, "I believe the Constitution protects the right to privacy." The full Senate prepared to vote. Then National Public Radio and *Newsday* reported that an employee of Thomas at the EEOC, thirty-five-year-old Oklahoma law professor Anita Hill, had made allegations of lewd remarks and inappropriate conduct. Seven women House members marched across the Capitol to demand a delay in a final confirmation vote. The white and male and handsy senators were flummoxed. The concept of sexual harassment had barely pierced their world. Judiciary Committee chair Joe Biden struggled to control the situation and flailed. Senator Strom Thurmond, the ninety-year-old father of an out-of-wedlock Black daughter, was so notorious that women were warned not to ride in an elevator with him. In the two decades after the death of Mary Jo Kopechne at Chappaquiddick, Ted Kennedy had long periods of licentious drunkenness. This all-white, all-male committee now would hear from Anita Hill.

Hill's testimony was painful and poised. "It is only after a great deal of agonizing consideration and a number of sleepless nights that I am able to talk of these unpleasant matters to anyone but my close friends," she said, continuing, "Telling the world is the most difficult experience of my life, but it is very close to having to live through the experience that occasioned this meeting." She described Thomas talking about pornography, pressuring her for dates, even as he mentored her. She recalled their last conversation as she left her job. "He made a comment I vividly remember," she testified. "He said that if I ever told anyone of his behavior, that it would ruin his career."

Thomas returned after she spoke. "This is a circus," he told the committee angrily. "It is a national disgrace. And from my standpoint, as a Black American, as far as I am concerned, it is a high-tech lynching for uppity Blacks who in any way deign to think for themselves, to do for themselves, to have different ideas, and it is a message that, unless you kowtow to an old order, this is what will happen to you, you will be lynched, destroyed, caricatured by a committee of the U.S. Senate, rather than hung from a tree."

The hearing had turned into a harrowing experience, a circus indeed, for Anita Hill. Senators questioned her mental state. After she left the room one accused her of perjury. Another claimed she was borrowing a scene from the novel *The Exorcist.* Four other women contacted the committee to back Hill or report similar encounters with Thomas but Biden did not call them. The Senate finally voted to confirm Thomas 52 to 48, the closest vote in decades. The topic of sexual harassment was widely discussed nationally for the first time, leading private companies and organizations to step up trainings and awareness. Voters' disgust about the hearings led to the "Year of the Woman" in the 1992 election, tripling the number of women senators from two to six.

On the day Thomas was confirmed, he told his clerks he planned to serve on the Court until 2034. Why that long? one asked. "The liberals made my life miserable for forty-three years, and I'm going to make their lives miserable for forty-three years." Ginni Thomas was barely more circumspect in public. "Clarence will give everyone a fair day in court," she told *People* magazine. "But I feel he doesn't owe any of the groups who opposed him anything."

The drama and anguish of his confirmation obscured the significance of Thomas's role on the Court. He refused to talk from the bench, sitting silently for years as the other justices probed, jabbered, and bantered. Privately, those at the Court confirmed, he was loquacious and warm, beloved by courthouse personnel. Publicly he glowered. He also, opinion by opinion, carved his own path. If a prior case was wrongly decided, if it did not follow the original meaning of the constitutional provision as he saw it, he would vote to ignore it or overturn it.

Antonin Scalia was the Court's most prominent originalist. But he took seriously precedent, the structure of government, and the impact of rulings. When asked the difference between his jurisprudence and that of Clarence Thomas, Scalia had a succinct answer: "I am an originalist, but I am not a nut."

Some of Thomas's seeming extremism was rooted in indignant social analysis. For example, he was appalled by the post–Civil War Court's evisceration of the Fourteenth Amendment. The amendment's simplest and potentially most powerful provision was the "privileges and immunities" clause, which overturned the holding of *Dred Scott* that Black people could not be citizens. "Privileges and immunities" of citizenship, available to all, were specific and could be identified. But the justices ignored "privileges and immunities." Instead, they ruled based on "substantive due process." Instead of shrugging and accepting that the fuzzier standards were the basis of a century of law, Thomas rejected the whole enterprise.

Repeatedly he excavated what he saw as the racist roots of otherwise cherished laws or doctrines, even when he had to stretch to do so. *Citizens United* overturned the 1907 statute enacted after campaign finance scandals when insurance companies had contributed cash to Theodore Roosevelt's reelection campaign. Thomas had a different memory. "Go back and read why [Senator "Pitchfork Ben"] Tillman introduced that legislation," Thomas told a Florida audience. "Tillman was from South Carolina, and as I hear the story he was concerned that the corporations, Republican corporations, were favorable toward blacks and he felt that there was a need to regulate them." But from this insight he decided that all efforts to protect unenumerated rights, those implied in the Constitution, were illegitimate.

At first Thomas often stood alone in his views. He did so in a concurrence in 1997, when the Court blocked part of a new federal gun law named after James Brady, Reagan's press secretary who was wounded in an attempted assassination of the president. The Court had last addressed the Second Amendment in 1939, and it repeatedly held that its provisions protected the "well regulated militia," not individual gun ownership. "Perhaps, at some future date, this Court will have the opportunity to determine whether Justice Story was correct when he wrote that the right to bear arms 'has justly been considered, as the palladium of the liberties of a republic,'" Thomas wrote. Nine years later, his solo and seemingly cranky view had become the Court's opinion. Two years later the Court applied its new reading of the Second Amendment to the states, striking down Chicago's strict handgun law. Thomas wrote for himself, again. He excavated the history showing that a purpose of the Fourteenth Amendment was to ensure that formerly enslaved, newly freed Black men could carry guns to protect themselves against the Ku Klux Klan. "Without federal enforcement of the inalienable right to keep and bear arms, these militias and mobs were tragically successful in waging a campaign of terror against the very people the Fourteenth Amendment had just made citizens."

By the time of the supermajority, Thomas was the longest serving justice. His legal views had gone from being the far-right fringe to an invisible gravitational force pulling the Court his way. Colleagues and observers tried to square the Thomas they once knew, an energetic but mainstream conservative, with the sullen silence and judicial radicalism of his time on the Court. The God-fearing, protect yourself, pick-up-a-gun ethos of the terrorized rural South now was a vision for the country. Abner Mikva, chief judge on the federal appeals court where Thomas had sat, speculated that the confirmation hearings changed him. "Such an embittering experience . . . may have shaped how he has been as a judge. He was nowhere near that far out when he was on our court. He was much more moderate," Mikva said.

When a chief justice is in the majority, he assigns the writing of the opinion. When Roberts did not vote with the winning side, Thomas was the senior justice, and he chose the author. Increasingly, it was Thomas's court. This was his moment. All of which made the controversies swirling ever more visibly around his wife a problem not just for him but for the institution.

Virginia Thomas's seeming embrace of delusional QAnon conspiracy theories was especially surprising because she herself had been an anti-cult activist.

She came to that activism based on personal experience. When she arrived in Washington, D.C., as an ambitious young business lobbyist in the 1980s, she joined a program called Lifespring, which she came to call a "cult." She realized she needed to be "deprogrammed." Thomas became active in the Cult Awareness Network, alumni of different sects who campaigned to alert the public about the brainwashing they had experienced. "When you come away from a cult, you've got to find a balance in your life as far as getting involved with fighting the cult or exposing it," she said in 1986. Repeatedly she asked herself "what was it that made you get into that group." When her texts parroting QAnon became public, some of her fellow activists from that era noted that once again she seemed to have joined a cult.

She was a generic party supporter, but not a prominent militant, until she attended a raucous rally at the Capitol in 2009. It was organized by FreedomWorks, a well-funded flagship conservative organization led by former congressman Dick Armey, that had taken to posing as the hard edge of the Tea Party movement. This angry mobilization of conservatives began amid the economic vertigo following the 2008 stock market collapse, the first months of the Great Recession, and not incidentally, the first months of the administration of the first Black president. That summer Tea Party protesters disrupted Democratic members of Congress as they tried to hold town hall meetings. They directed their ire at the Affordable Care Act, Obama's sweeping effort to reform the bloated health care system and extend coverage to all uninsured Americans. It was the long-sought-for goal of Democratic presidents since 1949. Bill Clinton's health plan had failed in Congress, and the rancor was so great it helped cost his party the Congress.

Ginni Thomas drew energy from her time on the Tea Party barricades. "They say a storm is coming," she told a protest at the U.S. Capitol in 2010. "They ain't seen nothing yet!" She became an omnipresent opponent of Obama and his administration. "America is in a vicious battle for its founding principles," as she put it, Already she was the most politically visible spouse in Supreme Court history. There was no precedent for her fervent, partisan political organizing against legislation that would assuredly land on the Court's docket.

In October 2011, her activism earned a front-page scolding in *The New York Times*: "Activism of Thomas's Wife Could Raise Judicial Issues." The story pointed out that a new organization she led was funded by undisclosed large contributions, the kind of money now flowing into the political system in the wake of the *Citizens United* decision for which her husband had provided the deciding vote. At 7:30 the next morning, she called Anita Hill and left a voice message. "Anita Hill, this is Ginni Thomas, and I just wanted to reach across the airwaves and the years and ask you to consider something. I would love you to consider an apology sometime and some full explanation of why you did what you did with my husband." She urged Hill to "pray about this." She ended on a cheery note: "O.K., have a good day!" (She subsequently put out a statement saying she was extending an "olive branch.")

As the decade went on, and Clarence Thomas's influence in the Court grew, his wife's political entanglements became a bigger problem. No longer was she a protester on the barricades; now she was a regular visitor at the White House, meeting with the president, and working to build support for Trump administration initiatives that were later adjudicated by the Supreme Court. Trump's campaign strategist called her "one of the most powerful forces in the MAGA movement—a force of nature." Others, anonymously, told *Politico* she was just a "harmless busybody" of the type that hover around all administrations. At one meeting with Trump, she urged him to purge aides who were part of the "deep state" as other attendees prayed for an end to same-sex marriage.

Now, in the spring of 2022, the House of Representatives committee investigating the January 6 insurrection was preparing its public hearings. The Justice Department issued subpoenas to an ever-widening group of officials and operatives. News stories began to report that Ginni Thomas had gone beyond enthusiasm—she was, it appeared, part of the effort to stop the peaceful transfer of power and overthrow the election.

The investigations focused on Trump and Eastman's scheme to enlist "fake electors" as an alternative to the ones chosen by voters. In May the *Washington Post* reported Thomas had pressured twenty-nine Arizona legislators to use their "plenary powers" to set aside the voters' choice of Biden and Harris and proclaim instead a "clean slate of Electors." The Arizona plot was one of the most advanced and, in the words of one participant, "wild." One organizer explained it in a rather candid email. "We would just be sending in 'fake' electoral votes to Pence so that 'someone' in Congress can make an objection when they start counting votes, and start arguing that the 'fake' votes should be counted," the activist wrote. He followed up with a suggestion: " 'alternative' votes is probably a better term than 'fake' votes," and added a smiley-face emoji.

It was all an unprecedented bit of public controversy kicking up the debris from the insurrection around the Court. It underscored one more unusual fact: the Supreme Court is the only court in the country, state or federal, with no ethics code or mechanism to police conflicts of interest.

Other federal judges must comply with a code enacted in 1973. Those rules put forward broad canons: judges should "uphold the independence and integrity of the judiciary," should not get involved in politics, and so on. Other rules are more specific. (Don't comment on a pending case, for example.) When judges are accused of violating the code, the chief appeals judge in their region will investigate, perhaps referring the matter to a committee of other judges. Punishment may even include a request that the judge retire. Alcatraz, it isn't, but it is something that judges take seriously.

The need for such a code, for some set of rules for the Supreme Court, grew throughout the decade. The judges who made up the supermajority were enmeshed in the corporate and conservative legal world before they joined the bench, and they stayed active and visible. On the day in 2017 that the Supreme Court agreed to hear a major case that would eventually hinder the work of labor unions, *Janus v. AFSCME*, Neil Gorsuch gave a speech to a foundation supported by the same conservative donors who funded the lawsuit. Clarence Thomas was even more energetic on the Republican and conservative dinner circuit. Ginni and her husband often attended the soirees and conferences together. They gave every impression of working as a team.

Justice Thomas managed to run afoul of the few existing rules that govern conduct. The good government group Common Cause charged in 2012 that he had not disclosed nearly $700,000 of payments to his wife by the conservative Heritage Foundation. He had to amend twenty years of financial filings. When he failed to recuse from the decision about the January 6 Committee and its subpoena of documents, he surely must have known his own wife's involvement would arise.

But the stark fact remains: the Supreme Court largely is exempt from the standards that govern all other government officials. At the very least there should be a binding code of ethics, adopted either by the Court itself or imposed by Congress. Some have suggested that an advisory group (say, of retired judges) could counsel the justices about when they need to recuse. But it appears there is little that Roberts or others on the Court can do to convince Thomas to change his conduct.

When it comes to policing itself, the Supreme Court remains largely lawless terrain.

CHAPTER TWELVE

THE LEAK

O N THE WARM AFTERNOON OF MAY 2, 2022, an event was held at the Supreme Court to honor John Paul Stevens, the gentle justice from Chicago, who had died two years earlier at age ninety-nine.

Stevens was from another time: baseball fans knew that, rather incredibly, he had been at Wrigley Field in 1932 when Babe Ruth "called his shot," pointing to a spot in the bleachers where he would park the next pitch. His jurisprudence came from another time as well. A Chicago Republican, solidly moderate, he had drifted left over the course of three decades on the bench as the Court moved right, finally retiring after stumbling with emotion as he read a furious dissent in *Citizens United*. The service could not take place during the pandemic, but now the grand hallway outside the courtroom filled with lawyers, journalists, and former clerks.

All awaited the arrival of the justices so the ceremony could begin. One after another, they slumped into seats in front.

As speakers honoring Stevens droned on, observers started to stir. Something, they whispered, was wrong. Some of the justices were scowling. Some glumly looked at their feet. Alito, one attendee observed, looked like he was going to punch someone. Barrett wore an ineffable face of beatific sadness. Surely she wasn't that broken up about the late justice, with whom she never had served? Attendees speculated at a reception. What was *that* all about?

A few hours later, they all found out, as the website *Politico* published an astonishing bombshell: a leaked draft of the majority opinion in *Dobbs v. Jackson Women's Health*, the long-awaited case on abortion rights.

The justices had voted to overturn *Roe v. Wade*. They also overturned *Planned Parenthood v. Casey*, the case that reaffirmed *Roe* three decades ago. Alito wrote the draft. Thomas, Gorsuch, Kavanaugh, and Barrett had voted with him.

The draft was raw and rough. It rang with Alito's caustic voice. "*Roe* was egregiously wrong from the start," *Politico* reported it saying. "We hold that *Roe* and *Casey* must be overruled," Alito wrote. "It is time to heed the Constitution and return the issue of abortion to the people's elected representatives. . . . *Roe* expressed the 'feel[ing]' that the Fourteenth Amendment was the provision that did the work, but its message seemed to be that the abortion right could be found *somewhere* in the Constitution and that specifying its exact location was not of paramount importance." The draft adopted language from the most uncompromising antiabortion forces about the rights of the fetus.

It seemed to taunt, as well. The draft listed fourteen cases that protected the right to privacy: contraception, gay sex, marriage equality, interracial marriage, and more. This case was different, it said, though the draft did not really explain why. "They do not support the right to obtain an abortion, and by the same token, our conclusion that the Constitution does not confer such a right does not undermine them in any way." (Nice right to privacy you have there. Pity if something should happen to it.) Plainly the reasoning used here would also undermine all those other constitutional protections based on unenumerated rights, those rights implied but not specifically spelled out.

The leak was an astounding news story: the surprise, the finality of seeing *Roe* overturned in cold type, the collapse of the wall of secrecy that surrounds the Court. After oral arguments, the justices meet on Wednesdays and Fridays to cast preliminary votes, with nobody else present. Then they retreat for months, writing drafts and dissents. The silence stretches until late spring, when the ruling is revealed with fanfare to the world. The monastic silence is a key part of the semireligious aura the Court strives to create for itself. People were simply flabbergasted by the fact that the draft of the biggest case in years was now public.

The next morning the Court confirmed the document as "authentic." In a statement it stressed that the draft was not "a decision by the Court." Roberts furiously denounced "a singular and egregious breach of . . . trust." He assigned the Court's marshal to investigate. She was the official who would call out "Oyez, oyez" to begin the public sessions, and while she had been a senior military lawyer, she had never conducted such a high-profile probe.

Critics quickly zeroed in on the threat to all other privacy-based rights. President Biden, on the way to his helicopter, told reporters, "It would mean that every other decision relating to the notion of privacy is thrown into question." At times the seventy-nine-year-old Biden could be halting and tentative; here he spoke with passion and reminded reporters about his questioning of Robert Bork three decades before. "If the rationale of the decision as released were to be sustained, a whole range of rights are in question."

Two days later, a grim eight-foot-high security fence was erected around the Court. Warning signs on each section of the fence declared: AREA CLOSED. Black and foreboding, it went up after the Capitol Police issued a security alert, warning that right-wing groups might attack pro-choice protesters. The jitters may have been understandable: less than two years before, the mob of pro-Trump insurrectionists had besieged the Capitol across the street. But the looming fence kept citizens away from the Court's building at the very moment of the greatest interest in decades in the work inside.

This was not the first leak of a major ruling in the Court's history. As we have seen, *Dred Scott* was disclosed in advance in 1857—to the incoming president, who all but announced it in his Inaugural Address, rather than to journalists. There, too, the leak was wildly controversial, the case was massive in its implications, and the disclosure had a political purpose. Over the years justices might whisper inside information to friendly presidents, as Abe Fortas did to his friend and former client Lyndon Johnson.

There had been other public leaks before, not all accurate. In 1974, a front-page *New York Times* story reported that six justices had voted to force Richard Nixon to turn over his Watergate tapes to a grand jury, but that Chief Justice Warren Burger along with Harry Blackmun would dissent, and were seeking other supporters. In fact, five days later, the Court voted unanimously to require Nixon to comply. *Roe v. Wade* itself leaked in 1973, apparently by accident. A clerk had given a heads-up to *Time* magazine, but then the justices delayed announcing the ruling by a week. A story headlined "The Sexes: Abortion on Demand" appeared on newsstands hours before the ruling was announced from the bench.

But nothing in memory compared to this. Who leaked the draft of *Dobbs*? It was the ultimate true crime podcast. Theories abounded.

Immediate suspicion fell on liberal staff members at the Court. Occam's razor reminds us that the simplest explanation is the most likely. A young progressive clerk was outraged by the opinion, the surmise went, and wanted the world to know. Maybe public clamor could shake the Court. Conservatives on Twitter targeted one clerk and accused her, with no evidence, of having been the leaker.

Liberals, in turn, pointed to conservatives. They noted a pattern and practice of past leaks, all from within the tight network of former clerks and legal activists, all aimed at preventing apostasy by one or another of the justices. Here the goal would have been to prevent the wily chief justice from peeling off a vote or two, presumably Kavanaugh, perhaps Barrett.

The most notorious recent breach had come in 2012 in the major case that upheld the constitutionality of the Affordable Care Act, *NFIB v. Sebelius*. The health care law, known to all as Obamacare, required individuals to buy insurance to ensure that risks be spread throughout the population. Heritage Foundation experts had first proposed this "individual mandate," and Republican governor Mitt Romney of Massachusetts made it the basis for his state's health plan. But now that Obama had embraced it, the Heritage Foundation labeled the requirement for minimum coverage unconstitutional after all, and Scalia and other conservatives insisted it exceeded Congress's power to regulate the economy under the Commerce Clause. John Roberts agreed with them and cast the fifth vote. This would have been an epic resuscitation of a long-buried attack on the regulatory state; ever since the "switch in time" in 1937, the Supreme Court never had blocked a major economic regulatory law on the basis of the Commerce Clause. It would have been an explosive move politically—a five-to-four vote to strike down the centerpiece domestic policy achievement of the Democratic Party and its president, less than two years after *Citizens United*, in the middle of an election.

In April and May 2012 Roberts grew uneasy and sought a way to uphold Obama's law. He found it in the taxing power, which had received glancing mention at the argument. (Recall the precedent for this, also from the New Deal era: "The taxing power, my dear, the taxing power. You can do anything under the taxing power.")

Word got out. As one libertarian put it, "a right-wing bat signal went out, with a clear message: we need to tell the chief justice to grow a backbone." The *National Review* warned that ACA supporters were "threatening dire consequences for the reputation of the Supreme Court and especially for Chief Justice John Roberts if he joins a majority of the justices to strike down the individual mandate." Two days later conservative George F. Will rushed to print with a column that claimed liberals were putting pressure on Roberts, "waging an embarrassingly obvious campaign, hoping he will buckle beneath the pressure of their disapproval and declare Obamacare constitutional." Will "had heard from a law student who had heard from a law clerk that Roberts was vacillating," Jeffrey Toobin recounted. Then a *National Review* editor told a Princeton University panel discussion that "based on people I talk to at the Supreme Court," Roberts "seems to be going a little wobbly. So right now, I would say, [the outcome of the case] is a little bit up in the air." Unerringly accurate. Other journalists fanned the leak.

When *NFIB v. Sebelius* was issued, at first reporters misunderstood it. CNN's correspondent breathlessly announced on the Court's steps that the Affordable Care Act had been overturned. "Wow," blurted anchor Wolf Blitzer. Only six minutes later did the reporter find the passage where the chief justice voted with the liberals to uphold it on different ground—Roberts's very own "switch in time." Observers correctly noted that the dissent read as if it originally had been drafted to be a majority ruling.

The conservative bat signal seemed to have been fired up again in 2020. In a group of cases known as *Bostock v. Clayton County*, two federal appeals courts had split on whether the Civil Rights Act of 1964 protected against discrimination due to sexual orientation or gender identity. In one case, a Georgia county employee had been fired for playing in a gay softball league: conduct "unbecoming." In another, a New York skydiving instructor was fired after mentioning he was gay. Surely a protection for LGBTQ employees was not what members of Congress intended in 1964, at a time when sodomy was still illegal, but the statute's language does prohibit discrimination "because of . . . sex." Elena Kagan had pointed to the text at the argument, but then

silence descended. Suddenly as the decision day approached conservative journalists started warning Gorsuch not to be taken in by Kagan, to
stand his ground, and so on. One writer speculated, "has there been a
leak?" In fact, Gorsuch wrote the opinion, in which he relied on close
textual analysis to prohibit the discrimination. Alito angrily dissented.

Then came *Dobbs*. There were many leaks, it seemed. The week
before the *Politico* detonation, *The Wall Street Journal* editorial page expressed concern about what was happening behind the Court's closed
doors. The flagship conservative organ previously had scoffed at fears
the Court would overrule *Roe*. "The abortion scare campaign," headlined one 2018 editorial reassuring readers that reproductive rights
were safe in Brett Kavanaugh's hands. Now as the Court deliberated,
the *Journal* fretted the justices might flinch from their duty. It warned
that Roberts would try to find a middle ground, and "may be trying to
turn another Justice now." Just savvy court-watching, perhaps, but the
writer had a rather precise sense of the Court's internal dynamics.

A week after it published the draft, *Politico* ran another scoop: "Alito's draft opinion overturning *Roe* is still the only one circulated inside
Supreme Court." None of the five conservative justices had switched
their votes. It was hard to see how this level of detail could have come
from the liberals, since they were not likely privy to any erosion of Alito's majority.

The leak and the investigation seemed to paralyze the Court. Investigators demanded that the clerks sign affidavits and turn over cell
phone records. Presumably some hired lawyers. The time of year when
the chambers would be abuzz, with clerks discreetly checking in with
staff members in other chambers, negotiating language, appeared frozen. The release of opinions slowed to a crawl. By the end of the term,
no prosecutions or dismissals had been announced, and the class of
clerks scattered to lucrative law firm jobs or other perches. The atmosphere within the chambers remained tense, accusatory, and suspicious.

Finally, later than usual, the Court began to release opinions.

One case addressed the question of whether a Maine county that
lacked a high school could pay for students to attend public schools
nearby as well as secular private academies, but not religious schools.
Roberts wrote that the state must pay for tuition at the religious schools,

even though the curriculum for one of them teaches students "to spread the word of Christianity." The topic was narrow (few school districts are so small as to lack a high school). The opinion, limited as it was, opened the way to further governmental support for religious institutions. Roberts explained the holding: "The State pays tuition for certain students at private schools—so long as the schools are not religious. That is discrimination against religion" and thus "violates the Free Exercise Clause of the First Amendment." Bit by bit, the Court eroded the notion that there is an interest in providing public, secular education to children. Indeed, Roberts suggested that the idea that public funds should be limited to secular schooling is a smokescreen for "discrimination against religion."

The Supreme Court in recent years had relentlessly ruled for religious interests, increasingly granting exemptions from human rights law or government policy if the claim was based on faith. In an earlier day religious freedom cases involved minorities, such as Jehovah's Witnesses; now they involved large and not oppressed denominations. In *Masterpiece Cakeshop v. Colorado Civil Rights Commission*, the Court allowed a baker to refuse to serve a gay couple because their marriage offended his religious views. The Court's ruling was narrow; it chided the state human rights agency for enforcing its rules against a religious baker but not against others who also had refused customers, calling it "religious hostility on the part of the State itself." In several cases over the previous decade, conservative Christians had objected to participating in the Affordable Care Act. In 2014, the Court had allowed the retail chain Hobby Lobby, owned by evangelicals, to refuse to provide insurance coverage for contraception for employees. A group of nuns, Little Sisters of the Poor, repeatedly sought exemption from having to participate in any way in the health insurance system that covered contraception, eventually prevailing by seven to two in 2020. Often the victories seemed not for religion but for Christianity. In 2014, the Court upheld a practice in one small town to begin each public meeting with a Christian prayer, with no outreach to the community's Jews or Muslims.

All this was now expected. More startling was the opinion in a case involving public prayer and high school football, itself a nearly religious experience in much of the country.

Neil Gorsuch narrated the story in the majority opinion. Coach

Joseph Kennedy lost his job in Bremerton, Washington, "because he knelt at midfield after games to offer a quiet prayer of thanks." One imagines a Norman Rockwell painting. "He offered his prayers quietly while his students were otherwise occupied." The school district worried that allowing the prayers by its employee would be seen as government endorsement of a religious view, in line with a half-century-old Supreme Court precedent on the First Amendment's "Establishment Clause," an eight-to-nothing ruling in *Lemon v. Kurtzman*. The coach in turn insisted his prayers were an expression of his "free exercise," also under the First Amendment. Framed this way, courts hear this kind of case all the time. The two parts of the First Amendment often are at odds, as judges wrestle with the thorny question of whether a government action seemed to promote religion, or conversely, would squelch religious freedom. At times Breyer or Kagan would vote with the conservatives. This time, the supermajority backed the coach. Instead of ruling narrowly, it used the heartwarming case to strike down the long-standing precedent. The religious conservatives were playing offense.

What revealed the frayed trust at the Court was the revelation in Sonia Sotomayor's dissent: it charged that the majority had knowingly misrepresented the facts of the case. Far from being a wistful loner wandering off in a reverie, the dissent observed, Coach Joe had staged an increasingly clamorous religious spectacle at the fifty-yard line. Sotomayor included three photographs showing the coach, holding aloft the helmets of both teams, surrounded by dozens of kneeling players, proud parents, and photographers. The dissent did not merely call the majority wrong; with photographs and receipts, it said, in effect, the majority justices were lying.

In this and other cases, as the term neared an end, Sotomayor stepped into a role she had increasingly come to occupy: the dissenter. As the Supreme Court radicalized, hers had become the voice of alarm.

She grew up in public housing in the South Bronx, in what she called "a tiny microcosm of Hispanic New York." Her alcoholic father died soon after she was diagnosed with diabetes at age eight. Another striver, Sotomayor attended Princeton and Yale Law School. As a Puerto Rican woman she faced slights and discrimination, just as Thomas and Alito said they did. She did not seem as wounded by the experience.

Sotomayor worked as a prosecutor under Manhattan district attorney Robert Morgenthau, in the office made legendary by twenty-one seasons of *Law & Order*. For seventeen years she was a federal judge, first trial and then on the appeals court. She was a visible presence among her peers and at the courthouse. To this day, restaurants around the federal courthouse at the edge of Manhattan's Chinatown proudly display photos of her posing with waitstaff. Later in her career she would regularly return to swear in new citizens and talk with lawyers at the Immigrant Justice Corps, a group founded by Robert Katzmann, the appeals court's chief judge, whom she called her *hermano* (brother).

A few questioned her intellectual reach. Obama wasn't buying it. "Maybe because of my own background in legal and academic circles— where I'd met my share of highly credentialed, high-IQ morons and had witnessed firsthand the tendency to move the goal posts when it came to promoting women and people of color," he wrote in his memoir, "I was quick to dismiss such concerns." Republicans attacked her for a speech in which she suggested, "I would hope that a wise Latina woman with the richness of her experiences would more often than not reach a better conclusion than a white male who hasn't lived that life," a bit of rhetorical braggadocio. In the end she received sixty-eight votes.

She became the first Latina on the Court, and only the third woman. After she was confirmed, she smilingly asked Obama if he noticed anything. She had painted her fingernails a muted color during her hearing, but now they were bright red.

She aimed to bring some grit into the abstract and rarefied chambers of the Court. In a dissent in an affirmative action case in 2014, she wrote that the majority was "out of touch with reality." In a powerful and perhaps autobiographical passage, she wrote:

> Race matters to a young man's view of society when he spends his teenage years watching others tense up as he passes, no matter the neighborhood where he grew up. Race matters to a young woman's sense of self when she states her hometown, and then is pressed, "No, where are you really from?," regardless of how many generations her family has been in the country. Race matters to a young person addressed by a stranger in a foreign language, which he does not understand

because only English was spoken at home. Race matters because of the slights, the snickers, the silent judgments that reinforce that most crippling of thoughts: "I do not belong here."

Roberts bristled. "It is not 'out of touch with reality,'" he wrote, "to conclude that racial preferences may themselves have the debilitating effect of reinforcing precisely that doubt, and—if so—that the preferences do more harm than good." Two years later, Sotomayor explained to the other justices how "[f]or generations, black and brown parents have given their children 'the talk'—instructing them never to run down the street; always keep your hands where they can be seen." Later she said her own brother had been given "the talk."

Her dissents turned journalistic. In Trump's frenzied last months in office the federal government began executing prisoners after a seventeen-year hiatus. In a January 2021 dissent, she named all thirteen of the people executed. "To put that in historical context, the Federal Government will have executed more than three times as many people in the last six months than it had in the previous six decades."

Now in 2022, with the supermajority preparing to announce its major rulings of the year, Sotomayor's dissents increased in frequency and urgency. In June she and her clerks were working on six of them, all to be released on the last day of the term. All dealt with criminal justice, in cases where the Court had rejected criminal appeals without explanation. They were attached to a dry-as-dust shadow docket list of procedural orders.

The new reality now was fully in view. There was little reason to hold back. Kagan joined Sotomayor now frequently in dissent, not always previously the case. Breyer's retirement meant Sotomayor would be assigning authorship of dissents. The liberal *Nation* magazine called her the Court's "minority leader."

Earlier Sotomayor had explained why she would send up flares. "Often, you're talking to Congress; sometimes, you're talking to the executive branch; sometimes, you're talking to the public," she explained. As the *Nation*'s Elie Mystal wrote, "Sotomayor's opinions read like the ringing of an alarm bell."

"There are days I get discouraged, there are moments where I am deeply disappointed," she told progressive law students in June 2022 at the American Constitution Society, a group that aimed to be the liberal version of the Federalist Society. "Every time I do that, I lick my wounds for a while, sometimes I cry, and then I say: 'Let's fight.'"

Another anguished dissent came from within the house of conservatives. Coloradan Neil Gorsuch had shown himself unusually sensitive to the rights and interests of Native Americans.

Two years before, in 2020, he had authored a decision about a rape prosecution in Oklahoma. "On the far end of the Trail of Tears was a promise," he began; the Creek Indians driven from Georgia in 1838 were given land in Oklahoma, and the federal government signed a treaty. Under federal law, half of Oklahoma was "Indian country," and crimes must be pursued in tribal or federal court, not state court. Gorsuch hewed close to the statutory and treaty text, and produced one of the more unexpected and farsighted opinions in recent years. Tulsa and much of the eastern half of the state now was, technically at least, governed by Native American law. Political conservatives were outraged. "Neil Gorsuch & the four liberal Justices just gave away half of Oklahoma, literally," warned Senator Ted Cruz. "Manhattan is next."

In 2022, with one new justice added to the mix, the Court ruled again on a question of Native American rights in *Oklahoma v. Castro-Huerta*, and abruptly swung in the opposite direction. Oklahoma had not changed; the condition of the Creek Indians had not changed; only the personnel on the Court changed. The justices undid much of the previous case, restoring power to the Oklahoma state government (in this case, allowing it to prosecute a child neglect case against a non-Indian). Gorsuch noted that the Court's 1832 opinion protecting the Cherokees was one of its finest moments. "Where this court once stood firm, today it wilts." The majority simply ignored history and context, he wrote, and "failed to honor the nation's promises." He added: "Truly, a more ahistorical and mistaken statement of Indian law would be hard to fathom."

With protesters kept far from the Supreme Court building after the *Dobbs* leak, pickets converged on the homes of the justices. Activists posted their addresses online.

Judges from all political backgrounds recoil when their residences and families are targeted in this way. They sentence defendants, who are often potentially violent, and jealously guard their privacy. They point to the recent time when a gunman came to the home of federal trial judge Esther Salas, and murdered her son as he sought to protect his parents. Many judges use Post Office boxes for mail and try to keep voter registration information secret.

Elected officials, in turn, tended to roll their eyes at these concerns. Senator Chuck Schumer was asked if he was comfortable with the demonstrations at justices' homes. "If protests are peaceful, yes. There's protests three to four times a week outside my [apartment] house. The American way to peacefully protest is okay."

The Court's security officers put out urgent calls to police in the suburbs, home to most of the justices. Brett Kavanaugh lives in Chevy Chase, Maryland, just across the line from the capital district. A man flew from California, carrying weapons, duct tape, and burglary tools. When he arrived at Kavanaugh's home in the middle of the night on June 8, he saw two armed U.S. marshals standing guard, and stepped away. A block later he turned himself in. Angry about the draft abortion opinion, he allegedly told police he had suicidal thoughts and was planning to murder the justice, "to give his life purpose." According to the FBI he had confided to friends his goal was to "remove" at least one justice. The man was charged with attempted assassination.

In most terms tensions among the justices stayed behind the velvet drapes. The Court's legitimacy depends on at least some notion that it is comprised of dispassionate judges, calling "balls and strikes," or at least priests performing an arcane ritual to divine the meaning of the Constitution, not partisan participants in the country's polarized and fractured politics. Not in 2022. In the season of the leak, justices made few efforts to hide their feelings.

Four days after *Politico* published, Clarence Thomas vented about the clerks at the Court in a speech before lawyers and judges. "It bodes ill for a free society," he said. Institutions can't "give you only the outcome you want, or . . . be bullied." Even as he decried threats to the Court as an institution, he mocked the idea that the justices should follow precedent. "We use *stare decisis* as a mantra when we don't want to think."

A week later he went to Dallas to speak before a conference of conservatives and libertarians, a gathering organized by the American Enterprise Institute, the Hoover Institution, and the Manhattan Institute. (The Manhattan Institute, at times an innovative think tank, was most recently known for its senior fellow, Christopher Rufo, who led the national campaign against "critical race theory" and warned that teachers were "grooming" children "into a sexual identity.") Thomas appeared to take direct aim at John Roberts. Before 2005, Thomas said—the year Roberts joined the Court as its leader—"we actually trusted each other. We may have been a dysfunctional family, but we were a family, and we loved it." He likened the leak to a marital breach. "You begin to look over your shoulder. It's like kind of an infidelity, that you can explain it, but you can't undo it." He seemed ready to opine about the danger of so many former clerks joining as justices, but then stopped short. "I wonder how long we're going to have these institutions at the rate we're undermining them. And then I wonder when they're gone or destabilized, what we're going to have as a country." Thomas not surprisingly made no mention of the controversy about his refusal to recuse from hearing cases about the insurrection because of his wife's activity, or its impact on the legitimacy of the institution.

Samuel Alito sounded more downcast when he spoke to students at the Antonin Scalia Law School at George Mason University. Pro-choice students protested on the campus, decrying the looming overruling of *Roe v. Wade*. Alito spoke six miles away, by video, from a room at the Supreme Court building. A student asked about what it was like at the Court. Did the justices in fact dine together? "I think it would just be really helpful," the questioner said, "for all of us to hear, personally, are you all doing okay in these very challenging times?"

Given the chance to spout about how the justices were all friends, how they all shared camaraderie, Alito pointedly declined.

"The Court right now," he said after a pause, "we had our conference this morning, we're doing our work. We're taking new cases, we're headed toward the end of the term, which is always a frenetic time as we get our opinions out." He concluded his appearance, "So that's where we are."

As the Court began its most consequential month in years, with major rulings due on abortion, guns, and environmental regulation, the Gallup Poll released new results. Public approval had plunged 11 points in one year. Only 25 percent of adults polled expressed a "great deal" or "quite a lot" of confidence in the Court. Many power centers lost trust during the pandemic, but the collapse of public support for the Supreme Court was twice that faced by other institutions.

For decades before the Covid pandemic, the Court would announce its decisions with some grandeur. The public would not be told in advance which case would be announced. Lawyers would be tipped off, though, and spouses and administration officials might show up for a big case. There would be suspense, at times, and a gasp when an unexpected justice read the majority opinion (as when Warren Burger began to announce the Nixon tapes case). Justices would orate, pause, declaim. Reporters might dash for phones to relay the big news in the era before cell phones. When justices wrote a dissent, sometimes, but not always, they would summarize it, too, from the bench. Before modern communication, reports of the spoken opinion would spread throughout the country as if it were a rumor. Newspapers first reported *Dred Scott* based on Taney's courtroom rendition, not the full and often confusing opinion. More recently, with cameras still prohibited, reporters and courtroom sketch artists can scrutinize expressions and convey drama and majesty. Audiotapes are released the same day.

In 2022, the Court heard arguments in person, but the tradition of announcing decisions vanished. Opinions were simply released online as PDF files. Thousands log onto the court's website or SCOTUSblog, the aficionados' website, tapping to refresh every few seconds. No audio was released of a justice declaring (for example) that a major precedent has been overturned. The three most important Supreme Court rulings of 2022 were issued in silence.

PART THREE

THREE DAYS
IN JUNE

CHAPTER THIRTEEN

BRUEN (JUNE 23, 2022)

O N MAY 14, 2022, A TEENAGER drove two hundred miles from his home in rural Conklin, New York, to a Tops supermarket in Buffalo. He chose the location because the zip code had a high percentage of African Americans. As he arrived at the store, he switched on a livestream camera and began to broadcast to twenty-two followers. The teen opened fire as he charged into the market. A security guard who had recently retired from the Buffalo police department, Aaron Salter Jr., shot the intruder. Body armor deflected the bullet; the teen turned and killed Salter. Ten people died, most of them elderly, all but one of them Black. The attacker's racist manifesto was already online.

When *New York State Rifle & Pistol Association v. Bruen* was argued before the justices the previous November, the case drew relatively little attention: a newspaper article here, a tweet there. In the ensuing months, though, the nation passed through an agonizing season of mass killings, culminating in the massacre of schoolchildren in Uvalde, Texas. Public anguish and anger grew so intense that Congress prepared to pass a national gun safety bill, the first in thirty years, despite opposition from the National Rifle Association. Then on June 23, 2022, the Supreme Court ruled and radically curbed government's ability to legislate gun safety.

Not until 2008 had the Supreme Court even ruled that the Constitution protects an individual right to gun ownership. Before that, it had repeatedly ruled otherwise. But *District of Columbia v. Heller*, as significant as it was, only addressed whether there is a constitutional right to keep a handgun to protect "hearth and home." It said little on nearly all other aspects of the law—what the Second Amendment covered, how courts should decide that question, how dangerous was too dangerous. *Bruen* was the most significant ruling on the Second Amendment in fourteen years. It may turn out to be the most significant such ruling ever. Certainly it was the most radical intervention by the courts to block gun safety laws in the country's history—at a time when bodies were being buried, in a country that now has more guns than people.

The Second Amendment comes to us from a time almost unimaginably different from ours. It reads in its entirety:

> *A well regulated militia, being necessary to the security of a free state, the right of the people to keep and bear arms, shall not be infringed.*

These militias were central governmental institutions in the American colonies. All free men ages sixteen to sixty—eventually, all white men—were required to join, and to own a weapon for their militia service. These citizen-soldiers, engaged in what we would regard as compulsory military service, were how communities were kept safe before police forces or an army. They were also seen as a bulwark against tyranny. Americans ardently opposed a standing army, a professional military force commanded by the central government (what we would now recognize as the U.S. Army). At Lexington and Concord, the Minutemen were militias; the Redcoats were a standing army. The archetypes burned deep into the rhetorical and philosophical vision of the new nation.

Reality soon intruded. Militias fought poorly. The part-time farmers and tradesmen often fled at the sound of gunfire. George Washington quickly realized that to prevail he needed to build an actual army: "To place any dependence upon Militia, is, assuredly, resting upon a broken staff." He and the other young nationalists who wrote the new Constitution had something different in mind from the sentimentalism of the shot heard round the world.

The Constitution thrust toward more centralized government. It very notably did not bar a standing army, and while it preserved the state militias, it made clear they, too, could be brought under federal control. To win enough support for the new Constitution from those wary of national power, James Madison reluctantly agreed to support changes to the Constitution. When the first House of Representatives convened, he proposed twenty amendments, on topics ranging from guaranteeing freedom of religion to regulating congressional pay.

One of them dealt with the militia, and gave Quakers and other pacifists conscientious objector status. Madison's draft read, "The right of the people to keep and bear arms shall not be infringed; a well armed and well regulated militia being the best security of a free country: but no person religiously scrupulous of bearing arms shall be compelled to render military service in person." Twelve congressmen spoke on the floor of the House as it marked up the Second Amendment in public; none of them mentioned a constitutional right to have a gun for self-defense. The amendment protected the individual right to a gun . . . to fulfill the duty to serve in a militia. Within months after the amendment was ratified, Congress passed a law that indicated what the founding generation thought it meant: white men had to join a militia, had to purchase guns, bayonets, and other equipment, and had to register their guns with the government.

Then the militia system collapsed. People did not want to show up for duty. The institution persisted largely in the form of slave patrols in the South. The country expanded, and there were plenty of guns, and also plenty of gun laws. At the time of the Second Amendment, Boston prohibited keeping a loaded gun at home, since the ammunition tended to catch fire. New York, Boston, and cities throughout Pennsylvania prohibited firing weapons. States imposed curbs on gun ownership. People deemed dangerous were barred from owning weapons. People expected to be able to own a gun, something they drew from common-law practices dating back to England, but knew that right was limited by many local gun laws. Public safety was always at issue.

And always, always, there were limits and even bans on carrying weapons outside the home. That was especially true in regions outside the South—but it was true nationwide. Restrictions were stricter in urban areas than in the countryside. In many towns on the frontier carrying of weapons was strictly prohibited, and there were few homicides as a result.

One document from the early decades shows how nonchalant

Americans were about gun regulation. On October 4, 1824, the Board of Visitors of the University of Virginia met to establish the new university, which would open its doors a year later in Charlottesville. The trustees approved buying land, agreed upon schedules for language classes, authorized assistant professors to help teach large lectures, and prohibited students from keeping "a servant, a horse or dog." The board also declared students could not "keep or use weapons or arms of any kind, or gunpowder . . . [or] appear in school with a stick, or any weapon." Among those voting to keep guns off campus were James Madison and Thomas Jefferson. Evidently they did not think this violated the sacred right to bear arms.

The country grew more individualistic over time. After the Civil War the Fourteenth Amendment was enacted in part to permit Black communities to arm themselves to protect against white terrorists in the South. Even in the Wild West era, though, gun laws were all-American. In Dodge City, Kansas, an iconic photo from 1879 shows a dusty main street surrounded by saloons and hitching posts. In the middle of the road is a sign: "The Carrying of Fire Arms Strictly Prohibited." When visitors arrived at a frontier town, often they would leave their weapons with the sheriff, and receive a token, like a coat check.

Courts generally did not assume the Second Amendment protected the right to carry a weapon. As the Tennessee Supreme Court wrote in 1840, interpreting the state's law, which was modeled after the U.S. Constitution's provision, "A man in the pursuit of deer, elk, and buffaloes might carry his rifle every day for forty years, and yet it would never be said of him that he had borne arms; much less could it be said that a private citizen bears arms because he has a dirk or pistol concealed under his clothes, or a spear in a cane."

In the early twentieth century, gun laws modernized as cities thronged with immigrants and factory workers. The most important protections were enacted as New York State's Sullivan Act, known as the revolver law, passed in 1911. Gun violence had jumped 50 percent that year. The legislature passed it after a dockworker shot the mayor of New York City as he prepared to leave on a cruise. "Big Tim" Sullivan, a leader of the Tammany Hall Democratic machine, carried the measure in Albany. The law required a license to own a handgun in New York City and prohibited concealed carrying of weapons. Licenses were awarded only to those with a specific need, such as a security guard or someone who faced a violent threat made against them. It amounted to a ban on carrying handguns. Soon other states followed suit, and it became the norm for much of the twentieth century.

There was no organized gun rights movement in those days. When the federal government passed a firearms act in 1934, the National Rifle Association witness testified, "I have never believed in the general practice of carrying weapons. . . . I do not believe in the general promiscuous toting of guns. I think it should be sharply restricted and only under licenses." A lawmaker asked him whether the proposal violated any part of the Constitution. The witness responded, "I have not given it any study from that point of view." The Supreme Court ruled only four times on the question of what kind of right the Second Amendment recognized. The most important and most explicit declaration came in 1939. It upheld a federal ban on sawed-off shotguns, a weapon fancied by bank robbers such as Bonnie and Clyde. Unless such guns have "some reasonable relationship to the preservation or efficiency of a well regulated militia, we cannot say that the Second Amendment guarantees the right to keep and bear such an instrument."

Warren Burger, the rock-ribbed conservative chief justice of the United States, restated the consensus of two centuries when he decried the notion that the Constitution protected an unfettered individual right to gun ownership. "This has been the subject of one of the greatest pieces of fraud, I repeat the word 'fraud,' on the American public by special interest groups that I have ever seen in my lifetime."

What changed that was a thirty-year campaign for constitutional change, one of the most successful in American history.

The National Rifle Association had formed after the Civil War, and focused on hunting and firearm safety. It spoke for the interest of sportsmen. It even announced it would move its headquarters from Washington, D.C., to Colorado in 1976 to signal its retreat from politics. At its annual meeting the next year, still known as the "Revolt in Cincinnati," extreme gun rights activists protested and took over the organization. It was part of the swing to the right in the 1970s among many old-line American institutions, such as Protestant churches and farm organizations. The NRA became militant and increasingly partisan. Its new headquarters no longer was emblazoned with signs lauding FIREARMS SAFETY EDUCATION, MARKSMANSHIP TRAINING, SHOOTING FOR RECREATION. Instead, on the lobby wall was an edited version of the Second Amendment: ". . the right of the people to keep and bear arms shall not be infringed." Half the amendment—the first part, about the "well-regulated militia"—was simply deleted. (Even the ellipses had only two dots.)

This all coincided with the rise of "originalism" among conservative lawyers. But little scholarship described what the original intent, or original public meaning, of that obscure sentence about the "well regulated militia" actually meant. Gun rights activists—the NRA had now rebranded itself, as it says on its website, as "America's longest-standing civil liberties organization"—did not begin by going to court. They seeded scholarship, including providing funds to researchers who churned out law review articles. This fusillade of scholarship and pseudo-scholarship insisted that the traditional view—shared by judges and scholars—was wrong. There had been a colossal constitutional mistake. Two centuries of legal consensus, they argued, must be overturned. Law professors eagerly snipped quotes out of context. For example, a foundational book bore the title, *Let Every Man Be Armed.* The phrase was plucked from Patrick Henry's speech opposing the Constitution at Virginia's ratifying convention in 1788. But a look at the full text shows that far from a ringing declaration of freedom, Henry was complaining about the cost of both the federal and state governments arming the militia. "The great object is, that every man be armed," he said. "At a very great cost, we shall be doubly armed." In other words: Sure, let every man be armed, but only once!

Having funded and encouraged scholarship, the NRA still did not go to court. It worked to defeat lawmakers who pressed for gun regulation. (In 1994, after enacting a waiting period for gun purchases and an assault weapons ban, Democrats lost control of Congress. Bill Clinton groused, "The NRA is the reason the Republicans control the House.") Through it all public opinion shifted. Citizens came to believe there was an individual right protected in the Constitution—even if the courts had not yet recognized it. By the time the Supreme Court aligned with public opinion in 2008, the ruling was like a ripe apple falling from a tree.

The gun group was still so nervous about the outcome that it tried to derail the suit. Instead the case was brought by libertarian lawyers associated with the Cato Institute, the think tank funded by the Koch brothers. *District of Columbia v. Heller* featured a sympathetic plaintiff—a security guard fearful for his safety—taking on the country's only outright ban on owning a handgun in the home.

Antonin Scalia wrote the opinion in *Heller*. He later proudly called it the greatest "vindication of originalism." The amendment's long-ago purpose, to give people the power to fight central government tyranny via compulsory service in a local militia, was left far behind. "[W]hatever else [the Second Amendment] leaves to future evaluation, it surely elevates above all other interests the right of law-abiding, responsible citizens to use arms in defense of hearth and home," he wrote. However, the opinion went on,

> Like most rights, the right secured by the Second Amendment is not unlimited. From [the English legal writer William] Blackstone through the 19th century cases, commentators and courts routinely explained that the right was not a right to keep and carry any weapon whatsoever in any manner whatsoever and for whatever purpose. . . . Although we do not undertake an exhaustive historical analysis today of the full scope of the Second Amendment, nothing in our opinion should be taken to cast doubt on longstanding prohibitions on the possession of firearms by felons and the mentally ill, or laws forbidding the carrying of firearms in sensitive places such as schools and government buildings, or laws imposing conditions and qualifications on the commercial sale of arms.

These rules, Scalia wrote, were "presumptively lawful." This interjection presumably was the price to get the vote of Anthony Kennedy. It turned out to be very significant indeed. John Paul Stevens wrote an authoritative dissent, using originalist methods to tell the real story of the Second Amendment. Stephen Breyer wrote more tersely, asking, how could courts interpret the individual right now that it had been established?

Soon scholars began to chip away at Scalia's showy use of history. He had explained that to "bear arms" must mean to carry a handgun, since "bear" meant "carry." Several years after *Heller*, scholars looked again at the phrase "bear arms." They used a database built at conservative

Brigham Young University in Utah—a massive trove of founding era materials, searchable and analyzable digitally, to enable judges to better ascertain the "original public meaning" of phrases from the 1780s. Many sources had been unavailable in 2008 when Scalia wrote. They found, to their surprise, that Scalia had misunderstood "bear arms." Nearly every use in more than 1,500 instances from the founding era used "bear arms" or "bearing arms" to refer to military service. It was a term of art describing service in a military force such as a "well regulated militia." (Frankly, it wasn't that hard to figure out. This author conducted a similar search in 2013 on a much smaller database of the papers of the six leading founders—Washington, Adams, Jefferson, Franklin, Madison, and Hamilton—and found the same thing.)

All of which raises yet again the sheer weirdness of trying to make social policy today based on long-buried evidence from 230 years ago. Push a button and the computer will tell you what to do. Why do we care what some pamphlet writer in New Hampshire in 1789 meant if the meaning of a provision has evolved since then? And if, as in the case of firearms regulation, the law understood it to mean something else for the better part of two centuries?

Heller was a jurisprudential earthquake—the first time the Court recognized a right to gun ownership, the first major originalist decision in the modern era, indeed, the first major opinion written by Scalia. Politically it fell lower on the Richter scale. Republican John McCain and Democrat Barack Obama both praised it. Two years later with far less fanfare the Court applied *Heller*, which involved a federal jurisdiction, to the states, where the vast majority of criminal law and gun law is established, in *McDonald v. City of Chicago*.

But it became clear quickly that the impact on gun policy in the United States would be less than hoped or feared. It had enshrined the right; it had given the Court's imprimatur to the view of gun rights advocates. But the ruling was limited, and its instructions vague.

In the following decade, judges and juries interpreted *Heller* and *McDonald* in thousands of cases. Yes, they ruled, there was an individual right, now recognized by the Supreme Court. But as with all individual rights, there could be limitations. Society had rights, too. Public safety and its dictates must be balanced against that individual right. Two professors, Eric Ruben of Southern Methodist University and Joseph Blocher of Duke, conducted the most comprehensive research on the cases in the years after *Heller*. Their first look covered rulings up to 2016. The Supreme Court in *McDonald* had warned that guns should not be treated as a "second class right." The researchers found that the judges generally took the job seriously, reviewing law, doctrine, and facts. Overwhelmingly, when they did, they upheld gun safety laws. All told, they found, out of 1,153 cases they surveyed, Second Amendment challenges succeeded only 9 percent of the time. Federal judges and appeals courts upheld assault weapons bans, limitations on who could carry weapons, waiting periods, licensing requirements, and more— the whole panoply of gun laws. All but one court of appeals, they noted, agreed on the right approach. First, courts ask if the weapon or practice was covered by the Second Amendment. If so, judges chose a level of scrutiny—mostly, "intermediate scrutiny," borrowed from First Amendment law. In practice courts balanced the individual right against society's needs, especially public safety.

As federal and state courts fashioned this jurisprudence, the Supreme Court kept silent. It let the rulings stand. For a decade it did not even consider another major Second Amendment case. To take a case requires four votes. It seems that the justices did not know where a fifth vote would land. Perhaps it was Kennedy, who had insisted on the language authorizing gun safety rules. Maybe Roberts kept the reins pulled tight, steering from controversy. In any case, Clarence Thomas regularly chafed at the Court's reticence. "The right to keep and bear arms is apparently this Court's constitutional orphan," he complained in 2018 in a fourteen-page dissent. The NRA charged that judges were engaged in "massive resistance" to the Supreme Court, likening the rulings to the noncompliant South's response to *Brown v. Board of Education*.

In these years, crime continued to drop. "We are still living through one of the safest periods in American history," one analyst reported. Before the 2012 election, Barack Obama barely ever mentioned the issue of guns. But a month after Obama won a second term, a deranged twenty-year-old man entered the Sandy Hook Elementary School in Newtown, Connecticut. He massacred six adults and twenty children ages six and seven. It was the worst day of his presidency, Obama tearfully confessed.

Efforts to restrict guns began again. A bipartisan bill to strengthen background checks supported by 90 percent of the public, introduced by Democrat Joe Manchin of West Virginia and Republican Pat Toomey of Pennsylvania, won majority Senate support but was blocked by a filibuster. A revived gun safety movement began to raise funds and awareness after decades in hibernation. New York mayor Michael Bloomberg, a billionaire who was the city's richest man, formed and funded Everytown for Gun Safety, a powerhouse organizing and research organization. Gabby Giffords, a member of Congress, was shot in the head at a community event. She survived and formed a gun safety organization with her husband, astronaut Mark Kelly, himself later elected to the U.S. Senate from Arizona.

Gun safety groups had new visibility. Meanwhile, the NRA and other gun rights advocates continued to win new victories.

State legislatures now were the most receptive and most conservative parts of government at any level. Twenty-five states passed laws to let people carry weapons with no license at all. They called it "constitutional carry." Federalism fights no longer solely pitted national officials versus states: now legislators in Republican states took aim at cities governed by Democrats. In some states, liberal city governments tried to regulate gun sales or bar carrying weapons, but legislatures passed laws to preempt those efforts.

In 2016, Hillary Clinton was far more vocal, far more confrontational, than Obama had been. She vowed to "take on the gun lobby." At the Democratic convention tearful family members of victims of a mass shooting at a gay nightclub in Orlando, Florida, spoke from the podium. Clinton's campaign bragged it was the first time that gun control had been the subject of a main presentation at a political convention. In part the former secretary of state wanted to hypercharge turnout of suburban women. But Donald Trump found unexpected intense support in rural areas, the very parts of the country where gun owners lived. Pennsylvania, as political consultant James Carville has quipped, is "Pittsburgh in the west, Philadelphia in the east, and Alabama in between." In 2016 "Alabama" voted in such large numbers that Trump squeezed out a victory in Pennsylvania, as well as Michigan and Wisconsin.

The National Rifle Association, meanwhile, was busy falling apart. It had spent an unprecedented amount of money on Trump's behalf.

Then its leaders began to accuse each other of misconduct. New York State attorney general Letitia James sued Wayne LaPierre, the NRA's executive vice president, and the group, accusing him of grifting and massive theft. (After the stress of mass shootings, LaPierre would escape on a luxury yacht moored in the Bahamas named *Illusions*.) LaPierre denounced the suit as an "affront to democracy." The NRA declared bankruptcy. An aphorism attributed to philosopher Eric Hoffer aptly notes, "Every great cause begins as a movement, becomes a business, and eventually degenerates into a racket."

But even as a sputtering hulk, the organization lived on in the lifetime judicial appointments it had helped engineer. The NRA strongly backed all three of Trump's Supreme Court nominees. Kavanaugh replacing Kennedy was key. The new justice had been one of the few federal judges to argue that a ban on AR-15 assault weapons was unconstitutional. (His surprising dissent caught the eye of gun rights promoters, who would boost him for the high court. Think of it as a supplemental college admissions essay, showing the applicant really would go the extra mile to get in.)

The Supreme Court waved away cases involving the Second Amendment and firearms until in 2019, when it heard a challenge brought by the New York State Rifle & Pistol Association, the NRA's state chapter. It was a peculiar lawsuit, however, challenging a New York City rule that prohibited city residents who had gun licenses from bringing their firearms to their country homes. It could not have applied to many people. It turned out the rule dated from the time of Mayor Rudy Giuliani and his police commissioner Bernard Kerik, who by decade's end were bumptious Trump allies. It was all bizarre, and would have been shaky ground for a big ruling. After the justices agreed to hear the case, New York state and city officials scrambled and repealed the rule. During oral argument, the justices mostly seemed annoyed. In an unsigned ruling they dismissed the case as moot.

Two years later the same NRA offshoot challenged another gun law—this one, the long-standing state restriction on the concealed carrying of weapons. The supermajority, firmly in place, took the case. The court faced a barrage of amicus briefs. Nearly all the ones from New York City backed the safety law, enacted in 1911. A quarter of the briefs filed on behalf of the NRA were filed by people or groups who had at one point received funding from the gun group. Unlike most Supreme Court cases, this ruling would immediately affect millions of people. As conservative federal judge Richard Posner had observed criticizing *Heller*, when something is a constitutional right, it means that Montana and Manhattan must be governed under the same rule, even if the circumstances (such as the speed with which police might respond to an alarm) are utterly different.

The case was heard one month into the term. The *Heller* argument in 2008 had been marred by justices ineptly trying to sound knowledge-able about colonial era gun practices, musing that West Coast grizzly bears had somehow threatened East Coast settlements. This time the justices sounded like confused tourists trying to navigate the Big Apple.

Samuel Alito startled New York State's lawyer, Barbara Underwood, with a question: "There are a lot of armed people on the streets of New York and in the subways late at night right now, aren't there?" Alito added, "All these people with illegal guns: they're on the subway, walking around the streets, but ordinary, hardworking, law-abiding people, no. They can't be armed."

Underwood mustered a reply that "the idea of proliferating arms on the subway is precisely, I think, what terrifies a great many people." Alito's sense of city life seemed derived from watching 1970s Betamax tapes of *The Warriors* or *Death Wish*. That dystopian depiction of the transit system had not been the reality in decades, if ever. Indeed, in Essex County, New Jersey—where Alito lived with his family, population approximately 800,000—there were more than two hundred shootings the year of the argument. New York City's subway system recorded just three shootings in the same time frame, while moving hundreds of millions of passengers.

It was clear the supermajority would likely strike down the gun law. Roberts repeatedly turned to whether rules could be different in crowded or unusually dangerous places. The justices and the lawyers tangled in confusion. Yankee Stadium, sure. Campuses, as well. But as former Manhattanite Kagan asked the NRA's lawyer Paul Clement, what about New York University, whose buildings sit on city streets in Greenwich Village? "You know, anybody can walk around the NYU campus." Clement responded, "Well, NYU doesn't have much of a campus." The factual groping was a reminder of the challenge when judges, with sometimes limited knowledge, try to parse social policy through their decisions.

Three decades ago, as one expert group reminded the justices, there were more than 2,200 homicides in New York City, and stray bullets killed ten children. Gun-related homicides soared even as other crime declined. Then the city introduced the CompStat computer system, which used data to target police work, and began to strictly enforce gun laws. Major crimes fell from 527,257 a year to 95,589. For years, New York had become the safest big city in the United States.

But soon crime there started to spike, as in many other cities. Covid and its social disruption was one reason. Courts were essentially closed for months, with prosecutions and police response lagging. Another influence likely was the conflict between police and comunities during protests over the murder of George Floyd during the summer of 2020. And transit police had pulled back from enforcing many public order laws (such as those designed to deter fare beaters). As the pandemic ground on for months and then years, the subways and city streets became alarming places of disorder, with homeless people, often visibly mentally ill, camped out in train cars, sharing space with commuters. Attacks on people of Asian descent spread fear. Crime was still lower than it had been before, rising only to the level of the last year of Michael Bloomberg's celebrated administration, but the feeling of disorder began to return.

Alito's question seemed obtuse in November 2021. But in the subsequent months a cluster of terrifying shootings rattled subway riders.

On April 12, a man dressed as a construction worker with an orange vest and pushing a cart rode the R train through the immigrant neighborhoods of Brooklyn. As the subway rumbled through Sunset Park, home of the city's second largest Chinatown and thousands of Mexican immigrants, he set off two smoke grenades and pulled out a gun, firing wildly into the car and hitting ten people, mostly in the leg. Transit officials surmise he had been headed for a deadlier mass shooting in Manhattan before his mishap. Terrified passengers staggered out of the car at the 36th Street station. The gunman shed his construction worker costume and strolled unnoticed onto the express train waiting across the platform. A citywide manhunt searched for a full day before he called his location in to police on the Lower East Side in Manhattan after eating lunch at Katz's Deli.

On Sunday morning May 22, a man with eleven previous arrests paced back and forth in a train car, pulling out a gun as it crossed the Manhattan Bridge. He shot a Goldman Sachs employee named Daniel Enriquez in the chest, killing him, left the station, handed the weapon to a homeless bystander, and disappeared into the city streets. The chaos summoned by Alito's questions seemed a bit less fanciful. People who two years before demanded "defund the police" now feared traveling on the subway due to safety concerns.

And as the end of the Supreme Court term approached, rising gun violence and the mass shootings that unfolded with a steady rhythm raised public focus and changed public attitudes. The Brooklyn subway shoot-'em-up came first. The shooter's motives were unclear: he had posted videos mocking New York mayor Eric Adams, and bragging that the state's gun laws could not stop him.

A month later, the teenager from Conklin, New York, drove to Buffalo to commit mass murder. Shortly before he arrived the eighteen-year-old posted a white supremacist manifesto on social media. It espoused the "Great Replacement Theory," which claims nonwhite people were being brought into the United States to take over its political system. Often Jews are blamed for this nefarious plot. The theory became visible when neo-Nazis marched in Charlottesville, Virginia, in 2017, chanting somewhat mysteriously, "Jews will not replace us!" The man who killed eleven people at a Pittsburgh synagogue and the one who shot twenty-three people at a Walmart in El Paso to stop a "Hispanic invasion of Texas" embraced the theory. Tucker Carlson, the highest-rated host on cable news, had featured the claim repeatedly in the previous two years. Carlson decried "global political elites" and figures such as Jewish financier George Soros, who aimed to replace white Christians, whom he called "legacy Americans." The Buffalo shooter blamed Jews for the country's changing demographics, but "they can be dealt with in time."

According to the Gun Violence Archive, in 2019 there were 417 mass shootings in the United States; in 2020, as the pandemic ripped through the country, there were 611; in 2021, almost 700 mass shootings. Many more people died every week by everyday gun violence: domestic violence, gang conflicts, street crime, and suicides. But the mass murders—so gory, so frequent, and so unique to the United States—began to stir public opinion.

Then came the massacre in Uvalde, Texas.

There, a teenage boy waited until his eighteenth birthday so he could legally purchase two AR-15 style rifles, as well as 375 rounds of ammunition. (So much for the idea that gun laws do not deter behavior.) For months he had told friends on social media he would do something big, while his friends teased him as a "school shooter." On the morning of May 24, he shot his grandmother, then drove to the nearby Robb Elementary School. A security guard saw him entering, heavily armed, but did not fire for fear of hitting children at play. Police arrived at the school almost immediately, but did not storm the building, as terrified students called for help on cell phones and panicked parents demanded action. Finally, over an hour into the siege, police shot the attacker. He had murdered nineteen children and two teachers.

In response to previous massacres, gun rights advocates had insisted, as the NRA's Wayne LaPierre put it, "The only thing that stops a bad guy with a gun is a good guy with a gun." In Buffalo, where the shooter was outfitted for combat, the good guy with a gun, a security guard, was no match. After earlier shootings the NRA had called for armed security guards at schools. In Uvalde, as criticism mounted of the inept police response, with video showing officers cowering down the hall from the gunman, it was clear the fact that the shooter had an AR-15—a weapon of war—deterred those good guys with guns.

Something changed. According to the Gallup Poll, support for stricter gun laws soared to 66 percent of the public (with the share wanting laws to stay as they are now falling 10 points to 25 percent). Only 8 percent wanted gun laws loosened—exactly what the Supreme Court was poised to do. For the first time in three decades, Democratic and Republican members of Congress began to work together rapidly on national firearms legislation. It would not meet the demands of many gun safety advocates, but the political logjam appeared to be breaking. A final legislative package expanded background checks for those who buy weapons between ages eighteen and twenty-one, the years when mental illness and aggression burst forth with such violence in so many young males. It addressed the "boyfriend loophole"—prohibiting people from buying a gun if they have committed domestic violence against a partner, not just a spouse. The proposed legislation provided funding for states to enhance "red flag laws," under which family members or law enforcement can ask a court to remove guns from dangerous individuals. As the plan headed to a vote in the Senate, it seemed to suggest that the country was finally moving toward action—the first significant new federal gun safety law since the 1990s. The NRA announced its opposition but that did little to slow momentum. The measure was due for a vote on Thursday evening, June 23.

That morning, the Supreme Court issued the first of its blockbuster rulings in the term, the case on guns. As the country seemed to be moving, slowly but perceptibly, in one direction, the Court veered in a very different one.

Clarence Thomas wrote the opinion. Roberts, Alito, Gorsuch, Kavanaugh, and Barrett joined him.

Of the possible permutations of the ruling, Thomas produced the most uncompromising, most extreme. It began with stately cadence: "the Second and Fourteenth Amendments protect an individual's right to carry a handgun for self-defense outside the home." (Recall that only through the Fourteenth Amendment do the provisions of the Bill of Rights, whatever they might be, apply to the states.) The Court struck down New York's law prohibiting the carrying of concealed weapons, which had been in place since 1911.

The opinion was truly odd. It made no mention of gun violence, modern crime, the reality of life today, let alone the reasons why some states might enact restrictions. Only once in sixty-three pages did Thomas mention "public safety"—and only in a footnote, to disparage a case that had cited that rationale for gun laws.

Three things stood out. The first was the way it sought to justify the Court's action through a reliance on history. Thomas, of course, often had stood alone, willing to ignore or strike down centuries of practice or understanding of the Constitution if he concluded the framers meant something different. Here was his big chance to use his method. He flailed. The Constitution's "meaning is fixed according to the understandings of those who ratified it," Thomas wrote. In *Heller*, at least, plenty of evidence had suggested that people had guns in their homes in the founding era, even if they did not think they were enshrining the right to own them in the Constitution. But when it comes to carrying weapons, inconveniently, there was overwhelming evidence throughout history that Americans have mostly thought prohibitions on carrying concealed weapons were just fine. That posed a problem for the author.

The opinion rather frenetically dug examples out of the often contradictory morass of the past to make its point, all while claiming to be relying on the original public meaning of the amendment. The reader lurches to and fro.

There was, to start, a long tradition of English laws prohibiting carrying of weapons. Thomas mocked "the ink the parties spill" over the Statute of Northampton, a British law from 1328 that prohibits carrying weapons. Having to care about such an ancient law is bizarre indeed. Such musty history took up much of Scalia's opinion in *Heller*, but here, it would cut hard against Thomas's view—so it "has little bearing upon the Second Amendment adopted in 1791." Three state laws around the time of the Constitution banned the carrying of weapons. "One 1786 Virginia statute provided that 'no man, great nor small, [shall] go nor ride armed by night nor by day, in fairs or markets, or in other places, in terror of the Country,'" Thomas admitted, and Massachusetts and Tennessee had similar rules. They didn't count, though, because the law required that the weapons inspire "terror." Then restrictive laws spread. "Only after the ratification of the Second Amendment in 1791 did public-carry restrictions proliferate." In other words, there were bans on carrying weapons before and after the amendment.

Then came the Fourteenth Amendment, enacted at a time of low-grade guerrilla war between the races in the South. White southerners passed laws to disarm Black people, who were under siege by the Ku Klux Klan and other terrorist groups. In South Carolina, a U.S. Army general issued orders: "The constitutional rights of all loyal and well-disposed inhabitants to bear arms will not be infringed; nevertheless this shall not be construed to sanction the unlawful practice of carrying concealed weapons." *Bruen* minimized or ignored all this and other late nineteenth-century evidence as well.

Then the opinion just stopped. It never told the reader why the revolver law was passed in 1911, or how it worked, or why Americans did not think it violated the right to keep and bear arms. "We will not address any of the twentieth-century historical evidence" either,

Thomas sniffed primly in a footnote. Such evidence "does not provide insight into the meaning of the Second Amendment when it contradicts earlier evidence." The ruling discussed Texas laws from 1871 and 1875—but not 1971 or 1975. When in doubt, it treated *Heller* not as a legal precedent but as an undisputed source of historical fact, such as Scalia's misreading of what "bear arms" meant.

In his dissent, with Dr. Seuss–like cadence, Stephen Breyer mocked:

> In each instance, the Court finds a reason to discount the historical evidence's persuasive force. Some of the laws New York has identified are too old. But others are too recent. Still others did not last long enough. Some applied to too few people. Some were enacted for the wrong reasons. Some may have been based on a constitutional rationale that is now impossible to identify. Some arose in historically unique circumstances. And some are not sufficiently analogous to the licensing regime at issue here.

The second noteworthy thing about the opinion was its vagueness. It struck down New York's long-standing law, an action with immediate practical consequences in the nation's biggest city. At oral argument the justices suggested they would spell out how to restrict guns to "sensitive places." Yet the ruling gave practically no guidance at all. Schools and courthouses were "sensitive," since *Heller* had said they were, but the fact that a place is where lots of people gather and police provide safety is not enough. "Put simply, there is no historical basis for New York to effectively declare the island of Manhattan a 'sensitive place' simply because it is crowded and protected generally by the New York City Police Department." These were baffling instructions. New York City had 33,000 residents in 1791 when the Second Amendment was ratified. In 2022, it had 8.8 million residents. The density, complexity, and potential for a chain reaction of violence differed dramatically.

The most radical thing about *Bruen*, though, was not how it treated New York's law, but its impact on the rest of the country. It set out a new standard that applied to every gun law, one far more restrictive than any put forward by the Supreme Court before.

Thomas acknowledged that courts of appeals over twelve years "have coalesced" around a two-step approach to assess Second Amendment claims. (Again, first to ask whether the activity in question is covered by the amendment, and then to assess whether public safety outweighed the individual right.) "Despite the popularity of this two-step approach, it is one step too many. . . . Instead, the government must affirmatively prove that its firearm regulation is part of the historical tradition that delimits the outer bounds of the right to keep and bear arms." In other words, gun laws are constitutional solely based on "history" and "tradition." It is up to the litigants to bring historical arguments to the Court. But judges can discard or ignore ones they don't like.

This meant that the 1,500 cases decided by courts in the previous dozen years used the wrong standard. Every one of these statutes would now be open to challenge. The NRA and gun rights lawyers would get a do-over. Perhaps not incidentally, many of the federal judges hearing those cases will not be those appointed by Obama or by George W. Bush, whose Justice Department had not backed *Heller*, but by Donald Trump, the beneficiary of the gun group's biggest expenditure. By the time Trump was defeated after one term in office, he had appointed one quarter of all appeals court judges. Every firearms safety law now stood on shakier ground.

Bans on assault weapons, limits on ammunition, background checks, and more—judges will scratch their heads and search for relevant historical analogies. How best to assess that "history" and "tradition"? After all, the 1911 New York law had been on the books for a longer time than at least three of the curbs on dangerous weapons *Heller* had said were "presumptively lawful." Breyer asked:

> How can we expect laws and cases that are over a century old to dictate the legality of regulations targeting "ghost guns" constructed with the aid of a three-dimensional printer? Or modern laws requiring all gun shops to offer smart guns, which can only be fired by authorized users? Or laws imposing additional criminal penalties for the use of bullets capable of piercing body armor?

Brett Kavanaugh and John Roberts voted for the opinion. They then filed a concurrence that tried to dismiss its radicalism, attempting to spell out "the limits of the Court's decision." They reprinted the now iconic *Heller* paragraph making clear many gun laws are allowed. They explained New York's law was flawed because it was not "objective." But nowhere did they explain how to square their blasé concurrence with the wild-eyed originalism of the opinion, an opinion with six votes and the force of law. Were all gun rules from 1791 "objective"? With back-of-the-envelope math, one could add their temperamentally different approach to that of the three dissenters, but that may not add up to a sturdy majority for a slimmed-down regime of gun licenses.

Samuel Alito filed his own peeved statement. He reproached the dissenters for their reference to the victims of gun violence, as if the topic was a rude intrusion. "In light of what we have actually held, it is hard to see what legitimate purpose can be served by most of the dissent's lengthy introductory section. Why, for example, does the dissent think it is relevant to recount the mass shootings that have occurred in recent years?" If Thomas's opinion could have been written by an eccentric if long-winded history professor, Alito's concurrence evoked "American carnage." New Yorkers "must traverse dark and dangerous streets in order to reach their homes after work or other evening activities," he warned. They should have the right to be armed. (Presumably, since nearly all New Yorkers ride the subway, they should be able to pack heat on the F Train.) "[S]ome of these people reasonably believe that unless they can brandish or, if necessary use a handgun in the case of attack, they may be murdered, raped, or suffer some other serious injury."

To be clear: New York City is still the safest big city in the country. The rate of homicides there in 2021 was still less than a fifth of what it was in 1990. Alito was unambiguous in his hoped-for outcome: a flood of guns into the most crowded city in the country, a city where most illegal guns were purchased legally elsewhere.

In the twentieth century, civilized society embraced the idea famously articulated by the German sociologist Max Weber, that "a state is a human community that (successfully) claims the monopoly of the legitimate use of physical force within a given territory." Now the Supreme Court had a different message to citizens: arm yourselves. Police cannot protect you; your only choice is to protect yourself.

Breyer wrote the dissent, which was joined by Sonia Sotomayor and Elena Kagan. It was his final dissent as lead author. Breyer's equanimity rarely faltered. Here he was too clinical, offering an arched eyebrow rather than a shout of warning. "I fear the court's interpretation ignores these significant dangers . . ." Erasing the work of the lower courts? "That is unusual. We do not normally disrupt settled consensus among the Court of Appeals . . ." Breyer seemed defeated, deflated. Perhaps he remembered the fate of his own dissent in *Heller*. It had effectively sketched out the approach that courts would take. But this time the majority left lower courts much less room than before to uphold public safety laws. He had spent the prior year insisting that the Court was not a political body. His dissent radiated palpable sadness that in fact it is.

Still, only in the dissent did the real world intrude, the fears and facts of the United States in 2022. It started soberly:

> In 2020, 45,222 Americans were killed by firearms. Since the start of this year (2022), there have been 277 reported mass shootings—an average of more than one per day. Gun violence has now surpassed motor vehicle crashes as the leading cause of death among children and adolescents.

Citations pointed not to originalist law review articles or mid-nineteenth-century court cases, but current sources such as the Centers for Disease Control, *The New England Journal of Medicine*, and the Bureau of Justice Statistics. Breyer pointed out that civilians owned over 390 million guns in the United States, about one and a half firearms per adult. Guns kill or send to the emergency room 100,000 people each year. No other country in the world comes close to such a sustained level of armed civilian mayhem.

Breyer's dissent noted an alarming trend. Gun violence, for years, actually had fallen, along with other crime and violence. But recently, among other things as states loosened gun laws in the wake of *Heller*, violence increased. Gun-related deaths rose by 25 percent between 2015 and 2020.

Ubiquitous firearms, weapons in the hands of people convinced they are a "law-abiding citizen," a "good guy with a gun," predictably intensified anger, conflict, and tension in an era of Covid. "In 2021, an average of forty-four people each month were shot and either killed or wounded in road rage incidents, double the annual average between 2016 and 2019," the dissent narrated. Domestic disputes become much more dangerous for women when their partner has a gun. The dissent also sagely noted that tensions between police and community members are magnified enormously by the proliferation of guns. (American exceptionalism includes not only the legacy of racism but the fact that police know they may be facing an armed confrontation at any moment.)

In *Bruen*, the Court in a stroke struck down the work of democratically elected bodies enacted over the course of a century. Not just the rules in New York and the seven other states with strict bans on carrying weapons, but hundreds of other laws now must pass through the sieve of "history" and "tradition." "Balancing these lawful uses against the danger of firearms is primarily the responsibility of elected bodies such as legislatures," Breyer wrote. Handguns are the most popular weapons for defense of the home. "But handguns are also the most popular weapons chosen by perpetrators of violent crime." Cities may have different conditions than the countryside, and states might also tolerate different degrees of risk.

The Court's liberals and conservatives still were uncertain about when to laud the duty of judges to protect individual rights, and when to lionize the legislatures. If the Court's progressives were going to craft a robust defense of judicial restraint, this ruling would have been a good place to start. Inconveniently, the majority and the minority would adopt the opposite positions in the abortion case that would be announced the next day.

That points to one of the most significant aspects of the ruling. Why is "history" and "tradition" the right way to understand how we today should apply the Constitution (especially when, as in Thomas's sloppy approach, the "history" is merely treated as a cupboard to be raided for supplies)? Other constitutional rights are powerful but can be limited. One cannot falsely shout "fire" in a crowded theater to induce a panic, the Court once told us, even if there is no colonial era law prohibiting it. We have a First Amendment right to speak, but child pornography is illegal, libel and slander can be subject to lawsuit, and courts have resisted giving securities fraud and other forms of white-collar crime protection of free speech.

Breyer asked with a weary sigh, "will the Court's approach permit judges to reach the outcomes they prefer and cloak those outcomes in the language of history?"

New York officials rushed to respond. The state's century-old law now was invalid. "The decision ignores this shocking crisis of gun violence every day, engulfing not only New York, but engulfing our entire country," Mayor Eric Adams railed to a press conference. "The opinion claims to be based on the nation's historical past but does not account for the reality of today." Governor Kathy Hochul called the legislature into emergency session the week after the ruling. Quickly it established a new licensing system for the state. The new law defined "sensitive places" to include houses of worship, schools and universities, subways, hospitals, theaters, bars and restaurants where alcohol is served, and Times Square, among other locations. People cannot carry a concealed weapon at a political demonstration, either. Private property owners were presumed to not want concealed handguns brought onto the premises, unless they affirmatively said they did—and they would need to post a sign to that effect. The Concealed Carry Improvement Act also required sixteen hours of classroom and two hours of live-fire training. The law limited licenses to individuals who show good "moral character," and to that end applicants would share their social media accounts—sensible in a season where mass killers post warnings online, but sure to be challenged. The NRA called the whole law "obnoxious" and gun rights groups did not wait until the law went into effect to sue.

Early forays into the courts verged on parody. One judge in western New York blocked much of the law, declaring that two examples of colonial era rules were only a "mere trend"; it took three to make a "tradition." Guns were banned in schools, but the court "cannot find these historical statutes analogous to a prohibition on 'summer camps,'" which of course did not exist in 1791. Same for a ban on carrying guns in subways: where were the early American laws on underground trains? He upheld the ban on carrying guns in churches, however. Just three weeks later, though, another upstate judge, scrutinizing the same "history and tradition," ruled that the state could *not* ban guns in houses of worship.

One federal judge blasted the Supreme Court for its use of dimly understood history. Carlton Reeves of Mississippi was asked to rule on long-standing laws banning felons from having guns. "This Court is not a trained historian. The Justices of the Supreme Court, distinguished as they may be, are not trained historians. . . . And we are not experts in what white, wealthy, and male property owners thought about firearms regulation in 1791. Yet we are now expected to play historian in the name of constitutional adjudication." Stuck with the task of applying the past, he announced he might appoint a trained historian to advise the court.

Across the country, other states undid safety rules to comport with the Supreme Court's newly maximalist protection for gun rights. In California, for example, police were ordered not to enforce the state's new ban on high-capacity magazines (which hold more than ten rounds of ammunition), until the courts could consider whether they were constitutional under *Bruen*. In Maryland the number of people asking to carry guns went up over sevenfold in a month.

The volley of lawsuits challenging long-standing laws also began in the weeks after the Court ruled. In California, for example, an innovative statute had required dealers to sell only "safe" guns, including those with microstamping technology to enable police to track bullets used in crimes. It offered hope that technology could help diminish gun deaths, as had occurred with auto safety regulation, for example. Courts upheld the law twice. Now the California offshoot of the NRA challenged it, demanding to know what the colonial era analogy was for such a law. In Colorado a town had banned assault weapons after a 2021 mass shooting at a supermarket in Boulder left ten people dead including a police officer. Now gun groups sued to overturn it: where is the "history and tradition" analogy from colonial times?

That almost baffling question will now proliferate—and gun laws across the country could topple like bowling pins.

CHAPTER FOURTEEN

DOBBS (JUNE 24, 2022)

T HE DAY AFTER *BRUEN*, SHORTLY AFTER ten in the morning, the Supreme Court released its opinion in *Dobbs v. Jackson Women's Health Organization*. This was the moment toward which the conservative legal movement had built for almost a half century. It was long expected yet still shocking. Every woman of childbearing age in the United States had lived her life with a constitutionally protected right to abortion. With the release of the opinion—the posting of a PDF document—the federal constitutional protection was gone. It was the first explicit repeal of a judicially recognized fundamental right in the country's history.

When the Court took the case, it had asked whether "all pre-viability prohibitions on elective abortions are unconstitutional." Now it ruled that there were no constitutional protections at all.

The opinion changed little from the draft as leaked the month before. Alito wrote it. Thomas, Gorsuch, Kavanaugh, and Barrett joined him. The five votes had, in fact, held. Roberts wrote separately, as many suspected he would, trying to craft a middle ground, an earnest memo to the file. The three liberals wrote an anguished dissent.

The opinion lost little of its blunt force for being expected.

> *Roe* was egregiously wrong from the start. Its reasoning was exceptionally weak, and the decision has had damaging consequences. And far from bringing about a national settlement of the abortion issue, *Roe* and *Casey* have enflamed debate and deepened division.

It is time to heed the Constitution and return the issue of abortion to the people's elected representatives.

The opinion was poorly written: repetitive, with sloppy grammar and misguided sourcing. It repeated the epithet "egregiously wrong" seven more times. It did not even pretend to focus on the interests of women who now would be forced by the government to carry a pregnancy to term. It read, in fact, as if the justices were frozen in place by the leak. *We'll show them, we won't change a thing.* It read like a first draft. A long first draft: it clocked in at 108 pages, including an appendix of state laws banning abortion from the past. (I wrote you a long letter. If I had time I would have written you a shorter one.)

The opinion slashed and mocked *Roe v. Wade*, noting that its reliance on "privacy" as the basis for the right to an abortion was flimsy, and that its different rules in each trimester read more like a legislative enactment than a constitutional opinion. It cited liberal critics such as professor John Hart Ely and Ruth Bader Ginsburg. It made the point that *Roe* effectively struck down the abortion laws of every state in 1973, and cited liberal icon Laurence Tribe as the source. It was the takedown generations of conservatives had dreamed of writing, and Alito was not going to let the opportunity pass by. *Roe* had long faced criticism. But what mattered for nonexperts was its establishment of a right to reproductive rights, embedding it in the Constitution and society's expectations. The real action came in *Casey*, the 1992 case that had reaffirmed *Roe* while largely jettisoning its reliance on "privacy" and rooting its position in the fact that *Roe* was two decades old.

The leaked draft had only intermittently addressed *Casey*. While most things did not change, perhaps recognizing that as a practical matter *Casey* rather than *Roe* was being overturned, the majority justices went at it hard. The 1992 opinion, written as it was by three Republican-appointed justices, failed because it did not "end the debate on the issue." *Casey* had not relied on the right to privacy, but on a ringing affirmation of the cherished American constitutional value of "liberty." *Dobbs* mocked *Casey*'s florid prose—"At the heart of liberty is the right to define one's own concept of existence, of meaning, of the universe, and of the mystery of human life"—surely written then by Anthony Kennedy, and now skewered by his two former clerks, Kavanaugh and Gorsuch.

The *Dobbs* opinion was radical in many dimensions. Even more than its overturning of the two key cases, it went well beyond where it might have. In its repeated invocation of the rights of the "fetus," including its right to "potential life," and its repeated embrace of the statute's reference to the "unborn human being," it echoed the language of antiabortion activists. Taking that phrasing and logic to its next step, the opinion pointed toward national legislation to ban all abortions, and toward a jurisprudence that recognized fetal personhood. It did not require states to strike any kind of balance at all, thus allowing them to ban abortion even when the woman's life was threatened. Those women would have "no rights which the law is bound to respect," to paraphrase an earlier case.

Rather abruptly, the opinion cut off what Alito called "yet another potential home for the abortion right": the argument that reproductive decisions are protected by "equal protection of the law." This was, as all knew, Ruth Bader Ginsburg's proposal. The majority serenely cited "our precedents" which "establish that a State's regulation of abortion is not a sex-based classification." (This after several "gotcha" style citations of the deceased justice.) Three leading feminist scholars, Reva Siegel, Serena Mayeri, and Melissa Murray, had written, "Abortion bans expressly target women and require them to continue pregnancy, imposing motherhood over their objections." They made the same argument to the Court. Alito took note of their brief, and dismissed it curtly with what Siegel called "an unargued sentence fragment." That flick of the hand, she later fumed, "was simply startling in its spitefulness."

Indeed, the words "woman" or "women" appear only three times in the first seven pages of the *Dobbs* ruling. The only place the phrase "poor women" appears, it is to dismiss concern for them: "The dissent has much to say about the effects of pregnancy on women, the burdens of motherhood, and the difficulties faced by poor women. These are important concerns. However, the dissent evinces no similar regard for a State's interest in protecting prenatal life."

It found no middle ground, as both *Roe* and *Casey* had purported to do. Admittedly both Mississippi (after Amy Coney Barrett joined the Court) and the Center for Reproductive Rights told the Court the same thing, with the abortion rights group telling the Court that "no half-measures" were available to uphold the state's law.

Alito was most persuasive when he insisted that the complexities of abortion are best sorted out by the politically accountable, democratically elected branches of government. The issue must be "returned to the people and their elected representatives." The opinion used such language sparingly; Alito was so appalled by abortion that he hardly would cheer if legislatures protected its availability by statute. Still there is a jarring disconnect between the *Dobbs* case and the *Bruen* case issued the day before. There, it was the dissent that sang a song of democracy: "the question of firearm regulation presents a complex problem—one that should be solved by legislatures rather than courts." Such decisions are not best made by judges, brandishing the absolutist language of rights, but "through democratic processes."

The lengthy opinion has been dissected at length in hundreds of forums. Three things stand out.

The first is its full embrace of a nuance-free originalism. "[T]he Constitution makes no mention of abortion," Alito complains. And when something is not specifically "mentioned" in the Constitution, rights will only be protected if they are "deeply rooted in this Nation's history and tradition" and "implicit in the concept of ordered liberty." This formulation comes from a 1997 case, *Washington v. Glucksberg*, that refused to recognize a right to assisted suicide. It had become a totemic mantra, recited repeatedly by nominees such as Ketanji Brown Jackson at confirmation hearings.

As interpreted by this Court, that means that only rights widely recognized in 1868—when the Fourteenth Amendment was ratified— would be protected. Applied to this most consequential of issues, this is an epochal shift in how the Constitution is interpreted. History, human progress, the understanding of human freedom, stopped in 1868. That sounds like an exaggeration, but it is not. "Indeed," the opinion explained, "when the Fourteenth Amendment was adopted, three quarters of the States made abortion a crime at all stages of pregnancy." (And women could not vote.) Alito did not ask whether concepts such as privacy, intimate relations, family, and home were established as part of what liberty meant at the time. Nor did he explore the fact that slavery had just been abolished, with its control over the bodies of Black women. Instead he looked only to whether abortion rights were specifically understood as part of liberty—which has the predictable effect of preserving in amber nineteenth-century social norms.

The majority insisted that *Roe v. Wade* had misused history, in the earlier case's claim that abortions before "quickening" (when a pregnant woman can feel movement) were largely tolerated. The history as deployed in *Roe* was debated. The way Alito sought to prove a long provenance for antiabortion laws, though, was unexpectedly revealing. To make the case that abortions were illegal in one form or another long before 1868, the opinion reached back to the 1200s. Repeatedly, Alito cites Sir Matthew Hale, a curious and rhetorically disastrous choice. Hale was a British jurist from the 1600s. He wrote that a woman had no rights in her marriage, and indeed formulated the doctrine saying that a husband could not be charged with raping his wife because "by their mutual matrimonial consent and contract the wife hath given up herself." Hale had sentenced two women to death for witchcraft. Alito quoted him as an expert for the proposition that an abortion of a quick child was "a great crime" and a "great misprision." (NBC's *Saturday Night Live*, after the draft leaked, led with a sketch featuring the newly famous Hale, played by Benedict Cumberbatch in a Renaissance costume. Future scholars would marvel, he bragged. "There's no need to update this at all. We nailed it in 1235.") Much of the actual opinion bordered on satirical, too. It quoted a judge in 1732 who, referring to abortion, scowled that he had "never met with a case so barbarous and unnatural." A 1602 indictment described abortion as "against the peace of our Lady the Queen, her crown and dignity."

The dissent and scholars criticized Alito's draft for misreading all this history. Before the mid-nineteenth century, in fact, abortion before "quickening" was not illegal in many places. As of 1800, no laws banned abortion in the United States. It was only in the middle of that century that a wave of statutes banned the practice, as Alito acknowledged. Scholars argue that was part of a general crackdown by the newly professionalized ranks of physicians (men) on midwives (women) who previously had been largely responsible for obstetric care. Other historians disagree. It is, again, unique to our country and to the very modern notion of originalism that historic debates over such long-ago topics would tip the balance in contemporary social policy disputes.

But even if the history had not been misread, the implications were stark: progress stopped in 1868. The laws governing abortion before that time were made entirely by men. Not only were women barred from voting—they could not serve on juries, own property if they were married, and so on. (And for nearly all of that time, Black people were enslaved.) Indeed the Fourteenth Amendment defined all citizens as "male" for the first time. It is a constitutional freeze frame. To the vast majority of Americans, 80 percent of whom today are fifty years or younger, the constitutionalized right to choose is emphatically part of their own story—happily or not, they have not known anything else.

And it cannot be stressed enough—this was not how constitutional law has been done at any point in the country's history up until now. Originalism was sold originally as a neutral way to tether modern decision making to some factually ascertainable standard, to avoid loosey-goosey constitutionalism embodied by *Roe v. Wade.* The implications of this alternative—literally of turning back a century and a half of social evolution—are startling, perhaps untenable, and utterly new.

The second big point about the decision is what it says about the Supreme Court and its approach to past decisions. Little is left of stare decisis. After all, the Supreme Court had upheld *Roe v. Wade* at least sixteen times since 1973. Now, suddenly, it was "egregiously wrong," disappeared from the law books.

They say hypocrisy is the tribute vice pays to virtue; this opinion pays a great deal of tribute to principles of stare decisis while blithely ignoring them. Courts have developed standards that set out when precedent should govern, and when an earlier opinion should be overturned. Alito and the others in the majority never really grapple with that. They simply asserted, repeatedly, that *Roe* was a bad decision, that *Casey* never ended agitation over abortion, and that the Supreme Court had overturned other cases, too. *Plessy v. Ferguson, Lochner,* and the case supplanted during the New Deal to produce the "switch in time," each are mentioned multiple times, like melodrama villains, brought out to elicit boos.

Standard reasons why a case might be overturned, for example, include new facts. Here there were few new facts, though Alito made a halfhearted point of noting the significance of ultrasound in possibly changing expecting parents' views of the issue. Stare decisis also offers certainty and predictability to the rest of society about how to order affairs, what expectations we all have of how our lives can be lived. Alito mocks this as a "reliance" interest and says that the only legitimate such concerns are financial—such as "those that develop in cases involving property and contract rights." As for "the effect of the abortion right on society and in particular on the lives of women," well, that's just too hard for the Supreme Court to assess.

The reason that the justices made this ruling less than two years after Amy Coney Barrett joined the Court is that they could. The supermajority now has essentially adopted Clarence Thomas's view that precedent is for suckers, and that if this Court disagrees with an earlier ruling, it can feel free to erase it.

The third major implication of the ruling is what it portends for many other issues and interests.

The majority opinion expressed surprise that anyone could think its logic might threaten other unenumerated rights not "deeply rooted in this Nation's history and tradition." It helpfully lists other cases protecting those rights, just to reassure the reader that they are perfectly safe: *Griswold* and its protection of the right to contraception, *Lawrence v. Texas* and its protection of the intimacy of gay couples, *Obergefell v. Hodges* and its protection of marriage equality, cases protecting against involuntary sterilization, upholding the right to make decisions about educating children, and so on. The more insistent Alito was that these rights are secure, entirely different because they do not involve "fetal life," the more nervous a reader should grow. At points the opinion could not help itself: *Roe* "held that the abortion right, which is not mentioned in the Constitution, is part of a right to privacy, which is also not mentioned."

The dissent homed in on the illogic of Alito's logic. "So one of two things must be true. Either the majority does not really believe in its own reasoning. Or if it does, all rights that have no history stretching back to the mid-nineteenth century are insecure. Either the mass of the majority's opinion is hypocrisy, or additional constitutional rights are under threat. It is one or the other."

Clarence Thomas's concurrence made this point plainly. The concurrence shocked many readers, but only those who had never read anything by Thomas. It was amusingly self-referential: he quoted or cited himself twenty-one times. He argued that the majority opinion's logic required a repudiation of other "demonstrably erroneous" cases rooted in the right to privacy and other unenumerated rights. Thomas's list of cases to be overturned mostly included the same greatest hits mentioned by the majority. Caustic observers noted one he left out: *Loving v. Virginia*, the 1967 case that protected the right to interracial marriage. A justice of the Connecticut Supreme Court, a gay man who is himself married, posted on Facebook that day, "Mr. Justice Thomas had much to say today about my loving marriage. Oddly he didn't have much to say about his 'Loving' marriage." That case, too, depended on an expansive reading of the Constitution, and there can be no doubt that most of the drafters of the Fourteenth Amendment did not expect or want to protect "race mixing." Thomas is in an interracial marriage, in the state of Virginia, no less.

John Roberts sought a middle path, or at least what he regarded as a middle path. In a concurrence he pledged loyalty to "a simple yet fundamental principle of judicial restraint: If it is not necessary to decide more to dispose of a case, then it is necessary *not* to decide more." He would have let the state restrict abortions after fifteen weeks, thus overturning *Roe* and also *Casey*'s "undue burden" test. He would ensure that the Constitution protects some right of a woman to bodily autonomy and the decision whether to terminate pregnancy, so long as she has a "reasonable opportunity" to do so. When women decide to end a pregnancy, it happens during the first trimester the vast majority of times. It is not clear how the new approach he proposed would have ever satisfied the majority; antiabortion forces would hate it just as much as the *Casey* status quo.

Roberts was unambiguous in his dismay over the hit to the Court's credibility and legitimacy from a five-to-four decision reversing *Roe v. Wade*—"a serious jolt to the legal system." *Brown v. Board of Education* had overturned a precedent, but it was unanimous and required only eleven pages to make its point. He decried Mississippi's mid-litigation switch to demanding a reversal of *Roe* once Barrett replaced Ginsburg.

The Court's public disquiet spilled onto the page. The majority saved most vinegary snark for the chief justice. His "quest for a middle way would only put off the day when we would be forced to confront the question we now decide. The turmoil wrought by *Roe* and *Casey* would be prolonged." The justices congratulated themselves repeatedly for their own courage. The chief's concern about legitimacy was just a euphemism for cowering to the mob. That they would not do.

Kavanaugh also wrote a concurrence. Why? One must assume

that Roberts's missive had aimed to persuade him. His response, basically, was, "sorry Chief, I have to do this." Kavanaugh insisted that the Supreme Court must be "neutral" on the subject of abortion. "The Constitution is neither pro-life nor pro-choice. The Constitution is neutral and leaves the issue for the people and their elected representatives to resolve." In truth, since abortion rights had been judicially protected for half a century, yanking them away would hardly feel neutral to millions of women who live in states with antiabortion legislatures. The success of the right-to-life movement in state politics in the previous decade rang loudly to Kavanaugh. Twenty-five states asked the Court to rule this way. That number would have been much lower before the Republican sweep of state legislatures in 2010 amid the Great Recession.

Three justices jointly authored the dissent. Like the majority ruling, it bore the mark of the tumultuous drafting process. Things were said multiple times, seemingly in the varying voices of Breyer (pained and puzzled), Sotomayor (quietly seething), and Kagan (conversationally feisty). It did not get around to asserting that *Dobbs* would entirely rescind an individual right "for the first time in history" until fifty-four pages in, and then in the middle of a paragraph.

Yet if the majority opinion strenuously avoided the topic of women and their rights, the dissent focused firmly on that central point. Women were mentioned seven times in the first paragraph. The justices continued:

> Whatever the exact scope of the coming laws, one result of today's decision is certain: the curtailment of women's rights, and of their status as free and equal citizens. Yesterday, the Constitution guaranteed that a woman confronted with an unplanned pregnancy could (within reasonable limits) make her own decision about whether to bear a child, with all the life-transforming consequences that act involves. . . . But no longer. As of today, this Court holds, a State can always force a woman to give birth, prohibiting even the earliest abortions. A State can thus transform what, when freely undertaken, is a wonder into what, when forced, may be a nightmare.

The dissenters expressed a chilled recognition that the majority opinion imposed no restrictions on government as it works to prevent women from having abortions. "Most threatening of all, no language stops the Federal Government from prohibiting abortions nationwide, once again from the moment of conception and without exception for rape or incest." Alito's opinion had no "to be sure" paragraph. It's open season.

The dissent hits the central fact about the majority opinion, summarizing it: "Because laws in 1868 deprived women of any control over their bodies, the majority approves States doing so today. Because those laws prevented women from charting the course of their own lives, the majority says States can do the same again."

Above all the dissent focused on stare decisis. Without something new—new facts, for example—the Supreme Court is not supposed to simply decide if it likes an earlier opinion, and if not, overturn it. The majority repeatedly cites the overturning of *Plessy v. Ferguson* as an example. But even pursuing *Brown v. Board of Education*, Thurgood Marshall had carefully navigated from point to point, building on precedent, persuading the Court first to strike down segregation at law schools, then in other graduate schools, and so on, building precedents which Warren and his colleagues could extend.

Yet the dissent shunned a key task. If friend and foe agree that the right to privacy was weak, the justices could have articulated a different rationale for abortion rights. Ginsburg and others had argued that the Fourteenth Amendment's Equal Protection Clause was a sturdier "limb," since forced pregnancy so clearly affects women in dramatically unfair ways. As mentioned, Alito's opinion waved away that idea, in a tone that one attorney called "owning the libs." But the dissent was silent on this approach as well. It laid out no alternate theory (as Thomas's dissents often did) or even breadcrumbs for future cases and advocacy.

Breyer, Kagan, and Sotomayor did try to articulate an alternative view to the nineteenth-century originalism of Alito's opinion. They quote John Marshall: the Constitution is " 'intended to endure for ages to come,' and must adapt itself to a future 'seen dimly,' if at all." The dissent speaks in a voice that would long have been the standard way for justices to interpret the grand but broad terms of the Fourteenth

Amendment. "[A]pplications of liberty and equality can evolve while remaining grounded in constitutional principles, constitutional history, and constitutional precedents."

The decision had a visceral and immediate impact. Demonstrations erupted in cities across the country. Stunned receptionists at health clinics called patients to tell them their appointments had been canceled.

The opinion professed merely to be sending the topic of abortion to the states for the political process to work its will. But that was illusory. In many states, sometimes without much public debate, laws were already in place, ready to be enforced. In others, the ruling led to a confusing scramble involving legislators, courts, and law enforcement, with women and health care providers bewildered and often terrified. We were finding out what it meant to have something deemed a fundamental right in one state and a felony in the state next door.

All told, twenty-two states had laws in effect that would ban or severely restrict abortion if *Roe v. Wade* were overturned. Within three weeks after the ruling, nine states had banned it: Alabama, Arkansas, Missouri, Mississippi, Oklahoma, South Dakota, Texas, West Virginia, and Wisconsin. Most offered no exception for rape or incest. Other states had restrictive laws long on the books but never removed after the 1973 ruling. In Michigan, a statute prohibiting all abortions dated from 1931. Governor Gretchen Whitmer, scrambling after the leaked draft, went to the state supreme court to seek a ruling that the Michigan constitution still protected reproductive rights. A court blocked the 1931 law, but the status was unclear for months, with abortion even banned statewide for a few hours due to dueling rulings.

It is hard to think of another decision by five government officials—for that is who the justices are—with a more immediate, disruptive impact on more lives. Abortion clinics shuttered across the country. In early July, after a waiting period, Jackson Women's Health—the clinic that sued to challenge Mississippi's law—closed its doors. As had been the case in Texas the previous summer, dismayed staff members told panicked and distraught women that the planned procedures could not be performed. According to one study, one in four abortion clinics nationwide could be forced to shut. Journalist Laura Bassett wrote an early assessment three weeks after the ruling:

> I expected these horrifying, dystopian stories to trickle out over the next six months to maybe a year, forcing people to acknowledge a reality that had long been just hypothetical.
>
> Instead, the stories have sprayed out like a firehose: A 10-year-old rape survivor had to travel to another state to get safe abortion care, and politicians immediately went after the doctor who helped her; a Texas hospital let a woman with an ectopic pregnancy bleed until she almost died to avoid getting sued; Idaho Republicans overwhelmingly voted to let women die before giving them care. The dystopia is upon us, and it arrived faster than anyone expected.

Particularly agonizing was the story of the child who had been raped. The ten-year-old lived in Ohio, which had banned abortion after six weeks on the day the Supreme Court ruled. Her mother brought her to Indiana to obtain the necessary medication. The president brought the story to national attention. "She was forced to have to travel out of the state to Indiana to seek to terminate the pregnancy and maybe save her life," Biden said in the Roosevelt Room at the White House. "Ten years old—ten years old!—raped, six weeks pregnant, already traumatized, was forced to travel to another state."

Supporters of *Dobbs* charged that the story was fishy, or even made up. The *Wall Street Journal* editorial board called it a "fanciful tale." A *National Review* writer labeled it "a fictive abortion and a fictive rape." Ohio attorney general Dave Yost went on Fox News, and told *The Columbus Dispatch*, "Every day that goes by the more likely that this is a fabrication," adding, "there is not a damn scintilla of evidence."

The next day, police arrested a twenty-seven-year-old man who allegedly confessed to the crime. The outrage brigade barely paused. Indiana attorney general Todd Rokita went on Fox News, as well, and said he would investigate the physician who helped the ten-year-old. He falsely charged she had hidden the procedure from authorities. James Bopp, the antiabortion lawyer who had won *Citizens United* at the Supreme Court, said he thought the girl should have been forced to

give birth. Eventually, he said, "we would hope that she would understand the reason and ultimately the benefit of having the child."

———

Democrats nationally seemed to be caught flat-footed by the Court,
hard to imagine given the long advance notice. (Months, at least, and
arguably years.) Biden and Harris made no immediate public statement just after the ruling, supposedly because they somehow thought
it would not come that day. Eighty-two-year-old House Majority Whip
James Clyburn all but shrugged: "it was a little anticlimactic."

The federal government had some tools it could use through legislative action, but politically those were out of reach. After the leak but
before the decision, the House passed and the Senate debated legislation to codify abortion rights nationwide. The proposal failed to attract
a simple majority of senators. Activists and lawmakers spun out increasingly frantic ideas: that the federal government could establish abortion clinics on federal property such as military bases, for example.
That would not work, since federal law banned the use of government
money to support abortion services. In September the Department of
Veterans Affairs announced it would make abortion counseling available and permit abortions when the life of the veteran is at risk, even
in states with different laws.

Meanwhile, Mitch McConnell mused that Republicans might try
to pass a national law to ban abortion everywhere in the country. This
may have been a feint, designed to rattle Democrats who ached to end
the filibuster. Republicans, having pushed for this moment, were notably muted in their exultation. In the widely used analogy—overused,
in fact, but still apt—they were the dog that caught the car. What do
you do with it? They knew that broad protection of abortion rights was
popular, and that the Supreme Court's ruling to overturn *Roe v. Wade*
seemed abrupt and unpopular.

How would the ruling affect the shape of American politics? Would
a national movement responding to *Dobbs* galvanize and eventually
prevail as the movement to overturn *Roe* eventually did? (And would
it take as long?) Or would the Court's move to yank the abortion issue
into the maelstrom of politics lead to anything other than continuing
polarized combat—might there be a political consensus for abortion

rights, abortions that are "safe, legal, and rare"? Could the *Casey* compromise in effect be enacted?

These questions will stretch far into the future and cannot be answered so soon after the convulsive events set in motion by the reversal of *Roe v. Wade.*

One thing is surely likely, of great relevance to the future of the Supreme Court and its supermajority: there will be a lot of litigation.

According to the majority in *Dobbs*, the status quo—which barred states from imposing an "undue burden" on abortion rights—was a mess. It assigned judges "an unwieldy and inappropriate task." In fact, as the definitive study of the legal landscape concluded, "the opposite is true: overturning *Roe* and *Casey* will create a complicated world of novel interjurisdictional legal conflicts over abortion." It will be a welter of conflicts among states, efforts by state governments to enforce their laws in other states, and head-butting between the federal government, states, counties, and courts.

One legal conundrum had to do with pharmaceutical abortion. Already, in 2022 most pregnancies were terminated not with a surgical procedure but through medication. The Food and Drug Administration approved mifepristone for use in 2000. That approval had taken a circuitous route. The French manufacturer was afraid to sell it in the United States due to boycott fears, and rights to the product passed back and forth between the Population Council, a large nonprofit, and private firms. Once approved, for twenty years it became the quiet alternative to surgical abortions, combined with the drug misoprostol. Together they induce a process similar to a miscarriage. FDA rules required a visit to a clinic or physician to obtain a prescription. In December 2021, two weeks after the lawyers argued *Dobbs*, the FDA lifted those restrictions and allowed the pills to be sent by mail. During the pandemic, doctors prescribed Mifeprex (the brand name) using telemedicine. Can a state bar its people from helping women obtain the medication? Could governments make it impossible for women to get the pills sent across state lines?

Travel was another potential legal quagmire. Americans have the right to travel from state to state. Yet that right—dating from the Articles of Confederation, thus older than the Constitution itself—is not explicitly spelled out. Can a legislature bar its own citizens from leaving a state for the purpose of getting an abortion? Democrats tried to pass federal legislation guaranteeing the right to move from state to state for reproductive health reasons. One Republican senator, James Lankford of Oklahoma, blocked the move. "Does that child in the womb have the right to travel in their future?" Lankford said in objecting. "Do they get to live?" What about abortion clinics over the border in Canada or Mexico? Issues of federal authority versus state power will proliferate.

Many of the legal issues evoke those of another ugly era: the time of the Fugitive Slave Laws, before the Civil War. That federal statute was used by slaveowners to hunt down and kidnap people who had fled bondage and found their way into free states. Local officials in free states were enlisted to help, thus ensnaring governments in the North. Many officials in the North refused to participate, and the Underground Railroad helped as many as 100,000 to flee. The Texas vigilante law, S.B. 8, does not limit its bounty hunter system to punishing only those who help someone procure an abortion within the state. A vigilante could profit by fingering those who help others leave Texas.

Lawmakers in other states announced that they, too, were considering legislation to punish those who help women go out of state to end a pregnancy. In his concurrence, Brett Kavanaugh found a reassuring answer: "[M]ay a State bar a resident of that State from traveling to another State to obtain an abortion? In my view, the answer is no based on the constitutional right to interstate travel." But the dissent was far less sanguine. It quoted three scholars who have looked at the post-*Roe* legal terrain. "Abortion travel will become an essential part of the post-*Roe* reality, but there will be attempts to outlaw it," they predict. Indeed, the National Right to Life Committee's model law prohibits helping minors "regardless of where an illegal abortion occurs." Meanwhile seventeen states had laws guaranteeing the right to an abortion. California was expected to host 200,000 people each year on an urgent mission to obtain reproductive health care. A first study of the impact of *Dobbs* released five months later showed many women traveling for the procedure, part of an overall 6 percent drop in abortions performed at clinics nationwide, with many more women availing themselves of pharmaceutical options.

Dobbs and *Bruen* conversed with one another—in the majority, in the dissents, and across all dimensions.

In *Bruen*, for example, judicial activism led to a ruling striking down a century-old law, soon to be joined by similar laws undone in six other states. With the new standard for review of firearms regulation, the ruling will imperil dozens of laws, state and federal, all of which had already been found constitutional. It was an act, as *Dobbs* might say of *Roe*, of judicial imperialism. It resembled earlier rulings in areas as varied as campaign finance and voting rights in expressing disdain for the expertise and efforts of legislators. The dissent sang a Walt Whitmanesque song about the glories of democracy; the majority spoke in the language of rights, upheld and ennobled.

In *Dobbs*, of course, the two sides swapped clothes. The majority with blasé assurance said it was simply sending the issue of abortion back to the democratic process in states where it should have been all along. Though it's worth noting that Alito does not spend much rhetorical energy lauding the democratic process and the chance that it could lead to expanded protection of reproductive rights. Yet even the assurance that women could exert their will in state politics rings hollow. The states that had already enacted the most extreme antiabortion laws were also the states, for example, where gerrymandering has produced the most unrepresentative legislative maps. Texas not only had the earliest abortion ban, it also had the most extreme gerrymandering, as well as among the country's harshest voting laws.

The most significant connection between the two decisions had to do with how they were reasoned. They speak most loudly in their joint embrace of originalism.

Again, that has not been the way the Supreme Court has interpreted the Constitution for the previous two centuries. Indeed, only one recent major ruling—*Heller* in 2008—proclaimed itself originalist. (In that case, fans of the ruling explained that since the Supreme Court had rarely considered the Second Amendment before, there were few cases to cite as precedent—so off to the founding era we went.) Arguably, the other major ruling in American history that rooted its analysis so thoroughly on the original public meaning of the Constitution was *Dred Scott*. That opinion's notoriety was one reason the approach fell out of favor.

The Supreme Court has almost always ruled using a synthesis of the text and original meaning of a provision—but more than that. The structure of the government. The values behind the language. And a keen eye for the practical consequences of its rulings (predictions not always accurate, but certainly seen as legitimate). That is the only way it is possible to imagine a society handing over so much power to one unelected group of nine people. There is no "history and tradition" of making major constitutional rulings using originalism.

Thomas's opinion in *Bruen* shows that for all its pretense, originalism in the hands of this Court was fake. Alito's originalism in *Dobbs* shows it to be dangerous and reactionary.

Bruen, as we've noted, found it necessary to ignore much history to uphold the idea that the decision was rooted in history. It required cherry-picking examples, excising evidence, excusing bad facts, and ripping quotes out of context. An opinion rooted accurately and honestly in history would have upheld New York's law.

In *Dobbs*, the originalism was drunk pure. It left little doubt about the implications of the approach. Scalia, Bork, and Meese (among other early proponents) soft-pedaled the consequences of turn-back-the-clock constitutionalism. It was merely an attempt to find an unchanging and predictable approach to constitutional law. Yet by insisting that the Constitution's "meaning is fixed according to the understandings of those who ratified it," then it matters when it was fixed and by whom. The implications of recognizing only those rights familiar in either 1791 or 1868 are now evident, and are uncontrovertibly retrograde. Is it really true that human understanding of rights and equality and the role of women have not evolved since then? The Constitution may be frozen but does anybody think society is?

It is hard to put the two opinions next to each other, ultimately, and avoid the conclusion that the justices decided the outcome first, and then worked backward to the rationale. This is the very results-oriented jurisprudence of which conservatives long accused liberals.

And the next time the Supreme Court made a major ruling, in the last big case of the year, decided days later, the Court jettisoned originalism altogether. As it began to rein in the ability of the federal government to protect the environment, the Court decided it could just make it up.

CHAPTER FIFTEEN

WEST VIRGINIA V. EPA (JUNE 30, 2022)

O N THE TERM'S FINAL DAY FOR decisions, the Supreme Court addressed an issue less raw than abortion or guns—but which has extraordinary and broad impact on our future. The topic was climate change. The case was *West Virginia v. Environmental Protection Agency*, the EPA. For once the caption captured the essence of the case. The Court blocked many of the agency's potential efforts to curb carbon emissions from facilities that burn coal and other fossil fuels.

This was a key moment in a decades-old crusade for the men and women who had invested in the project of packing the courts with conservatives. Pro-business Manhattanites who quietly supported abortion rights and would be embarrassed to be seen carrying a gun had invested in a zip code's worth of think tanks and legal groups aiming for such a result. *Dobbs* and *Bruen* were for the Republican Party voters; *West Virginia v. EPA* was for the paying customers. Together these three cases reflected the coalition of religious conservatives, white rural voters, and business interests that have made up the Republican Party since the 1970s.

Significantly, there is every reason to think that *West Virginia v. EPA* will be just the first such major case to collar the regulators. It shows that the supermajority may be willing to act to curb the power of government and roll back the clock—perhaps not to 1868, but to 1937.

That was the year everything went wrong, as far as some legal activists and scholars are concerned. Franklin Roosevelt's threat of court expansion followed by the Supreme Court's sudden turn away from its accustomed role of blocking extensive economic and social regulation launched the modern constitutional era. In 1937 the Court validated much of the New Deal. The next year, in *Carolene Products*, in that famous footnote number four, it made clear it would uphold economic regulations unless they were unreasonable.

Americans went on to build a modern government. The far-reaching regulatory laws policing Wall Street, governing labor relations, instituting the minimum wage, and more were upheld throughout the mid-twentieth century. In the rebellious 1960s and its aftermath, a new slew of regulatory laws sought to address the excesses of economic growth. They protected clean air and water, ensured worker safety, created the Environmental Protection Agency and the Occupational Safety and Health Administration (OSHA), established agencies to police auto and consumer product safety, and more. A new environmental movement sparked by Rachel Carson's book *Silent Spring* first pushed to ban dangerous pesticides, then to address the full panoply of pollution and toxic chemicals. Dense smog enveloped major cities, and the Cuyahoga River near Cleveland, Ohio, caught on fire. Even the first photos of earth from space heightened environmental awareness. Richard Nixon presented to Congress a thirty-seven-point message imploring it to enact laws to clean up the environment. In 1970 Congress passed the Clean Air Act with only one dissenting vote.

At the same time Ralph Nader, who had exposed the dangers of the Corvair car—"sporty" but prone to roll over—organized a consumer movement even more robust than that of the Progressive Era. In the 1950s a cabinet secretary had said, "What's good for General Motors is good for America." But in 1966 when the auto company sent a private detective to trail Nader, it caused such a scandal that GM's chief executive was forced to apologize to the crusader in front of a congressional committee. With money he won from suing the company Nader formed a fleet of consumer and environmental citizens organizations. In the 1970s it seemed as if their lawyerly approach, focused not on revolution but regulation, had unstoppable momentum. New agencies proliferated; everything from seatbelts in cars to nutrition labels on food, so much of the fabric of modern life, came from this era of expanded consumer activism.

Having enacted these laws in the first flush of enthusiasm for environmental and consumer protection, Congress then largely pulled back from effective policymaking, stymied by intense lobbying, a radically changed campaign finance system, and an increasingly antigovernment Republican caucus. Congress became mired in dysfunction. Agencies staffed with experts were left the task of implementing the law on topics of often fiendish scientific and economic complexity.

Business leaders for many years had been powerful but cautious, content to whisper to friendly congressional committee chairs and confident that regulatory agencies would serve industry as much as the public interest. Major corporations were unprepared for the consumer and environmental wave. Lewis Powell was a lawyer in Richmond, Virginia, who wrote a now legendary memorandum in 1971 for the U.S. Chamber of Commerce, warning in dire terms of an imminent socialist takeover of the country. He urged businesses to mobilize, establish organizations, and map a political strategy to push back. Business would need to engage in "the neglected political arena." And he focused, too, on "The Neglected Opportunity in the Courts." "American business and the enterprise system have been affected as much by the courts as by the executive and legislative branches of government. Under our constitutional system, especially with an activist-minded Supreme Court, the judiciary may be the most important instrument for social, economic and political change." Powell's memo later attained near mythological status; in fact, as one journalist later wryly noted, it was "little noticed and little heeded at the time." Indeed, corporations already had begun to launch think tanks and lobby groups. Still, Powell was prescient in precisely describing the massive, lavish influence operation that would soon be built. Within months he would be named to the Supreme Court.

In 1977 and 1978, in a first major test for new president Jimmy Carter, corporate lobbying defeated legislation to create a new Consumer Protection Agency, as even liberal Democrats recoiled from overregulation at a time of rising inflation. (Also, the new campaign finance system produced by the Supreme Court's ruling in *Buckley v. Valeo* meant that

Democratic incumbents now had to chase campaign funds from business.) New regulation stalled. But libertarians and those who funded them wanted not just to slow but to roll back the regulatory state. They sought a way to declare it unconstitutional.

In the intellectual ferment on the right, one idea took hold among a few activist professors: the Court's surrender to FDR had been a ghastly mistake. They called it the "Constitution in Exile." They believed that economic freedom was a natural right and that there were sharp limits on how much government could infringe upon it. They were convinced the Court had been doing its job up until 1937. The "Constitution in Exile" was a phrase coined by Douglas Ginsburg, the judge whom Reagan had nominated for the Supreme Court but who was forced to withdraw over his past marijuana use. "[T]he Great Depression and the determination of the Roosevelt Administration placed the Supreme Court's commitment to the Constitution as written under severe stress in the 1930s, and it was then that the wheels began to come off," he told a libertarian audience. An influential 2005 *New York Times* article by Jeffrey Rosen identified John Roberts, not yet named to the Supreme Court, as a judge who might be willing to use the Constitution to restrict regulation.

The conservative legal expats cast about for ways to curb government's power over the economy.

Some strategies were misfires. One involved an expanded definition of private property rights. Richard Epstein, a libertarian scholar at the University of Chicago, proposed using the Fifth Amendment's Takings Clause, which says that government cannot seize property without paying just compensation. Epstein had argued that government should pay not only if it took land through eminent domain, but if it regulated a business in a way that hurt its economic interests. He chided the Court, for example, when it let New York City government stop a massive skyscraper from being built atop Grand Central Terminal, all without paying the train station owners. When Clarence Thomas testified at his confirmation hearing, Joe Biden theatrically waved a copy of Epstein's dense book and demanded to know whether it influenced the nominee's thinking. In any event, the Supreme Court rarely bought the idea that regulation amounted to seizing property.

Then the activists took a run at the Commerce Clause, that capacious constitutional provision that empowered the federal government to regulate the national economy. John Marshall had described the clause as a potent instrument of federal power, ruling in 1824 that it "may be exercised to its utmost extent." During the *Lochner* era, the business-protective justices said the federal government could not apply its laws to manufacturing or the economy more broadly, only to sales of products across state lines. In 1937, as part of their headlong retreat during the court packing fight, the justices again recognized the federal government's ability to organize the market. We had a huge, intricate, interconnected national economy, increasingly linked to trade and the flow of capital around the world. A major multibillion-dollar industry such as health insurance was practically the definition of interstate commerce.

But in 2012 five justices voted to strike down the Affordable Care Act's requirement that people purchase private health insurance as beyond the reach of the Commerce Clause. The Constitution, they wrote, did not give the federal government the power to make people buy insurance, even as part of a broader national scheme for universal coverage. The case showed how conservative legal arguments had now moved from the periphery to the center of debate as if flung by a slingshot.

For example, none other than John Eastman—not yet infamous as the coup plotter who urged Mike Pence to overturn the 2020 election—went on Fox News to say, "If the government can order you to buy health insurance it can order you to buy broccoli, it can order you to buy General Motors cars." Soon enough at oral argument Scalia mocked, "Everybody has to buy food sooner or later. Therefore, you can make people buy broccoli." Scalia and three other conservatives wanted to rule that the failure to buy insurance was not an act "affecting commerce," so the whole law would fall. Roberts agreed with them on the Commerce Clause, but upheld the law anyway on other constitutional grounds. The Affordable Care Act survived.

For years, it seemed the Court might be able to sharply limit regulation by curbing the authority of agencies themselves, effectively shifting power instead to federal judges. Over the past century Congress has created about one hundred separate regulatory agencies to make rules on topics ranging from auto safety to pension funds: topics, in other words, requiring significant technical expertise. Sometimes Congress—deadlocked between interest groups—gives a broad charge to an agency, passing responsibility along with legislation. In 1984 the Supreme Court ruled that courts will defer to expert agencies when they interpret a law with ambiguous wording. Judges will not second-guess that approach if the agency has made a reasonable choice. This is called "*Chevron* deference," after the case in which the doctrine was first propounded. The Supreme Court has applied it over one hundred times. It has been the basis of thousands of legal decisions (or nondecisions) throughout the federal courts.

Surprisingly, this notion of giving latitude to regulatory agencies came from conservatives. When he swept into office, Ronald Reagan appointed New Right activists to run the agencies. Many wanted to eliminate the offices where they worked altogether, and they collaborated closely with industry to pursue deregulation. *Chevron*—which involved a case brought by environmental advocates at the Natural Resources Defense Council—was seen as a way to protect conservative regulators from interference by federal courts, which then were stacked with liberal judges. Antonin Scalia championed this permutation of judicial restraint.

Indeed, *Chevron* came in an era when the Environmental Protection Agency itself was consumed with scandal and drama. Its administrator, Anne Gorsuch, was a charismatic thirty-eight-year-old Colorado state legislator who led a faction called the "House Crazies." The *Rocky Mountain News* wrote admiringly, "She could kick a bear to death with her bare feet." The second-highest-ranking woman in the Reagan administration, she became one of its most flamboyant and controversial officials. As EPA administrator she cut staff by 22 percent in one year and filled senior ranks with alumni of the industries they now regulated. Environmentalists denounced and Congress investigated. *The New York Times* admonished she had "inherited one of the most efficient and capable agencies of government. She has turned it into an Augean stable, reeking of cynicism, mismanagement and decay."

One scandal involved the administration of the Superfund program, which cleaned up toxic waste sites. Following White House orders, Gorsuch refused to turn over documents to congressional investigators and became the first agency head ever to be cited for contempt of Congress. "A year in jail and a $1,000 fine versus faithfully serving the President of the United States? I will continue faithfully serving," she declared.

Gorsuch was forced to resign in 1983, complaining that "it's hard to lead a normal life when there are people camped in your front yard." Her memoir recounts her teenage son Neil responding angrily to her stepping down. "You raised me not to be a quitter. Why are you a quitter," he demanded. "He was really upset," she added. The administration cast her adrift, forcing her to pay for her own legal defense. In her memoir, she called it an "expensive mid-life education." Reagan tried to reward her with a minor advisory job. The Senate voted 74 to 19 to oppose her getting the post. She responded by calling the job a "nothingburger." (Her usage was the first time the word appeared in the news pages, though it had been used earlier by *Cosmopolitan*'s Helen Gurley Brown. Credit Gorsuch for its ubiquity in politics.) Washington, D.C., she charged at the time, was "too small to be a state but too large to be an asylum for the mentally deranged."

By 2022, her son Neil Gorsuch had sat on the Supreme Court for five years. Instead of seeking to give the EPA more autonomy to deregulate, he sought to curb its power, now that the agency was peopled not by Reagan Revolutionaries but rather the entrenched "administrative state." He was as sober and buttoned-down as his mother was hot-blooded; she wanted to curb the EPA's authority from within, he wanted to curb it from the bench, but they had similar goals: limiting regulation of business.

For years it seemed the Court was ready to undo *Chevron*, or at least to trim it significantly. Scalia was the doctrine's great champion. After he died the Court essentially stopped citing it. Each June environmentalists and business lawyers waited expectantly. And each June, the justices pulled back.

A typically tantalizing example came in mid-June 2022. A case brought by the American Hospital Association challenged the Health and Human Services department for interpreting federal law in a way that reduced prescription drug reimbursements for some hospitals. Antiregulation groups pelted the Court with briefs demanding that it at last repudiate *Chevron*. The Koch brothers' influential Americans for Prosperity group proclaimed, "Nowhere in the Constitution does it say or even suggest the People have agreed to be ruled by unelected, politically unaccountable government 'experts.'" In a season of judicial radicalism, with precedents toppling, this seemed like the moment.

But while the Court ruled unanimously for the hospitals, it avoided any mention at all of *Chevron* deference. Another punt on the issue.

Then came the final decision of the term, which relied on a doctrine that had never been articulated, had inspired no reams of law review articles, and which threatened to blow open a hole in the regulatory state.

The case came out of a tangle of legislative and White House attempts to address climate change.

For decades scientists worldwide had all but screamed that carbon emissions threatened to devastate human life. "It's now or never," wrote the United Nations secretary-general in the spring of 2022, releasing yet another assessment by hundreds of scientists. Indeed, the world was suffering through its warmest decade on record, with six of its hottest years ever. Over the previous summer fires from the Northwest woods spewed smoke over much of the country. Floods walloped towns in Kentucky. Hurricanes ravaged the South. Even Texas was enveloped in a winter storm that led to power outages, a storm worsened by climate change.

America's broken political system now had a global impact. Among the major democracies, only in the United States did the more conservative of the political parties now deny the existence of the crisis. Fewer than one in three Republicans believe that climate change is real and has begun to have effects. Policies veered abruptly. Bill Clinton, who signed an international agreement on climate change, was followed by George W. Bush, who withdrew from it. The night Barack Obama clinched the Democratic nomination in 2008, he proclaimed that "this was the moment when the rise of the oceans began to slow and our planet began to heal." He was followed by Donald Trump, who called climate change a "hoax" concocted by China.

Divided government produced paralysis. America's system of checks, balances, and veto points where special interests could thwart policy moves made it worse. For all but twelve years in the past half century Republicans and Democrats have split control of the White House and at least one chamber in Congress. With the two parties polarized, pulled by voters and campaign funds to ideological poles, and hardened in tactics, basic legislation stalled, let alone major efforts to impose short-term pain for long-term gain—or survival.

It had been decades since Congress passed a major environmental regulatory law. Meanwhile presidents increasingly turned in frustration to executive action and administrative measures. (When their allies control Congress, chief executives act with less bravado, out of sensitivity to congressional egos and prerogatives.) Democratic presidents, in particular, relied on executive action to advance domestic policies. Elena Kagan's long scholarly article before she joined the Court, "Presidential Administration," was about this very topic. Republican presidents tended to argue for expanded executive power in foreign affairs and war making, claiming the "unitary executive" had allowed "enhanced interrogation methods" and other tortured interpretations. Trump melded both archetypes: he focused especially on immigration, such as when he declared a national emergency to secure funds to try to build a wall on the border with Mexico.

Congress's struggle to find a way to reduce carbon emissions was nothing new. In 2003, when Republicans controlled government, John McCain unsuccessfully tried to pass legislation to create a system of carbon trading, where companies could sell their right to pollute, at an overall diminishing rate, marrying market methods to environmental goals. In 2009, despite the economic crash and high unemployment of the Great Recession, Congress tried again. The House passed an ambitious climate bill, but it was blocked by a Senate filibuster, a resistance spurred by the political power of fossil fuel companies and fear of job loss. (Coal companies staged protests where miners held signs reading COAL KEEPS THE LIGHTS ON, while the American Petroleum Institute ran ads calling for "more jobs, not more taxes.")

Meeting with his cabinet for its first session of 2014, Obama declared he would go it alone. "I've got a pen, and I've got a phone," he said. He would use executive orders and administrative action to advance goals, with climate change a top priority. The EPA launched a Clean Power Plan to limit emissions of greenhouse gases and encourage utilities—responsible for a third of carbon emissions—to shift from coal to cleaner technologies including natural gas, wind, and solar power. By 2030 the plan would produce a 32 percent cut in carbon pollution from 2005 levels, according to agency estimates. The much hyped plan never went into effect. Trump canceled it upon taking office and appointed an EPA administrator who had denied that carbon caused climate change, and who suggested a warmer planet would be a good thing. Meanwhile, by 2019 the power industry had reduced carbon emissions to the target level, eleven years ahead of schedule, because state governments had acted and natural gas prices had fallen so low. Lawsuits drifted along like smog. The Biden administration indicated it would start over. Long after Obama's plan had been repudiated by the Trump administration, the Supreme Court heard a lawsuit challenging its legal basis.

West Virginia brought the case. Coal once dominated, and still played an outsized role in the state's gritty self-image. By now, West Virginia produced only 13 percent of the coal mined in the United States, and its number of coal miners had fallen sharply over the decade. But the extraction industry still loomed large in the state's economy. The state government and a coal company charged that the EPA had exceeded its statutory authority in devising the Clean Power Plan. The Supreme Court had already confirmed that the agency had broad authority to try to address climate change. Carbon dioxide—even though it was invisible and safe to breathe—was deemed a pollutant given its catastrophic effect. To impose Obama's new rules the EPA relied on the Clean Air Act, the law last amended in 1990 that gave it broad authority. The law also let the agency regulate power plants and determine the "best for emissions reduction." At first, West Virginia pursued a narrow agenda, arguing the environmental agency had misread the statute. Then when Barrett replaced Ginsburg, the state swung for the fences—arguing that the agency had not misread the statute, but that the Constitution blocked such action.

Once again, the Supreme Court attracted amicus briefs like metal filings to a magnet. Once again, the briefs were from an array of groups, many with similar-sounding names, often funded by a few fossil fuel companies and trade groups.

John Roberts wrote the opinion in *West Virginia v. EPA*, joined by the other conservatives. Kagan, Breyer, and Sotomayor dissented. The justices ruled that the long-canceled Clean Power Plan could not go into effect. The Court did not claim that the agency had misread the statute; it had not. It did not, in the end, address the *Chevron* doctrine or hold that Congress could not delegate its power. Rather, it articulated a new "major questions doctrine," one that limited the power of agencies to act when a matter was really important. It was, as former

NYU Law dean Richard Revesz summarized, the most important environmental ruling in over a decade, one that threatened all future regulation.

The opinion held, in essence, that Congress could not have meant to give the EPA the power to act on something so important without being clear about it, even if the statutory language let the agency act. Roberts wrote: "Extraordinary grants of regulatory authority are rarely accomplished through modest words, vague terms, or subtle device[s]. Nor does Congress typically use oblique or elliptical language to empower an agency to make a radical or fundamental change to a statutory scheme." The part of the Clean Air Act on which the agency relied was a "backwater," Roberts wrote, a "gap filler."

> In certain extraordinary cases, both separation of powers principles and a practical understanding of legislative intent make us reluctant to read into ambiguous statutory text the delegation claimed to be lurking there. To convince us otherwise, something more than a merely plausible textual basis for the agency action is necessary. The agency instead must point to clear congressional authorization for the power it claims.

The agency had a "plausible textual basis" for acting, Roberts admitted. But even so, the agency couldn't do it, because of the plan's "economic and political significance." Given that, Congress must give explicit authority. Boiled down, the new doctrine says that if a topic is so important, so urgent, that action is essential, then that means the agency cannot act. It is a constitutional Catch-22.

The opinion never measured how much "economic and political significance" was too significant. The regulation never went into effect, after all, and industry had already met its goals ahead of schedule. Instead, the Court mostly fretted about how the plan was just too novel. Evidently, since EPA never did it before, it could not do so now, even if the text of the statute allows it to.

The new "doctrine" will check government's ability to meet emergencies, short- or long-term. It purported to honor the role of elected members of Congress, but they have already voted for laws with broad empowering language. So in fact, the decision about what health and safety measures can proceed now would be made by federal judges assessing agency actions, a disproportionate number of whom are now dogmatic conservatives with lifetime appointments and little political accountability.

And that is where Neil Gorsuch came in. Roberts wrote the *West Virginia* opinion. But for Gorsuch, finding a way to curb the power of regulatory agencies is a crusade—intellectual, political, even moral. The majority opinion never says when a topic is so "major" that the regulatory agency cannot follow the law to issue regulations, but Gorsuch expounded with relish in a concurrence joined by Alito. Its implications are, not surprisingly, major.

He took direct aim at a core principle of government for the past century: that some complex problems require scientific, medical, or economic expertise—and that Congress has the power to delegate major responsibility to address these issues to government agencies. Gorsuch began the treatise with an oddly intense footnote aimed at Woodrow Wilson. The takedown of the long-ago president is a dog whistle, highly meaningful to some, baffling to most. Wilson became a target of revisionist right-wing pop historians such as Glenn Beck and Jonah Goldberg who claimed his attempt to build a regulatory state was incipient dictatorship. Liberalism, they insist, was just fascism with an American accent. More recently, those on the left object to Wilson's virulent racist views (he segregated the civil service and premiered the pro-Klan film *The Birth of a Nation* at the White House). Once Wilson was admired by Richard Nixon and echoed by George W. Bush, but by decade's end, the former president had his name stripped from the public policy school at Princeton (an institution which was Alito's alma mater and an object of much of his ire).

With gusto, Gorsuch then offered a defense of lawmaking by elected officials. Legislating "is difficult," he admits. But by "effectively requiring a broad consensus to pass legislation, the Constitution sought to ensure that any new laws would enjoy wide social acceptance, profit from input by an array of different perspectives during their consideration, and thanks to all this prove stable over time." All true, and admirable. Yet again Congress has repeatedly passed and strengthened clean air laws, and given the EPA wide latitude to figure out what pollutants should be limited and how to do so. Gorsuch's highly articulate defense of lawmakers, stirring as it is, would be more persuasive if he had not just days before signed the opinion that stripped those same politicians of much of their ability to balance goals by crafting gun safety laws. (Gorsuch also joined in the opinion eviscerating Congress's version of the Voting Rights Act, one of the cases from *Citizens United* onward that blocked the democratically elected branch from protecting democratic rights.)

Roberts's implicit vision of "major questions" is, "I know it when I see it." Or, as the dissent charges and the opinion embraces, when it "raises an eyebrow." Gorsuch was more specific. Agencies could not act without "clear congressional authorization" when the matter has "political significance" or affects "a significant portion of the American economy." Similarly agencies cannot act if a rule "intrudes" on something typically covered by state law. He calls these "triggers"—it seems a regulation could trip any of them. The electric power industry is just too big, and the impact of the Clean Power Plan just too significant, for the agency to rely only on the language of environmental statutes.

Kagan wrote the dissent with some bafflement and, perhaps, horror. This was, she pointed out, the very first time that any Supreme Court governing opinion used the phrase "major questions doctrine." She noted that "a key reason Congress makes broad delegations . . . is so an agency can respond, appropriately and commensurately, to new and big problems." The statute authorized the agency to act. Indeed, the majority did not really dispute that the law did this. "Some years ago, I remarked that we're all textualists now. . . . It seems I was wrong. The current Court is textualist only when being so suits it. When that method would frustrate broader goals, special canons like the major questions doctrine magically appear as get-out-of-text-free cards."

Gorsuch's concurrence, with its detail and erudition (and snark), marked his full emergence as the voice of regulatory rollback within the supermajority.

Gorsuch spent most of his legal career in Washington, D.C. When his mother moved to the capital to run the EPA he enrolled at Georgetown Prep, the Catholic school in Maryland where he was two years behind Brett Kavanaugh. He was there when his mother resigned and became a punch line in editorial cartoons and even comic strips. This very particular inside-the-Beltway trauma was Gorsuch's origin story. He attended Columbia University, Harvard Law School, and Oxford, and wrote a well-regarded book on the ethics and law of assisted suicide.

He chose to practice law at a small start-up firm in the capital rather than join a lobbying powerhouse, and then was appointed to a federal appeals court in Colorado.

He landed on Trump's list of could-be-justices during the 2016 campaign, the roster prepared by the Federalist Society and approved by its leader Leonard Leo. Trump was known to pick cabinet secretaries by whether they "looked the part"; lean, square-jawed Gorsuch surely did. A fluffy *Washington Post* article gushed that "when it comes to laws, Gorsuch, like Scalia, is a textualist, who believes that only the actual words written in a statute matter—not legislators' intent or any potential consequences of a judge's decisions." It predicted he would find "a homespun truth somewhere in between" left and right.

Mostly, once on the bench Gorsuch found his homespun truth on the far right. In his first fifteen cases, according to the data-crunching website *FiveThirtyEight*, he voted with Thomas each time, and even joined in all of Thomas's concurrences. In earlier eras conservative justices might surprise by drifting toward the center and even landing on the left. The Federalist Society's vetting-in-advance has made that increasingly unlikely. Gorsuch managed to annoy the other justices from the start. Writing in dissent on the first case he heard, he schooled his colleagues: "If a statute needs repair, there's a constitutionally prescribed way to do it. It's called legislation." In his first few months, Gorsuch wrote on his own seven times. Roberts seemed to rebuke him in a speech. "You do have to take into account other people's views," he said without naming names, adding, "It's not just about you."

Over time Gorsuch etched out an occasionally idiosyncratic path. Earlier jurists appointed by Richard Nixon embodied that president's "law-and-order" backlash. Gorsuch arrived at a time when left and right coalesced on the need for criminal justice reform, perhaps briefly. Motivations differed. Progressives focused most on mass incarceration's harsh racial impact. (An example: Black and white people used marijuana at the same rate, but nationwide Black people were nearly four times more likely to be arrested for possession.) Conservatives and libertarians had multiple motives—worries about cost, religious conviction—and above all, a libertarian distrust of government overreach. The Koch brothers were reliable and committed reformers. To them, it seemed, mass incarceration was just as bad as the tyranny of the FDA, all a part of a big government leviathan.

Soon after Gorsuch was confirmed, crime again began to rise, and the issue began to be a subject of intense polarization once more. In rulings and dissents, even before he joined the Court, he had a noteworthy dedication to the Fourth Amendment. At one oral argument in 2019, he mused to a government attorney, "We live in a world in which everything has been criminalized. Some professors have even opined that there's not an American alive who hasn't committed a felony." In that case, he and the other justices ruled unanimously that a police officer who chased a driver into his own garage, and there administered a sobriety test, which the unfortunate individual failed spectacularly, had needed a search warrant.

Before *West Virginia v. EPA*, no doubt, he would have wanted to be known for his devotion to textualism. That's a close cousin to originalism: it looks not at the Constitution (with its often deliberately vague language) but statutes. Throughout most of the country's history, courts not only scrutinized the clauses and commas of statutes for instructions, but also looked at the legislation's purpose, for example. They took seriously the legislative history—often voluminous committee reports or debates in the *Congressional Record*—where lawmakers explained their goals in great detail. Judges asked what members of Congress were trying to do, and took the answers seriously. As Robert Katzmann, a judge who urged a realistic view of how the world actually worked, noted, "If Congress passes energy legislation with an accompanying committee report providing detailed direction to the Department of Energy, it is unfathomable that the Secretary of Energy or any other responsible agency officials would ignore that report, let alone not read that report."

Textualists scorned legislative history. Scalia, for example, seemed to regard elected officials as crass, shallow, and endlessly lusting for the love of a fickle public. To him it did not matter that Congress itself, in creating the laws, intended the legislative history to matter. Textualism shared with originalism a focus on the "original public meaning" of the words on the page, relying, as ever, on dictionaries. There were limits: textualism was supposed to be abandoned when the result would be "absurd," for example.

Somehow, though, in practice textualism often magically seemed to align with conservative policy preferences or Republican dogma.

Gorsuch to his credit was more willing than most to break with that. Most notably he did so in the *Bostock* case, the breakthrough ruling on gay rights that appeared to have leaked to the conservative-lawyer-gossip-circuit, and thence to the media. Gorsuch's adherence to the text of the Civil Rights Act compelled him to agree that it did prohibit discrimination based on sexual orientation or identity. Surely that was not what the cigar-chomping politicians of 1964 had in mind. Indeed, Lyndon Johnson's top White House aide Walter Jenkins had to resign after he was arrested for "disorderly conduct" at a YMCA just a few months after the act was signed into law. Gorsuch—again, reflecting personal character as well as generational ethos—had a history of friendship with gay people, and presumably was not entirely averse to ruling as he did. Carrie Severino of the Judicial Crisis Network, which had spent $10 million campaigning for Gorsuch's confirmation, was aghast. Gorsuch had "bungled textualism," she wrote, "for the sake of appealing to college campuses and editorial boards."

In *Bostock* rigid textualism proved a powerful if surprising tool for justice. But in *West Virginia v. EPA*, with Gorsuch's larger project of reining in government and its power at stake, he flinched.

Clarence Thomas bent the Court to his lone dissents over many years. Gorsuch seems determined to do the same—focusing on the very topic that was the source of *his* childhood drama, the battle between corporate interests and zealous environmentalists. Aiming for an even broader and more radical result than produced by "major questions," Gorsuch has begun to urge his colleagues to once again use the "nondelegation doctrine" to strike down rules they do not like. This is the idea that Congress, which is given the lawmaking power by the Constitution, cannot delegate that power to expert agencies—even if it wants to.

The Supreme Court has not struck down a statute on nondelegation grounds since it did so three times in 1935 and 1936 during its doomed war with the New Deal (for some, the true Lost Cause). Gorsuch rattled the cage by dissenting from an otherwise unremarkable case on sex abuse sanctions, and brought Roberts and Thomas along to call for a full reexamination of nondelegation. In *Gundy v. United States*, Gorsuch launched a flare, marking out a position to which he could return in future cases, and which other judges lower down in the court system would see. By "directing that legislating be done only by elected representatives in a public process," he wrote, "the Constitution sought to ensure that the lines of accountability would be clear: The sovereign people would know, without ambiguity, whom to hold accountable for the laws they would have to follow." Ringing words, but the implications would be to reorder the entire shape of the federal government, and given the reality in Congress and the country, prevent effective action on much of what the country wants government to do.

In *West Virginia v. EPA* the Supreme Court did not obliterate the federal government's ability to act on climate change. Later in the summer, senators reached agreement on long-stalled budget legislation. The Inflation Reduction Act (rebranded from Build Back Better) included $369 billion to encourage a transition to clean energy. It was the biggest climate change bill ever enacted in the United States. Significantly, it achieved progress not by regulating but by spending. That was partly due to Senate rules. A bill regulating carbon, say, would effectively require 60 votes and hence Republican support to pass. Budget reconciliation bills can pass with a simple majority if they spend (or save) significant governmental funds. The Senate parliamentarian watches with an eagle eye to ensure that any merely regulatory language does not slip into such legislation. Senate dysfunction combined with the newly launched Supreme Court rollback of regulatory authority creates perverse incentives: major bills can be enacted only if they spend gobs of money.

Buried in the budget bill was language designed to strengthen the EPA's hand. It defined greenhouse gasses as "pollution" for some spending programs and made clear that the agency should try to address climate change. Republicans discovered the provision as the legislation hurtled toward final passage. Frantically late at night they implored the Senate parliamentarian to strip it from the bill. She issued her ruling: the language stayed, shortly before the legislation passed with Vice President Kamala Harris breaking the tie. (Another oddity of American government: the little-known parliamentarian rules whether language can remain in a budget bill—it must spend or save money— and Senate Democrats obey her rulings with the ardent intensity of a Federalist Society acolyte following the jottings of James Madison.) Some hyperventilating media reports suggested this act "overturned" *West Virginia v. EPA*. It did not: the Inflation Reduction Act did not give the EPA the power to restart the "generation shifting" program (perhaps because West Virginia senator Manchin was the key vote for the bill). Still, it was a quick example of the ways Congress can allay the impact of a Court ruling.

West Virginia v. EPA, as some observers breathed relief, was not as bad as it could have been. "More gloom than doom," one headline explained, trying to be helpful. After all, the plan's emissions targets already had been rendered moot. The Court did not overturn *Chevron* altogether. Conservatives celebrated: it was "a long-overdue step to rein in an agency that has exerted hydra-like control over much of the U.S. economy through its regulations on virtually every activity that uses energy," exulted one writer at *National Review*. But as with the ruling on the Second Amendment, the impact will likely come not today but in its logical implication for dozens of other laws and rules.

"Major questions" is just a minor variation on nondelegation. "The contours of the major questions doctrine will be unknowable until the Supreme Court decides additional cases," scholar Ricky Revesz wrote. "But in the meantime, enterprising red-state attorneys general will aggressively invoke the major questions doctrine to challenge the Biden administration's regulatory programs."

The supermajority's response to government regulation has just begun to take shape. Throughout the term the Court issued a mixed set of rulings curbing government authority, especially around Covid. The worker safety agency OSHA could not require workplaces to have employees vaccinated or masked and tested, for example. States, however, could do much the same thing, following a hundred-year-old public health precedent. Health agencies could not extend a moratorium on evictions, a position that even the Biden White House at first admitted might be right. Each time, Gorsuch and others ruled against regulatory powers the government had taken for granted for decades.

But the Supreme Court is only the final stop. Throughout the federal system, judges—mostly appointed by Trump—are issuing rulings that would have seemed outlandish just a few years ago, decisions that would cripple government's ability to protect safety.

It all offers a window on how the new notes from the high court echo and amplify across the country.

Meet Kathryn Mizelle, a Federalist Society member and graduate of Covenant College who had clerked for Clarence Thomas. Just thirty-three years old, she was an associate at a law firm when Trump nominated her to be a federal judge. The American Bar Association rated her "Not Qualified." The Senate confirmed Mizelle nonetheless on a party-line vote weeks after Trump lost the 2020 election. In 2022 she struck down one of the main responses to Covid-19, ruling that the Centers for Disease Control lacked the authority to require masks on airplanes and trains in a global pandemic. The judge did not rule that the mask mandate had outlived its usefulness, or that enough people were now vaccinated. Rather, she ruled that the nation's premier public health agency could not make a rule in the first place to protect against a fast-moving and deadly threat to public health. "At first blush," she admitted in the opinion, what CDC did would appear to be "closely related to the powers granted" by law. The law creating the CDC gives it the power "to make and enforce such regulations as in [its] judgment are necessary to prevent the introduction, transmission, or spread of communicable diseases." In the next sentence, it explains, "for purposes of carrying out and enforcing such regulations," the CDC "may provide for such inspection, fumigation, disinfection, sanitation . . . and other measures as in [its] judgment may be necessary." A mask mandate surely sounds like a rather snug fit. Baffled by the ruling, a conservative professor wrote, "It seems to me that mandatory masking to prevent the spread of a respiratory virus at least plausibly fits within the meaning of 'sanitation.' "

Not to Mizelle. The law has been "rarely invoked. . . . At least until recently." (It is true that we had not had any epic global pandemics of late.) "Sanitation," she reasoned over a twelve-page analysis, means something like taking out the trash, scrubbing the floors, or "measures to keep something clean." For this insight she relied on dictionaries from the 1940s. She admitted that the requirement for masks on airplanes and in subways to help keep the passengers clean fits the statute . . . but she preferred another definition of sanitation that did not. The opinion read like a parody by someone spoofing textualism.

Writing in *The New Yorker*, attorney Fabio Bertoni found what may be the perfect way to explain what could be so maddening about such rulings: the children's book character Amelia Bedelia. The eager housekeeper takes words hyper-literally, out of context, and thus misreads their meaning in ways preschoolers find hilarious. (Told to "put the lights out," she unscrews the bulbs and carefully hangs them outdoors.) "We are all textualists now," but increasingly, "we are all Amelia Bedelia."

The mask ruling came two years into the pandemic, when people were sick of wearing masks and even many who had dutifully complied now doubted how necessary it still was. Perhaps the pandemic was shifting to something endemic, something we all lived with. The young judge lived in a state where the governor had reaped political benefit by loudly opposing masks. After her decision was announced, cell phone videos showed passengers on airplanes cheering midflight. But the ruling's logic did not apply only to health crises two years in; it would apply, too, to future pandemics, to the next time we live through terrifying days like those at the start of Covid-19.

The Biden administration was so flummoxed by the court's action that it wavered about what to do. Eventually it decided not to appeal to the Supreme Court, out of fear that the supermajority might issue a ruling that would be truly catastrophic for public health. The lower courts are now dotted with Judge Mizelles, Federalist Society true believers with lifetime appointments and many years ahead of them. Due to an unresolved issue in federal law, these judges have taken to issuing nationwide injunctions to stop government policies, and strategically minded litigants have found ways to steer litigation into their courtrooms. (Liberal groups did this, too, when Trump was president; now conservatives know to head straight to Amarillo, Texas, or Tampa, Florida, to block Biden.)

Lower courts now are issuing rulings that—if appealed to the Supreme Court—could provide the next opportunity to hack away at government's authority, rulings with more destructive potential than the *West Virginia* case. Perhaps the most unnerving such ruling came in Texas, in July 2022. More or less out of nowhere, it declared unconstitutional the principal way the Securities and Exchange Commission polices against securities fraud.

Since the earliest days of the New Deal, the SEC has regulated the stock market and sought to protect investors against fraud. Its success has been one of the main reasons the economy no longer swerves from speculative bubble to ruinous crash. Congress gave it new power after the economic collapse in 2008, at a time when the country suffered from home foreclosures, bankruptcies, toxic mortgage-backed securities, multimillion-dollar frauds by the likes of Bernie Madoff, and failing investment banks. Under the Dodd-Frank law, which modernized financial regulation, investors and others could bring actions before administrative law judges at the SEC. The agency could level fines aimed at those engaged in misconduct. This became a principal way the agency protected against securities fraud, and let consumers and investors avoid the cost and length of filing a lawsuit. Think of it as a kind of "small claims court" for investors.

Indeed, administrative law judges appointed by the president play a similar role at dozens of other regulatory agencies. UCLA professor Blake Emerson explains, "Administrative adjudication is a key aspect of how modern government functions. Congress has required federal agencies to decide large numbers of cases regarding issues such as labor rights, race and sex discrimination, workplace safety, immigration, disability and veterans' benefits, unfair trade practices, and much more." If individuals are unhappy with the result, they can appeal to a federal court. But vast stretches of the everyday work of government is done this way. These public protections are very popular. Congress does not usually want to undo them. And congressional paralysis works both ways—as hard as it was to pass the Affordable Care Act, for example, Republicans never could muster the votes to undo it. As a structural matter, then, conservatives turn to the courts to accomplish what they cannot do legislatively.

Wall Street was reeling when the Dodd-Frank law was enacted in 2010, but soon recovered nicely. Its ruddy vigor restored, it began to mount a full attack on the new enforcement regime—with lawsuits, conferences, articles, and more lawsuits. After a decade, advocates found receptive judges on the fervently conservative Fifth Circuit Court of Appeals. Judge Jennifer Elrod wrote the opinion. Active in the Federalist Society even after she was appointed to the federal bench, Elrod earlier had upheld the harsh Texas abortion law that was vetoed by the U.S. Supreme Court in 2016. In May 2022, Elrod and Andrew Oldham—a former counsel to Texas governor Greg Abbott who had clerked for Alito—declared that the Securities and Exchange Commission's entire system of using administrative judges to hear claims of securities fraud was unconstitutional. "The Seventh Amendment guarantees Petitioners a jury trial because the SEC's enforcement action is akin to traditional actions at law to which the jury-trial right attaches," they thundered, quoting Thomas Jefferson, John Adams, and others in the pantheon of American freedom. (The opinion is filled with Easter Eggs for conservatives, too. At one point it quotes Ronald Reagan saying "the most terrifying nine words in the English language" but not identifying what they were. Only buffs would know them: "I'm from the government, and I'm here to help." It even blames the whole thing on Woodrow Wilson, claiming erroneously that he was "the instigator of the agency that became the SEC." It cites a book promoted by Glenn Beck on Fox News.)

The judges did not make a technical ruling or follow the practice of "constitutional avoidance." They chose constitutional confrontation. The two judges say that these administrative proceedings deprive accused fraudsters of their right to a jury trial. More significantly, they ruled that the fact that Congress gave the administrative law judges themselves the power to make these rulings was itself unconstitutional. The Supreme Court has not formally revived "nondelegation," so these judges leapt ahead. Moreover, the provisions protecting those SEC officials from political retaliation were unconstitutional, too. Presidents could pressure these regulators or fire them at will, the judges ruled.

This all lays bare an internal contradiction in conservative legal theory. Aren't these the same people who want maximum presidential power? The same judicial activists who want to curb the power of regulators (by eliminating *Chevron* deference) also believe in the "unitary executive theory," the idea that the president has been given complete control over all activities of the executive branch and can set its policy with little restraint. The seeming contradiction is less than it appears. In effect, federal courts would police the expert agencies. Meanwhile, presidents personally would exert nearly unfettered control, constrained only by a weak Congress. In recent years, that conservative Republicans have most often controlled the courts and the presidency—but not always Congress or the regulatory agencies—suggests this emerging doctrine may aim above all to consolidate ideological and even partisan power, wrapped in the garb of constitutional theory.

The pre-1937 Constitution may still be in exile, but perhaps not for long.

PART FOUR

THE FIGHT
AHEAD

CHAPTER SIXTEEN

RACE AND DEMOCRACY

B Y THE TIME THE SUPREME COURT completed its term, the country was in an uproar.

Some rituals and rhythms remained. The justices' clerks, their golden careers now clouded by suspicion of leaking, left for their next jobs with the whodunit unsolved. Ketanji Brown Jackson formally took her seat. Justices left to teach, or for junkets to meet with other jurists in picturesque locations. Each justice is responsible for a circuit of the court, and often they speak at conferences of judges. Usually those speeches are circumspect. At times clues are dropped. (Ruth Bader Ginsburg told one meeting before the Affordable Care Act case was announced that it had been an unusually "taxing" term, though few got the hint about how the health law would be upheld.)

A few weeks after the term ended, Elena Kagan spoke to the judges of the Ninth Circuit, which includes California and other western states, at the Big Sky Resort in Montana. Kagan looked drained, in no mood for wisecracks. A panel of judges interviewed her. They asked an obvious if painful question: how could the Supreme Court maintain its legitimacy? Kagan plainly had thought through her answer. Her tone was even but her warning was dire.

"I'm not talking about any particular decision or even any particular series of decisions, but if over time the court loses all connection with the public and with public sentiment, that's a dangerous thing for a democracy," she said. After all, "nobody can throw the bums out."

Kagan continued:

The way the Court retains its legitimacy and fosters public confidence is by acting like a court. By doing the kinds of
things that do not seem to people political or partisan. By not
behaving as though we are just people with individual political,
or policy, or social preferences that we are making everybody
live with. But that instead, we are acting like a court, doing
something that is recognizably law-like.

And that's where we gain our legitimacy. Not because we
have better opinions than anybody else. There is no reason
why the nine of us should be able to make the rules for democracy. Nine unaccountable people, people who haven't been
elected. There is no reason why the nine of us should have the
right to have their opinions hold sway, except for the fact that
they are due in law and that they are advancing the rule of law
in everything they do.

The Court, she said, could retain its legitimacy if it honored precedent, if it followed consistent rules for decision making (such as textualism or originalism even when they do not produce the desired
outcomes), and when it held back from being activist. "If one justice
leaves the Court or dies, and another justice takes his or her place—
and all of sudden the law changes on you," she said, "that doesn't seem
like law." Kagan quoted Roberts's maxim approvingly: if a court is not
required to act, it is required not to act.

She had another warning. This was not the only time this had happened. There have been other times, she said, when the Supreme Court
was "unconstrained and undisciplined," when justices "really just attempted
to basically enact their own policy or political or social preferences."

Kagan, Breyer, and Sotomayor had signed their *Dobbs* dissent in
"sadness." Weeks later that had not dissipated.

Samuel Alito struck a different tone in a different locale. His was
a victory lap. He went to Rome to speak to yet another audience affili-
ated with Notre Dame Law School—its new Religious Liberty Initiative,
which had filed friend of the court briefs in *Dobbs* and other cases,
with a perfect winning record. The institute's director—who had taken
a leave to clerk for Neil Gorsuch in the recent tumultuous term—
introduced Alito. "This is a man who has done much for religious liberty and other important values," she said earnestly, "at great sacrifice

to himself and his family, and with extraordinary courage." Sporting a raffish beard and wearing a tuxedo, basking in applause from the audience of donors and professors, Alito interrupted his written speech to sarcastically mock critics of the Court.

"I had the honor this term of writing I think the only Supreme Court decision in the history of that institution that has been lambasted by a whole string of foreign leaders," Alito said, noting they felt "perfectly fine commenting on American law." "One of these was former prime minister Boris Johnson. But he paid the price," Alito continued, closing his eyes as the audience laughed and clapped. (The frenetic British leader recently had announced his resignation.) He mentioned French president Emmanuel Macron and Canadian prime minister Justin Trudeau.

"But what really wounded me—what really wounded me," he mocked, "was when the Duke of Sussex addressed the United Nations and seemed to compare the decision 'whose name may not be spoken' with the Russian attack on Ukraine." (Prince Harry had called 2022 "a painful year in a painful decade," mentioning both Russia's aggression and the "rolling back of constitutional rights here in the United States.")

The bulk of Alito's half hour keynote focused on the benefits of religious liberty, on winning "the battle for religious freedom in an increasingly secular society." "Religious liberty is fragile. And religious intolerance and persecution have been recurring features throughout human history." He cited the torture of early Christians in Rome, anti-Semitic attacks, and China's persecution today of Muslim Uighurs. He analogized these assaults to the view that secular and societal goals should supplant religious claims. "[China's] Cultural Revolution did its best to destroy religion, but it was not successful. It could not extinguish the religious impulse," he said. "Our hearts are restless until we rest in God. And, therefore, the champions of religious liberty who go out as wise as serpents and as harmless as doves can expect to find hearts that are open to their message."

Throughout the summer of 2022, public support for the Supreme Court drained away. A Marquette University poll taken after the term was over found that 61 percent of respondents said they disapproved of the Court, while 38 percent said they approved; a year before, the numbers were almost precisely reversed, with 60 percent approval and 39 percent disapproval. Later in the summer an NBC News poll showed that many more people disapproved of the Supreme Court than approved of it, the first time that was the case since the pollster began asking that question three decades ago.

American politics can turn on single surprising election results. Sometimes they are overinterpreted. Sometimes, though, it is possible to feel the first tremors of something much bigger. Those tremors could not be mistaken in the weeks after the term ended.

On August 1, 2022, voters in Kansas considered a ballot measure that sought to remove the protection for abortion rights in the state's constitution. Kansas is a conservative, Republican state. A buzzy 2004 book, *What's the Matter with Kansas?*, had persuaded a generation of Democrats that somehow the state's voters had been beguiled to ignore their economic interests through a focus on abortion and other social causes. A 2019 state supreme court ruling had found a right in the Kansas constitution, and now the state was abutted by others where the practice was banned. Antiabortion forces pushed for the ballot measure and scheduled it for a day when turnout would likely be low. Many more Republicans voted than Democrats. But women made up seven of every ten Kansans who registered to vote in the weeks after *Dobbs*. And the antiabortion ballot measure to end constitutional protection was overwhelmingly, decisively rejected. The "no" vote won by 18 points. Pro-choice majorities piled up not only in progressive cities such as Wichita but in suburbs and even rural counties. Some pro-choice television ads spoke of individual freedom and even warned, "Kansans don't want another government mandate," while showing a picture of a sign requiring the wearing of a mask to prevent Covid.

Indiana, like Kansas, is a storied exemplar of middle America, portrayed by sociologists as the typical "Middletown." There, legislators acted a few days after Kansas voters spoke. They passed a new law that fully banned all abortions, and which allowed exceptions for rape, or incest, or even the health of the mother only within the first two months of pregnancy. That was not enough for the National Right to Life Committee, which denounced the bill because it did not impose criminal penalties, among other things. James Bopp, the antiabortion lawyer who lives in the state, called it a "wolf in sheep's clothing." On the other hand, Indianapolis-based pharmaceutical giant Eli Lilly opposed the law, worrying that it would now be hard "to attract diverse scientific, engineering and business talent from around the world."

Yet despite the turmoil and anger, the political machine that installed and supports the supermajority grew stronger, too. The public got a glimpse of the workings of that machine, and how well oiled it was.

Rev. Rob Schenck was once a religious conservative leader who raised $30 million over eighteen years for antiabortion causes. One of them was "Operation Higher Court," which recruited wealthy religious conservatives and assigned them the task of befriending the justices. Donors were encouraged to become trustees of the Supreme Court Historical Society. Schenck told his "stealth missionaries" to "See a justice— boldly approach." Eventually Schenck switched sides. In 2022 he wrote to John Roberts claiming that a decade before, Alito had leaked the *Hobby Lobby* decision to the effort's conservative backers. Alito and the woman who supposedly received the leak both denied the charge. Harder to deny was the influence campaign, one that risked making the Court look like nothing more than a political body and a venue for influence peddling. After Democrats demanded an ethics probe, the Court took the extraordinary step of issuing a statement refusing to act.

Then we learned more about the money that fueled the machine. Only after the term was over did the public find out that a single donor in 2020 had quietly given Leonard Leo, de facto leader of the Federalist Society, *$1.6 billion*. Leo spends the funds through a series of innocuous-sounding groups and entities under the umbrella of the Marble Freedom Trust. It gave $153 million to a Rule of Law Trust to urge appointment of conservative judges, for example. Leo's group also backed a new Honest Elections Project pushing a legal theory before the Supreme Court that would reshape American elections.

The legal conservative movement may have started as a student club, but now it is a dark money operation unprecedented in American history.

The supermajority's second full term began in October 2022. It, too, promised to shatter precedent. The new court's first full term had focused on long-standing goals of key Republican interest groups—overturning *Roe v. Wade*, expanding gun rights, blocking environmental regulation. For the second term the justices chose to take cases about race and democracy.

For much of the past seventy years, the Court spoke with passion and moral leadership on race. Justices realize that *Brown* was the high point of the Court's history and the source of much of its legitimacy. Justices point to it at every opportunity, to steel themselves when they are doing something big, as they did in *Dobbs*. If *Plessy* is the hissed-at villain, the lion-hearted and heedless justices of the Warren Court are heroes of the drama, allying with the courageous civil rights activists who risked all. Even before *Brown*, federal courts had begun to strike down racial discrimination. After, the Court allowed and encouraged myriad efforts to undo the legacy of discrimination and slavery. Signs suggest that all could change now.

The marquee cases concern affirmative action in education. Students for Fair Admissions challenged the system at Harvard and at the University of North Carolina at Chapel Hill. The group is led by Edward Blum, an activist lawyer who brought the *Shelby County* challenge to the Voting Rights Act and numerous suits against affirmative action. The Court decided to split the cases, since Ketanji Brown Jackson had recused herself from hearing the challenge to Harvard, where she sat on an alumni board. The question posed is stark: "Should this Court overrule" its earlier cases "and hold that institutions of higher education cannot use race as a factor in admissions?"

Every decade or so the justices address the topic. In 1978, in *Bakke*, a splintered Court ruled that race itself could not be the sole reason for admission or rejection—but that schools benefit from "diversity" and thus could take race into consideration. This gave the high court's imprimatur to a shift from equal opportunity as a central goal, toward a more explicit recognition of group identity. Foes wanted more. As with abortion, advocates repeatedly tried to undermine or undo affirmative action. Here, too, society had developed "reliance" interests apart from legal technicalities.

In 2003, a white applicant challenged the University of Michigan's use of race in admissions. *Grutter v. Bollinger* pivoted on friend of the court briefs as much as learned arguments. Major institutions stressed that managing America's racial diversity was a critical goal, and that it would be catastrophically disruptive to end a system that was working. Former president Gerald Ford quietly organized a brief supporting the consideration of race in admissions signed by retired military leaders. The submission by former chairs of the Joint Chiefs, joined by "Stormin' Norman" Schwarzkopf (who led the ground forces in Operation Desert Storm), had a concussive impact. Here was a concrete example of society's "reliance interest": "a highly qualified, racially diverse officer corps educated and trained to command our nation's racially diverse enlisted ranks," with its officers drawn from ROTC on campuses. Facts mattered. A brief detailing a sharp drop in minority attendance after a ballot measure ended affirmative action in California shook Sandra Day O'Connor. She wrote the controlling opinion, which held that since applicants are considered one at a time, schools could consider race as one factor since doing so did not guarantee acceptance or rejection. This was not a permanent remedy, however. "The Court expects that twenty-five years from now, the use of racial preferences will no longer be necessary to further the interest approved today."

Clarence Thomas is the only justice on the Court today who participated in *Grutter*. Back then, he seethed. He quoted Frederick Douglass: "'What I ask for the negro is not benevolence, not pity, not sympathy, but simply justice.' Like Douglass, I believe blacks can achieve in every avenue of American life without the meddling of university administrators." The Constitution, he insisted, "abhors classifications based on race . . . because every time the government places citizens on racial registers and makes race relevant to the provision of burdens or benefits, it demeans us all." John Roberts, meanwhile, may find his deep aversion to race-based policies—"The way to stop discrimination on the basis of race is to stop discriminating on the basis of race"—at odds with his unease over the Court's ebbing legitimacy. On race, the center point for the new majority likely has shifted hard to the right.

The country has changed since earlier cases, with patterns not always easy to discern. Today the country is far more diverse but identity is more kaleidoscopic. When *Bakke* was decided in 1978, issues of racial justice starkly focused on Black aspirations. In 2003, after the continued immigrant surge that began in 1965, Latinos made up 13 percent and Asians less than 5 percent of the country. Now Latinos make up one fifth of the American population (though half of them also identify as white), while Asians have grown to 6 percent, those identifying as being multiracial have exploded, the Black population remained static, and the white population shrank as a share of the total. Half of all young Americans identify as people of color. Diversity is not a catchphrase; it is a description.

The Harvard case, in particular, poses thorny issues of equity and aspiration. Athletes and children of alumni continue to receive unspoken affirmative action. Unsettling evidence showed that Asian American applicants were often downgraded on "personal" ratings. It reminded many of the ways Ivy League schools excluded Jews in earlier decades, using geographic diversity as a genteel quota. Yet the share of Black students continues to shrink at many top schools. It seemed an inauspicious time to jettison affirmative action.

In the summer of 2022, friend of the court briefs by the dozens were posted on the Court's website. Once again, business and military leaders practically begged for well enough to be left alone. Asian American activists pledged solidarity in the civil rights struggle. Others pointed to steady gains in enrollment by students of color, gains that could be threatened in an instant. This time, those arguments may not matter. The *Dobbs* majority made it clear it took pride in ignoring the real-world impact of its rulings.

When the case is argued and decided—given new personnel lineup, and political and ideological polarization—the Court may well rule that race cannot be used at all as a factor in admissions. No doubt we will hear John Marshall Harlan, thundering in his *Plessy* dissent that "Our constitution is color-blind, and neither knows nor tolerates classes among citizens," or Dr. King at the March on Washington dreaming his children would be judged not by the color of their skin but by the "content of their character." We will read statistics, too, about Asian aspiration. If the Court follows the pattern of its first year, it will discover timeless principles that previous generations somehow had missed, and make a maximalist ruling. Rip the Band-Aid off.

This term the Court may also effectively finish off the federal law against racial discrimination in voting.

The Voting Rights Act was born in Alabama. The judicial project of dismantling the act had Alabama roots as well. Shelby County is a suburb of Birmingham. The Court made clear even as it ruled in

Shelby County v. Holder that the act's Section 2 still remained. Then in *Brnovich,* Alito and others in the supermajority made it much harder to undo restrictive voting laws. But it was still available as it had been for years, to stop racial gerrymandering and the "dilution" of the power of Black and other minority voters.

Alabama, again. When the lawmakers there drew new congressional maps in 2021, they reduced from two to one the number of districts likely to elect a Black member of Congress. Three federal appeals court judges, two of them named by Trump, ruled that the map was racially discriminatory. On its shadow docket, with no opinion to explain what it was doing, the Supreme Court stopped that ruling from taking effect—thus Alabama held its 2022 elections using maps already declared illegal and discriminatory. Kagan wrote a twelve-page dissent. The appeals court had gathered massive amounts of evidence and applied the law as it now stood. Maybe that law needs to be revisited, she wrote, but "such a change can properly happen only after full briefing and argument—not based on scanty review this Court gives matters on its shadow docket." The Supreme Court's action was so abrupt—in effect, rewriting the Voting Rights Act without a hearing and with no explanation—that John Roberts, despite his long opposition to the law, dissented as well.

Now the Alabama redistricting got a full hearing. Perhaps the Court will uphold or modify the Voting Rights Act's long application to racial gerrymandering. Perhaps it will do what it did in *Brnovich*—leave Section 2 standing but as a frail, empty shell. Some urged the Court to go all the way, as Clarence Thomas has previously recommended, and declare that the special justification for national supervision of race in voting is no longer needed.

The case was argued on the second day of the Court's term in October 2022. Alabama's solicitor general fared poorly. The state claimed that Section 2 did not prohibit discriminatory "results," but required proof of racism. The justices were incredulous. All knew, if none pointed out, that John Roberts had started his career bemoaning precisely that fact.

Ketanji Brown Jackson was in only her second day on the bench. Alabama's lawyer insisted that the Voting Rights Act required that remedies to discrimination must be "race neutral." She pinned him back. The whole point of the Fourteenth Amendment was to ensure equal rights for freed slaves, she said. "That's not a race-neutral or race-blind idea in terms of the remedy." The drafters of the amendment wanted it to align with the Civil Rights Act of 1866, "to make sure that the other citizens, the Black citizens, would have the same as the white citizens." It was a jolt of progressive originalism. Jackson's presence seemed to embolden Kagan and Sotomayor. Not every case aligns so neatly with the purpose of the Fourteenth Amendment, but it was an early taste of what the liberal justices—likely united in dissent on this and other cases—could do. Of course, given the hostility by Roberts and others to the Voting Rights Act, even a good day at oral argument may not give much comfort.

The real-world impact of the Court's long assault on democracy has been felt. In 2021 all states redistricted their legislatures and congressional maps. It was the first time in half a century they did so without the benefit of full federal protection for voting rights. In parts of the country, state court decisions or redistricting commissions (created by ballot measures, as in California and Michigan) produced fairer elections. It helped to have divided government, too, where the parties were forced to negotiate. However, in much of the country single-party control, combined with no effective Voting Rights Act, led to egregious gerrymandering.

Journalists scrutinized the muddled partisan implications but the impact on representation is stark. The 2020 census showed that all the population growth in the country came in the South and Southwest, and over 90 percent of that came in Latino, Asian, and other communities of color. But the lines drawn in new legislative and congressional maps would actually lead to less representation for many minority communities.

A third major case in the term could have catastrophic consequence for the political system. In *Moore v. Harper*, the Court decided to consider a fringe claim that would hand extraordinary power over federal elections to state legislators without checks and balances from state courts, constitutions, or governors. It could rival *Citizens United* and *Shelby County* in undermining American democracy.

The Supreme Court has never supported this idea—indeed, has

rejected it repeatedly, most recently in 2015. It has no foundation at the time of the Constitution or in the centuries since.

Backers call it the independent state legislature theory, or the ISLT. It rests on a misreading of the little-known Elections Clause, which reads, "The Times, Places and Manner of holding Elections for Senators and Representatives, shall be prescribed in each State by the Legislature thereof; but the Congress may at any time by Law make or alter such Regulations, except as to the Places of chusing Senators."

James Madison insisted on this language because he emphatically did not trust state legislatures. That disdain was one reason the Constitutional Convention was called in the first place. Madison believed legislatures were corrupt, would be captured by "factions" (today, most notably, parties), and would engage in what we would call vote suppression or gerrymandering. (They did not call it that, of course. And Elbridge Gerry was standing right there!) Delegates from South Carolina, a notably malapportioned state, tried to strip the provision out. Madison retorted that the section used "words of great latitude" because "it was impossible to foresee all the abuses" to come. He warned astutely: "Whenever the State Legislatures had a favorite measure to carry, they would take care so to mold their regulations as to favor the candidates they wished to succeed."

The notion is that because a provision to curb the power of legislatures uses the word "legislature," that must mean it gives *all* the power to legislators. There is no historical evidence for this. The framers knew perfectly well that legislatures were established under state constitutions, and sought to curb the role of those bodies. This makes no more sense than a claim that that "Congress may at any time" means the president does not get to sign or veto federal election laws. Amelia Bedelia, meet James Madison.

Donald Trump and his legal team first floated the idea during the effort to overturn the 2020 election. Four of the sitting justices showed themselves to be ISLT-curious, at the very least. What about John Roberts? In 2015 the chief justice dissented when the Court upheld voters' power to pass ballot measures on democracy issues, such as those creating redistricting commissions. More recently, though, in 2019, Roberts wrote the opinion where federal courts were barred from policing partisan gerrymandering. Not to worry, he explained:

state courts under state constitutions could do so, as could voters using ballot measures.

Moore v. Harper itself shows the danger of an unwise ruling. North Carolina is politically divided, with a Democratic governor, Republican senators, and tight presidential margins. Democrats slightly outnumber Republicans. Yet the legislature produced a map that would likely yield eleven Republican members of Congress, and only four Democrats. The state supreme court invalidated that illegal gerrymander under North Carolina's constitution. The legislature's response to the court: you have no role here.

What would happen if the Court fully embraces the claim? Legislatures could pass restrictions, say, ending early voting for most, eliminating vote by mail or drop boxes, limiting polling place hours, and so on, without risk of a governor's veto or a state court override. With the Voting Rights Act gutted, racially discriminatory laws might face few obstacles. Thousands of rules set by constitutions and ballot measures would be invalid—in forty-four states, for example, it is the constitution that establishes the secret ballot. In many states, voter ID laws passed by conservative ballot measures would suddenly be invalid, too. There could be administrative chaos, as rules differ for federal and state races. Federal judges would be called on to referee even the most minor matters of election law, topics today reserved to local judges.

At the oral argument few of the justices seemed ready to embrace the North Carolina legislature's most outlandish claims. It seemed they might rule that federal courts can police state courts to see if they violated the Elections Clause, but not disturb the way elections are run throughout the country.

This idea is so outlandish, one must ask: why did the Court take the case? State legislatures today are the most conservative partisan redoubt for Republicans. The case came as Trump and his supporters continued to insist falsely that the 2020 election was stolen. Former federal judge J. Michael Luttig is a conservative icon, a mainstay of the Federalist Society. George W. Bush almost named him to the Supreme Court twice. He famously advised Vice President Mike Pence that he could not, in fact, overturn American democracy, an encounter he described in sober testimony to the January 6 Committee. Luttig calls the ISLT claim part of "the Republican blueprint to steal the 2024 election." He called the case "the most important case for American democracy in the almost two and a half centuries since America's founding."

The jurist felt so strongly that he joined the team arguing before the Court. No doubt the justices took note. At the same time, perhaps they noticed that the Honest Elections Project had weighed in with equal force on the other side: the new group started by Leonard Leo, the man who did so much to put them in their seats.

Dozens of other questions came before the Court in the 2022–23 term. Two key cases tested the use and limits of the First Amendment.

In one, a Colorado artist refused to create a website for a same sex wedding. As in *Masterpiece Cakeshop*, the state's antidiscrimination law is at issue. But in taking the case the Court chose to focus on whether the state's law violates the artist's freedom of speech (rather than religious liberty). It may be another case where a small proprietor wins rights that will be most aggressively used by big corporations after that.

And one of the most significant cases of the term—hard to predict on ideological grounds—will be the first time the Supreme Court assesses the reach of Section 230 of the telecommunications laws. This is the rule that gives social media companies and other online platforms broad immunity from libel and other laws. It helped usher in the creative and frenetic online universe. At the same time, it has allowed multibillion-dollar companies to monetize hate speech and disinformation with no consequence. The family of a terrorism victim, in this instance, is suing Google over YouTube's distribution of ISIS recruitment videos.

In its first year the supermajority showed itself in no mood to trim or wait. It overturned *Roe v. Wade*, radically expanded gun rights, and launched a new doctrine that will make it harder for environmental officials to act on anything important. Its second term includes cases touching on American history's rawest nerves. They may accelerate the dramatic social change ushered by, as Elena Kagan put it, "nine unaccountable people." Perhaps an abrupt end to affirmative action in school admissions. Maybe the final evisceration of the Voting Rights

Act. Even, if outlandishly, a potential grant of untrammeled authority to state legislatures to run American elections as they see fit, free of judicial review, depriving voters of free and fair elections.

The Court continues down this path with rancor and drama. It is not, again to quote Kagan, "acting like a court." As in earlier eras, all this has touched off a political conflagration, a backlash that will stretch across years. Politics may realign; it has happened before. What can be done about it?

CONCLUSION:
WE THE PEOPLE

T HAT A SMALL GROUP OF PEOPLE has seized so much power and wields it so abruptly, energetically, and unwisely poses a crisis for American democracy. As we have seen, the Court has overreached before. *Dred Scott, Lochner* and the New Deal Court, and the rulings of the late 1960s and early 1970s all provoked backlash, political mobilization, and even realignment. We may be at the start of such a moment of conflict today. How will the response play out? A response requires passion and patience in equal measure.

No equal and opposite reaction will instantly counter the Court's provocation. Efforts to enshrine gun rights and overturn abortion rights began in the 1970s but did not achieve victory until now. But they and other movements helped create a new political coalition that reshaped politics and law in myriad ways.

It is too early to know the shape and intensity of the backlash, but the 2022 election five months after the supermajority's first full term ended suggested it would be strong. In a midterm election, political trends normally would have weighed against the Democrats: 8 percent inflation, rising crime, and the tendency of voters to punish the party that controls the White House. A president's party on average loses 29 seats in a midterm. Reaction to *Dobbs*, however, helped produce the best midterm for a party in power in decades.

Democrats not only held control of the U.S. Senate but gained a seat. Republicans gained only nine seats and took control of the

House by just four votes. Governors in Pennsylvania, Michigan, Wisconsin, and New York won by pledging to support reproductive rights against opponents who lauded the Court. In Michigan, Vermont, and California, voters used ballot measures to enshrine abortion rights in state constitutions. In Kentucky, whose senator Mitch McConnell had worked for years to pack federal courts with antiabortion judges, voters defeated an antiabortion measure. National exit polls showed that 59 percent of voters wanted abortion to be legal in all or most cases, and a similar number were "dissatisfied" or "angry" about *Dobbs*. A quarter said that the issue was the most important (second only to inflation) and overwhelmingly they backed Democrats. To independent voters, in particular, "election denial" by candidates who backed Donald Trump's false claim of a stolen election, and the overturning of *Roe v. Wade* after a half century, combined as evidence of extremism. Yet this is just the first wave of response, and it is not yet clear how it will reshape the electorate. In states with unified Republican control, where governors already had backed antiabortion measures, incumbents faced little electoral penalty.

Congress, too, can respond to the Court's radicalism. Sometimes new laws can undo misguided decisions. In the 1990s Lilly Ledbetter was a middle manager at Goodyear Tire & Rubber. She discovered that for years she had been paid less than men doing similar jobs. In 2007 an Alito opinion ruled that she could not recover for the years of discrimination, since she did not file her case within 180 days of her first unequal paycheck—long before she even knew about it. Ginsburg in her dissent announced, "the ball is in Congress' court." Two years later President Obama signed a law named after Ledbetter that ensured more time to sue. Such legislative responses used to be much more common than today, as partisan divisions now hinder congressional action. In 2022, federal voting rights legislation would have undone *Brnovich* and *Shelby County*, but received no Republican votes when it fell to a filibuster.

Congress can also steer around the Court without directly confronting it. The Inflation Reduction Act in 2022 was at long last a major piece of climate legislation. But as has been noted, the law took the form of spending, not government regulation of business. That policy choice was dictated by political calculus, budget rules, and Senate procedures that allowed passage with a simple majority and no filibuster. It happens to be the case that paying businesses to create green energy is more popular than curbing their carbon emissions. A more aggressive regulatory regime might also have fallen afoul of one or another conservative legal doctrine. Spending and tax powers, by contrast, still are largely constitutionally sacrosanct. A similar calculus was visible in the bipartisan gun safety law signed two days after the Supreme Court ruled in *Bruen*. The goal was to show that a bill opposed by the NRA could pass. That bill, too, focused on spending—for mental health treatments, to help states enforce "red flag" laws to take guns from dangerous people, and so on. It danced away from any substantive regulation that might run afoul of the extremist Second Amendment doctrine of the Court.

An obstinate Court can force rethinking of policy goals. If our public discourse seems stuck in the 1960s, the constitutional era that started then may be one of the reasons. Adversity can spur innovation, new thinking for a very different country and time. Much progress toward equality in elections, for example, may be best advanced by automatic voter registration and national voting standards, universal measures resting on constitutional doctrines even this Supreme Court has upheld.

Then there are the courts. As federal courts close their doors to claims of rights and equality, state courts will matter more. Every state constitution but one, for example, includes a guarantee of a right to vote stronger than that in the U.S. Constitution. After the U.S. Supreme Court said federal jurists would not police partisan gerrymandering in 2019, state courts in Alaska, Maryland, New York, North Carolina, and Ohio struck down or changed legislative maps. Abortion rights, racial equality, and environmental rules, among other issues, may be fought out increasingly in state courtrooms, not at the Marble Palace. Until now states largely interpreted their constitutions in lockstep with the U.S. Supreme Court. That will need to change. Few professors study state constitutional law, and law students crave federal, not state clerkships. But activists at last have taken note. For example, the Brennan Center, which I lead, in 2022 launched a new program to focus on state courts and constitutions. Its website, statecourtreport.org, will let advocates, scholars, and judges learn in real time what similar strategies are being pursued in states around the country.

Even beyond Congress and states, activists must think with ambition and audacity about strategy. The framers expected there would be many constitutional amendments, but it turned out it was too hard to change the document. Mostly we've relied since on court rulings and broad changes in public understanding. Even so, amendments come in clusters every half century or so. We are overdue. Often these have overturned misguided court decisions. The House of Representatives already passed an amendment to undo *Citizens United* and other misguided campaign finance rulings, for example. There may be a push to revive an Equal Rights Amendment for women. Conservatives, in turn, have pushed for a "Convention of States" to revise the Constitution and require a balanced budget.

All these fights will play out amid the clamor of politics, not the hush of a courtroom. Activists will need to accept the inevitable compromises of the legislative realm. On this one, John Roberts has a point. "Federal courts are blunt instruments when it comes to creating rights," he wrote in his *Obergefell* dissent. "They have constitutional power only to resolve concrete cases or controversies; they do not have the flexibility of legislatures to address concerns of parties not before the court or to anticipate problems that may arise from the exercise of a new right." Ruth Bader Ginsburg made a similar argument about abortion. So, too, did Barack Obama as a young law lecturer. He found it one of "the tragedies of the civil rights movement" that it "became so court focused." Only through "actual coalitions of power [do] you bring about redistributive change," he added. Such change is deeper, more rooted in public opinion, and more durable. Yet that can pose uncomfortable strategic dilemmas, especially where public opinion challenges the binary choices forced by rights-based litigation. One in four women have had an abortion. Three quarters happen in the first ten weeks of pregnancy, and nearly all before the fifteenth week. A broad and stable consensus supports the procedure being legal, with some restrictions. That outcome may be achievable through the legislative process—or not. Will activists accept less than unfettered freedom for reproductive autonomy?

Columbia Law School scholar Jamal Greene identifies "a common but unrecognized problem in American law: in striving to take rights seriously, we take them too literally. We believe that holding a right means getting a judge to do whatever the right protects." Courtroom combat over rights, he argues, pushes us to ignore valid arguments on all sides of an issue. Yet we cannot minimize the impact of a court ruling. It can confer legitimacy on an otherwise unlikely point of view.

Same sex marriage gained ground each time a court ruled on it. *Roe* may have atrophied organizing muscles on the pro-choice side, but it stood for a half century and women still had that right, battered and diminished as it was. We may hope for more durable protections for reproductive freedom won at the ballot box, but that is cold comfort today to many Americans.

And there are three other people whose voices now must ring loudly to the public: the likely dissenters, Justices Sotomayor, Kagan, and Jackson. In an earlier era, "Holmes and Brandeis dissent" was a repeated and revered phrase. Those justices narrated the injustices of the *Lochner* Court. They knew they had a wider audience, and they did not hold back. The jolt of energy visible in the oral arguments in the 2022–23 term suggests that the liberals may be ready to play this role.

When norms are broken, reform often follows. The Supreme Court itself is now ripe for such a response.

Start with life tenure. Our Constitution is the world's oldest, and while some of its features once seemed quaint, increasingly they seem fateful. They combine to entrench minority rule. The U.S. Senate features equal representation for each state. In 1787, the biggest state, Virginia, had thirteen times the population of the smallest, Delaware. Today, California's senators represent a state sixty-seven times bigger than Wyoming. Then there's the Electoral College, once a charming bit of Americana, which now routinely misfires. For well over a century, the electoral vote matched and ratified the popular vote. But the popular vote loser became president twice in the past two decades—in 2000 and 2016—and it almost happened in 2004 as well. Lifetime tenure for justices, too, once was tolerable. Now it has egregious consequences.

The United States is the only major constitutional democracy that does not limit terms or impose a retirement age for its high court judges. The same is true in states: only in Rhode Island do justices serve for life. Such limits rely on the same insight that prompted George Washington to retire: no person, no matter how valuable, should hold that much power for too long. With younger nominees and longer lifespans, U.S. Supreme Court justices now serve far longer than they used to. On average Amy Coney Barrett will hold power until 2052.

Term limits could be implemented by a constitutional amendment.

Many argue they could be set by statute, too. The Constitution says judges serve so long as they are "on good behavior," but past cases have suggested that justices could be moved to "senior status." These judges are still be paid, and sit on some cases, but are semiretired. Naturally, the final decision would be made by . . . the justices themselves.

Most plans would limit justices to an eighteen-year tenure. Presidents would make one nomination every two years. Regular terms and appointments would bring predictability and stability without sacrificing independence. Nominations simply would matter less. True, candidates might feel compelled to say whom they would choose—thus effectively adding Supreme Court justices to the ticket. That might worsen politicization, or it might just bring the politics into public view. Term limits would help demystify the Supreme Court. Justices are government officials, not mysterious wizards empowered to divine the meaning of the past. Simple math would make it less likely that a supermajority of left or right could be installed. It would all be part of "rightsizing" the Supreme Court and its role in our system.

In a May 2022 Quinnipiac poll, 69 percent favored ending lifetime appointments. Democrats and independents strongly backed the idea, as did six in ten Republicans. An annual survey conducted by professors finds stable and growing support. It is rare to find such broad enthusiasm for a novel policy idea.

I saw this when I served as a member of a Presidential Commission on the Supreme Court of the United States that convened in 2021 to consider reforms. Joe Biden announced he would establish such a panel during the presidential campaign, in part to evade pressure from party activists who pressed to expand the Court. Blue-ribbon commissions are a hoary Washington way to ensure nothing happens, and we were ordered not to make any recommendations.

Yet something did happen. The commission heard public testimony from dozens of witnesses, twenty-seven in one day. Speakers disagreed on many things. Strikingly, though, witnesses of left and right said they supported term limits. The panel's final report noted the idea "enjoyed considerable, bipartisan support." Perhaps this should not surprise. The year before, the National Constitution Center had asked separate groups of "progressive" and "conservative" scholars to propose constitutional changes; both groups supported an eighteen-year term for justices. A nascent national consensus backs the idea, reflected in the presidential panel's report.

By contrast, proposals to expand the Supreme Court would likely fare poorly.

Congress has changed the Court's size before. There were six justices at first, then five justices, then seven, then ten, then eventually nine in 1869. Some of the variation came because justices were on the road riding circuit. As the country grew, that meant more circuits, hence more justices needed. Lawmakers also acted from partisan motives: backers of Jefferson, Jackson, and Lincoln all wanted to put friendly faces on the bench.

But there are reasons to be skeptical. A retaliatory spiral could follow. Democrats might add five seats; the next time Republicans could, they would add five; soon dozens of justices would crowd the courtroom. There are also risks to judicial independence. Authoritarians around the world have expanded court size when rulings threatened their power. Hugo Chávez in Venezuela, Recep Tayyip Erdoğan in Turkey, and others have done so in recent years.

Another reason to tread carefully: the idea is truly unpopular. Yes, the Supreme Court's approval ratings are low; yes, millions are angry at the right's power grab. But those reactions could shift fast if the response also seems illegitimate. In 1937 Franklin Roosevelt had just won the biggest electoral landslide yet, and his party held an all-but-unthinkable 70 percent of seats in the U.S. Senate. Yet his court reorganization plan crossed a previously unseen line. Jeff Shesol writes it was "not the cause, but the catalyst that helped fracture the New Deal coalition; reawaken the GOP; unite conservatives across party lines; and shatter the myth of FDR's omnipotence." Today, neither party has anything like those landslide margins to squander.

No doubt it would be viscerally satisfying to meet hardball with hardball. Republicans packed the Court to attain this supermajority. Why should those appalled by this Court refrain from doing everything possible to right the situation? At some point there may be little choice. If the Court threatens democracy, then the democratic system cannot be afraid to respond.

There are other steps to take. An enforceable ethics code would help. We can also buttress other parts of the federal judicial system.

Congress last created a big batch of lower court federal judgeships in 1990, and the country has grown by 89 million people since then. The Judicial Conference of the United States led by John Roberts has called for seventy-nine new judges. That would ease overcrowded dockets. It would also offer the chance to bolster diversity and build a judiciary that looks more like the country it serves. Other ideas are more far-fetched. Congress can strip jurisdiction from the Supreme Court to take away its power to rule on certain types of cases, for example. Such proposals and more—some wise, some not—will be debated. For decades supporters asked every Republican candidate: what will you do about the Supreme Court? In the future, every person running for office on the left will be asked the same question.

There must be a response in the realm of ideas, too. When Republicans first advanced originalism in the 1980s, Meese, Bork, and others insisted "a jurisprudence of original intent" would stop liberal judges from imposing their personal views. Quickly it switched styles, becoming "original public meaning," asking what the phrases meant to Americans at the time of ratification. Hence the prolific use of dictionaries—as though ordinary people in 1791 consulted dictionaries. (In fact, the first fully American dictionary, Noah Webster's, would not be published until forty-one years later.) An industry of law professors parse variations on originalism, "new originalism," and more.

Now originalism is having its big moment, and its flaws are on full display.

One comes from the very notion that the Constitution's meaning was "fixed" by the people who ratified it. They disagreed vehemently among themselves or changed their minds rapidly. (Just four years after James Madison wrote *Federalist* 10 denouncing "faction" and political parties, he had organized one. So he began writing—again, anonymously—that anyone who did not see the need for two parties was historically illiterate.) Much of the portrayal of the past is fanciful. An example: in the cases that beckon the "Constitution in Exile," judges simply assume that early lawmakers did not delegate much to regulatory agencies or the executive branch. In fact, the Founders delegated plenty.

But even if the meaning of the past was clear, that only magnifies the absurdity of purporting to rewrite current mores and laws in that light. The framers were from a different time—thank heavens! Many owned slaves, or abhorred democracy. Nearly all disdained women's equality. Most Americans lived isolated in villages and farms. Why should their views govern in 2023? To privilege their prejudices and notions, let alone insist that they should control us, would hurl the country backward. It is also simply odd. When Great Britain today considers gun safety legislation, parliamentarians do not first ask, "Well, what did King George III think?"

Let's shed any illusions: today's justices are not conservative because they are originalists; they are originalists because it is conservative. They fly a flag of convenience. Today's reigning doctrine is a product of a half century of political organizing to change how the Supreme Court and country understood the Constitution. Having at last achieved success, proponents act as if this newly minted vision is unchanging, and unchallengeable. It is, in fact, a form of living constitutionalism.

But you cannot beat something with nothing. When it comes to the Constitution, progressives have largely fallen silent. They huddle in a defensive crouch. It was painful to watch Justice-to-be Ketanji Brown Jackson and other nominees find it necessary to make ritual originalist incantations, without uttering so much as a peep in protest.

What would be a better approach?

Franklin Roosevelt said it well in 1937: "The Constitution of the United States was a layman's document, not a lawyer's contract." It reflects profound values. Liberty and equality, individual autonomy and a well-ordered community. When later generations decided that the Constitution allowed a more expansive federal government, they did not misread the charter—they embraced its adaptability to new needs. Such moments create new constitutional understandings. The country has changed, people's expectations of their humanity has changed, and a modern Constitution reflects that change. The past matters; the framing matters. But that must be only the beginning of the analysis. It's important to know what happened in 1787. *And what happened after that?* It lacks the punchy meme-worthiness of "originalism," but it is how the Court always has understood history. We have been a country that always looked forward, not backward.

Above all, we must find a way to read the Constitution as a charter for a thriving and equal democracy. That word "democracy" appears nowhere in the Constitution. But "federalism" and "separation of powers" are not mentioned either. They are implied throughout. Individual rights have now been weaponized not to bolster democracy but to undermine it, whether it is a fetishized version of the First Amendment destroying campaign finance law or trumped-up claims of religious freedom used to poke loopholes in public health and education measures.

Amid surging demographic change our only hope is to build a system of representative government that will reflect the country as it is and as it is becoming. Few societies have seen so many demographic and economic shifts without severe disruption. Arguably we have not escaped that fate, with the convulsive 2016 rise of Trump and his white nationalist movement. We must have a modern Constitution that enables American society to govern itself in 2023 and beyond.

As part of this, liberals once again must make a case for judicial restraint. In recent years, right and left have traded rhetoric depending on the issue. But throughout most of American history progressives sought ways for the democratically accountable branches of government to act. Such restraint would have led to a more just, more equal, and more free society over time. For a short time judges aggressively moved to protect rights from abuse by elected majorities. A very short time, as it turns out.

Nineteenth-century abolitionists such as Frederick Douglass and twentieth-century reformers, people such as Louis Brandeis and Theodore Roosevelt and Florence Kelley, had no illusions. They condemned the Court's arrogance. Today the supermajority's decisions are the work of a little group of willful men and women, ripping up long-settled aspects of American life for no reason beyond the fact that they can do so. Would a critique of judicial overreach sometimes preclude important rulings? It's a tough question. *Obergefell v. Hodges* was a landmark in human liberty. But by the time the Court ruled, it reflected a hard-won if rapidly evolving consensus. Public support for same sex marriage rose from 27 percent in 1996 to 60 percent when the Court ruled in 2015. (Support stands at over 70 percent today.) The country affirmed marriage equality before the Court ever did. On the other hand, only a ruling of this kind guarantees the freedom to marry in all states. Would

Alabama or Mississippi allow same-sex marriage even today if the protection of federal courts were withdrawn?

Above all, liberals must fall out of love with the Supreme Court. Until recently polling showed higher support for the Court among Democrats than Republicans. Perhaps this reverence mostly reflected generational nostalgia. I live this contradiction myself. I lead a think tank named after one of the great liberal jurists of the twentieth century. Every day at work, I am reminded of the reality: Justice Brennan's portrait is on the wall at the Brennan Center, but Justice Alito sits on the bench.

A young scholar, Nikolas Bowie, delivered one of the most compelling statements before the Supreme Court commission. He described a long list of major cases where judicial review struck down laws. In every instance but one, that power was wielded against legislative bids to build a stronger democracy or to advance economic and racial justice. Bowie acknowledged the significance of *Brown* as a moral statement but noted that a decade later southern schools were still segregated. He speaks for a new generation that never knew the Supreme Court as a beacon of hope or even as a wistful aspiration. "As absurd as it was" at the time of the Declaration of Independence "for a continent to be perpetually governed by an island, it is equally absurd now for a nation of 300 million to be perpetually governed by five Harvard and Yale alumni," he wrote.

Thus the most profound casualty of the supermajority's reign may be the legitimacy of the Supreme Court itself. Justice Robert Jackson was only partly right when he famously quipped, "We are not final because we are infallible, but we are infallible only because we are final." Legitimacy must be earned. Instead it is being squandered. If that yields a more realistic understanding and more effective strategy than dreamed-of victories in the courts, that may turn out to be a positive development. But it will be a shift with costs and consequences for many of the most vulnerable.

After World War II Americans grew accustomed to uniform national rights. On free speech, legislative representation, criminal justice protections, and more, the national government set a floor, sometimes through the courts, often through legislation. Now we are not drifting but driving toward two social systems, one in states run by Republicans, the other in states dominated by Democrats. Your rights will differ based on where you live. New doctrines are being concocted or "rediscovered" once again to limit our national government. Above it all, the Supreme Court has systematically knocked down the protections for our democratic institutions, which abets this momentum toward polarization.

American democracy faces extraordinary pressure. The former president tried to stop the peaceful transfer of power and overthrow the constitutional order. That coup attempt was shambolic and clownlike. Future attacks on American democracy will be more systematic and more effective. Today much of the country falsely believes our democracy is rigged, riddled with fraud, and illegitimate. The future of our democratic system is on the line.

Three days in June 2022, the supermajority made its move. In coming years it will be up to the country to respond. In the term that started in the summer of 2021 and culminated with such force in the summer of 2022, the United States Supreme Court showed itself to be one of those threats to American democracy. Its role matters. Its membership matters. These concerns will now be at the center of our politics. That's as it should be. Conservatives long understood, and liberals now are remembering, that the only way to win meaningful legal and policy change is first to win in the court of public opinion. It turns out that the most important words in the Constitution are "We the People."

Acknowledgments

This book is a first draft of history. I wrote it to trace the significance of what is happening at the U.S. Supreme Court, and why I think it is bad for the country. And I wanted to draw on the lessons of history to understand how we got here and what will happen next. I wanted to make the case that robust debate about the Supreme Court is not a transgression—it is the way the country always has responded when jurists go too far.

At Simon & Schuster I have been extraordinarily fortunate to have the commitment and engagement of which authors dream. Bob Bender conceived of this book, my first full project with him. He is focused and encouraging, sharp-eyed and wise. Thank you to Johanna Li, who has worked on every step of this project, together with Fred Chase, Lisa Healy, Lewelin Polanco, and Beth Maglione. Thank you as well to Jonathan Karp for supporting my writing, with this, my fourth book with S&S. Carolyn Levin provided invaluable legal assistance.

Rafe Sagalyn has been my agent for over two decades. He, too, pushed me to do this book, offered sharp edits, and came up with the title (as he did for the last two!). His enthusiasm and encouragement mean the world to me—and, I know, to his other authors as well.

Thank you, too, to experts and friends who read all or parts of the manuscript. They have such deep knowledge of the country, its history, its politics, and its laws, and I benefited from all of it. They include Jonathan Alter, Gary Ginsberg, Daniel Kummer, Peter Lehner, Richard Revesz, Kate Shaw, Jeff Shesol, Cliff Sloan, George Stephanopoulos, Hana Vizcarra, Ben Waldman, Steven Waldman, Susannah Waldman, and Jennifer Weiss-Wolf. Of course, opinions and especially errors are mine! Thank you, as well, to experts including Larry Kramer, Jesse Wegman, Melissa Murray, Reva Siegel, Kenji Yoshino, Julian Zelizer, and Sherrilyn Ifill for insights and suggestions as the work unfolded. Opinions and any errors, again, are still mine alone.

I wrote this book while leading the Brennan Center for Justice at NYU School of Law. I am privileged to be part of a special institution that works to strengthen, reform, and defend the systems of democracy and justice so they work for all Americans.

I am so fortunate to have a wonderful team of colleagues who have been unfailingly helpful to me in this intense project. Alan Beard, policy strategist in the office of the president at the Center, organized our squad for research and editing. Amanda Bart, my executive assistant, joined the team and has been extraordinarily helpful and a valuable editor. Jeanine Chirlin, the Brennan Center's chief of staff, was insightful and engaged, and understands so well the power of books to move ideas. I had the chance to work with four interns: Elizabeth Byrnes-Mandelbaum, an NYU Law student, who provided sharp editing, writing, and research, and three tremendous undergraduate interns, each of whom has a great future: Itai Grofman, Chloe Kellison, and Nathan Platt.

Numerous Brennan Center colleagues generously offered insight, read the manuscript, checked facts, or shared expertise. Special thanks to Alicia Bannon, Alice Clapman, Chisun Lee, Elisa Miller, Mekela Panditharatne, Chrissy Teeter, Cherie Vu, and Dan Weiner for going above and beyond, and to our colleagues Patrick Berry, Madiba Dennie, L. B. Eisen, Ames Grawert, Ethan Herenstein, Doug Keith, Martha Kinsella, Maya Kornberg, Chris Leaverton, Michael Li, Sarah Mazzarella, Peter Miller, Sean Morales-Doyle, Kevin Morris, Larry Norden, Brian Palmer, Yurij Rudensky, Sonali Seth, Hernandez Stroud, Ram Subramanian, Eliza Sweren-Becker, Ian Vandewalker, Wendy Weiser, and Tom Wolf. Eric Ruben, our Second Amendment fellow and a professor at SMU, offered his insight in so many ways. Amanda Powers helped with early research on these topics even before this book was under way while I was a member of the Presidential Commission on the Supreme Court of the United States. And thank you to Adriana Monzon, a skilled paralegal on the Center's staff.

Thank you to our friends at Paul, Weiss for pro bono help, especially to Megan Gao for expert legal assistance, and to Robert Atkins for making it possible.

Thank you as well to Robert Raben and Jeremy Paris, who worked with the Center to organize private discussions on the Court's originalism and its impact.

This book touches on issues of law and strategy that go to the heart of what we do at the Brennan Center. So many colleagues (150 plus) are so passionately and expertly engaged in the fight for democracy, justice, the rule of law, and the Constitution. They worked so well during this time and also gave me encouragement and time away from the office to write. Thank you to our executive team—Lisa Benenson, Tony Butler, Jeanine Chirlin, Jaemin Kim, John Kowal, Elisa Miller, Manuel Monge, and Wendy Weiser—for their leadership and for making it possible for me to focus on this project. Special thanks as well to Larry Norden, Faiza Patel, Liza Goitein, L. B. Eisen, and Ted Johnson. Our Board of Directors, especially cochairs Patricia Bauman and Bob Atkins, have been unfailingly supportive, as have the other members of our board, including Dean Troy McKenzie of NYU Law and his predecessor, Trevor Morrison.

I am deeply grateful for the generosity and partnership of the Brennan Center's generous supporters—now 27,000 strong—who are fiercely committed to the health and longevity of our democracy. Special thanks go to our leading supporters of this work, including Arnold Ventures, Bainum Family Foundation, the Bauman Foundation, the Arthur M. Blank Family Foundation, Bohemian Foundation, Susan Burden and Carter and Charmaine Burden, Carnegie Corporation of New York, Cynthia Crossen and James Gleick, Marc Fasteau and Anne Fredericks, Ford Foundation, Sibyl Frankenburg and Steven Kessel, Jerome L. Greene Foundation, William and Flora Hewlett Foundation, Joyce Foundation, JPB Foundation, Kaphan Foundation, Klarman Family Foundation, Lakeshore Foundation, Leon Levy Foundation, Mai Family Foundation, John and Wendy Neu Foundation, Craig Newmark Philanthropies, Rockefeller Brothers Fund, Solidarity Giving, Someland Foundation, Bernard and Anne Spitzer Charitable Trust, Wilf Family Foundations, and the Zegar Family Foundation. I also want to especially thank the late Nancy Kohlberg and the Kohlberg Foundation for their extraordinary leadership and support.

I was honored to serve as a member of the Presidential Commission on the Supreme Court of the United States. I learned a great deal during my time on the panel, and want to thank Bob Bauer and Cristina Rodriguez, its chairs, for organizing it and steering it to unexpectedly productive ground.

Finally, to my family. My mother, Sandra Waldman, turned ninety years old during the writing of this book. She played an important role in one aspect of the history recounted here: for years, as communications director of the Population Council, she worked to make pharmaceutical options available to give women the choice of reproductive rights. She carefully and astutely edited this volume. My brother Steve Waldman, too, carefully read the manuscript and gave tremendous guidance, based on his own years of writing books—and his expertise on religion and the Constitution. Thank you to him and his family, Amy Cunningham, Gordon Waldman, and Joe Waldman for all their interest and encouragement. Thank you as well to Katrina Northrop and Emily Carlson for bringing love into our lives.

Then there is my wife, Liz Fine. During the entire time I wrote this book, she has been in a whirlwind of activity with an exciting job as Counsel to the Governor of New York. She was intimately involved in so many of the issues discussed here (including, of course, the response to the Supreme Court's egregious ruling striking down New York's gun law). She's insightful, funny, warm, giving, and as ever, shockingly energetic.

And finally I come to our three children—Ben, Susannah, and Josh. When I wrote previous books they were toddlers, or teenagers, or off to college. Now they are remarkable adults. Two of them were studying law as I wrote this: Ben, a former U.S. Army officer, has infectious enthusiasm for its theories and intricacies. And I am inspired and challenged by Susannah's soulful, extraordinary, and passionate commitment to those caught up in an unjust criminal justice system. Josh, with brilliant wit and insight, works to ensure that millions of people benefit from the American Rescue Plan through his work in the White House. They each challenge my thinking, expand my horizons, offer vital new perspectives from their very different angles, and push me to see the Court and law and Constitution in ways that went past where my own views might have been. I'm proud of them. They have been supportive and caring and enthusiastic, and I am honored to dedicate the book to them and the world they will make.

Michael Waldman
New York City
December 2022

Notes

INTRODUCTION

1 *It overturned* Roe: *Dobbs v. Jackson Women's Health,* 597 U.S. ___, 142 S. Ct. 2228 (2022).

1 *radically loosened curbs on guns: New York State Rifle & Pistol Association v. Bruen,* 597 U.S. ___, 142 S. Ct. 2111 (2022).

1 *It hobbled the ability: West Virginia v. Environmental Protection Agency,* 597 U.S. ___, 142 S. Ct. 2587 (2022).

2 *Clarence Thomas:* Throughout this book, I do not use the title "Justice" every time a justice's name appears, for reasons of readability and repetitiveness.

2 *nine scorpions in a bottle:* Noah Feldman, *Scorpions: The Battles and Triumphs of FDR's Great Supreme Court Justices* (New York: Twelve, 2010), iv.

2 *Democrats won the popular vote:* From 1992 to 2020, Republicans won the popular vote only in 2004. Roberts and Alito were appointed by George W. Bush (who lost the popular vote in 2000, though they were appointed in his second term after he had won it). Donald Trump appointed Gorsuch, Kavanaugh, and Barrett.

3 *"It is a Constitution we are expounding": McCulloch v. Maryland,* 17 U.S. 4 Wheat. 316 (1819).

4 *Most of the time the Court has reflected:* Barry Friedman documents how the Court's rulings generally track public opinion. See Barry Friedman, *Will of the People: How Public Opinion Has Influenced the Supreme Court and Shaped the Meaning of the Constitution* (New York: Farrar, Straus & Giroux, 2010). Another approach, taken by Keith Whittington, looks less at public opinion and more at the governing regime. He borrows the typology developed by political scientist Stephen Skowronek. Some presidents are "reconstructive," creating a new governing coalition and approach in repudiation of a weakened earlier one (Lincoln, McKinley, FDR, Reagan). Some are "orthodox innovators" trying to invigorate an existing model (LBJ, George W. Bush). Some try to carry on the previous "regime," at times presiding over its dissolution (Hoover, George H. W. Bush). A few are oppositional presidents who have not won a majority and stand in opposition to the governing coalition (Wilson, Nixon, Clinton—all

"preemptive presidents," borrowing policies and ideas from the majority, and all of whom had constitutional crises). See Stephen Skowronek, *The Politics Presidents Make: Leadership from John Adams to Bill Clinton*, rev. ed. (Cambridge, MA: Belknap Press, 1997). Whittington argues that the Supreme Court largely adapts and ratifies the governing approach of the majority party in an ongoing regime. Keith E. Whittington, *Political Foundations of Judicial Supremacy: The Presidency, the Supreme Court, and Constitutional Leadership in U.S. History* (Princeton: Princeton University Press, 2007), 104–20. In an influential article in 1957, the political scientist Robert Dahl wrote that the Court is a political as well as a legal institution. "The fact is, then, that the policy views dominant on the Court are never for long out of line with the policy views dominant among the lawmaking majorities of the United States." Robert A. Dahl, "Decision-Making in a Democracy: The Supreme Court as a National Policy-Maker," *Journal of Public Law* 6, no. 2 (Fall 1957): 279, 285. Lucas Powe has a more basic explanation: "I see it as part of a ruling regime doing its bit to implement the regime's policies." Lucas Powe Jr., *The Supreme Court and the American Elite, 1789–2008* (Cambridge: Harvard University Press, 2009), ix. In any case, the Supreme Court proves itself exquisitely responsive to public trends and opinion.

5   *Public support:* Jeffrey M. Jones, "Confidence in U.S. Supreme Court Sinks to Historic Low," Gallup Poll, June 23, 2022, https://news.gallup.com/poll/394103/confidence-supreme-court-sinks-historic-low.aspx.

ONE: AMERICAN ARISTOCRACY

9   *"no Constitution would ever have been adopted":* Richard Beeman, *Plain, Honest Men: The Making of the American Constitution* (New York: Random House, 2009), 83.

9   *For three months:* John P. Kaminski, *Secrecy and the Constitutional Convention* (Madison, WI: Center for the Study of the American Constitution, 2005), 7.

9   *"As states are a collection of individual men":* Notes of Debates in the Federal Convention of 1787, reported by James Madison (Athens: Ohio University Press, 1985) (June 29, 1787), 215. The notes were first published in vols. 2–3 of *The Papers of James Madison* (Washington, D.C., 1840).

10   *"a considerable pause ensuing":* Ibid. (June 1, 1787), 45.

10   *"tho' we cannot":* Kaminski, *Secrecy and the Constitutional Convention*, 17.

10   *"Laws may be unjust":* Notes of Debates (July 21, 1787), 337.

10   *"by degrees the lawgiver":* Ibid. (August 15, 1787), 463.

10   *Before the Revolution, in the colonies:* William E. Nelson, *Marbury v. Madison: The Origins and Legacy of Judicial Review*, 2nd ed. (Lawrence: University Press of Kansas, 2018), 11–22.

11   *"the higher law":* Larry D. Kramer, *The People Themselves: Popular Consti-*

tutionalism and Judicial Review (Oxford: Oxford University Press, 2004), 24–27.

11 *The state eliminated the property requirement:* See Michael Waldman, *The Fight to Vote,* rev. ed. (New York: Simon & Schuster, 2022), 14–16. The new state constitution gave the right to vote to "freemen." This was ambiguous: did it include Black men? As a practical matter, the decision was left to local officials who ran elections. In many counties Black men could vote, though Philadelphia effectively barred them by not adding them to the tax rolls. Edward Price, "The Black Voting Rights Issue in Pennsylvania, 1780–1900," *The Pennsylvania Magazine of History and Biography* 100, no. 3 (July 1976): 356–73.

11 *Instead of a governor:* For a discussion of the general radicalism of the Pennsylvania revolution, see generally Gordon S. Wood, *Creation of the American Republic* (New York: W. W. Norton, 1969), 83–90.

11 *"Fundamental law":* For a discussion of the ways state laws helped prompt growing support for judicial review among the drafters of the Constitution, see Michael J. Klarman, *The Framers' Coup: The Making of the United States Constitution* (New York: Oxford University Press, 2016), 159–62.

11 *"was at the same time at a loss":* Wood, *Creation of the American Republic,* 455.

12 *In the end the Constitution did not grant:* Only in one key area did it give Congress the power to "make or alter" state laws: voting and elections. The Elections Clause included these "words of great latitude," Madison explained, because of expected abuses by partisan state legislators. See Eliza Sweren-Becker and Michael Waldman, "The Meaning, History, and Importance of the Elections Clause," *Washington Law Review* 96, no. 3 (2021): 997.

12 *some form of judicial review had become commonplace:* William Treanor, "Judicial Review Before *Marbury,*" *Stanford Law Review* 58 (2005): 455.

12 *while the men who wrote the constitution:* Kramer, *The People Themselves,* 73–75.

12 *"In some states": Notes of Debates* (June 4, 1787), 61.

12 *And members of the founding generation disagreed:* See Jack N. Rakove, *Original Meanings: Politics and Ideas in the Making of the Constitution* (New York: Alfred A. Knopf, 1996), for a Pulitzer Prize–winning exploration of the differences among the framers.

13 *as Julius Caesar could attest:* Long before the Ides of March, Brutus's ancestor Lucius Julius Brutus led the expulsion of Rome's last king and the creation of the Roman Republic. Mary Beard, *SPQR: A History of Ancient Rome* (New York: Liveright 2015), 123.

13 *"operate to a total subversion of the state judiciaries":* Brutus, no. 11 (January 31, 1788), in Herbert J. Storing, *The Complete Anti-Federalist* (Chicago: University of Chicago Press, 1981), https://press-pubs.uchicago.edu /founders/documents/a3_2_1s19.html.

13 *"least dangerous to the political rights": Federalist* 78, in Alexander Hamilton,

James Madison, and John Jay, *The Federalist Papers*, ed. Lawrence Goldman (New York: Oxford University Press, 2008), 380.

14   *As the infant institutions:* See Charles Warren, "The First Decade of the Supreme Court of the United States," *University of Chicago Law Review* 7 (1940): 4.

14   *James Wilson:* Maeva Marcus, "Wilson as a Justice," *Georgetown Journal of Law & Public Policy* 17 (2019): 147.

14   *"energy, weight, and dignity":* "To John Adams from John Jay, 2 January 1801," Founders Online, National Archives, https://founders.archives .gov/documents/Adams/99-02-02-4745.

14   *fractured into factions:* The phrase, of course, comes from *Hamilton*. Lin-Manuel Miranda and Jeremy McCarter, "Washington on Your Side," *Hamilton: The Revolution* (New York: Grand Central Publishing, 2016), 199.

14   *An ambassador sent by the French Revolution's Convention:* For the story of Citizen Genet, see Gordon S. Wood, *Empire of Liberty: A History of the Early Republic, 1789–1815* (Oxford: Oxford University Press, 2009), 185–89.

14   *Matthew Lyon:* Geoffrey R. Stone, *Perilous Times: Free Speech in Wartime* (New York: W. W. Norton, 2004), 17–20; Aleine Austin, *Matthew Lyon: "New Man" of the Democratic Revolution, 1749–1822* (University Park: Pennsylvania State University Press, 1981).

15   *"to the seditious attempts":* Stone, *Perilous Times*, 49–50.

15   *From prison:* Stanley Elkins and Eric McKitrick, *The Age of Federalism: The Early American Republic, 1788–1800* (New York: Oxford University Press, 1993), 710–11.

15   *"have retired into the judiciary":* "From Thomas Jefferson to John Dickinson, 19 December 1801," Founders Online, National Archives, https://founders .archives.gov/documents/Jefferson/01-36-02-0090. Original source: *The Papers of Thomas Jefferson*, vol. 36, *1 December 1801–3 March 1802*, ed. Barbara B. Oberg (Princeton: Princeton University Press, 2009), 165–66.

16   *"Marshall knew that such a decision":* Cliff Sloan and David McKean, *The Great Decision: Jefferson, Adams, Marshall, and the Battle for the Supreme Court* (New York: PublicAffairs, 2009), 161.

17   *Later generations of justices:* Ibid., 173–77.

17   *school segregation in Little Rock: Cooper v. Aaron*, 358 U.S. 1 (1958).

17   *Watergate special prosecutor: United States v. Nixon*, 418 U.S. 683 (1974), 703.

17   *Every so often: McCulloch v. Maryland*, 17 U.S. 4 Wheat. 316 (1819). Opinions from John Marshall's tenure included those making clear the Supreme Court could hear appeals from state courts on federal constitutional issues, *Martin v. Hunter's Lessee*, 14 U.S. (1 Wheat.) 304 (1816), and *Fletcher v. Peck*, 10 U.S. (6 Cranch) 87 (1810), which ruled that a state law had violated the U.S. Constitution's Contracts Clause (which was designed to keep states from changing laws to get out of contracts), the first time the Court struck down a state statute.

17   *Georgia law: Worcester v. Georgia*, 31 U.S. (6 Pet.) 515 (1832).

17   *"John Marshall has made his decision":* The quotation appeared twenty
     years later in a book by Horace Greeley. Jackson did tell an associate,
     "The decision of the Supreme Court has fell still born, and they find that
     it cannot coerce Georgia to yield to its mandate." Jon Meacham, *Amer-
     ican Lion: Andrew Jackson in the White House* (New York: Random House,
     2008), 204. Sean Wilentz notes that the sentiment behind the quote was
     consistent with Jackson's belief that the democratically elected branches
     of government each must interpret the Constitution, and need not fol-
     low Supreme Court rulings with which they disagreed. Sean Wilentz, *An-
     drew Jackson* (New York: Times Books, 2005), 141.

18   *"The American aristocracy":* Alexis de Tocqueville, *Democracy in America*,
     abridged with introduction by Sanford Kessler; translated by Stephen D.
     Grant (Indianapolis: Hackett Publishing, 2000), 122.

18   *"The lawyer belongs to the people":* Ibid., 121.

18   *"There is almost no political question":* Ibid., 122.

TWO: "NO RIGHTS"

19   *a part of the constitutional system:* Noah Feldman, *The Broken Constitution:
     Lincoln, Slavery, and the Refounding of America* (New York: Farrar, Straus &
     Giroux, 2021), 109.

19   *lucrative railroad routes:* The competition between those who wanted rail-
     road routes to the West Coast to run through the North, and thus spread
     "free soil" west, and those who wanted routes to run through slave states,
     is fascinatingly described in Sidney Blumenthal, *Wrestling with His Angel:
     The Political Life of Abraham Lincoln, vol. 2, 1849–1856* (New York: Simon
     & Schuster, 2017), 92–101.

20   *"blot on our national character":* Timothy S. Huebner, "Roger B. Taney and
     the Slavery Issue: Looking beyond—and before—*Dred Scott*," *Journal of
     American History* 97, no. 1 (June 2010): 17–38, https://doi.org/10.2307
     /jahist/97.1.17.

20   *antislavery senator William Seward:* James F. Simon, *Lincoln and Chief Justice
     Taney: Slavery, Secession, and the President's War Powers* (New York: Simon &
     Schuster, 2006), 99.

20   *"For one, I may say":* *New-York Daily Tribune*, December 19, 1855, https://
     www.loc.gov/item/sn83030213/1855-12-19/ed-1/.

20   *The Supreme Court made its move: Dred Scott v. Sandford*, 60 U.S. 393 (1857).

21   *"Seldom, if ever":* Sidney Blumenthal, *All the Powers of Earth: The Political
     Life of Abraham Lincoln, vol. 3, 1856–1860* (New York: Simon & Schuster,
     2019), 277–78.

21   *"Slavery promises to exist":* Simon, *Lincoln and Chief Justice Taney*, 116.

21   *"We have thought it due to you":* Letter from Justice Robert Cooper Grier
     to James Buchanan, quoted in Don E. Fehrenbacher, *The Dred Scott Case:*

Its Significance in American Law and Politics (New York: Oxford University Press, 1978), 312. Buchanan's eagerness for the Court to rule as it did had a decisive impact on the justices. See Roy Franklin Nichols, *The Disruption of American Democracy* (New York: Free Press, 1948), 77–78.

21   *"We said, when the Kansas-Nebraska bill passed":* "The Triumph of Slavery Complete, March 5, 1857," *New-York Daily Tribune,* March 9, 1857, https://www.loc.gov/resource/sn83030213/1857-03-09/ed-1/?sp=5&st=pdf.

22   *the Missouri Compromise:* The Kansas-Nebraska Act repealed the Missouri Compromise.

22   *The first major originalist opinion:* For a full evisceration of *Dred Scott* as the first major originalist opinion, see Sol Wachtler, *"Dred Scott:* A Nightmare for the Originalists," *Touro Law Review* 22, no. 3 (2014): 1; Cass R. Sunstein, "Constitutional Myth-Making: Lessons from the *Dred Scott* Case" (Occasional Papers No. 37, 1996), http://nrs.harvard.edu/urn-3:HUL.InstRepos:12942329. *Dred Scott* is a rather embarrassing ancestor for originalists. Neil Gorsuch gamely tried to argue that the case repudiated originalism, in Neil M. Gorsuch, *A Republic, If You Can Keep It* (New York: Crown Forum, 2019), 115–16.

22   *"a riot of originalism":* Christopher L. Eisgruber, "Dred Again: Originalism's Forgotten Past," *Constitutional Commentary* 141, no. 10 (1993): 46, https://scholarship.law.umn.edu/concomm/14.

22   *they were dicta:* David M. Potter, *The Impending Crisis: America Before the Civil War, 1848–1861,* Don E. Fehrenbacher, ed. (New York: Harper & Row, 1976), 279–86.

23   *Readers across the country:* Jill Lepore, *These Truths: A History of the United States* (New York: W. W. Norton, 2018), 269.

23   *"entitled to just so much moral weight":* New-York Daily Tribune, March 7, 1857, https://www.loc.gov/resource/sn83030213/1857-03-07/ed-1/?sp=4&st=image&r=-0.073,0.364,0.689,0.257,0. Another reporter wrote, "If epithets and denunciation could sink a judicial body, the Supreme Court of the United States would never be heard of again," https://www.loc.gov/resource/sn83030213/1857-03-07/ed-1/?sp=5&r=0.084,0.922,0.468,0.175,0.

23   *"We scarcely know how to express":* The newspaper reactions North and South are related in Fehrenbacher, *The Dred Scott Case,* 417–19.

23   *The "infamous decision of the slaveholding wing":* David W. Blight, ed., *Frederick Douglass: Speeches and Writing* (New York: Library of America, 2022), 292.

24   *"an astonisher in legal history":* Lincoln's denunciation of the opinion offers a taste of his wit and skill on the stump. "It is the first of its kind; it is an astonisher in legal history. [Laughter] It is a new wonder of the world. [Laughter and applause.]" Abraham Lincoln, "Speech at Chicago, July 10, 1858," in Don E. Fehrenbacher, ed., *Lincoln: Speeches and Writings, 1832–1858* (Des Moines: Library of America, 1989), 451.

24 *"A house divided'"*: "House Divided Speech at Springfield Illinois," June 16, 1857, ibid., 426–434.

24 *"The taste is in my mouth"*: David Herbert Donald, *Lincoln* (New York: Simon & Schuster, 1996), 241.

24 *"He searched through the dusty volumes"*: Harold Holzer, *Lincoln at Cooper Union: The Speech That Made Abraham Lincoln President* (New York: Simon & Schuster, 2004), 28.

24 *In his hourlong address:* "Speech at the Cooper Institute, New York, February 27, 1860," Don E. Fehrenbacher, ed., *Lincoln: Speeches and Writings, 1859–1865* (Des Moines: Library of America, 1989), 111–29.

25 *"There shall be neither Slavery"*: Northwest Ordinance, July 13, 1787, Avalon Project, Yale Law School, http://avalon.law.yale.edu/18th_century /nworder.asp.

25 *"the position assumed by some"*: "First Inaugural Address," Fehrenbacher, *Lincoln: Speeches and Writings, 1859–1865*, 220–21.

25 *Abolitionists criticized:* For a discussion of Frederick Douglass's reaction, see John Stauffer, *Giants: The Parallel Lives of Frederick Douglass and Abraham Lincoln* (New York: Twelve, 2009), 219.

26 *Danielle Allen's sleuthing:* Most later printed versions of the Declaration placed a period after "life, liberty, and the pursuit of happiness." (The transcription on the National Archives website reads that way, for example.) The next sentence tied those ideals to the notion of a government being legitimate only when it rested on the "consent of the governed." In fact, Harvard professor Allen realized on scrutinizing the parchment that the period was a comma; it was all one sentence. Its dramatic conclusion was not about rights but about self-government. See Danielle Allen, *Our Declaration: A Reading of the Declaration of Independence in Defense of Equality* (New York: W. W. Norton, 2014), 275; Jennifer Schuessler, "If Only Thomas Jefferson Could Settle the Issue: A Period Is Questioned in the Declaration of Independence," *New York Times*, July 2, 2014.

26 *the fight already emerging:* The "three fifths compromise" partly counted the enslaved toward electoral representation and thus gave added weight to the South in the Electoral College and Congress, and the fugitive slave clause bound northern state governments to cooperate in returning escaped slaves. See Sean Wilentz, *No Property in Man: Slavery and Anti-Slavery at the Nation's Founding* (Cambridge, MA: Harvard Univ. Press, 2018).

26 *Gettysburg Address responded to* Dred Scott: Lincoln's transmogrification of the meaning of the country, including the substitution of 1776 for 1787 as the nation's founding, was brilliantly expounded in Garry Wills, *Lincoln at Gettysburg: The Words That Remade America* (New York: Simon & Schuster, 1992). See also Michael Waldman, *My Fellow Americans: The Most Important Speeches of America's Presidents, from George Washington to Barack Obama*, rev. ed. (Naperville, IL: Sourcebooks, 2010), 53–56.

27 *"Second Founding"*: See, e.g., Eric Foner, *The Second Founding: How the Civil*

War and Reconstruction Remade the Constitution (New York: W. W. Norton, 2019).

28   *In 1875 Congress passed:* The Supreme Court struck it down in the *Civil Rights Cases*, 109 U.S. 3 (1883).

28   *"an act of surrender":* Steve Luxenberg, *Separate: The Story of* Plessy v. Ferguson, *and America's Journey from Slavery to Segregation* (New York: W. W. Norton, 2019), 257.

28   *in one key voting case, Giles v. Harris*, 189 U.S. 475 (1903). For a discussion of the case, see Michael Waldman, *The Fight to Vote*, rev. ed. (New York: Simon & Schuster, 2022), 86–88; and Richard H. Pildes, "Democracy, Anti-Democracy and the Canon," *Constitutional Commentary* 17 (2000): 603.

28   *150 cases:* Foner, *The Second Founding*, 127.

28   *"counter-revolution of property":* W. E. B. Du Bois, *Black Reconstruction in America, 1860–1880* (New York: Free Press, 1992), 580.

28   *The notorious low point: Plessy v. Ferguson*, 163 U.S. 537 (1896).

28   *Black leaders including Frederick Douglass opposed:* Peter S. Canellos, *The Great Dissenter: The Story of John Marshall Harlan, America's Judicial Hero* (New York: Simon & Schuster, 2021), 333.

THREE: "NINE OLD MEN"

30   *Between 1860 and 1900:* In 1860 it was 32 million people; by 1900 it had grown to 76 million. Bureau of the Census, *Historical Statistics of the United States, Colonial Times to 1970, Part 1*, A 1–8, https://www.census.gov/li brary/publications/1975/compendia/hist_stats_colonial-1970.html.

30   *the national wealth:* Bureau of the Census, *Historical Statistics of the United States, 1789–1945*, https://www.census.gov/library/publications/1949 /compendia/hist_stats_1789-1945.html.

30   *The wealthiest one percent:* Steven R. Weisman, *The Great Tax Wars* (New York: Simon & Schuster, 2002), 179–80.

31   *U.S. Senators chosen by "the people":* U.S. Constitution, Amendment XVII.

31   *Germany:* T. H. Tulchinsky, "Bismarck and the Long Road to Universal Health Coverage," *Case Studies in Public Health* (2018): 131–79, doi:10 .1016/B978-0-12-804571-8.00031-7.

31   *Only in the United States:* The closest analogy in a major country was the effort by Great Britain's House of Lords to veto the "People's Budget" in 1911. That led to constitutional reform that ended the power of the Lords to block legislation. See Bruce Murray, "The 'People's Budget' a Century On," *Journal of Liberal History* 64 (Autumn 2009): 4–13.

31   *it held twenty-one unconstitutional:* William E. Nelson, *Marbury v. Madison: The Origins and Legacy of Judicial Review*, 2nd ed. (Lawrence: University Press of Kansas, 2018), 121.

32   *"We are all of opinion that it does":* For a saucy narrative of how Roscoe

Conkling seemed to have concocted the legislative history of the Fourteenth Amendment, and its impact on the Court, see Adam Winkler, *We the Corporations: How American Businesses Won Their Rights* (New York: Liveright, 2018), 114–60. The announcement of corporate personhood was included in the headnote to *Santa Clara County v. Southern Pacific R. Co.*, 118 U.S. 394, 397 (1886), and became established fact after that.

32 *"monopolize, or attempt to monopolize":* Sherman Antitrust Act of 1890, 15 U.S.C. §§ 1–38.

32 *the "Sugar Trust":* United States v. E.C. Knight Company, 156 U.S. 1 (1895).

32 *it upheld the use of an injunction: In re Debs,* 158 U.S. 565 (1895).

32 *He thundered to the Court:* Weisman, *The Great Tax Wars,* 150–51.

33 *The "boy orator" set off on an unheard-of speaking tour:* Michael Kazin, *A Godly Hero: The Life of William Jennings Bryan* (New York: Alfred A. Knopf, 2006), 63–76.

33 *"Our criticism of the Supreme Court":* "Bryan Tammany's Guest; The Wigwam Crowded to Hear the Boy Orator," *New York Times,* September 30, 1896.

33 *cities and states rather than Congress:* Theda Skocpol, *Social Policy in the United States: Future Possibilities in Historical Perspective* (Princeton: Princeton University Press, 1995), 97.

33 *At the turn of the century:* Paul Kens, *Lochner v. New York: Economic Regulation on Trial* (Lawrence: University Press of Kansas, 1998), 8.

33 *In 1905: Lochner v. New York,* 198 U.S. 45 (1905).

34 *it did not protect the rights of people:* During the *Lochner* Era, from 1897 to 1937, the Supreme Court used substantive due process 212 times to strike down laws, according to the long-accepted analysis. Benjamin F. Wright, *The Growth of American Constitutional Law* (Chicago: University of Chicago Press, 1942), 148.

35 *"If my fellow citizens":* Oliver Wendell Holmes to Harold J. Laski, March 4, 1920, in Mark de Wolfe Howe, ed., *Holmes-Laski Letters,* vol. 1, abridged by Alger Hiss (New York: Atheneum, 1963), 194.

35 *"The tendency of State Legislatures":* "Ten Hour Decision," *New York Times,* April 28, 1905.

35 *"a great husky Irish woman":* Melvin Urofsky, *Louis D. Brandeis* (New York: Random House, 2009), 213.

35 *"the right to privacy":* Joseph Warren and Louis Brandeis, "The Right to Privacy," *Harvard Law Review* 4, no. 5 (1890): 193.

36 *Brandeis produced a brief:* Urofsky, *Louis D. Brandeis,* 212–19. The brief is available at "The Brandeis Brief—in Its Entirety," Louis D. Brandeis School of Law Library, https://louisville.edu/law/library/special-collec tions/the-louis-d.-brandeis-collection/the-brandeis-brief-in-its-entirety.

36 *The argument spoke to the justices':* Skocpol, *Social Policy in the United States,* 127–28.

36 *Chief Justice Walter Clark:* William G. Ross, *A Muted Fury: Populists,*

Progressives, and Labor Unions Confront the Courts, 1890–1937 (Princeton: Princeton University Press, 1994), 94–96.

37 *"a nation of Constitution-worshipers":* Richard Hofstadter, *The Age of Reform* (New York: Vintage, 1955), 200.

37 *Theodore Roosevelt bounded off the ship:* "Million Join in Welcome to Roosevelt," *New York Times,* June 19, 1910.

37 *But the New York Court of Appeals: In Re Jacobs,* 98 N.Y. 98 (NY 1885). In addition to finding that the ban violated the cigar manufacturers' private property, it noted that tobacco was not "injurious to the public health." The employers had claimed it was "a disenfectant."

37 *"It was this case which first waked me":* Theodore Roosevelt, *An Autobiography* (New York: Macmillan, 1913), 89.

38 *"Everywhere he went":* "Denver Shouts Wild Welcome for Roosevelt," *Los Angeles Herald,* April 30, 1910.

38 *"strained to the utmost":* Theodore Roosevelt, "Judges and Progress," *Outlook,* January 6, 1912.

38 *"[W]hen a judge decides":* Theodore Roosevelt, *A Charter of Democracy: Address Before the Ohio Constitutional Convention* (February 21, 1912) (Washington, D.C.: Government Printing Office, 1919), https://www.loc.gov /item/19027679/.

38 *"the craziest article":* "The Short Way with the Courts," *New York Times,* January 6, 1912.

38 *"My hat is in the ring":* James Chace, *1912: Wilson, Roosevelt, Taft & Debs— The Election That Changed the Country* (New York: Simon & Schuster, 2004), 105–6. A boxer would toss a hat into the ring to signal a challenge to a fight.

38 *His attack on the courts:* Sidney M. Milkis, *Theodore Roosevelt, the Progressive Party, and the Transformation of American Democracy* (Lawrence: University Press of Kansas, 2009), 54–62, 75–122.

38 *"will never give up":* "All Taft Wants Is a Square Deal," *New York Times,* March 20, 1912.

39 *seven governors:* Chace, *1912,* 105.

39 *"an untrammeled and independent judiciary":* Republican Party Platform of 1912, online, by Gerhard Peters and John T. Woolley, The American Presidency Project, https://www.presidency.ucsb.edu/node/273327.

39 *"We stand at Armageddon":* H. W. Brands, *T.R.: The Last Romantic* (New York: Basic Books, 1998), 719.

39 *"A second class mind":* Jonathan Alter, *The Defining Moment: FDR's Hundred Days and the Triumph of Hope* (New York: Simon & Schuster, 2006), 233–34. As Alter describes, some historians now think Holmes may in fact have been referring to TR, whom he knew well, rather than FDR, whom he barely knew. The quote is nearly universally assumed to refer to FDR, and was widely known at the time.

40   *a plan by the president:* Jeff Shesol, *Supreme Power: Franklin Roosevelt vs. the Supreme Court* (New York: W. W. Norton, 2010), 87–106.

40   *Within weeks:* See Kenneth S. Davis, *FDR: The New Deal Years, 1933–1937* (New York: Random House, 1986), 42–157.

40   *"had been a remote authority":* V. O. Key Jr., *The Responsible Electorate* (New York: Vintage, 1968), 31.

40   *a law designed to help farmers:* Louisville Joint Stock Land Bank v. Radford, 295 U.S. 555 (1934).

40   *FDR lacked the power:* Humphrey's Executor v. United States, 295 U.S. 602 (1935). The obstreperous commissioner died shortly after being fired, and his estate was suing for back pay. For the story of the case, see William E. Leuchtenburg, *The Supreme Court Reborn: The Constitutional Revolution in the Age of Roosevelt* (New York: Oxford University Press, 1995), 52–80.

40   *Supreme Court struck down the National Recovery Administration:* A. L. A. Schechter Poultry Corporation v. United States, 295 U.S. 495 (1935).

40   *an estimated 85 percent of businesses:* "Johnson Tells NRA Rally Depression Is 25% Lifted by Roosevelt's Program," *New York Times*, September 13, 1933

41   *In September 1933:* "Over 1,500,000 Cheer Vast NRA Parade; March of 250,000 City's Greatest; Demonstration Lasts Until Midnight," *New York Times*, September 14, 1933.

41   *"The most important":* "The Goal of the National Industrial Recovery Act—A Statement by the President on Signing It, June 16, 1933," in *The Public Papers and Addresses of Franklin D. Roosevelt, Volume 2, The Year of Crisis, 1933* (New York: Random House, 1938), 246.

41   *"This is the end of this business":* Arthur M. Schlesinger Jr., *The Politics of Upheaval, 1935–1936* (New York: Houghton Mifflin, 1960), 280.

41   *Roosevelt held a furious press conference:* "The Two Hundred and Ninth Press Conference, May 31, 1935," in *The Public Papers and Addresses of Franklin D. Roosevelt, Volume 4, The Court Disapproves, 1935* (New York: Random House, 1938), 201–5.

41   *farm program:* U.S. v. Butler, 297 U.S. 1 (1936).

42   *New York law requiring:* Morehead v. New York ex rel. Tipaldo, 298 U.S. 587 (1936).

42   *"'no-man's-land'":* "The Three Hundredth Press Conference (Excerpts), June 2, 1936," in *The Public Papers and Addresses of Franklin D. Roosevelt, Volume 5, The People Approve, 1936* (New York: Random House, 1938), 192.

42   *"'the taxing power'":* Frances Perkins, "The Roots of Social Security," Speech to the Social Security Administration, October 23, 1962.

42   *"Never before":* "Campaign Address at Madison Square Garden, New York City, 'We Have Only Just Begun to Fight,' October 31, 1936," in *Public Papers and Addresses of Franklin D. Roosevelt, Volume 5*, 568-69.

43 *Supporters from fifteen states:* David E. Kyvig, "The Road Not Taken: FDR, the Supreme Court, and Constitutional Amendment," *Political Science Quarterly* 104, no. 3 (Autumn 1989): 463, 475.

43 *"Cowards! Cowards!":* Sidney Fine, *Sit-Down: The General Motors Strike of 1936–1937,* rev. ed. (Ann Arbor: University of Michigan Press, 2020), 6–7.

43 *"Tomorrow morning, I shall personally enter":* David M. Kennedy, *Freedom from Fear: The American People in Depression and War, 1929–1945* (New York: Oxford University Press, 1999), 313; Irving Bernstein, *Turbulent Years: A History of the American Worker* (Boston: Houghton Mifflin, 1971), 548. Lewis was leader of the United Mine Workers. With the other industrial unions, the UMW formed the Committee for Industrial Organizations. The American Federation of Labor expelled them in 1938, and they formed the rival Congress of Industrial Organizations. The two groups later merged to become the AFL-CIO.

44 *"Roosevelt's first instinct":* Eric Alterman, *When Presidents Lie* (New York: Viking, 2004), 26.

44 *"I feel too much like a conspirator":* Samuel I. Rosenman, *Working with Roosevelt* (New York: Harper & Brothers, 1952), 154.

44 *"Roosevelt's presentation":* Shesol, *Supreme Power,* 295.

45 *"Boys, here's where I cash in my chips":* Joseph Alsop and Turner Catledge, *The 168 Days* (Garden City: Doubleday, 1938), 67. A year later, after Roosevelt's plan crashed and the remark was made public, Representative Hatton Sumners claimed what he had really said was, "Boys, here's where I cash in," meaning he would save Roosevelt and his effort to reshape the Court, and perhaps reap political reward. Josiah M. Daniel III, "What I Said Was 'Here Is Where I Cash In': The Instrumental Role of Congressman Hatton Sumners in the Resolution of the 1937 Court-Packing Crisis," *UIC John Marshall Law Review* 54 (2021): 379.

45 *"The question was debated":* Leuchtenburg, *The Supreme Court Reborn,* 136.

45 *National Committee to Uphold Constitutional Government:* Shesol, *Supreme Power,* 359.

45 *"the most unsparing":* Ibid., 380.

45 *"has been acting not as a judicial body":* Franklin D. Roosevelt, Fireside Chat, March 9, 1937, https://www.presidency.ucsb.edu/documents/fireside-chat-17.

46 *the Court overruled a 1923 case: Adkins v. Children's Hospital,* 261 U.S. 525 (1923).

46 *"the protection of law against the evils": West Coast Hotel v. Parrish,* 300 U.S. 379 (1937).

46 *National Labor Relations Act: National Labor Relations Board v. Jones & Laughlin Steel Corporation,* 301 U.S. 1 (1937).

46 *Two upheld:* Unemployment compensation was upheld in *Steward Machine Co. v. Davis,* 301 U.S. 548 (1937).

46 *"The conception of the spending power": Helvering v. Davis,* 301 U.S. 619

(1937). The Spending Clause (U.S. Constitution, Article I, Section 8, Clause 1) broadly authorizes spending for the "general Welfare." The Necessary and Proper Clause (U.S. Constitution, Article I, Section 8, Clause 18) gives Congress power to condition receipt of the funds. These provisions provoked an early debate among the Founders. Madison later claimed that the "general welfare" language merely referred to other enumerated powers in the Constitution; Hamilton argued that "the clause confers a power separate and distinct from those later enumerated." The Court had first embraced the Hamiltonian position in 1936, in *U.S. v. Butler*, even as it struck down the New Deal farm program on other grounds.

46 *"the switch in time":* John Q. Barrett, "Attribution Time: Cal Tinney's 'A Switch in Time'll Save Nine,'" *Oklahoma Law Review* 73 (2020): 229. Barrett, the biographer of Justice Robert Jackson, was the first to find the original quipster, long forgotten by history. The line is a pun on the adage, "a stitch in time saves nine."

47 *Polls never supported his plan:* Gallup poll, March 3–8, 1937, in Lydia Saad, "Gallup Vault: A Supreme Court Power Play," February 26, 2016, https:// news.gallup.com/vault/189617/supreme-court-power-play.aspx.

47 *Administrative Procedure Act:* P.L. 79-404, 60 Stat. 237 (1946). The APA is codified at 5 U.S.C. § 551 *et seq.* For the business effort to pass the law, see Roni Elias, "The Legislative History of the Administrative Procedure Act," *Fordham Environmental Law Review* 27, no. 2 (2015): 207.

48 *Libertarian strategist Randy Barnett:* Randy E. Barnett, "Restoring the Lost Constitution, Not the Constitution in Exile," *Fordham Law Review* 75 (2006): 669.

48 Carolene Products: *United States v. Carolene Products Company*, 304 U.S. 144 (1938). The quotes from footnote four have been edited to eliminate the lengthy case citations within.

48 *"filled milk":* The now obscure issue was once hotly contested. See Geoffrey P. Miller, "The True Story of Carolene Products," *The Supreme Court Review* 1987 (1987), 397. Even the margarine example was fraught. Congress had allowed oleomargarine, but under pressure from the dairy industry, had taxed it at a prohibitively high rate. States later banned the use of yellow color in margarine, which made it look too much like butter.

49 *Japanese Americans: Korematsu v. United States*, 323 U.S. 214 (1944).

49 *It let school districts:* In *Minersville School District v. Gobitis*, 310 U.S. 586 (1940), the Court allowed a school district to require Jehovah's Witnesses to say the Pledge of Allegiance and salute the flag. Just three years later, the Court reversed course in *West Virginia State Board of Education v. Barnette*, 319 U.S. 624 (1943), holding that the First Amendment protected students' right not to salute or say the pledge.

50 *"almost bombastically pretentious":* Stone refused to move into his chambers.

Clare Cushman, *Courtwatchers: Eyewitness Accounts in Supreme Court History* (Lanham, MD: Rowman & Littlefield, 2011), 110.

FOUR: THE WARREN COURT

51   *its most revered case:* Brown v. Board of Education of Topeka, 347 U.S. 483 (1954). The classic account of *Brown* is Richard Kluger, *Simple Justice: The History of Brown v. Board of Education and Black America's Struggle for Equality* (New York: Random House, 1975).

52   *Black also had once been a member of the Ku Klux Klan:* William E. Leuchtenburg, *The Supreme Court Reborn: The Constitutional Revolution in the Age of Roosevelt* (New York: Oxford University Press, 1995), 180–212.

52   *"This is the first indication":* Brad Snyder, *Democratic Justice: Felix Frankfurter, the Supreme Court, and the Making of the Liberal Establishment* (New York: W. W. Norton, 2022), 569.

52   *"I can't escape":* Bernard Schwartz, *A History of the Supreme Court* (New York: Oxford University Press, 1993), 292.

52   *Warren waged a high-EQ campaign:* Jim Newton, *Justice for All: Earl Warren and the Nation He Made* (New York: Riverhead Books, 2006), 313.

53   *"If we are wrong":* Taylor Branch, *Parting the Waters: America in the King Years, 1954–1963* (New York: Simon & Schuster, 1988), 140–41.

53   *the Democratic Party platform had come out:* 1948 Democratic Platform (July 12, 1948), https://www.presidency.ucsb.edu/documents/1948-democratic-party-platform.

53   *"growing in alarming proportions":* Mary Dudziak, "Brown as a Cold War Case," *The Journal of American History* 91, no. 1 (June 2004): 32, 37.

53   *Voice of America radio network:* "'Voice' Speaks in 34 Languages to Flash Court Ruling to World," *New York Times*, May 18, 1954.

53   *Just days after the announcement:* Michael Murakami, "Desegregation," in *Public Opinion and Constitutional Controversy*, Nathaniel Persily, Jack Citrin, and Patrick J. Egan, eds. (New York: Oxford University Press, 2008), 21.

53   *segregation in streetcars and buses:* Browder v. Gayle, 142 F. Supp. 707 (M.D. Ala.), affirmed, 352 U.S. 903 (1956) (per curiam).

53   *Gallup Poll two years later:* Gallup Organization, Lydia Saad, "Gallup Vault: 60 Years Ago, the End of 'Separate but Equal,'" November 11, 2016 (Washington, D.C.), https://news.gallup.com/vault/197372/gallup-vault-years-ago-end-separate-equal.aspx.

54   *"all deliberate speed":* Brown v. Board of Education of Topeka (II), 349 U.S. 294 (1955).

54   *"clear abuse of judicial power":* Michael J. Klarman, *From Jim Crow to Civil Rights: The Supreme Court and the Struggle for Racial Equality* (New York: Oxford University Press, 2004), 320.

54   *He lost to a more extreme candidate:* Dan T. Carter, *The Politics of Rage: George*

Wallace, the Origins of the New Conservatism, and the Transformation of American Politics, 2nd ed. (Baton Rouge: Louisiana State University Press, 2000), 96.

54 *"Earl Warren does not have enough brains"*: Ed Cray, *Chief Justice: A Biography of Earl Warren* (New York: Simon & Schuster, 1997), 11.

54 *Little Rock Central High School:* David Strauss, "Little Rock and the Legacy of *Brown*," *University of Saint Louis Law Review* 52 (2008): 3, https://scholarship.law.slu.edu/cgi/viewcontent.cgi?article=1593&context=lj.

54 *The Supreme Court responded with force: Cooper v. Aaron*, 158 U.S. 1 (1958).

54 *"long-settled doctrine":* Josh Blackman, "The Irrepressible Myth of *Cooper v. Aaron*," *Georgetown Law Journal* 107 (2019): 1135, https://www.law.georgetown.edu/georgetown-law-journal/wp-content/uploads/sites/26/2019/05/The-Irrepressible-Myth-of-Cooper-v.-Aaron.pdf.

55 *"I couldn't serve there":* "You're Goddamn Sure Going to Serve," Transcript of calls between Lyndon Johnson and Richard Russell, November 29, 1963, "Lyndon Johnson and Richard Russell on 29 November 1963," Tape K6311.05, PNO 7; and "Lyndon Johnson and Richard Russell (President Johnson joined by Albert Moursund) on 29 November 1963," Tape K6311.06, PNOs 14, 15, and 16, Presidential Recordings Digital Edition. Also: *The Kennedy Assassination and the Transfer of Power*, vol. 1, ed. Max Holland (Charlottesville: University of Virginia Press, 2014–). URLs: http://prde.upress.virginia.edu/conversations/9010161; http://prde.upress.virginia.edu/conversations/9010184.

55 *"It hadn't even taken that long":* Robert A. Caro, *The Passage of Power: The Years of Lyndon Johnson*, vol. 4 (New York: Alfred A. Knopf, 2012), 445–46.

56 *only red-baiter Joseph McCarthy:* Seth Stern and Stephen Wermiel, *Justice Brennan: Liberal Champion* (New York: Houghton Mifflin, 2010), 114.

56 *reopened America's borders to immigrants:* For the story of the 1965 law, see Jia Lynn Lang, *One Mighty and Irresistible Tide: The Epic Struggle over American Immigration, 1924–1965* (New York: W. W. Norton, 2020), 233–61.

56 *a nationwide regime:* For a recent laudatory look at the Warren Court, see Geoffrey Stone and David Strauss, *Democracy and Equality* (New York: Oxford University Press, 2020).

57 *In 1962, the Supreme Court banned them: Engel v. Vitale*, 370 U.S. 421 (1962).

57 *school-sponsored Bible reading: Abington School District v. Schempp*, 374 U.S. 203 (1963).

57 *It barred the introduction in criminal trials: Mapp v. Ohio*, 367 U.S. 643 (1961). The ruling applied the Fourth Amendment's prohibition against unreasonable searches and seizures of evidence applied to state governments as well as the federal government. This was done through the process of partial "incorporation," applying the Bill of Rights to the states through the Fourteenth Amendment.

57 *had to be represented by a lawyer: Gideon v. Wainwright*, 372 U.S. 335 (1963).

57 *police needed to warn suspects: Miranda v. Arizona*, 384 U.S. 436 (1966).

57 *First Amendment applied to libel law: New York Times Co. v. Sullivan*, 376 U.S. 254 (1964).

57 *"political questions": Luther v. Borden*, 48 U.S. 1 (1849).

57 *In 1920:* The failure to reapportion in the 1920s is told in Charles W. Eagles, *Democracy Delayed: Congressional Reapportionment and Urban-Rural Conflict in the 1920s* (Athens: University of Georgia Press, 2010), 32–84.

57 *"in nineteen states":* J. Douglas Smith, *On Democracy's Doorstep: The Inside Story of How the Supreme Court Brought "One Person, One Vote" to the United States* (New York: Hill & Wang, 2014), 18.

58 *Los Angeles County:* Ibid., 16.

58 *Supreme Court waded into the thicket: Baker v. Carr*, 369 U.S. 186 (1962).

58 *"one person, one vote": Reynolds v. Sims*, 377 U.S. 533 (1964).

58 *"conspicuously reluctant":* Stone and Strauss, *Democracy and Equality*, 6.

58 *only the power of the federal government: Barron v. Baltimore*, 32 U.S. 243 (1833).

59 *"among the fundamental personal rights": Gitlow v. New York*, 268 U.S. 652 (1925).

59 *Benjamin Gitlow:* "Benjamin Gitlow Is Dead at 73; Leader in U.S. Communist Party," *New York Times*, July 20, 1965.

60 *"He plays an interesting game of poker":* Roosevelt said this in a meeting with seven political leaders as they mulled the vice presidential selection. Joseph Lelyveld, *His Final Battle: The Last Months of Franklin Roosevelt* (New York: Alfred A. Knopf, 2016), 166.

60 *"he left his third wife":* Jeffrey Rosen, "Courting Trouble," review of Bruce Allen Murphy, *Wild Bill*, *Washington Post*, May 9, 2003.

60 *P. T. Barnum:* John W. Johnson, *Griswold v. Connecticut: Birth Control and the Constitutional Right of Privacy* (Lawrence: University Press of Kansas, 2005), 5.

60 *Prescott Bush:* Jacob Weisberg, *The Bush Tragedy* (New York: Random House, 2008), 18.

60 *the nickname "rubbers":* Jon Meacham, *Destiny and Power: The American Odyssey of George Herbert Walker Bush* (New York: Random House, 2015), 140.

61 *"When the long arm":* Stern and Wermiel, *Justice Brennan*, 281, citing Fowler W. Harper's Jurisdictional Statement in Brief for the Appellants, 1960 WL 98679 *2, *Poe v. Ullman*, 376 U.S. 497 (1961) (No. 60-61).

61 *"[T]he full scope of the liberty": Poe v. Ullman*, 367 U.S. 497 (1961) (Harlan, J., dissenting).

61 *"Specific guarantees": Griswold v. Connecticut*, 381 U.S. 479 (1965).

61 *Ninth Amendment:* Ibid. (Goldberg J. concurring).

61 *"If the right of privacy means anything": Eisenstadt v. Baird*, 405 U.S. 438 (1972).

62 *Consumer advocates won:* Adam Winkler, *We the Corporations: How American Businesses Won Their Rights* (New York: Liveright, 2018), 289–300.

FIVE: THE LONG BACKLASH

63   *"sooner or later":* Alexis de Tocqueville, *Democracy in America*, abridged with introduction by Sanford Kessler; translated by Stephen D. Grant (Indianapolis: Hackett Publishing, 2000), 122.

64   *"raw and naked power":* Rick Perlstein, *Before the Storm: Barry Goldwater and the Unmaking of the American Consensus* (New York: Hill & Wang, 2001), 425.

64   *Committee for Government of the People:* Michael Waldman, *The Fight to Vote*, rev. ed. (New York: Simon & Schuster, 2022), 140.

64   *"the whole secret of politics":* Garry Wills, *Nixon Agonistes: The Crisis of the Self-Made Man* (New York: Houghton Mifflin, 1970), 265. The young aide wrote a manifesto for the Southern Strategy. See Kevin P. Phillips, *The Emerging Republican Majority* (The James Madison Library in American Politics) (Princeton: Princeton University Press, 2015).

64   *"What's shakin', Chiefy baby?":* Bob Woodward and Scott Armstrong, *The Brethren: Inside the Supreme Court* (New York: Simon & Schuster, 1979), 67.

64   *"stick it to":* John Ehrlichman, *Witness to Power* (New York: Simon & Schuster, 1982), 118.

65   *"There are a lot of mediocre judges":* Hruska added, "We can't have all Brandeises, Frankfurters, and Cardozos." By coincidence, no doubt, all were Jewish. (At the time, after Abe Fortas resigned from the Court, there was no Jewish justice, and there would be none until 1994.)

65   *"Find a good federal judge":* Richard Reeves, *President Nixon: Alone in the White House* (New York: Simon & Schuster, 2001), 160.

65   *"I am Southern":* "Carswell Disavows '48 Speech Backing White Supremacy," Associated Press, January 22, 1970.

65   *The Burger Court:* The argument that the Burger Court was more significant than understood in pushing the law in a conservative direction is made by Michael J. Graetz and Linda Greenhouse, *The Burger Court and the Judicial Right* (New York: Simon & Schuster, 2016).

65   *"Play it tough":* Transcript of Oval Office conversation, June 23, 1972, in Stanley I. Kutler, *Abuse of Power: The New Nixon Tapes* (New York: Free Press, 1997), 68–69.

65   *In a jumbled opinion: Buckley v. Valeo*, 424 U.S. 1 (1976). For a full critique of *Buckley*, see E. Joshua Rosenkranz, *Buckley Stops Here: Loosening the Judicial Stranglehold on Campaign Finance* (New York: Century Foundation Press, 1998); E. Joshua Rosenkranz, ed., *If Buckley Fell: A First Amendment Blueprint for Regulating Money in Politics* (New York: Century Foundation, 1999).

65   *"Money is speech": Buckley v. Valeo*, transcript of argument, November 10, 1975, 24.

66   *"These death sentences are cruel": Furman v. Georgia*, 408 U.S. 238 (1972).

Dozens of states rewrote their laws to bring order to their use of the death penalty, and many codified it for the first time. New laws were upheld in *Gregg v. Georgia*, 428 U.S. 153 (1976). Thereafter the number of executions began to rise.

66   *States had begun to ease abortion laws:* Mary Ziegler, *Abortion and the Law in America: Roe v. Wade to the Present* (New York: Cambridge University Press, 2020), 13–20.

67   *Political conservatives and evangelical Christians:* Richard K. Williams, *Defenders of the Unborn: The Pro-Life Movement Before Roe v. Wade* (New York: Oxford University Press, 2016), 67.

67   *"Catholic issue":* For a discussion of how abortion politics forged a coalition between evangelicals and Catholics, two communities long hostile to one another, see Steven Waldman, *Sacred Liberty: America's Long, Bloody, and Ongoing Struggle for Religious Freedom* (New York: HarperCollins, 2019), 232–33.

67   *A March for Life:* The first march in Washington attracted six thousand people, according to contemporary press reports. See Nancy Hicks, "Both Sides Press Abortion Views," *New York Times*, January 23, 1974. In recent years antiabortion groups claim there were in fact many more people there.

67   *"manslaughter, if not murder":* The stirrings of opposition to *Roe v. Wade* are described in Rick Perlstein, *The Invisible Bridge: The Fall of Nixon and the Rise of Reagan* (New York: Simon & Schuster, 2014), 300–301.

67   *the now annual march drew:* Rick Perlstein, *Reaganland: America's Right Turn, 1976–1980* (New York: Simon & Schuster, 2020), 47.

67   *The 1972 Republican platform:* The 1972, 1976, and 1980 Republican Party platforms are found at Gerhard Peters and John T. Woolley, The American Presidency Project, https://www.presidency.ucsb.edu/node/273420.

67   *He ran as an angry voice of backlash:* An eye-opening look at Reagan's belligerent early days in politics is Matthew Dallek, *The Right Moment: Ronald Reagan's First Victory and the Decisive Turning Point in American Politics* (New York: Oxford University Press, 2004). The impact on Reagan's demeanor of his near assassination is visible in *American Experience: Reagan*, PBS.

67   *His team mapped an audacious strategy:* Office of Legal Policy, United States Department of Justice, *The Constitution in the Year 2000: Choices Ahead in Constitutional Interpretation*, October 11, 1988 (Washington, D.C.: Government Printing Office).

68   *"roam[ing] at large":* Attorney General Edwin Meese III, "Speech Before the American Bar Association," Washington, D.C., July 19, 1985, in Steven G. Calabresi, ed., *Originalism: A Quarter-Century of Debate* (Washington, D.C.: Regnery, 2007), 287–96.

69   *"dead, dead, dead!":* Scalia used that line often, winning raucous laughter from audiences. An example is described in Ushma Patel, "Scalia Favors

'Enduring,' Not Living, Constitution," Princeton University Office of Information, posted December 11, 2012.

69 *One estimate is that one in three:* See Barry J. McMillon, "Supreme Court Nominations, 1789 to 2020: Actions by the Senate, the Judiciary Committee, and the President," Congressional Research Service, March 8, 2022, https://crsreports.congress.gov.

69 *"stunned as if by a bomb":* Alpheus Thomas Mason, *Brandeis: A Free Man's Life* (New York: Viking, 1946), 465.

69 *"He is a muckraker":* Melvin Urofsky, *Louis D. Brandeis* (New York: Random House, 2009), 438.

69 *"Where others were radical":* Ibid., 439.

69 *"The participation of the Negro in politics":* Gilbert Jonas, *Freedom's Sword: The NAACP and the Struggle Against Racism, 1909–1969* (New York: Routledge, 2005), 120.

70 *went before the Judiciary Committee:* See Wil Haygood, *Showdown: Thurgood Marshall and the Supreme Court Nomination That Changed America* (New York: Viking, 2015), especially 3–10.

70 *"Well, Senator, the word 'voluntary'":* Ibid., 99.

70 *"wreak yourself upon the world!":* Dale Russakoff and Al Kamen, "Bork's Appetite Is Whetted for Place on Supreme Court," *Washington Post,* July 28, 1987.

70 *Bork had revolutionized antitrust:* See Robert H. Bork, *The Antitrust Paradox: A Policy at War with Itself* (New York: Basic Books, 1978).

70 *"curse of bigness":* For a recent assessment of Brandeis's views and how they were supplanted by those of Bork, see Tim Wu, *The Curse of Bigness: Antitrust in the New Gilded Age* (New York: Columbia Global Reports, 2018).

70 *For Bork, the only measurable and thus legitimate test:* Ibid., 86–92.

71 *"judicial imperialism":* U.S. Congress, Senate, Committee on the Judiciary, *Confirmation of Federal Judges, Hearings Before the Committee on the Judiciary, United States Senate, Ninety-Seventh Congress, First Session, on the Selection and Confirmation of Federal Judges, July 14 and 28, September 15, October 6 and 22, 1981, Part 1,*1982, 5.

71 *He believed the First Amendment protected only political speech:* Ethan Bronner, *Battle for Justice: How the Bork Nomination Shook America* (New York: Doubleday, 1989), 242–48.

71 *"is itself a principle":* Robert Bork, "Civil Rights—A Challenge," *The New Republic,* August 31, 1963.

71 *"I don't want to be seen":* Garrett M. Graff, *Watergate: A New History* (New York: Simon & Schuster, 2022), 508.

71 *"Robert Bork's America":* Jack Farrell, *Ted Kennedy: A Life* (New York: Penguin, 2022), 457.

71 *People for the American Way:* "1987 Robert Bork TV ad, narrated by Gregory Peck," YouTube, accessed April 18, 2022, https://www.google.com

/search?q=youtube+peck+bork&rlz=1C1CHBF_enUS795US795&oq=you
tube+peck+bork&aqs=chrome..69i57j69i64j69i60.2753j0j9&sourceid=
chrome&ie=UTF-8.

71   *"You wouldn't vote":* Bronner, *Battle for Justice,* 179.

72   *"If your senators":* Ibid.

72   *Previously he had praised Bork:* "Say the administration sends up Bork and,
     after our investigations, he looks a lot like Scalia. I'd have to vote for him,
     and if the [special-interest] groups tear me apart, that's the medicine I'll
     have to take." George F. Will, "Biden v. Bork," *Washington Post,* July 2, 1987.

72   *he set out a new standard:* Bronner, *Battle for Justice,* 124–26.

72   *"In passing on this nomination":* "Excerpts from Opening Statements,"
     United Press International, September 16, 1987, https://www.upi.com
     /Archives/1987/09/16/Excerpts-from-opening-statements/717455876
     3200/.

73   *ninety activist leaders:* Michael Pertschuk and Wendy Schaetzel, *The People
     Rising: The Campaign Against the Bork Nomination* (New York: Thunder's
     Mouth Press, 1989), 299–302.

73   *"Borked":* William Safire, *Safire's New Political Dictionary,* rev. ed. (New
     York: Oxford University Press, 2008), 74–75.

73   *"rot and decadence":* Robert Bork, *Slouching Towards Gomorrah* (New York:
     HarperCollins, 1996), 63.

73   *Near the end of his life:* The university and its former professor settled for
     an undisclosed amount. Isaac Arnsdorf, "Robert Bork Settles $1 Million
     Lawsuit with Yale Club," *Yale Daily News,* May 12, 2008, https://yaledaily
     news.com/blog/2008/05/12/robert-bork-settles-1-million-lawsuit-with
     -yale-club/.

73   *"Greenhouse effect":* Martin Tolchin, "Press Is Condemned by a Federal
     Judge for Court Coverage," *New York Times,* June 15, 1992.

74   *"Souter-type candidate":* "GOP Senator Concerned About Miers' Abortion
     Views," ABC News, October 5, 2005, https://abcnews.go.com/GMA/Su
     premeCourt/story?id=1184984.

74   *Three conservative law students formed the Federalist Society:* See generally
     Amanda Hollis-Brusky, *Ideas with Consequences: The Federalist Society and the
     Conservative Counterrevolution* (New York: Oxford University Press, 2015);
     Michael Avery and Danielle McLaughlin, *The Federalist Society: How Con-
     servatives Took the Law Back from Liberals* (Nashville: Vanderbilt University
     Press, 2013); and a volume edited by the Federalist Society itself on its
     anniversary, Calabresi, ed., *Originalism.* The founding students were Cal-
     abresi, now a professor; Lee Liberman, later a George H. W. Bush aide;
     and David McIntosh, who became a member of Congress. The broader
     history of the movement is described in Steven M. Teles, *The Rise of the
     Conservative Legal Movement* (Princeton: Princeton University Press, 2008).
     Interestingly, in this book Leonard Leo's name appears on only two pages.

74   *only 15 percent of law professors:* Adam Bonica, Adam Chilton, Kyle Rozema,

and Maya Sen, "The Legal Academy's Ideological Uniformity," *Journal of Legal Studies* 47 (1) (2018): 1.

74 *"grew to become the most influential":* Noah Feldman with Lidia Jean Kott, *Takeover: How a Conservative Student Club Captured the Supreme Court* (Audible Audio Book, 2021).

74 *Eventually the Federalist Society had:* For information on chapters, see *2021 Annual Report*, Federalist Society for Law & Public Policy (2022), https://fedsoc-cms-public.s3.amazonaws.com/update/pdf/rcgSSFzDr EVXTh9aDQvr6YlLvvh9WSl7vIU8ZYIV.pdf. For information on active members and the pervasive reach of the society, see David Montgomery, "Conquerors of the Courts," *Washington Post Magazine,* January 2, 2019.

75 *Libertarians hatched the lawsuit:* Josh Blackman, *Unprecedented: The Constitutional Challenge to Obamacare* (New York: PublicAffairs, 2013), 41–43.

75 *Amy Coney Barrett was a little-known:* Zeke Miller, Colleen Long, and Michael Balsamo, "How It Happened: From Law Professor to High Court in Four Years," Associated Press, September 26, 2020.

75 *"judges project":* Montgomery, "Conquerors of the Courts."

75 *Leonard Leo of the Federalist Society:* Jeffrey Toobin, "The Conservative Pipeline to the Supreme Court," *The New Yorker,* April 10, 2017, https://www .newyorker.com/magazine/2017/04/17/the-conservative-pipeline-to-the -supreme-court.

76 *"beyond disingenuous":* Ruth Marcus, *Supreme Ambition: Brett Kavanaugh and the Conservative Takeover* (New York: Simon & Schuster, 2019), 24.

76 *$250 million:* Robert O'Harrow Jr. and Shawn Boburg, "A Conservative Activist's Behind the Scenes Campaign to Remake the Nation's Courts," *Washington Post,* May 21, 2019.

76 *"JCN has made more than 14,000 ad buys":* Captured Courts: The Impact of the Judicial Crisis Network's Dark-Money Scheme on Our Courts, Democratic Policy and Communications Committee, April 2022, https://www.demo crats.senate.gov/imo/media/doc/Captured%20Courts%20Report%20 4-5-22.pdf.

76 *It spent $15 million:* Richard Lardner, "Pro-Kavanaugh Group Received Millions from Anonymous Donors," Associated Press, November 27, 2018.

76 *the most conservative Democrat:* Morris E. Fiorina, *Unstable Majorities: Polarization, Party Sorting, and Political Stalemate* (Palo Alto: Stanford University Press, 2017), 18. Fiorina cites the widely used assessment of political scientists Keith T. Poole and Howard Rosenthal, who date this trend to the early 1970s. Keith T. Poole and Howard Rosenthal, *Ideology & Congress* (New Brunswick, NJ: Transaction Publishers, 2007).

77 *It summarized the trend:* Presidential Commission on the Supreme Court of the United States, *Final Report,* December, 2021, 16, https://www.white house.gov/pcscotus/final-report/. The author served as a member of the commission.

78 *Starting with Nixon:* Sandra Day O'Connor was a state court judge, and

Elena Kagan was serving as solicitor general when chosen. When chosen as associate justice, William Rehnquist was a Justice Department official, but was a member of the Supreme Court when elevated to chief justice.

78 *On several occasions he offered a seat:* George Stephanopoulos, *All Too Human* (New York: Little, Brown, 1999), 186–88. Cuomo had always been Clinton's first choice. But Clinton and Cuomo had an uneasy relationship. "Seeing them interact was like watching porcupines mate," Stephanopoulos wrote.

79 *Clinton tried to appoint Interior Secretary Bruce Babbitt:* John F. Harris, *The Survivor: Bill Clinton in the White House* (New York: Random House, 2005), 61.

79 *installed exclusively Catholic and Jewish justices:* Zachary Baron Shemtob, "The Catholic and Jewish Court: Explaining the Absence of Protestants on the Nation's Highest Court," *Journal of Law and Religion* 27, no. 2 (2011–12): 359, https://www.jstor.org/stable/23645136. Bush did nominate Protestant Harriet Miers, but she withdrew.

SIX: THE TRUMP COURT

80 *"balls and strikes":* U.S. Congress, Senate, Committee on the Judiciary, *Confirmation Hearing on the Nomination of John G. Roberts, Jr. to be Chief Justice of the United States,* 109th Cong., 1st Sess., September 12–15.

80 *"Figuring out where":* Marcia Coyle, "Only 'Balls and Strikes'? Sotomayor: Don't Ignore How Strike Zone Is Set," *National Law Journal,* May 21, 2021, https://www.law.com/nationallawjournal/2021/05/21/only-balls-and-strikes-sotomayor-dont-ignore-how-strike-zone-is-set/.

81 *a career marked:* John Roberts's early career is recounted in Joan Biskupic, *The Chief: The Life and Turbulent Times of John Roberts* (New York: Basic Books, 2019), 13–140.

81 *His boss, William Rehnquist:* Rehnquist's memos to Robert Jackson are described in Richard Kluger, *Simple Justice: The History of Brown v. Board of Education and Black America's Struggle for Equality* (New York: Random House, 1975), 613–15. Rehnquist's confirmation hearings, the controversy over his memos to Jackson, and his unpersuasive denials, are described in John A. Jenkins, *The Partisan: The Life of William Rehnquist* (New York: PublicAffairs, 2012), 215–22.

81 *"Circumstances have changed dramatically":* Political Staff of the *Washington Post, Deadlock: The Inside Story of America's Closest Election* (New York: PublicAffairs, 2001), 48.

82 *Brett Kavanaugh and Amy Coney Barrett also:* Joan Biskupic, "Supreme Court Is About to Have 3 Bush v. Gore Alumni Sitting on the Bench," CNN.com, October 17, 2020, https://edition.cnn.com/2020/10/17/politics/bush-v-gore-barrett-kavanaugh-roberts-supreme-court/index.html.

82 *"It is not often":* Biskupic, *The Chief,* 190.

82 *"It is a sordid business":* League of United Latin American Citizens v. Perry, 548 U.S. 399 (2006) (Roberts, C.J., concurring in part, dissenting in part).

82 *"The way to stop discrimination":* Parents Involved in Community Schools v. Seattle School District No. 1, 551 U.S. 701 (2007).

83 *"Every Chief Justice takes on a project":* Jeffrey Toobin, "The John Roberts Project," *The New Yorker*, April 2, 2014, https://www.newyorker.com/news /daily-comment/the-john-roberts-project.

83 *undid a century of campaign finance law:* Defenders of *Citizens United* insist it did not strike down a century of law, but they are mistaken. For decades statutes covered indirect spending as well as gifts to candidates. The Tillman Act, for example, banned "a money contribution in connection with any election to any political office." Tillman Act, Pub. L. No. 59–36, 34 Stat. 864, 865 (1907) (codified as amended at 2 U.S.C. § 441b(a) (2006)). Only one case, *First National Bank of Boston v. Bellotti*, 435 U.S. 765 (1978), struck down an outright ban on corporate contributions to state ballot initiative campaigns. The Court never extended that narrow ruling to candidate races or federal elections. See *Austin v. Michigan Chamber of Commerce*, 494 U.S. 652 (1990) (upholding ban on using corporate treasury funds for independent expenditures on political campaigns); *Nixon v. Shrink Missouri Government PAC*, 528 U.S. 377 (2000) (the principles of *Buckley v. Valeo* applied to state laws); *McConnell v. Federal Election Commission*, 540 U.S. 93 (2003) (upholding the McCain-Feingold law, the Bipartisan Campaign Reform Act). In *Austin* and *McConnell* the Court made clear that the law could treat contributions and spending by corporations differently from those of natural persons.

83 *The rule dated to 1907:* The story of the Tillman Act is told in Robert E. Mutch, *Buying the Vote: A History of Campaign Finance Reform* (New York: Oxford University Press, 2014), 45–61; Adam Winkler, *We the Corporations: How American Businesses Won Their Rights* (New York: Liveright, 2018), 218–20; and Michael Waldman, *The Fight to Vote*, rev. ed. (New York: Simon & Schuster, 2022), 99–104.

83 *"constitutional avoidance":* Some friend of the court briefs urged exactly that course of action. See *Citizens United v. Federal Election Commission*, Supplemental Brief of Former Officials of the American Civil Liberties Union as *Amici Curiae* on Behalf of Neither Party, July 31, 2009, https:// www.fec.gov/resources/legalresources/litigation/citizens_united_sc _08_acsb_formeraclu.pdf.

83 *"The censorship we now confront":* Citizens United v. Federal Election Commission, 558 U.S. 310, 354 (2010).

83 *"While American democracy is imperfect":* Citizens United v. Federal Election Commission, 558 U.S. at 479 (Stevens, J., dissenting).

84 *That gave birth to "super PACs":* A lower court ruling had extended *Citizens United*'s logic to allow the creation of committees that could accept

unlimited funds from individuals as well as corporations and unions. These were known as "super PACs." *SpeechNow.org v. Federal Election Commission,* 599 F.3d 686, 689 (D.C. Cir. 2010) (en banc).

84   *The next year: Arizona Free Enterprise Club v. Bennett,* 564 U.S. 721 (2011).

84   *the Court struck down a long-standing cap: McCutcheon v. Federal Election Commission,* 572 U.S. 185 (2014).

84   *"With all due deference":* The White House, "Remarks by the President in State of the Union Address," January 27, 2010, https://obamawhitehouse .archives.gov/the-press-office/remarks-president-state-union-address.

84   *super PACs spent $3 billion:* Ian Vandewalker, "Since *Citizens United,* a Decade of Super PACs," Brennan Center for Justice (2020), https://www .brennancenter.org/our-work/analysis-opinion/citizens-united-decade -super-pacs.

84   *According to the EPA:* Jane Mayer, *Dark Money: The Hidden History of the Billionaires Behind the Rise of the Radical Right* (New York: Doubleday, 2016), 275.

85   *In 2010 billionaires spent: Billionaires Buying Elections,* Americans for Tax Fairness, July 13, 2022, https://americansfortaxfairness.org/issue/re port-billionaires-buying-elections/.

85   *Peter Thiel:* See Andrew Gumbel, "Peter Thiel's Midterm Bet: The Billionaire Seeking to Disrupt America's Democracy," *The Guardian,* October 15, 2022, https://www.theguardian.com/technology/2022/oct/15/peter-thiel -who-is-he-republican-donor-tech-entrepreneur; Andrew Tobias, "Super PAC Discloses Raising, Spending Millions Helping J. D. Vance Win Ohio's U.S. Senate Republican Primary," Cleveland *Plain Dealer,* July 11, 2022. See also Alex Isenstadt, "A Mole Hunt, a Secret Website and Peter Thiel's Big Risk: How J. D. Vance Won His Primary," *Politico,* May 3, 2022, https://www.politico.com/news/2022/05/03/jd-vance-win-ohio -primary-00029881.

85   *the drive to deregulate money in politics:* See an important book, Mary Ziegler, *Dollars for Life: The Anti-Abortion Movement and the Fall of the Republican Establishment* (New Haven: Yale University Press, 2022).

85   *It found a right: District of Columbia v. Heller,* 554 U.S. 570 (2008).

85   *It declared that privacy: Obergefell v. Hodges,* 576 U.S. 644 (2015).

85   *Obama's lower court nominees:* John Gramlich, "Trump Has Appointed a Larger Share of Female Judges than Other GOP Presidents, but Lags Obama," Pew Research Center, October 2, 2018, https://www.pewresearch .org/fact-tank/2018/10/02/trump-has-appointed-a-larger-share-of-female -judges-than-other-gop-presidents-but-lags-obama/.

86   *A onetime liberal Republican:* Fred Wertheimer, "Meet a Younger Mitch McConnell as Bold Campaign Finance Reformer," *Democracy 21,* February 13, 2019, https://democracy21.org/news-press/press-releases/meet -a-younger-mitch-mcconnell-as-bold-campaign-finance-reformer. As for

the cat "Rocky," see Stefan Alexander MacGilliss, *The Cynic: The Political Education of Mitch McConnell* (New York: Simon & Schuster, 2014), 13.

86 *He fought against John McCain's bipartisan campaign finance:* McConnell v. Federal Election Commission, 540 U.S. 93 (2003).

86 *it was used only sparingly:* See Adam Jentleson, *Kill Switch: The Rise of the Modern Senate and the Crippling of American Democracy* (New York: Liveright, 2021), 68–71.

86 *In 1938 senators filibustered for thirty days:* "Filibuster Ended as Senate Shelves Anti-Lynch Bill," *New York Times*, February 22, 1938.

86 *The 1964 Civil Rights Act passed:* See Todd S. Purdum, *An Idea Whose Time Has Come: Two Presidents, Two Parties, and the Battle for the Civil Rights Act of 1964* (New York: Picador, 2014).

86 *At the LBJ Library in Austin:* Memorandum from Mike Manatos to Larry O'Brien, December 8, 1964, http://voices.washingtonpost.com/ezra-klein /obriencropped.jpg. See Ezra Klein, "How a Letter from 1964 Shows What's Wrong with the Senate Today," *Washington Post*, November 25, 2009.

86 *both John Roberts and Elena Kagan:* George H. W. Bush nominated Roberts to the D.C. Circuit Court of Appeals. The nomination expired when Bill Clinton became president. Clinton, in turn, nominated Kagan, one of his top aides, for the D.C. Circuit in 1999. That, too, expired when George W. Bush took office.

87 *In 2003 Democrats blocked Miguel Estrada:* For a critique of the treatment of the Estrada nomination, see Thomas Mann, "Estrada Caught in 'Poisonous' War Based on Ideology," Brookings Institution, March 5, 2003, https://www.brookings.edu/opinions/estrada-caught-in-poisonous-war -based-on-ideology/.

87 *Finally, in June 2013:* Megan Slack, "President Obama Announces Three Nominees for the D.C. Circuit Court," *The White House* (blog), June 4, 2013, https://obamawhitehouse.archives.gov/blog/2013/06/04/presi dent-obama-announces-three-nominees-dc-circuit-court; Patricia Millett, Nina Pillard, and Robert Wilkins all received "extremely qualified" ratings from the American Bar Association.

87 *After the third would-be judge:* Jeremy W. Peters, "Obama Pick for Court Is 3rd in a Row Blocked by Republicans," *New York Times*, November 18, 2013.

87 *"Four of my predecessor's six nominees":* The White House, "Statement by the President," November 18, 2013, https://obamawhitehouse.archives .gov/the-press-office/2013/11/18/statement-president.

87 *"You will regret this":* 157 Cong. Rec. S8416 (daily ed., November 19, 2013) (statement of Sen. McConnell).

88 *Cases involving LGBTQ Americans:* "legalistic argle-bargle" came from *U.S. v. Windsor*, 570 U.S. 744 (2013) (Scalia, J., dissenting). His mockery of

the majority's writing style: "If, even as the price to be paid for a fifth vote, I ever joined an opinion for the Court that began: 'The Constitution promises liberty to all within its reach, a liberty that includes certain specific rights that allow persons, within a lawful realm, to define and express their identity,' I would hide my head in a bag. The Supreme Court of the United States has descended from the disciplined legal reasoning of John Marshall and Joseph Story to the mystical aphorisms of the fortune cookie." *Obergefell v. Hodges*, 576. U.S. 655 (2015).

88   *presidents had chosen justices in an election year:* They were Abe Fortas (nominated by Lyndon Johnson in 1968, rejected by the Senate); William Brennan (recess appointed by Dwight Eisenhower in 1956, and confirmed in 1957); Frank Murphy (nominated by Franklin Roosevelt in 1940); Benjamin Cardozo (nominated by Herbert Hoover in 1932); John Clarke and Louis Brandeis (both nominated by Woodrow Wilson in 1916); Mahlon Pitney (nominated by William Howard Taft in 1912); George Shiras Jr. (nominated by Benjamin Harrison in 1892); Melville Fuller (nominated by Grover Cleveland in 1888); William Woods (nominated by Rutherford Hayes in 1880); Ward Hunt (nominated by Ulysses S. Grant in 1872); and Salmon Chase (nominated by Abraham Lincoln in 1864). Another nominee, Homer Thornberry, was chosen to fill Fortas's seat as associate justice when he was nominated for chief justice; the nomination became moot when the Senate rejected Fortas for the promotion. United States Senate, Supreme Court Nominations (1789–Present), accessed April 22, 2022, https://www.senate.gov/legislative/nominations/SupremeCourtNominations1789present.htm. In addition, Anthony Kennedy was confirmed in February 1988 after Ronald Reagan nominated him in November 1987.

88   *when the Senate was controlled by the opposition party:* Four times the nominee was confirmed by a chamber controlled by the opposition party. In 1957, Democrats controlled the Senate and confirmed Brennan; in 1888, Democrats confirmed Fuller; and in 1880, Democrats confirmed Woods. In addition, Republican Anthony Kennedy was confirmed by a Democratic Senate in 1988, though he had been nominated the year before.

88   *"The American people":* Burgess Everett and Glenn Thrush, "McConnell Throws Down the Gauntlet: No Scalia Replacement Under Obama," *Politico,* February 13, 2016, https://www.politico.com/story/2016/02/mitch-mcconnell-antonin-scalia-supreme-court-nomination-219248.

88   *"The president told me several times":* Dennis Romboy, "Hatch, Lee Resolve to Hold Up Supreme Court Nominee Confirmation," *Deseret News,* March 16, 2016.

89   *"One of my proudest moments":* "Sen. Mitch McConnell Speech, Fancy Farm 2016, KET," YouTube, August 6, 2016, https://www.youtube.com/watch?v=kP1G45maN4A.

89   *a previously unknown "Biden rule":* Julie Hirschfeld Davis, "Joe Biden

Argued for Delaying Supreme Court Picks in 1992," *New York Times*, February 23, 2016.

90   *"I am very pro-choice":* Donald Trump, interview on NBC's *Meet the Press*, October 24, 1999, https://www.nbcnews.com/meet-the-press/video/trump -in-1999-i-am-very-pro-choice-480297539914.

90   *Trump announced a list of jurists:* Ginger Gibson and Lawrence Hurley, "Trump Identifies 11 Potential Supreme Court Nominees," Reuters, May 18, 2016.

90   *But the point had been made:* Trump suggested he would put out a list at a meeting of lawmakers, lobbyists, and Federalist Society leaders at the Jones Day law firm, where Don McGahn was a partner. "The room reacted with joy." David Enrich, "How a Corporate Law Firm Led a Political Revolution," *New York Times Magazine*, August 25, 2022.

90   *"That was some weird shit":* Yashar Ali, "What George W. Bush Really Thought of Donald Trump's Inauguration," *New York*, March 29, 2017, https://nymag.com/intelligencer/2017/03/what-george-w-bush-really -thought-of-trumps-inauguration.html.

90   *a week after his inauguration:* Executive Order No. 13769, Protecting the Nation from Foreign Terrorist Entry into the United States. 82 Fed. Reg. 8977 (2017). The hectic effort to implement Trump's vow of a "total and complete shutdown" through an executive order is described in Peter Baker and Susan Glasser, *The Divider: Trump in the White House, 2017– 2021* (New York: Doubleday, 2022), 37–38.

90   *Volunteer lawyers rushed:* Robert Atkins, a top litigator at the firm, rushed to JFK Airport with a squad of lawyers on hearing of Trump's order. See Alison Frankel, "At JFK's Terminal 4, a Good Weekend to Be a Lawyer," Reuters, January 30, 2017.

91   *Federal courts fully or partly blocked:* Eventually the Supreme Court upheld the revised travel ban in *Trump v. Hawaii*, 585 U.S. ___ (2018), 138 S. Ct. 2392 (2018).

91   *"even consider the propriety":* Charles P. Pierce, "So, What's Neil Gorsuch Up to These Days," *Esquire*, September 25, 2017, https://www.esquire.com /news-politics/politics/a12465124/neil-gorsuch-mitch-mcconnell/.

91   *Trump would go on to appoint:* Trump named fifty-four, while Obama appointed just fifty-five. John Gramlich, "How Trump Compares with Other Recent Presidents in Appointing Federal Judges," Pew Research Center, January 13, 2021, https://www.pewresearch.org/fact-tank/2021/01/13 /how-trump-compares-with-other-recent-presidents-in-appointing-federal -judges/.

92   *"You never know":* Robert Dallek, *Flawed Giant: Lyndon Johnson and His Time, 1961–1973* (New York: Oxford University Press, 1998), 233.

92   *At Stevenson's gravesite:* Abner Mikva, personal conversation, August 7, 2010.

92   *no seat was available:* The intermediary who called was, in fact, Justice Abe

Fortas. For a compelling description of Johnson's manipulative skill in edging Tom Clark off the Court to open a seat for Marshall, see Laura Kalman, *The Long Reach of the 1960s: LBJ, Nixon, and the Making of the Contemporary Supreme Court* (New York: Oxford University Press, 2017), 85–96.

92 *Johnson sent Justice Clark:* Wil Haygood, *Showdown: Thurgood Marshall and the Supreme Court Nomination That Changed America* (New York: Viking, 2015), 15–16.

92 *"Say hello to your boy":* Adam Liptak and Maggie Haberman, "Inside the White House's Quiet Campaign to Create a Supreme Court Opening," *New York Times,* June 28, 2018.

92 *Kennedy's son:* David Enrich, *Dark Towers: Deutsche Bank, Donald Trump, and an Epic Trail of Destruction* (New York: Custom House, 2020), 174–76.

93 *Kavanaugh drove the focus:* Sean Wilentz, "Why Was Kavanaugh Obsessed with Vince Foster?," *New York Times,* September 5, 2018. Wilentz reports he examined Kavanaugh's files at the National Archives and found that the information that prompted Kavanaugh to reopen the probe of Foster's death came from Christopher Ruddy and other conspiracy theorists. "Mr. Kavanaugh's files in the National Archives make clear that they were some of the most ludicrous hard-right conspiracy-mongers of the time."

93 *Kavanaugh sought authority:* Ruth Marcus, *Supreme Ambition: Brett Kavanaugh and the Conservative Takeover* (New York: Simon & Schuster, 2019), 127.

93 *kept the probe going:* Jackie Calmes, *Dissent: The Radicalization of the Republican Party and Its Capture of the Court* (New York: Twelve, 2021), 77–83; Marcus, *Supreme Ambition,* 124–28. Ruddy continued to feed conspiracy theories to Trump. In 2016 the candidate told *The Washington Post* that Foster's death was "very fishy."

93 *faced harsh criticism:* William Safire, "The Big Flinch," *New York Times,* January 20, 1997.

93 *Kavanaugh demanded that prosecutors ask:* His memo is in Ken Gormley, *The Death of American Virtue: Clinton v. Starr* (New York: Crown, 2010), 541.

93 *Kavanaugh's defenders insisted:* He reportedly urged Starr to omit the pornographic details from the report submitted to Congress. Bob Woodward, *Shadow: Five Presidents and the Legacy of Watergate* (New York: Simon & Schuster, 2000), 452–54.

93 *Kavanaugh had long been seen as a potential:* See, for example, Waldman, *The Fight to Vote,* 207.

93 *Kavanaugh now argued:* Brett M. Kavanaugh, "Separation of Powers During the Forty Fourth Presidency and Beyond," *Minnesota Law Review* 93 (2009): 1454. For an explanation of Kavanaugh's views, see Michael Waldman, "Courting Disaster: The Trouble with Brett Kavanaugh's Views of Executive Power in the Age of Trump," New York *Daily News,* July 16, 2018.

94   *of all the possible nominees:* Dahlia Lithwick, "Brett Kavanaugh Was a Mistake," *Slate*, July 10, 2018, https://slate.com/news-and-politics /2018/07/brett-kavanaugh-supreme-court-donald-trump-just-handed -democrats-a-gift.html.

94   *"I am here today":* Calmes, *Dissent*, 291.

94   *Thurgood Marshall for gender equality:* Linda Greenhouse, *Justice on the Brink: The Death of Ruth Bader Ginsburg, the Rise of Amy Coney Barrett, and Twelve Months That Transformed the Supreme Court* (New York: Random House, 2022), 41–42; Jane Sharron De Hart, *Ruth Bader Ginsburg: A Life* (New York: Alfred A. Knopf, 2018), 104–276.

94   *"Doctrinal limbs too swiftly shaped":* Ruth Bader Ginsburg, "Speaking in a Judicial Voice," *New York University Law Review* 67, no. 6 (1992): 1185.

95   *Virginia Military Institute: United States v. Virginia*, 518 U.S. 515 (1996).

95   *It was not until 2018:* Mark Joseph Stern, "A Milestone for Ruth Bader Ginsburg," *Slate*, April 18, 2018, https://slate.com/news-and-politics /2018/04/ruth-bader-ginsburg-just-assigned-a-majority-opinion-for-the -first-time-ever.html.

95   *Barack Obama met with her:* Susan Dominus and Charlie Savage, "The Quiet 2013 Lunch That Could Have Altered Supreme Court History," *New York Times*, September 25, 2020.

95   *"Anybody who thinks":* Jessica Weisberg, "Remembering Ruth Bader Ginsburg in Her Own Words," *Elle*, September 21, 2020, reprinting an interview published in 2014, https://www.elle.com/culture/career-politics /interviews/a14788/supreme-court-justice-ruth-bader-ginsburg/.

95   *early voting had started in nine states:* Joey Garrison, "Election 2020: When Early Voting and Mail Voting for President Begins in Every State," *USA Today*, September 16, 2019.

95   *"use my words against me":* Matthew S. Schwartz, "'Use My Words Against Me': Lindsey Graham's Shifting Position on Court Vacancies," NPR, September 19, 2020, https://www.npr.org/sections/death-of-ruth-bader -ginsburg/2020/09/19/914774433/use-my-words-against-me-lindsey -graham-s-shifting-position-on-court-vacancies.

96   *"I think this [election] will end up":* Peter Baker, "Trump Says He Wants a Conservative Majority on the Supreme Court in Case of an Election Day Dispute," *New York Times*, September 23, 2020.

96   *Sixty-three courts ruled:* The quotes come from these cases: *Wisconsin Voters Alliance v. Wisconsin Elections Commission*, No. 2020AP1920-OA (Wis. December 4, 2020) (Hagedorn, J., concurring) ("flimsy"); *Costantino v. City of Detroit*, No. 20-014780-AW (Mich. Cir. Ct. November 13, 2020) ("incorrect and not credible"); *Donald J. Trump for President Inc. v. Boockvar*, 502 F. Supp. 3d 899, 906 (M.D. Pa. November 21, 2020) ("strained legal arguments").

96   *Texas sued Pennsylvania: Texas v. Pennsylvania*, 592 U.S. ___, 141 S. Ct. 1230 (2020).

98 *"Instead, the justices repeatedly defied":* Jeannie Suk Gersen, "The Supreme Court's Surprising Term," *The New Yorker,* June 27, 2021, https://www.newyorker.com/magazine/2021/07/05/the-supreme-courts-surprising-term.

98 *The legal director of the ACLU:* David Cole, "Surprising Consensus at the Supreme Court," *New York Review of Books,* August 17, 2021, https://www.nybooks.com/articles/2021/08/19/surprising-consensus-at-the-supreme-court/. Cole noted that an exception to the consensus was the *Brnovich* case on voting rights, discussed in the next chapter.

98 *Most of those involved:* Kimberly Wehle, "The One Area Where the Supreme Court's Six Conservative Judges Could Agree," *Politico Magazine,* August 3, 2021, https://www.politico.com/news/magazine/2021/08/03/the-one-way-the-supreme-courts-new-conservative-majority-lived-up-to-its-billing-502164.

SEVEN: MARCHING BACKWARD

101 *Americans remember Selma:* For a definitive narrative of the protests and the legislation, see Gary May, *Bending Toward Justice: The Voting Rights Act and the Transformation of American Democracy* (New York: Basic Books, 2013). John Lewis wrote a vivid memoir with Michael D'Orso, *Walking with the Wind: A Memoir of the Movement* (New York: Simon & Schuster, 1998), and also three graphic novels, John Lewis with Andrew Aydin and Nate Powell, *March Book 1* (Marietta, GA: Top Shelf, 2013), *Book 2* (2015), and *Book 3* (2016). The story is told in the Academy Award–winning film *Selma* directed by Ava DuVernay (2014), which featured John Legend's Grammy-winning song, "Glory." See also David J. Garrow, *Protest at Selma: Martin Luther King, Jr., and the Voting Rights Act of 1965* (New Haven: Yale University Press, 1978); Taylor Branch, *At Canaan's Edge: America in the King Years, 1965–68* (New York: Simon & Schuster, 2006); and Nick Kotz, *Judgment Days: Lyndon Baines Johnson, Martin Luther King, Jr., and the Laws That Changed America* (New York: Houghton Mifflin, 2005). LBJ's speechwriter describes backstage politics in Richard N. Goodwin, *Remembering America: A Voice from the Sixties* (Boston: Little, Brown, 1988).

101 *Days before: Brnovich v. Democratic National Committee,* 594 U.S. ___, 141 S. Ct. 2321 (2022).

101 *in its first five years:* Chandler Davidson, "The Voting Rights Act: A Brief History," Bernard Grofman and Chandler Davidson, eds., *Controversies in Minority Voting* (Washington, D.C.: Brookings Institution Press, 1992), 2.

101 *In Mississippi:* Richard M. Valelly, *The Two Reconstructions: The Struggle for Black Enfranchisement* (Chicago: University of Chicago Press, 2004), 207.

101 *for the first time opened the way for:* That was especially true when the act was amended in 1975 to explicitly cover Hispanic, Asian American, Native American and Native Alaskan voters: 42 U.S.C. S 1973b(b) (1976).

The inclusion of language minorities was authorized not by the Fifteenth Amendment but by the Fourteenth Amendment's Equal Protection Clause.

102   *All told the act stopped nearly 1,200:* Shelby County v. Holder, 570 U.S. at 571 (Ginsburg, J., dissenting).

102   *The Supreme Court had held:* Mobile v. Bolden, 446 U.S. 55 (1980).

102   *not just when there is proof of racist intent:* The Constitution already prohibited explicitly racist voting laws in the Fifteenth Amendment.

102   *He fired off memos:* Roberts's crusade to prevent the "results" test from being added to the Voting Rights Act is described in Joan Biskupic, *The Chief: The Life and Turbulent Times of John Roberts* (New York: Basic Books, 2019), 70–76; and Ari Berman, *Give Us the Ballot: The Modern Struggle for Voting Rights in America* (New York: Farrar, Straus & Giroux, 2015), 148–52.

102   *"Such an effort":* Roberts's arguments were forwarded to the Senate in "Why Section 2 of the Voting Rights Act Should be Retained Unchanged," in U.S. Congress, Senate, Committee on the Judiciary, Subcommittee on the Constitution, *Voting Rights Act: Hearings Before the Subcommittee on the Constitution of the Committee on the Judiciary, on S. 53, S.1761, 1975, S. 1992, and H.R. 3112, Bills to Amend the Voting Rights Act of 1965, Volume 2—Appendix*, 97th Cong., 2nd sess., February 1, 2, 4, 11, 12, 25, and March 1, 1982, 416.

102   *"the extra effort":* Berman, *Give Us the Ballot*, 155.

103   *"Whether conditions continue to justify":* Northwest Austin Municipal Utility District No. One v. Holder, 557 U.S. 193, 211 (2009).

103   Shelby County: *Shelby County v. Holder*, 570 U.S. 529 (2013). For the case and its background, see Michael Waldman, *The Fight to Vote*, rev. ed. (New York: Simon & Schuster, 2022), 229–33.

103   *"Even the name of it":* Shelby County v. Holder, transcript of argument, February 27, 2013, https://www.supremecourt.gov/oral_arguments/argument _transcripts/2012/12-96_7648.pdf.

104   *"Throwing out preclearance":* Shelby County, 570 U.S. 529 (Ginsburg, J., dissenting).

104   *After a lengthy trial:* Veasey v. Perry, No. 13-CV00193, 2014 WL 5090258 (S.D. Tex. October 9, 2014).

104   *"target African Americans with almost surgical precision":* North Carolina State Conference of NAACP v. McCrory, 831 F.3d 204, 226 (2016).

104   *Previously that part of the law:* After the Voting Rights Act was amended to make clear it prohibited discriminatory results, not just discriminatory intent, the Supreme Court only heard cases dealing with the application of Section 2 to redistricting or "vote dilution" rather than the "vote denial" that can come from unfair voting rules. See *Thornberg v. Gingles*, 478 U.S. 30 (1986).

104   *They claimed two technical provisions:* Arizona did not count the ballots of

citizens who voted on Election Day in the wrong precinct. Another rule governed the collection of mail ballots, and required them to be gathered only by family members, not by political campaigns or groups.

105 *"far from the most egregious"*: Rick Hasen, "A Partisan Battle in an Overreach of a Case," *SCOTUSblog*, February 22, 2021, https://www.scotus blog.com/2021/02/a-partisan-battle-in-an-overreach-of-a-case/.

105 *Governor Brian Kemp signed it:* Will Bunch, "Georgia Governor Signed a Voter Suppression Law Under a Painting of a Slave Plantation," *Philadelphia Inquirer*, March 25, 2021; Mark Niesse, Maya T. Prabhu, and Greg Bluestein, "Georgia Representative Arrested After Governor Signs Elections Bill," *Atlanta Journal-Constitution*, March 25, 2021.

106 *"nine of the eleven instances"*: Tonja Jacobi, Timothy R. Johnson, Eve M. Ringsmuth, and Matthew Sag, "Oral Argument in the Time of COVID: The Chief Plays Calvinball," *Southern California Interdisciplinary Law Journal* 30 (2020): 399.

106 *During one May 2020 argument:* Ashley Feinberg, "Investigation: I Think I Know Which Justice Flushed," *Slate*, May 8, 2020, https://slate.com /news-and-politics/2020/05/toilet-flush-supreme-court-livestream.html.

106 *"A state has long had"*: Brnovich v. DNC, transcript of argument, March 2, 2021, https://www.supremecourt.gov/oral_arguments/argument_tran scripts/2020/19-1257_1b7d.pdf.

106 *Alito often seemed consumed by anger:* Mark Joseph Stern, "The Rudest Justice—Surprise, It's Not Scalia! Why Is Samuel Alito So Nasty?," *Slate*, June 27, 2013, https://slate.com/news-and-politics/2013/06/justice -samuel-alito-why-hes-so-rude.html.

107 *After the Court had ruled:* In 1985, applying to the Justice Department for a job, Alito wrote, "I developed a deep interest in constitutional law motivated in large part by disagreement with Warren Court decisions, particularly in the areas of criminal procedure, Establishment Clause, and reapportionment." Questioned frequently about this at his confirmation hearing, Alito explained that his opposition to the reapportionment decisions was based on seeing his father try to find districts with exactly equal population. U.S. Congress, Senate, Committee on the Judiciary, *Confirmation Hearing on the Nomination of Samuel A. Alito, Jr. to be an Associate Justice of the Supreme Court of the United States, January 9–13, 2006*, 109th Cong., 2nd Sess., 381. He elaborated on the story in his private conversations with senators.

107 *His roommate said:* Rinker Buck, "Alito's Yale Years," *Hartford Courant*, November 20, 2005.

107 *"This is like meeting"*: Alito told the story to a Federalist Society dinner. David Lat, "More About the Fabulous Fed Soc Fête," *Above the Law*, November 19, 2007, https://abovethelaw.com/2007/11/more-about-the-fabulous-fed -soc-fete/. The colleague was Charles Fried. Margaret Talbot, "Justice Alito's Crusade Against a Secular America Isn't Over," *The New Yorker*,

September 5, 2022, https://www.newyorker.com/magazine/2022/09/05 /justice-alitos-crusade-against-a-secular-america-isnt-over.

108   *Scholars could not point to:* Ian Millhiser, "The Most Partisan Supreme Court Justice of All," *Think Progress,* July 2, 2014, https://archive.thinkprogress .org/the-most-partisan-supreme-court-justice-of-all-fd31c58a25aa/ https://archive.thinkprogress.org/the-most-partisan-supreme-court -justice-of-all-fd31c58a25aa/.

108   *His* Hobby Lobby *opinion: Burwell v. Hobby Lobby Stores, Inc.,* 573 U.S. 682 (2014).

108   *"To read his opinions":* Aziz Huq, "Alito: One Angry Man," *Politico Magazine,* May 18, 2022, https://www.politico.com/news/magazine/2022/05/18 /samuel-alito-angry-man-00033207.

108   *"like 'battling the Hydra'":* Brnovich v. DNC, 594 U.S. ___, 141 S. Ct. 2321, 2354 (2022) (Kagan, J., dissenting).

109   *"Like all Jews":* U.S. Congress, Senate, Committee on the Judiciary, *Nomination of Elena Kagan to Be an Associate Justice of the Supreme Court of the United States, Hearing Before the Committee on the Judiciary,* 111th Cong., 2nd Sess., June 28–30 and July 1, 2010, Serial No. J–111–98, 144. The tradition is described in Jennifer 8. Lee, *The Fortune Cookie Chronicles: Adventures in the World of Chinese Food* (New York: Twelve, 2008), 89–106. ("Chinese food on Christmas Day is as much an American Jewish ritual as the Seder on Passover (maybe even more so, once you take into account non-observant Jews).")

109   *moved easily in and out of the Oval Office:* This author worked with Kagan at the time. I describe one such scene in Michael Waldman, *POTUS Speaks* (New York: Simon & Schuster, 2000), 125. Clinton had angrily complained to me about a draft speech he was due to give vetoing legislation to curb product liability lawsuits. After the event went well, Kagan and I were walking by the Oval Office when the president opened the door and invited us in to rave about the event, never mentioning his prior eruption. Leaving the president, Kagan observed, "This is how presidents apologize."

109   *She was responsible:* Dana Milbank, "Wonderwonk," *The New Republic,* May 18, 1998.

110   *After leaving government:* Elena Kagan, "Presidential Administration," *Harvard Law Review* 114 (2000–2001): 2245.

110   *Her horse-trading skills:* Jeffrey Toobin, *The Oath: The Obama White House and the Supreme Court* (New York: Random House, 2102), 289.

110   *"We are all textualists now":* Elena Kagan, "Harvard Law School, The Antonin Scalia Lecture Series: A Dialogue with Justice Elena Kagan on the Reading of Statutes," YouTube video (November 25, 2015), https:// www.youtube.com/watch?v=dpEtszFT0Tg.

110   *"We are all Keynesians now":* This kind of thing used to be big news. "Nixon Reportedly Says He Is Now a Keynesian," *New York Times,* January 7, 1971,

https://www.nytimes.com/1971/01/07/archives/nixon-reportedly
-says-he-is-now-a-keynesian.html. Nixon said it to television news anchors
after an interview, and ABC's Howard K. Smith recounted it.

111 *Pennsylvania offered an extreme example:* The Pennsylvania Supreme Court
declared the congressional map illegal under the state constitution.
League of Women Voters of PA v. Commonwealth, 178 A.3d 737 (Pa. 2018).

111 *"For the first time ever":* Rucho v. Common Cause, 588 U.S. (2019) (Kagan, J.,
dissenting); 139 S. Ct. 2484.

111 *"At first, her voice":* Mark Joseph Stern, "You Can Now Hear Elena Kagan
Read Her Searing Dissent in the Partisan Gerrymandering Case," *Slate,*
October 25, 2009, https://slate.com/news-and-politics/2019/10/elena
-kagan-audio-partisan-gerrymandering-dissent.html.

112 *Voting Rights Act been at full strength:* See *Voting in America: A National
Perspective on the Right to Vote, Methods of Elections, Jurisdictional Boundar-
ies, and Redistricting,* Committee on Administration, Subcommittee on
Elections, U.S. House of Representatives, 117th Cong., 1st sess. (2021)
(written testimony of Michael Waldman), https://docs.house.gov/meet
ings/HA/HA08/20210624/112806/HHRG-117-HA08-Wstate-Waldman
M-20210624.pdf.

112 *"the most significant test of our democracy":* The White House, "Remarks by
President Biden on Protecting the Sacred, Constitutional Right to Vote,"
July 13, 2021, https://www.whitehouse.gov/briefing-room/speeches
-remarks/2021/07/13/remarks-by-president-biden-on-protecting-the
-sacred-constitutional-right-to-vote/.

113 *in four states in 2022:* "Redistricting Litigation Roundup," Brennan Center for Justice, November 18, 2022, https://www.brennancenter.org/our
-work/research-reports/redistricting-litigation-roundup-0. The states were
Alabama, Louisiana, Georgia, and Ohio. The five to seven seat swing calculus came from Dave Wasserman of the Cook Political Report. Michael
Wines, "Maps in Four States Were Ruled Illegal Gerrymanders. They're
Being Used Anyway," *New York Times,* August 6, 2022.

EIGHT: THE SHADOW DOCKET

114 *A conservative scholar coined:* See William Baude, "Foreword: The Supreme
Court's Shadow Docket," *NYU Journal of Law and Liberty* 9 (2015): 1.

115 *not even found in one place:* "The Supreme Court's Shadow Docket, Before the Subcommittee on Courts, Intellectual Property, and the Internet of the House Committee on the Judiciary," 117th Cong., 1st Sess.
(2021) (testimony of Stephen I. Vladeck), https://docs.house.gov/meet
ings/JU/JU03/20210218/111204/HHRG-117-JU03-Wstate-Vladeck
S-20210218-U1.pdf.

115 *future justice Abe Fortas:* Robert A. Caro, *Means of Ascent: The Years of Lyndon Johnson,* vol. 2 (New York: Alfred A. Knopf, 1990), 379–82.

115 *From the execution of the Soviet spies:* For historical examples of the deference typically given to the government when it asks for emergency relief, see Stephen Vladeck, "Symposium: The Solicitor General, the Shadow Docket and the Kennedy Effect," *SCOTUSblog*, October 22, 2022, https://www.scotusblog.com/2020/10/symposium-the-solicitor-general-the-shadow-docket-and-the-kennedy-effect/. On the emergency order that temporarily stopped the execution of convicted spies Julius and Ethel Rosenberg in 1953, *Rosenberg v. United States*, 346 U.S. 313 (Douglas, Circuit Justice, 1953), see Brad Snyder, "Taking Great Cases: Lessons from the Rosenberg Case," *Vanderbilt Law Review* 63, no. 4 (2010): 885. In an essay describing his frantic search for a justice who would allow a lower-court ruling to stand that halted the bombing of Cambodia, *Holtzman v. Schlesinger*, 414 U.S. 1316 (Douglas, Circuit Justice, 1973), former ACLU legal director Burt Neuborne writes, "In those days, the ACLU kept a 24-hour watch on the whereabouts of Justice William O. Douglas, in case an emergency vote was needed to slay a dragon, square a circle, or stay an execution." Douglas granted the order but the next day was overruled by a telephone poll of the Court conducted by Thurgood Marshall. Burt Neuborne, "I Fought the Imperial Presidency, and the Imperial Presidency Won," ACLU, September 27, 2019, https://www.aclu.org/issues/national-security/i-fought-imperial-presidency-and-imperial-presidency-won. The order where the Supreme Court halted the recount in Florida, days before the final ruling, was *Bush v. Gore*, 531 U.S. 1046 (2000).

115 *Starting in 2017:* Stephen I. Vladeck, "The Supreme Court, 2018 Term—Essay: The Solicitor General and the Shadow Docket," *Harvard Law Review* 133 (2019): 162, table 3.

115 *The federal government rarely had asked for emergency relief before:* Steve Vladeck, "The Supreme Court's 'Shadow Docket' Helped Trump 28 Times. Biden is 0 for 1," *Washington Post*, August 26, 2021. "From 2001 to 2017, the Justice Department sought emergency relief only eight times, across the very different presidencies of George W. Bush and Barack Obama."

115 *The Court acted:* For example, the Court issued two shadow docket orders allowing Trump's Muslim travel ban to go into effect before a lower court would have the chance to stop or delay it. *Trump v. Hawaii*, Orders of December 4, 2017, https://www.supremecourt.gov/orders/courtorders/120417zr_4gd5.pdf; and https://www.supremecourt.gov/court orders/120417zr_4gd5.pdf. Shoba Sivaprasad Wadhia, "Symposium: From the Travel Ban to the Border Wall, Restrictive Immigration Policies Thrive on the Shadow Docket," *SCOTUSblog*, October 27, 2020, https://www.scotusblog.com/2020/10/symposium-from-the-travel-ban-to-the-border-wall-restrictive-immigration-policies-thrive-on-the-shadow-docket/.

115   *"a now-familiar pattern":* *Wolf v. Cook County,* 589 U.S. ___, 140 S. Ct. 681
      (2020) (Sotomayor, J., dissenting on application for stay).

115   *Refugees long could claim asylum:* To establish eligibility for asylum or refu-
      gee status under U.S. law (8 U.S.C. § 1158), individuals must prove they
      meet the definition of a refugee (under 8 U.S.C. § 1101).

115   *Then a trial judge:* Judge Matthew Kacsmaryk was a particularly controver-
      sial nominee, having called homosexuality "disordered," opposed the
      legalization of premarital sex, and charged that the "sexual revolution"
      was the work of "secular libertines." Marriage and "even the unborn
      child must yield to the erotic desires of liberated adults," he warned.
      Matthew Kacsmaryk, "The Inequality Act: Weaponizing Same-Sex Mar-
      riage," *Public Discourse,* September 15, 2015, https://www.thepublic
      discourse.com/2015/09/15612/. The Senate confirmed him with 52
      votes. Colby Itkowitz, "Senate Confirms Trump Judicial Nominee Who
      Called Homosexuality 'Disordered,' " *Washington Post,* June 19, 2019.

116   *That would require the United States:* Ruth Marcus, "Thanks to the Supreme
      Court, a Federal Judge in Texas Is Making Foreign Policy Decisions,"
      Washington Post, August 25, 2021.

116   *in a single unsigned paragraph: Biden v. Texas,* Order in Pending Case, 594
      U.S. Order no. 21A21 (August 24, 2021). Justices Breyer, Sotomayor, and
      Kagan dissented.

116   *Nearly a year later: Biden v. Texas,* 597 U.S. ___, 142 S. Ct. 2528 (2022).

116   *The next week: Alabama Association of Realtors v. Department of Health and
      Human Services,* 594 U.S. ___, 141 S. Ct. 2485 (2021).

116   *"the justices have issued seven":* Steve Vladeck, "The Supreme Court Doesn't
      Just Abuse Its Shadow Docket. It Does so Inconsistently," *Washington Post,*
      September 3, 2021.

116   *The Court blocked that ruling: Barnes v. Ahlman,* No. 20A19, 591 U.S. ___,
      140 S. Ct. 2620 (August 5, 2020).

116   *"I have no idea":* Ian Millhiser, "The Supreme Court's Enigmatic 'Shadow
      Docket,' Explained," *Vox,* August 20, 2020, https://www.vox.com/2020
      /8/11/21356913/supreme-court-shadow-docket-jail-asylum-covid-immi
      grants-sonia-sotomayor-barnes-ahlman.

116   *"night court":* Greg Stohr (@gregstohr), Twitter, February 6, 2021, 1:02 p.m.,
      https://twitter.com/ GregStohr/status/1358113817696288769?s=20.

116   *In 2020, by a five-to-four vote:* "Texas's Unconstitutional Abortion Ban and
      the Role of the Shadow Docket, Hearing Before the Senate Committee
      on the Judiciary," September 29, 2021 (testimony of Stephen I. Vladeck),
      17, https://www.judiciary.senate.gov/imo/media/doc/Vladeck%20test
      imony1.pdf.

117   *"whenever a lower court can say with confidence":* Vetan Kapoor and Judge
      Trevor McFadden, *Symposium: The Precedential Effects of Shadow Docket
      Stays, SCOTUSblog* (October 28, 2020, 9:18 a.m.), https://www.scotusblog
      .com/2020/10/symposium-the-precedential-effects-of-shadow-docket

-stays/. McFadden was a member of the Federalist Society from 2003 until his appointment in 2017. U.S. Senate Judiciary Committee, "Nomination of Trevor McFadden to the U.S. District Court for the District of Columbia Questions for the Record Submitted July 5, 2017," https://www.judiciary.senate.gov/imo/media/doc/McFadden%20Responses%20to%20QFRs.pdf.

117   *Abortion is safer for women:* According to a federal district court ruling, quoting a medical expert, "Abortion is also one of the safest medical procedures. Fewer than 1% of pregnant people who obtain abortions experience a serious complication. And even fewer abortion patients—only approximately 0.3%—experience a complication that requires hospitalization. Abortion is far safer than pregnancy and childbirth." *U.S. v. Texas,* 1:21-CV-796-RP (October 6, 2021), https://storage.courtlistener.com/recap/gov.uscourts.txwd.1146510/gov.uscourts.txwd.1146510.68.0.pdf.

117   *The U.S. Supreme Court with an almost audible sigh: Whole Woman's Health v. Hellerstedt,* 579 U.S. 582 (2016).

117   *Now he joined the liberals: June Medical Services L.L.C v. Russo,* 591 U.S. ___, 140 S. Ct. 2013, 2133 (2020) (Roberts, C.J., concurring in judgment).

117   *"Chief Justice Roberts is at it again":* Ted Cruz, Twitter, June 29, 2020, 2:39 p.m.,https://twitter.com/sentedcruz/status/1277673169315344391.

118   *"What's next":* Jim Jordan, Twitter, June 29, 2020, 10:35 a.m., https://twitter.com/jim_jordan/status/1277611721516032000.

118   *Mississippi, enacted its new antiabortion law:* Gestational Age Act, ch. 393, § 1, 2018 Miss. Laws (codified at MISS. CODE ANN. § 41-41-191).

118   *Over 90 percent of abortions:* Katherine Kortsmit, Tara Jatlaoui, Michele Mandel, et al., "Abortion Surveillance—United States," Centers for Disease Control (2018), Morbity and Mortality Weekly Report, Surveillance Summary 2020; 69(No. SS-7):1–29, http://dx.doi.org/10.15585/mmwr.ss6907a1.

118   Planned Parenthood: *Planned Parenthood of Southeastern Pennsylvania v. Casey,* 505 U.S. 833 (1992).

118   *A federal appeals court blocked it: Jackson Women's Health Organization v. Dobbs,* 945 F.3d 265 (2019).

118   *Mississippi:* Kathryn Kost, "Unintended Pregnancy Rates at the State Level: Estimates for 2020 and Trends Since 2002," table 1, Guttmacher Institute (2015), https://www.guttmacher.org/sites/default/files/report_pdf/stateup10.pdf. The study was cited in *Dobbs v. Jackson Women's Health,* 2339 n.19 (2022) (Breyer, J., Sotomayor, J., and Kagan, J., dissenting).

118   *Lawmakers even balked:* Emily Wagster Pettus, "Mississippi Could Renew Push to Extend Medicaid for New Moms," Associated Press, March 14, 2022; Becky Gillette, "Expanding Medicaid Could Help Lift Mississippi Women off Bottom on Health Rankings," *Mississippi Business Journal,* April 29, 2022, https://www.djournal.com/mbj/expanding-medicaid-could-help-lift-mississippi-women-off-bottom-on-health-rankings/article_880907b4-5911-5873-acef-10feb103ae2e.html.

118 *five times more likely:* Susan A. Cohen, "Abortion and Women of Color: The Bigger Picture," Guttmacher Institute, August 6, 2008, https://www.gutt macher.org/gpr/2008/08/abortion-and-women-color-bigger-picture; Zoe Dutton, "Abortion's Racial Gap," *The Atlantic,* September 22, 2014, https://www.theatlantic.com/health/archive/2014/09/abortions-racial -gap/380251/.

119 *In 2018 he wrote an article:* Jonathan F. Mitchell, "The Writ of Erasure Fallacy," *Virginia Law Review* 104 (2018): 933, https://www.virginialawre view.org/articles/writ-erasure-fallacy/.

119 *The Supreme Court had ruled:* In the landmark case *Shelley v. Kraemer,* 334 U.S. 1, 14 (1948), the Court had ruled, "the action of state courts and judicial officers in their official capacities is to be regarded as action of the State."

120 *The Texas legislature, casting about for new ways:* Texas Heartbeat Act, Senate Bill No. 8, 87th Leg., Ch. 62 Reg. Sess. (Tex. 2021) (to be codified at Tex. Health & Safety Code §§ 171.203(b), 171.204(a)). The act prohibits physicians from "knowingly perform[ing] or induc[ing] an abortion on a pregnant woman if the physician detected a fetal heartbeat for the unborn child" unless a medical emergency prevents compliance. Tex. Health & Safety Code Ann. §§171.204(a), 171.205(a) (West Cum. Supp. 2021).

120 *Fifth Circuit Court of Appeals:* Whole Woman's Health v. Jackson, 13 F.4th 434 (5th Cir. 2021).

120 *Clinics rushed to the Supreme Court:* Emergency Application to Justice Alito for Writ of Injunction, and, in the Alternative, to Vacate Stays of District Court Proceedings, *Whole Woman's Health v. Jackson* No. 21-463 (August 30, 2021).

120 *Whole Woman's Health clinic in Fort Worth:* A gripping description of the scene as the deadline approached is Laurel Brubaker Calkins, "As Abortion Deadline Neared, 27 Women Waited in Texas Clinic," Bloomberg, September 2, 2022, "https://www.bloomberg.com/news/articles/2021 -09-01/as-abortion-deadline-neared-27-patients-huddled-in-texas-clinic. See also BeLynn Hollers, "Fort Worth Abortion Provider Says Waiting Rooms Filled as Texas 'Heartbeat Bill' Went into Effect," *Dallas Morning News,* September 1, 2021.

120 *A day later:* Whole Woman's Health v. Jackson, 594 U.S. ___, 141 S. Ct. 4294 (2021).

121 *"The statutory scheme before the Court":* Ibid., 594 U.S. ___, 141 S. Ct. 2494, 2496 (2021) (Roberts, C.J., dissenting).

121 *Sotomayor called the action "stunning":* Ibid., 594 U.S. ___, 141 S. Ct. 2494, 2498 (2021) (Sotomayor, J., dissenting).

121 *"illustrates just how far":* Ibid., 594 U.S. ___, 141 S. Ct. 2494, 2500 (2021) (Kagan, J., dissenting).

121 *"I drove six hours":* Sarah McCammon, Lauren Hodges, and Jonaki Mehta, "A Louisiana Clinic Struggles to Absorb the Surge Created by Texas'

New Abortion Law," NPR, October 6, 2021, https://www.npr.org/2021
/10/07/1044045564/a-louisiana-clinic-struggles-to-absorb-the-surge
-created-by-texas-new-abortion-l.

122   *"[if] the legislatures of the several states"*: *Whole Woman's Health v. Jackson*, 595
U.S. ___, 142 S. Ct. 522, 545 (2021) (Roberts, C.J., dissenting). Roberts
was quoting *United States v. Peters*, 5 Cranch 115, 136 (1809).

122   *Salesforce pledged to pay:* Jordan Novet, "Salesforce Offers to Relocate Employees and Their Families After Texas Abortion Law Goes into Effect,"
CNBC, September 10, 2021, https://www.cnbc.com/2021/09/10/sales
force-offers-to-relocate-employees-from-texas-after-abortion-bill.html.

122   *In October, Elon Musk announced:* Kara Carlson, "Tesla Moving HQ from
California to Austin: 'A Huge Feather in the Cap' for Region," *Austin
American-Statesman*, October 7, 2021.

123   *Red Mass:* 69th Annual Red Mass Sponsored by the John Carroll Society, Saint Matthew's Cathedral, Washington, D.C., October 3, 2021,
https://holyseemission.org/contents//statements/6160b2188dc5d
.php; Ian Shapira, "On Eve of Huge Supreme Court Term, a Prayer
from on High," *Washington Post*, October 3, 2021.

123   *"My goal today":* Mary Ramsey, "Justice Amy Coney Barrett Argues US
Supreme Court Isn't 'a Bunch of Partisan Hacks,'" Louisville *Courier-
Journal*, September 12, 2021.

124   *"I think the media makes it sound":* Carley Lanich, "Justice Clarence Thomas
Laments a 'Race-Obsessed World' in Lecture at Notre Dame," *South Bend
Tribune*, September 17, 2021.

124   *"The catchy and sinister term":* Nina Totenberg, "Justice Alito Calls Criticism
of the Shadow Docket 'Silly' and 'Misleading,'" NPR, September 30,
2021, https://www.npr.org/2021/09/30/1042051134/justice-alito-calls
-criticism-of-the-shadow-docket-silly-and-misleading; Adam Liptak, "Alito
Responds to Critics of the Supreme Court's 'Shadow Docket,'" *New York
Times*, September 30, 2021; Robert Barnes and Mike Berardino, "Alito
Defends Letting Texas Abortion Law Take Effect, Says Supreme Court
Critics Want to Intimidate Justices," *Washington Post*, September 30, 2021.

NINE: ARGUMENTS

127   *"At oral argument":* Nina Totenberg, "Gorsuch Didn't Mask Despite Sotomayor's COVID Worries, Leading Her to Telework," NPR, January 21,
2022, https://www.npr.org/2022/01/18/1073428376/supreme-court
-justices-arent-scorpions-but-not-happy-campers-either.

127   *"It will alter the balance of power":* Recording of Telephone Conversation between Lyndon B. Johnson and Abe Fortas, September 22, 1966,
8:30AM, WH6609.11, PNO 3-4, #10821-22, MC, cited in Laura Kalman,
*The Long Reach of the 1960s: LBJ, Nixon, and the Making of the Contemporary
Supreme Court* (New York: Oxford University Press, 2017), 88.

127 *"for an audience of one":* "[E]ight men may read our briefs, but the real au-
     dience is one woman. Sandra Day O'Connor, the only woman in Ameri-
     can history to sit on the United States Supreme Court, is in the position
     single-handedly to decide the future of abortion rights." Susan R. Estrich
     and Kathleen M. Sullivan, "Abortion Politics: Writing for an Audience
     of One," *University of Pennsylvania Law Review* 138, no. 1 (1989): 119, https://
     doi.org/10.2307/3312181.

128 *A Democratic governor signed a state law: Planned Parenthood of Southeastern
     Pennsylvania v. Casey,* 505 U.S. 833 (1992).

128 *his fulminating mockery had pushed her away:* Evan Thomas, *First: Sandra
     Day O'Connor* (New York: Random House, 2019), 237, 299–300. Scalia's
     "irrepressible need to lecture and needle—and write ad hominem dis-
     sents" pushed Kennedy away, too. Ibid., 280.

128 *"cannot be taken seriously":* Webster v. Reproductive Health Services, 492 U.S.
     490, 532 (1989) (Scalia, J., concurring).

129 Casey, *in turn:* For an argument that *Casey* tamped down conflict over
     the issue, see Neal Devins, "How Planned Parenthood v. Casey (Pretty
     Much) Settled the Abortion Wars," *Yale Law Journal* 118 (2009): 1318,
     https://scholarship.law.wm.edu/cgi/viewcontent.cgi?article=1364&con
     text=facpubs.

129 *women's health choices:* This book refers to those who have abortions as
     women, though transgender and nonbinary people can become preg-
     nant and need abortion care as well.

129 *"safe, legal, and rare":* See Caitlin Flanagan, "Losing the *Rare* in 'Safe, Legal,
     and Rare,'" *The Atlantic,* December 6, 2019, https://www.theatlantic.com
     /ideas/archive/2019/12/the-brilliance-of-safe-legal-and-rare/603151/.

129 *the abortion rate started to fall:* Sarah Kliff, "Surprise! The Abortion Rate
     Just Hit an All-Time Low," *Washington Post,* January 22, 2013.

129 *630,000 reported abortions:* Kortsmit K, Mandel MG, Reeves JA, et al. Abor-
     tion Surveillance—United States, 2019. Centers for Disease Control
     Mortality and Morbidity Weekly Report Surveillance Summary 2021; 70
     (No. SS-9): 4, https://www.cdc.gov/mmwr/volumes/70/ss/ss7009a1.htm
     ?s_cid=ss7009a1_w.

130 *More abortion restrictions:* "More State Abortion Restrictions Were Enacted
     in 2011–2013 than in the Entire Previous Decade," Guttmacher Insti-
     tute (January 2, 2014), https://www.guttmacher.org/article/2014/01
     /more-state-abortion-restrictions-were-enacted-2011-2013-entire-previ
     ous-decade.

130 *In Missouri:* Josh Merchant, "Nearly Half of Abortions in Kansas Are for
     Missouri Residents, but Voters Could End That," *Kansas City Beacon,*
     November 20, 2021, https://www.kcur.org/news/2021-11-20/nearly-half
     -of-abortions-in-kansas-are-for-missouri-residents-but-voters-could-end
     -that.

130 *Twenty-four states, nearly a majority: Dobbs v. Jackson Women's Health,* Brief for

the States of Texas, Alabama, Alaska, Arizona, Arkansas, Florida, Georgia, Idaho, Indiana, Kansas, Kentucky, Louisiana, Missouri, Montana, Nebraska, North Dakota, Ohio, Oklahoma, South Carolina, South Dakota, Tennessee, Utah, West Virginia, and Wyoming as *Amici Curiae* in Support of Petitioners, July 29, 2021, https://www.supremecourt.gov/Docket PDF/19/19-1392/185249/20210729123524687_19-1392%20Amicus %20Brief.pdf.

131   *would "happen automatically":* At the third general election presidential debate, moderator Chris Wallace asked Trump if his justices would overturn *Roe.* Trump: "Well, if we put another two or perhaps three justices on, that's really what's going to be—that will happen. And that'll happen automatically, in my opinion, because I am putting pro-life justices on the court. I will say this: It will go back to the states, and the states will then make a determination." Clinton retorted: "Well, I strongly support *Roe v. Wade,* which guarantees a constitutional right to a woman to make the most intimate, most difficult, in many cases, decisions about her health care that one can imagine." "October 19, 2016 Debate Transcript," Committee on Presidential Debates, https://www.de bates.org/voter-education/debate-transcripts/october-19-2016-debate -transcript/.

131   *As a young law professor:* Elena Kagan, "Confirmation Messes, Old and New," reviewing Stephen Carter, *The Confirmation Mess, The University of Chicago Law Review* 62, no. 2 (Spring 1995): 919.

131   *"a precedent of the Supreme Court":* U.S. Congress, Senate, Committee on the Judiciary, *Confirmation Hearing on the Nomination of Hon. Neil M. Gorsuch to Be an Associate Justice of the Supreme Court of the United States, March 20, 21, 22, and 23, 2017,* 115th Cong., 1st Sess., 77, https:// www.govinfo.gov/content/pkg/CHRG-115shrg28638/pdf/CHRG -115shrg28638.pdf.

131   *"important precedent of the Supreme Court":* U.S. Congress, Senate, *Confirmation Hearing on the Nomination of Hon. Brett M. Kavanaugh to Be an Associate Justice of the Supreme Court of the United States, Hearing Before the Committee on the Judiciary, September 4, 5, 6, 7, and 27, 2018,* 115th Cong., 2nd Sess., 115th Cong., 2nd Sess., https://www.govinfo.gov/content/pkg/CHRG -115shrg32765/pdf/CHRG-115shrg32765.pdf.

132   *"settled":* The Merriam-Webster Dictionary (Springfield, MA: Merriam-Webster, 2016), 658.

132   *"super-stare decisis":* Richmond Medical Center for Women v. Gilmore, 219 F.3d 376, 377 (4th Cir. 2000).

132   *"barbaric":* Adrian de Vogue, "Barrett Signed a 'Right to Life' Letter in Ad That Also Called to End Roe v. Wade," CNN, October 1, 2020, https:// www.cnn.com/2020/10/01/politics/amy-coney-barrett-abortion-rights /index.html.

132   *"all the rules of stare decisis":* Kevin Freking, "What GOP-Nominated Justices

Said About Roe to Senate Panel," Associated Press, May 7, 2022. Some
point to an earlier talk where Barrett seemed to say that *Roe* should not
be overturned. In fact, she was only speculating shortly before the 2016
election what Clinton or Trump appointees might do. "I think don't
think the core case—*Roe*'s core holding that, you know, women have a
right to an abortion—I don't think that would change. But I think the
question of whether people can get very late-term abortions, how many
restrictions can be put on clinics—I think that would change." "Hes-
burgh Lecture 2016: Professor Amy Barrett at the Jacksonville University
Public Policy Institute," November 3, 2016, https://www.youtube.com
/watch?v=7yjTEdZ81lI.

132   *one justice who almost certainly lied:* Thomas's defenders denied after the
hearings that he had testified he did not discuss *Roe.* The *Wall Street Journal* editorial board called that claim a "whopper." But that is precisely
what he said:

> **Sen. Patrick Leahy:** Have you ever had discussion of *Roe v. Wade*
>   other than in this [hearing] room? In the seventeen or
>   eighteen years it's been there?
> **Judge Clarence Thomas:** Only, I guess, senator, in the fact that,
>   in the most general sense, that other individuals express
>   concerns one way or the other, and you listen and you try to
>   be thoughtful. If you're asking me whether or not I've ever
>   debated the contents of it, the answer to that is no, senator.
> **Sen. Leahy:** Have you ever . . . stated whether you felt that it was
>   properly decided or not?
> **Judge Thomas:** Senator, in trying to recall and reflect on that, I
>   don't recollect commenting one way or the other.

> *Nomination of Judge Clarence Thomas to Be Associate Justice of the
> Supreme Court of the United States Hearings Before the Committee on
> the Judiciary, Part 1 of 4 Parts,* 112nd Cong., 2nd sess., 1991, 222.
> See Michael Kinsley, "Did He Say It?," *Washington Post,* Decem-
> ber 12, 1991. A biography of Thomas quoted Assistant Attorney
> General for Civil Rights Brad Reynolds, an ardent conservative,
> as saying he and Thomas discussed *Roe* at length and that the
> future justice opposed the decision. Andrew Peyton Thomas,
> *Clarence Thomas: A Biography* (San Francisco: Encounter Books,
> 2001), 246.

133   *Crowds of demonstrators:* "Demonstrators Rally Outside Supreme Court
During Arguments in Mississippi Abortion Case," *USA Today,* December 1, 2021.

133   *When state lawyers first appealed:* "To be clear, the questions presented in
this petition do not require the Court to overturn *Roe* or *Casey*," the state

wrote. Petition for Writ of Certiorari at 5, *Dobbs v. Jackson Women's Health Organization*, No. 19-1392 (U.S. June 24, 2022), https://www.supremecourt. gov/DocketPDF/19/19-1392/145658/20200615170733513_FINAL %20Petition.pdf.

133   *Mississippi passed another law:* Senate Bill 2116, passed in 2019, was blocked by a federal appeals court. *Jackson Women's Health v. Dobbs*, No. 19-60455 (5th Cir. 2020).

133   *"the fetus has an interest":* Dobbs v. Jackson Women's Health, transcript of argument, December 3, 2021, 66.

133   *"explicitly took into account":* Ibid., 45–46.

134   *Roberts quoted:* Ibid., 19.

134   *"In all fifty states":* Ibid., 56.

134   *Fifteen justices over the past thirty years:* Ibid., 14–15.

135   *California Senator Dianne Feinstein:* Other lawmakers told journalists of their concerns about Feinstein's deteriorating capacities. See Tal Kopan and Joe Garofoli, "Colleagues Worry Dianne Feinstein Is Now Mentally Unfit to Serve, Citing Recent Interactions," *San Francisco Chronicle*, April 14, 2022; Jane Mayer, "Dianne Feinstein's Missteps Raise a Painful Age Question Among Senate Democrats," *New Yorker*, December 9, 2020, https://www.newyorker.com/news/news-desk/dianne-feinsteins-mis steps-raise-a-painful-age-question-among-senate-democrats. Feinstein insisted, "I'm an effective representative." Aaron Parsley, "Sen. Dianne Feinstein Responds After Colleagues' Accounts That Her Memory Is Deteriorating," *People*, April 14, 2022, https://people.com/politics/law makers-concern-dianne-feinsteins-memory-senator-defends-service/.

135   *"a major victory for the Christian legal movement":* Daniel Bennett, "Amy Coney Barrett's Confirmation Would Be a Major Victory for the Christian Legal Movement," *Religion & Politics*, October 6, 2022, https://religion andpolitics.org/2020/10/06/amy-coney-barretts-confirmation-would -be-a-major-victory-for-the-christian-legal-movement/.

135   *moment for "religious conservatives":* United States Senate, 116th Congress, 2nd Session, "Sen. Josh Hawley, Bostock v. Clayton County, Georgia," 166 *Congressional Record* 111: S2999.

135   *"common good constitutionalism":* Adrian Vermeule, *Common Good Constitutionalism: Rediscovering the Classical Legal Tradition* (Medford, MA: Polity Press, 2022); "Beyond Originalism," *The Atlantic*, March 31, 2020, https:// www.theatlantic.com/ideas/archive/2020/03/common-good-constitu tionalism/609037/.

136   *such as speaking in tongues:* Michael Biesecker and Michelle R. Smith, "Barrett Tied to Faith Group Ex-Members Say Subjugates Women," Associated Press, September 29, 2020.

136   *embodies the alliance:* Margaret Talbot, "Amy Coney Barrett's Long Game," *The New Yorker*, February 7, 2022, https://www.newyorker.com/maga zine/2022/02/14/amy-coney-barretts-long-game.

136   *Her law review articles:* See, for example, Amy Coney Barrett, "Originalism
      and Stare Decisis," *Notre Dame Law Review* 92 (2017): 1921.

136   *She wrote a dissent: Kanter v. Barr,* 919 F.3d 437 (7th Cir. 2019) (Barrett,
      dissenting).

136   *"She seems like she was tailor made":* Elizabeth Dias, Rebecca R. Ruiz, and
      Sharon LaFraniere, "Rooted in Faith, Amy Coney Barrett Represents a
      New Conservatism," *New York Times,* October 11, 2020.

138   *Florida governor Ron DeSantis:* Hannah Knowles, "DeSantis Sells 'Don't
      Fauci My Florida' Merch as New Coronavirus Cases Near Highest in Na-
      tion," *Washington Post,* July 16, 2021.

137   *They died at twelve times the rate:* Amanda Montañez and Tanya Lewis,
      "How to Compare Covid Deaths for Vaccinated and Unvaccinated Peo-
      ple," *Scientific American,* June 7, 2022, https://www.scientificamerican
      .com/article/how-to-compare-covid-deaths-for-vaccinated-and-unvaccinated
      -people/.

137   *Roberts had "in some form":* Totenberg, "Gorsuch Didn't Mask Despite So-
      tomayor's COVID Worries, Leading Her to Telework."

137   *"NPR stands by its reporting":* Nina Totenberg, "Supreme Court Hears Ar-
      guments on Campaign Finance Law, Issues Statement on NPR Report,"
      NPR, January 19, 2022, https://www.npr.org/2022/01/19/1074169348
      /supreme-court-hears-arguments-on-campaign-finance-law-issues-state
      ments-on-npr-r.

TEN: KBJ MEETS Q

138   *"I am writing to tell you":* Hon. Stephen Breyer, Letter to President Joseph
      Biden, January 27, 2022, https://www.supremecourt.gov/publicinfo
      /press/Letter_to_President_January-27-2022.pdf.

138   *a not-so-quiet outside campaign to persuade the justice to quit:* Matt Viser, Tyler
      Pager, Seung Min Kim, and Robert Barnes, "Inside the Campaign to
      Pressure Justice Stephen Breyer to Retire," *Washington Post,* January 28,
      2022.

138   *"Political groups may favor a particular appointment":* Stephen Breyer, *The
      Authority of the Court and the Peril of Politics* (Cambridge: Harvard Univer-
      sity Press, 2021), 54.

139   *Noble Lie:* Laurence H. Tribe, "Politicians in Robes," *New York Review of
      Books,* March 10, 2022, https://www.nybooks.com/articles/2022/03/10
      /politicians-in-robes-justice-breyer-tribe/.

139   *"I don't live on Pluto":* Ariane de Vogue, "Breyer Defends State of Supreme
      Court in Interview with CNN's Fareed Zakaria," CNN, September 19,
      2021, https://www.cnn.com/2021/09/19/politics/breyer-fareed-zakaria
      -gps/index.html.

139   *"The person I will nominate":* Remarks by President Biden on the Retirement
      of Supreme Court Justice Stephen Breyer, https://www.whitehouse.gov

/briefing-room/speeches-remarks/2022/01/27/remarks-by-president
-biden-on-the-retirement-of-supreme-court-justice-stephen-breyer/.

140 *As Biden's candidacy reeled:* Edward-Isaac Dovere, *Battle for the Soul: Inside the
Democrats' Campaigns to Defeat Trump* (New York: Viking, 2021), 322–23.

140 *"affirmative racial discrimination":* Josh Lederman and Julie Tsirkin, "GOP
Sen. Wicker Compares Biden's Supreme Court Pledge to Affirmative Action," NBC News, January 29, 2022, https://www.nbcnews.com/politics
/supreme-court/gop-sen-wicker-compares-biden-s-supreme-court-pledge
-affirmative-n1288211.

140 *"offensive":* Andrew Zhang, "Ted Cruz Calls Biden's Vow to Nominate
First Black Woman to U.S. Supreme Court 'Offensive,'" *Texas Tribune,*
February 1, 2022, https://www.texastribune.org/2022/02/01/ted-cruz
-biden-supreme-court/.

140 *A Georgetown lecturer tweeted:* Lauren Lumpkin, "Incoming Georgetown
Law Administrator Apologizes After Tweets Dean Called 'Appalling,'"
Washington Post, January 27, 2022.

140 *"If it were not that Brandeis is a Jew":* A. L. Todd, *Justice on Trial: The Case of
Louis D. Brandeis* (New York: McGraw-Hill, 1964), 85. German Jews were
considered more cultured than supposedly vulgar Eastern European Jews.

141 *every New York City borough except Staten Island:* Antonin Scalia was from
Queens; Elena Kagan from Manhattan; Ruth Bader Ginsburg, Brooklyn;
and Sonia Sotomayor, the Bronx. All sat on the same Court.

141 *The last white Christian man:* That was Byron White. The last one before
that named by a Democratic president was Sherman Minton in 1949.
Lyndon Johnson nominated Homer Thornberry, but his nomination
became moot when the Senate denied Abe Fortas a promotion to chief
justice in 1968.

141 *"number of false and misleading accusations":* Ronald Reagan, Governor
Reagan's News Conference, online, by Gerhard Peters and John T. Woolley, The American Presidency Project, https://www.presidency.ucsb
.edu/node/285628, https://www.presidency.ucsb.edu/documents/governor
-reagans-news-conference; Lou Cannon, "Reagan Pledges He Would
Name a Woman to the Supreme Court," *Washington Post,* October 15, 1980.

141 *When Trump announced his first short list:* Ginger Gibson and Lawrence
Hurley, "Trump identifies 11 potential Supreme Court nominees,"
Reuters, May 18, 2016. After criticism of the first list, a second list released later in the year was more diverse, and also included Neil Gorsuch. "While the new list adds the name of just one more woman, it is
more racially and ethnically diverse—one African-American state court
judge, a Venezuelan-born federal judge and another federal judge of
South Asian descent." Nina Totenberg, "Donald Trump Unveils New,
More Diverse Supreme Court Short List," NPR, September 23, 2016,
https://www.npr.org/2016/09/23/495216645/donald-trump-unveils
-new-more-diverse-supreme-court-short-list.

141   *In twenty states:* Amanda Powers and Alicia Bannon, *State Supreme Court Diversity—May 2022 Update,* Brennan Center for Justice, (May 25, 2022), https://www.brennancenter.org/our-work/research-reports/state-su preme-court-diversity-may-2022-update.

142   *If even one woman:* See, for example, Christina L. Boyd, Lee Epstein, and Andrew D. Martin. "Untangling the Causal Effects of Sex on Judging," *American Journal of Political Science* 54, no. 2 (2010): 389–411, http://www .jstor.org/stable/25652213 (which found that having a woman on an appeals court panel increased the chance it would rule for a plaintiff in a sex discrimination case).

142   *Diversity of race or gender:* Summarized by Maya Sen, "Written Testimony on the Importance of Judicial Diversity," Subcommittee on Courts, Intellectual Property, and the Internet, March 25, 2021, https://docs.house .gov/meetings/JU/JU03/20210325/111405/HHRG-117-JU03-Wstate-Sen M-20210325-U1.pdf.

142   *Labor unions attacked her:* Jeff Stein and Seung Min Kim, "Labor Groups Wary of Potential Supreme Court Pick Backed by Top House Democrat," *Washington Post,* February 2, 2022,.

142   *Graham in turn accused critics:* Glenn Kessler, "Graham's False Claim That Arabella Advisors Targeted Judge Childs," *Washington Post,* March 22, 2022.

142   *Biden should have been ready:* Colbert I. King, "Biden Should Have Been Ready to Make His Supreme Court Pick," *Washington Post,* February 9, 2022.

143   *She presided over 1,278 cases:* Gloria Huang, *New Datasheet: Judge Ketanji Brown Jackson,* Lex Machina (a Lexis-Nexis Company), March 22, 2022, https://lexmachina.com/blog/new-datasheet-judge-ketanji-brown-jackson /#:~:text=During%20Judge%20Jackson's%20tenure%20as,rights%20 and%20social%20security%20cases).

143   *national police union:* Fraternal Order of Police, "FOP National President Patrick Yoes Statement on Nomination of Ketanji Brown Jackson to SCOTUS," February 25, 2022, https://fop.net/2022/02/fop-national -president-patrick-yoes-statement-on-nomination-of-ketanji-brown-jack son-to-scotus/.

143   *Sixth Amendment:* "In all criminal prosecutions, the accused shall enjoy the right to a speedy and public trial, by an impartial jury of the State and district wherein the crime shall have been committed, which district shall have been previously ascertained by law, and to be informed of the nature and cause of the accusation; to be confronted with the witnesses against him; to have compulsory process for obtaining witnesses in his favor, and to have the Assistance of Counsel for his defence." U.S. Constitution, Amendment VI.

143   *It was the Supreme Court itself: Gideon v. Wainwright,* 372 U.S. 335 (1963).

143   *Another case required: Argersinger v. Hamlin,* 407 U.S. 25 (1972).

143 *over one million Americans:* As of the end of 2021, 1.2 million people were in prison in the United States. *People in Prison in Winter 2021–22,* Vera Institute, February 2022, https://www.vera.org/downloads/publications /People_in_Prison_in_Winter_2021-22.pdf. According to the Justice Department, there were 10.3 million admissions to jail in 2019 (some are people detained more than once), though the number dropped sharply during 2020 and the Covid pandemic (to 8.7 million). U.S. Department of Justice, Office of Justice Programs, Bureau of Justice Statistics, *Jail Inmates in 2020,* December 2021, https://bjs.ojp.gov/content/pub /pdf/ji20st.pdf.

143 *Many are fortunate if they can give clients a few hours:* See *The Louisiana Project: A Study of the Louisiana Public Defender System and Attorney Workload 2017 Standards,* American Bar Association Standing Committee on Legal Aid and Indigent Defendants and Postlethwaite and Netterville, February 15, 2017, APAChttps://www.americanbar.org/content/dam/aba /administrative/legal_aid_indigent_defendants/ls_sclaid_louisiana _project_report.pdf.

143 *Over 90 percent:* In some places the number is even higher: 97 percent in large urban state courts in 2009, and 90 percent in federal courts in 2014. Ram Subramanian, Léon Digard, Melvin Washington II, and Stephanie Sorage, *In the Shadows: A Review of the Research on Plea Bargaining,* Vera Institute, September 2020, https://www.vera.org/downloads /publications/in-the-shadows-plea-bargaining.pdf.

143 *Lately it has rarely been sympathetic:* See, for example, *Shinn v. Martinez Ramirez,* 596 U.S. ____, 142 S. Ct. 1718 (2022). Clarence Thomas wrote the six-to-three opinion; Kagan, Sotomayor, and Breyer dissented.

144 *In the Second Circuit:* Pérez was director of the Voting Rights and Elections Program at the Brennan Center for Justice at NYU School of Law. See Myrna Pérez, *Election Integrity: A Pro-Voter Agenda,* Brennan Center for Justice (2017), https://www.brennancenter.org/our-work/policy-solutions /election-integrity-pro-voter-agenda.

144 *In 2004 the Supreme Court had ruled: Rasul v. Bush,* 542 U.S. 466 (2004).

145 *"Do you regret":* Carl Hulse, "As Jackson Faces Senators, Her Criminal Defense Record Is a Target," *New York Times,* March 16, 2022.

145 *Violent crime had fallen:* John Gramlich, "What the Data Says (and Doesn't Say) About Crime in the United States," Pew Research Center, November 20, 2020, https://www.pewresearch.org/fact-tank/2020/11/20/facts -about-crime-in-the-u-s/.

146 *"the soft-on-crime brigade":* United States Senate, 117th Congress, 2nd Session, "Sen. Mitch McConnell, Nomination of Ketanji Brown Jackson (Executive Session)," 168 *Congressional Record* 46: S1159.

146 *"meritless to the point of demagoguery":* Andrew C. McCarthy, "Senator Hawley's Disingenuous Attack Against Judge Jackson's Record on Child Pornography," *National Review,* March 20, 2022, https://www.nationalreview

.com/2022/03/senator-hawleys-disingenuous-attack-against-judge-jack sons-record-on-child-pornography/.

146 *a man carrying an assault weapon:* U.S. Department of Justice, U.S. Attorney, District of Columbia, "North Carolina Man Sentenced to Four-Year Prison Term for Armed Assault at Northwest Washington Pizza Restaurant," Press release no. 17-33, June 22, 2017, https://www.justice .gov/usao-dc/pr/north-carolina-man-sentenced-four-year-prison-term -armed-assault-northwest-washington.

146 *"The intel on this":* Adam Goldman, "The Comet Ping Pong Gunman Answers Our Reporter's Questions," *New York Times,* December 16, 2021.

147 *"For more than two decades, confirmation hearings":* Melissa Murray, "Republicans Won't Be Satisfied with Overturning Roe," *Washington Post,* March 25, 2022.

147 *no right to assisted suicide: Washington v. Glucksberg,* 521 U.S. 702 (1997).

147 *In that case, she said:* The conservative *National Review* hailed the exchange when similar wording was decried in the leaked opinion in *Dobbs.* See Dan McLaughlin, "What Ketanji Brown Jackson Said About Unenumerated Rights," *National Review,* May 12, 2022.

148 *"thoroughgoing rout":* Dan McLaughlin, "The Jackson Hearings So Far Are a Rout for Progressive Pieties," *National Review,* March 22, 2022, https:// www.nationalreview.com/corner/the-jackson-hearings-so-far-are-a-rout -for-progressive-pieties/.

149 *By the time the hearings were over:* "New Marquette Law School Poll National Survey Finds Two-Thirds of Public Support Confirming Ketanji Brown Jackson as a Supreme Court Justice," March 30, 2022, https://law .marquette.edu/poll/2022/03/30/marquette-law-school-supreme-court -poll-march-2022/.

149 *It confirmed her with a 53-to-47 vote:* U.S. Congress, Senate, "On the Nomination (Confirmation: Ketanji Brown Jackson, of the District of Columbia, to Be an Associate Justice of the Supreme Court of the United States)," 117th Congress, 2nd Session, April 7, 2022, https://www.senate.gov/leg islative/LIS/roll_call_votes/vote1172/vote_117_2_00134.htm.

149 *"It has taken 232 years":* The White House, "Remarks by President Biden, Vice President Harris, and Judge Ketanji Brown Jackson on the Senate's Historic, Bipartisan Confirmation of Judge Jackson to be an Associate Justice of the Supreme Court," April 8, 2022, https://www.whitehouse .gov/briefing-room/speeches-remarks/2022/04/08/remarks-by -president-biden-vice-president-harris-and-judge-ketanji-brown-jackson -on-the-senates-historic-bipartisan-confirmation-of-judge-jackson-to-be -an-associate-justice-of-the-supreme-court/.

ELEVEN: INSURRECTIONISTS

150   *"Biden crime family & ballot fraud":* The texts between Meadows and Ginni
       Thomas were revealed in Bob Woodward and Robert Costa, "Virginia
       Thomas Urged White House Chief to Pursue Unrelenting Efforts to
       Overturn the 2020 Election, Texts Show," *Washington Post,* March 24,
       2022.

150   *That, she later confirmed:* Select Committee to Investigate the January 6th At-
       tack on the U.S. Capitol, Interview of Virginia L. Thomas, September 29,
       2022, 84, https://www.documentcloud.org/documents/23559240-tran
       script-of-ginni-thomas-interview-with-house-january-6-committee.

151   *"My wife is my best friend":* Jeffrey Toobin, "Partners: Will Clarence and
       Virginia Thomas Succeed in Killing Obama's Health-Care Plan?," *The
       New Yorker,* August 22, 2011, https://www.newyorker.com/magazine/2011
       /08/29/partners-jeffrey-toobin.

151   *"LOVE MAGA people!!!!":* Mark Joseph Stern, "Ginni Thomas, Wife of
       Clarence, Cheered On the Rally That Turned into the Capitol Riot," *Slate,*
       January 8, 2021, https://slate.com/news-and-politics/2021/01/ginni
       -thomas-donald-trump-clarence-thomas-capitol-riot.html.

151   *Thomas left the rally:* Select Committee to Investigate the January 6th At-
       tack on the U.S. Capitol, Interview of Virginia L. Thomas, September 29,
       2022.

152   *write to party leaders:*   "Conservative Leaders: Remove Cheney and
       Kinzinger from House Republican Conference," Conservative Action
       Project, December 15, 2021, http://conservativeactionproject.com/con
       servative-leaders-remove-cheney-and-kinzinger-from-house-republican
       -conference/. She signed the letter as the president of Liberty Consulting.

152   *He lost in a unanimous appeals court ruling: Trump v. Thompson,* 20 F. 4th 10
       (CADC 2021).

152   *Only Clarence Thomas voted to shield the records: Trump v. Thompson,* 595
       U.S. ___, 142 S. Ct. 680 (2022), https://www.supremecourt.gov/opin
       ions/21pdf/21a272_9p6b.pdf.

152   *Thomas's life story is well known:* His time in the segregated South is vividly
       described in Clarence Thomas, *My Grandfather's Son* (New York: Harper-
       Collins, 2007), 1–32.

153   *"When I was sixteen":* Jeff Nesbit, "The Real Reason Clarence Thomas
       Rarely Speaks," *U.S. News & World Report,* March 30, 2016, https://www
       .usnews.com/news/articles/2016-03-30/why-clarence-thomas-rarely
       -speaks-from-the-supreme-court-bench.

153   *"There was no other purpose to the cross": Virginia v. Black,* transcript of argu-
       ment, December 11, 2002, 23–24.

153   *"as close to totalitarianism":* Clarence Thomas, "Why Black Americans
       Should Look to Conservative Policies," speech to the Heritage Foundation,

August 1, 1987, https://www.heritage.org/political-process/report /why-black-americans-should-look-conservative-policies.

153   *A compelling recent book:* Corey Robin, *The Enigma of Clarence Thomas* (New York: Metropolitan Books, 2019), 2–10.

153   *"racial paternalism":* Adarand Constructors v. Peña, 515 U.S. 200 (1995) (Thomas, J., concurring).

154   *"She gets mad":* Juan Williams, "Black Conservatives, Center Stage," *Washington Post,* December 16, 1980.

154   *"A new media fad":* Clarence Thomas, "Letters to the Editor: Campus Bias," *Wall Street Journal,* April 20, 1987.

154   *"Today . . . color conscious means":* William Raspberry, "Are the Problems of Blacks Too Big for Government to Solve?," *Washington Post,* July 17, 1983.

154   *"as an umpire would":* Jon Meacham, *Destiny and Power: The American Odyssey of George Herbert Walker Bush* (New York: Random House, 2015), 479.

154   *"Was race a factor":* George Bush, The President's News Conference in Kennebunkport, Maine, July 1, 1991, online, by Gerhard Peters and John T. Woolley, The American Presidency Project, https://www.presidency .ucsb.edu/node/268236.

155   *"I believe the Constitution protects the right to privacy":* U.S. Congress, Senate, Committee on the Judiciary, *Nomination of Judge Clarence Thomas to Be Associate Justice of the Supreme Court of the United States, J-102-N̄084, Pt. 1, September 10, 11, 12, 13, and 16* (testimony of Clarence Thomas), 102nd Cong., 1st Sess., 180. Thomas even testified that "the marital right to privacy, of course, is at the core of that, and that the marital right to privacy in my view and certainly the view of the Court is that it is a fundamental right." Ibid., 255.

155   *"It is only after a great deal":* U.S. Congress, Senate, Committee on the Judiciary, *Nomination of Judge Clarence Thomas to Be Associate Justice of the Supreme Court of the United States, J-102-40, Pt. 4, October 11, 12, and 13, 1991* (testimony of Anita Hill), 102nd Cong., 1st Sess., 36.

155   *"This is a circus":* Ibid., 157–58.

155   *The hearing had turned into a harrowing experience:* See Jane Mayer and Jill Abramson, *Strange Justice: The Selling of Clarence Thomas* (New York: Houghton Mifflin, 1994).

156   *"The liberals made my life miserable":* Neil A. Lewis, "2 Years After His Bruising Hearing, Justice Thomas Can Rarely Be Heard," *New York Times,* November 27, 1993.

156   *"Clarence will give":* She also told *People* of Anita Hill, "In my heart, I always believed she was probably someone in love with my husband and never got what she wanted." The cover of *People* was headlined, " 'How We Survived': Virginia Thomas Tells Her Story," *People,* November 11, 1991.

156   *If a prior case was wrongly decided:* He wrote in one of his concurrences, "In my view, if the Court encounters a decision that is demonstrably

erroneous—i.e., one that is not a permissible interpretation of the text—the Court should correct the error, regardless of whether other factors support overruling the precedent." *Gamble v. United States,* 587 U.S. ____, 139 S. Ct. 1960, 1984 (2019) (Thomas, J., concurring).

156 *"I am an originalist":* Among other times, Scalia said that during a question-and-answer session at the Spanish and Portuguese Synagogue on Central Park West in New York City. See Jeffrey Toobin, *The Nine: Inside the Secret World of the Supreme Court* (New York: Doubleday, 2008), 120.

157 *Repeatedly he excavated:* For a defense of his approach by a former Thomas clerk who is himself Black, see Stephen F. Smith, "Clarence X?: The Black Nationalist Behind Justice Thomas's Constitutionalism," *New York University Journal of Law and Liberty* 4 (2009): 583.

157 *"Go back and read":* Adam Liptak, "A Justice Responds to Criticism from Obama," *New York Times,* February 4, 2010.

157 *He did so in a concurrence in 1997: Printz v. United States,* 521 U.S. 898 (1997) (Thomas, J., concurring).

157 *the Court applied its new reading: McDonald v. City of Chicago,* 561 U.S. 742 (2010).

158 *"Such an embittering experience":* Abner Mikva, "Oral History Transcript," Miller Center, Presidential Oral Histories, Bill Clinton presidency, November 5, 2005, https://millercenter.org/the-presidency/presiden tial-oral-histories/abner-mikva-oral-history. Mikva had been a member of Congress and then served in the Clinton White House as counsel to the president.

158 *she herself had been an anticult activist:* Allan Smith and Alex Seitz-Wald, "The Untold Story of Ginni Thomas' Anti-Cult Activism—After She Was 'Deprogrammed,'" NBC News, June 14, 2022, https://www.nbcnews .com/politics/politics-news/untold-story-ginni-thomass-anti-cult-activ ism-was-deprogrammed-rcna22131.

158 *She came to that activism:* Marc Fisher, "I Cried Enough to Fill a Glass," *Washington Post,* October 25, 1987. The trainings used high-pressure tactics, humiliation, and isolation from friends and families, according to the *Post* article. "[Thomas] was confused and troubled by exercises such as one in which trainees listened to 'The Stripper' while disrobing to skimpy bikinis and bathing suits. The group then stood in a U-shaped line, made fun of fat people's bodies and riddled one another with sexual questions."

159 *"They say a storm is coming":* "Tea Party Activists March on Capitol Hill," Associated Press, July 1, 2010.

159 *"America is in a vicious battle":* Danny Hakim and Jo Becker, "The Long Crusade of Clarence and Ginni Thomas," *New York Times Magazine,* February 22, 2022.

159 *In October 2011:* Jackie Calmes, "Activism of Thomas's Wife Could Raise Judicial Issues," *New York Times,* October 8, 2010.

159   *"Anita Hill, this is Ginni Thomas":* Jane Mayer, "Virginia Thomas's Message
       for Anita Hill," *The New Yorker*, October 19, 2010, https://www.newyorker
       .com/news/news-desk/virginia-thomass-message-for-anita-hill.

160   *"harmless busybody":* Meredith McGraw and Daniel Lippman, "Is Ginni
       Thomas a Trumpworld Power Player or a Gadfly? It Depends on Who
       You Ask," *Politico*, March 31, 2022, https://www.politico.com/news/2022
       /03/31/ginni-thomas-trump-world-power-00022042.

160   *"deep state":* Jane Mayer, "Is Ginni Thomas a Threat to the Supreme
       Court?," *The New Yorker*, January 21, 2022.

160   *Thomas had pressured:* Emma Brown, "Ginni Thomas, Wife of Supreme
       Court Justice, Pressed Ariz. Lawmakers to Help Reverse Trump's Loss,
       Emails Show," *Washington Post*, May 20, 2022.

160   *The investigation focused:* See *The January 6th Report* (New York: Celadon
       Books, 2022), 341–371.

160   *"We would just be sending in 'fake' electoral votes":* Maggie Haberman and
       Luke Broadwater, "'Kind of Wild/Creative': Emails Shed Light on
       Trump Fake Electors Plan," *New York Times*, July 26, 2022.

160   *"I can't wait":* Shelby Talcott, "Ginni Thomas Says She Looks 'Forward to
       Talking to' January 6 Committee, Wants to 'Clear Up Misconceptions,'"
       Daily Caller, June 16, 2022, https://dailycaller.com/2022/06/16/ginni
       -thomas-talk-testify-january-6-committee-clear-up-thompson-eastman/.

160   *the only court in the country, state or federal:* Johanna Kalb and Alicia Ban-
       non, *Supreme Court Ethics Reform*, Brennan Center for Justice (2019),
       https://www.brennancenter.org/our-work/research-reports/supreme
       -court-ethics-reform.

161   *On the day in 2017:* Elizabeth Warren, "The Supreme Court Has an Ethics
       Problem," *Politico*, November 1, 2017, https://www.politico.com/mag
       azine/story/2017/11/01/supreme-court-ethics-problem-elizabeth-warren
       -opinion-215772/. In *Janus v. AFSCME*, the Court ruled five to four that
       public employees were not required to pay fees to a union if they are not
       members.

161   *he had not disclosed:* Clarence Thomas, letter to Committee on Fi-
       nancial Disclosure, January 21, 2011, https://www.wsj.com/public
       /resources/documents/Thomas.pdf; Peter Landers, "Justice Thomas
       Revises Disclosures After Criticism," *Wall Street Journal*, January 24, 2011.

TWELVE: THE LEAK

162   *he had been at Wrigley Field:* Jason Meisner, "Ex-Justice John Paul Stevens
       Coming Home for World Series," *Chicago Tribune*, October 25, 2016. Did
       Ruth actually call the shot? "Very definitely, he pointed his bat," Ste-
       vens insisted. "View from Bench: Former Supreme Court Justice Roots
       for Cubs," Associated Press, October 26, 2016. (Recently unearthed film
       suggests Ruth may have been pointing at the Cubs' dugout.)

162 Politico *published an astonishing bombshell:* Josh Gerstein and Alexander Ward, "Supreme Court Has Voted to Overturn Abortion Rights, Draft Opinion Shows," *Politico,* May 2, 2022, https://www.politico.com/news /2022/05/02/supreme-court-abortion-draft-opinion-00029473.

164 *"It would mean that every other decision":* "Remarks by President Biden Before Air Force One Departure," the White House, May 3, 2022, https:// www.whitehouse.gov/briefing-room/speeches-remarks/2022/05/03 /remarks-by-president-biden-before-air-force-one-departure-15/.

164 *it went up after the Capitol Police:* Whitney Wild, "Law Enforcement Officials Warn of Potential Violence in DC and Nationwide in Wake of Supreme Court Draft Opinion," CNN, May 5, 2022, https://www.cnn .com/2022/05/05/politics/law-enforcement-violence-supreme-court -draft-opinion-roe/index.html.

164 *a front-page* New York Times *story:* Warren Weaver Jr., "Justices Ruling on Tapes May Follow Vote by Panel," *New York Times,* July 20, 1974.

164 Roe v. Wade *itself leaked in 1973:* James Robenalt, *January 1973: Watergate, Roe v. Wade, Vietnam, and the Month That Changed America Forever* (Chicago: Chicago Review Press, 2015), 235.

165 *Heritage Foundation experts:* A plan published by the think tank in 1989 urged that government should "Mandate all households to obtain adequate insurance. Many states now require passengers in automobiles to wear seatbelts for their own protection. Many others require anybody driving a car to have liability insurance. But neither the federal government nor any state requires all households to protect themselves from the potentially catastrophic costs of a serious accident or illness. Under the Heritage plan, there would be such a requirement." Stuart M. Butler, "Assuring Affordable Health Care for All Americans," Heritage Foundation, October 1, 1989, https://www.heritage.org/social-security/report /assuring-affordable-health-care-all-americans. Embarrassed by his prescient apostasy, Butler later claimed that any attribution of the plan to him was in error. Stuart M. Butler, "Don't Blame Heritage for ObamaCare Mandate," Heritage Foundation, February 6, 2012, https://www.heri tage.org/health-care-reform/commentary/dont-blame-heritage-obama care-mandate. (As Orwell would say, we have always been at war with Oceana.)

165 *now that Obama had embraced it:* See Randy Barnett, Nathaniel Stewart, and Todd Gaziano, "Why the Personal Mandate to Buy Health Insurance Is Unprecedented and Unconstitutional," Heritage Foundation, Legal Memorandum No. 49, December 9, 2009, https://www.heritage.org /health-care-reform/report/why-the-personal-mandate-buy-health-insurance -unprecedented-and.

165 *the Supreme Court never had blocked a major economic regulatory law:* The most recent major cases involved social laws that had been justified by the Commerce Clause rather than core economic activities (such as buying

insurance or regulation of the multibillion-dollar health care industry). Three cases did limit federal action under the Commerce Clause. *Lopez* blocked the 1990 Gun Free Schools Zone law, which had relied on the Commerce Clause to bar guns near schools. *United States v. Lopez,* 514 U.S. 549 (1995). Gun possession was noneconomic and a subject for criminal law, the Court ruled. A few years later, the Court's conservatives held that part of the Violence Against Women Act also had exceeded the Commerce Clause by giving women the right to sue for damages for gender-based violence in federal courts. *United States v. Morrison,* 529 U.S. 598 (2000). But the Court upheld use of the Commerce Clause when Congress overrode states that had legalized medical marijuana. Here it was a socially conservative outcome, and Scalia joined the majority in finding this to be an acceptable assertion of federal power. Thomas dissented: "If Congress can regulate this under the Commerce Clause, then it can regulate virtually anything—and the Federal Government is no longer one of limited and enumerated powers." *Gonzales v. Raich,* 545 U.S. 1 (2004).

166 *"a right-wing bat signal"*: Josh Blackman, *Unprecedented: The Constitutional Challenge to Obamacare* (New York: PublicAffairs, 2013), 288.

166 *"threatening dire consequences"*: "Pressuring the Chief," *National Review,* May 24, 2012, https://www.nationalreview.com/2012/05/pressuring-chief -editors/.

166 *"an embarrassingly obvious campaign"*: George F. Will, "Liberals Put the Squeeze to Justice Roberts," *Washington Post,* May 25, 2012.

166 Will *"had heard from a law student"*: Jeffrey Toobin, *The Oath: The Obama White House and the Supreme Court* (New York: Random House, 2102), 288.

166 *"based on people I talk to"*: Orin Kerr, "More on the Supreme Court Leak," *The Volokh Conspiracy,* July 3, 2012, https://volokh.com/2012/07/03 /more-on-the-supreme-court-leak/.

166 *the dissent read as if it originally had been drafted:* See Avik Roy, "The Inside Story of How Roberts Changed His Supreme Court Vote on Obamacare," *Forbes,* July 1, 2012.

166 *In a group of cases:* Bostock v. Clayton County, 590 U.S. ___, 140 S. Ct. 1731 (2020).

167 *One writer speculated:* Josh Blackman, "Has There Been a Leak from the Supreme Court in Bostock?," *Reason,* November 25, 2019, https://reason .com/volokh/2019/11/25/has-there-been-a-leak-from-the-supreme -court-in-bostock/.

167 *"abortion scare campaign"*: "The Abortion Scare Campaign," editorial, *Wall Street Journal,* July 2, 2018.

167 *"may be trying to turn another Justice now"*: "Abortion and the Supreme Court," editorial, *Wall Street Journal,* April 26, 2022.

167 Politico *ran another scoop:* Josh Gerstein, Alexander Ward, and Ryan Lizza, "Alito's Draft Opinion Overturning Roe Is Still the Only One Circulated

Inside Supreme Court," *Politico*, May 11, 2022, https://www.politico.com
/news/2022/05/11/alito-abortion-draft-opinion-roe-00031648.

168   *The Supreme Court in recent years had relentlessly ruled:* The Roberts Court
found in favor of religious organizations over 50 percent more than previous courts since 1950, according to a statistical analysis. (The current
Court holds for religious groups over 81 percent of the time, compared
with 50 percent previously.) Eric A. Posner and Lee Epstein, "The Roberts Court and the Transformation of Constitutional Protections for Religion: A Statistical Portrait," *Supreme Court Review* 2021 (2022): 315.

168   *In an earlier day religious freedom cases:* See Steven Waldman, *Sacred Liberty: America's Long, Bloody, and Ongoing Struggle for Religious Freedom* (New
York: HarperCollins, 2019).

168   *"religious hostility":* Masterpiece Cakeshop v. Colorado Civil Rights Commission,
584 U.S. ___, 138 S. Ct. 1719, 1724 (2018).

168   *The Court had allowed the retail chain Hobby Lobby:* Burwell v. Hobby Lobby
Stores, Inc., 573 U.S. 682 (2014).

168   *A group of nuns:* Little Sisters of the Poor Saints Peter and Paul Home v. Pennsylvania, 140 S. Ct. 2367 (2020).

168   *In 2014, the Court:* Town of Greece v. Galloway, 572 U.S. 565 (2013).

169   *a half-century-old Supreme Court precedent:* Lemon v. Kurtzman, 403 U.S. 602
(1971).

169   *it used the heartwarming case:* The Court effectively overruled *Lemon v.
Kurtzman*. Gorsuch claimed the prior ruling had been long ago abandoned, but Sotomayor observes that, in fact, the Court was overruling it
in this opinion.

169   *"a tiny microcosm":* Sonia Sotomayor, *My Beloved World* (New York: Random House, 2013), 18.

170   *"Maybe because":* Barack Obama, *A Promised Land* (New York: Random
House, 2020), 389.

170   *"out of touch with reality":* Schuette v. Coalition to Defend Affirmative Action,
572 U.S. 291 (2014) (Sotomayor, J., dissenting).

171   *"[f]or generations":* Utah v. Strieff, 579 U.S. 232 (2016) (Sotomayor, J., dissenting).

171   *Later she said her own brother:* Irin Carmon, "Reintroducing Sonia Sotomayor," *New York*, February 1, 2021, https://nymag.com/intelligencer
/article/reintroducing-sonia-sotomayor.html.

171   *"To put that in historical context":* United States v. Justin Don Higgs, 592 U.S.
___, 141 S. Ct. 645, 647 (2021) (Sotomayor, J., dissenting in denial of
certiorari).

171   *On the last day of the term:* Grzegorczyk v. United States, 597 U.S. ___, 142 S.
Ct. 2580 (2022) (Sotomayor, J., dissenting from denial of certiorari);
Storey v. Lumpkin, 597 U.S. ___, 142 S. Ct. 2576 (2022) (Sotomayor,
J., dissenting from denial of certiorari); *Canales v. Lumpkin*, 597 U.S.
___, 142 S. Ct. 2563 (2022) (Sotomayor, J., dissenting from denial of

certiorari); *Ramirez v. Guadarrama*, 597 U.S. ___, 142 S. Ct. 2571 (2022) (Sotomayor, J., dissenting from denial of certiorari); *Cope v. Cogdill*, 597 U.S. ___, 142 S. Ct. 2573 (2022) (Sotomayor, J., dissenting from denial of certiorari); *Hill v. Shoop*, 597 U.S. ___, 142 S. Ct. 2579 (Mem) (2022) (Sotomayor, J., dissenting from denial of certiorari).

171   *"minority leader":* Elie Mystal, "How Sonia Sotomayor Became the Conscience of the Supreme Court," *The Nation*, August 22, 2022, https://www.thenation.com/article/politics/sonia-sotomayor-liberal-justice/.

171   *"Often, you're talking to Congress":* Justice Sonia Sotomayor and Linda Greenhouse, "A Conversation with Justice Sotomayor," *Yale Law Journal Forum* 123 (2014): 375, http://yalelawjournal.org/forum/a-conversation-with-justice-sotomayor.

171   *"Sotomayor's opinions read like":* Mystal, "How Sonia Sotomayor Became the Conscience of the Supreme Court."

171   *"There are days":* Lawrence Hurley, "Liberal Justice Sotomayor Says U.S. Supreme Court 'Mistakes' Can Be Fixed," Reuters, June 17, 2022.

172   *"On the far end of the Trail of Tears":* McGirt v. Oklahoma, 591 U.S. ___, 140 S. Ct. 2452 (2020).

172   *"Neil Gorsuch & the four liberal justices":* Ted Cruz, @tedcruz, Twitter, 12:52 p.m., July 9, 2020, https://twitter.com/tedcruz/status/1281269895519514625?lang=en.

172   *the Court ruled again on a question of Native American rights:* Oklahoma v. Castro-Huerta, 597 U.S. ___, 142 S. Ct. 2486 (2022).

172   *Gorsuch noted that the Court's 1832 opinion:* This was *Worcester v. Georgia*, 31 U.S. 515 (1832), the case where Andrew Jackson supposedly said, "John Marshall has made his ruling—now let him enforce it," and in any case where the federal and state governments ignored the Court.

173   *"If protests are peaceful, yes":* Natalie Prieb, "Schumer Says He Sees No Issue with Peaceful Protests at Houses of Supreme Court Justices," *The Hill*, May 10, 2022, https://thehill.com/homenews/senate/3483411-schumer-says-he-sees-no-issue-with-protests-at-houses-of-supreme-court-justices/amp/.

173   *A man flew from California:* Dan Morse, "Man Accused in Kavanaugh Assassination Plot Pleads Not Guilty," *Washington Post*, June 22, 2022; https://www.documentcloud.org/documents/22056105-us-v-nicholas-john-roske-charging-documents. For his explanation about *Roe*, alleged in a search warrant application, see Holmes Lybrand and Tierney Sneed, "FBI Says Man Accused of Attempting to Kill Brett Kavanaugh Said He Was 'Shooting for 3' Justices," CNN, July 27, 2022, https://www.cnn.com/2022/07/27/politics/kavanaugh-roske-arrest-warrant/index.html.

173   *Thomas vented about the clerks:* Robert Barnes, "Clarence Thomas Says He Worries Respect for Institutions Is Eroding," *Washington Post*, May 6, 2022.

174   *The Manhattan Institute:* See Jonathan Chait, "Christopher Rufo Foments a School-Rape Panic," *New York*, July 2022, https://nymag.com/intelli

gencer/2022/07/christopher-rufo-foments-a-school-rape-panic.html; Christopher F. Rufo, @realchrisrufo, Twitter, 7:04 PM, May 12, 2022, https://twitter.com/realchrisrufo/status/1524888386682531842?lang =en.

174 *"we actually trusted each other"*: Shawna Mizelle and Joan Biskupic, "Thomas Says Supreme Court After Leaked Draft Opinion Is 'Not the Court' of Ginsburg's Era," CNN, May 14, 2022, https://www.cnn.com/2022/05/14 /politics/clarence-thomas-supreme-court-rbg/index.html.

174 *Samuel Alito sounded more downcast:* Robert Barnes and Lauren Lumpkin, "Alito Reluctant to Discuss State of Supreme Court After Roe Leak," *Washington Post,* May 12, 2022.

175 *Public approval had plunged:* Jeffrey M. Jones, "Confidence in U.S. Supreme Court Sinks to Historic Low," Gallup Poll, June 23, 2022, https:// news.gallup.com/poll/394103/confidence-supreme-court-sinks-historic -low.aspx.

THIRTEEN: *BRUEN* (JUNE 23, 2022)

179 *On May 14, 2022:* Office of New York State Attorney General, "Investigative Report on the Role of Online Platforms in the Tragic Mass Shooting in Buffalo on May 14, 2022," October 18, 2022, 9–10, https://ag.ny.gov /sites/default/files/buffaloshooting-onlineplatformsreport.pdf.

179 *"hearth and home"*: *District of Columbia v. Heller,* 554 U.S. 270 (2008).

180 *more guns than people:* According to the Small Arms Survey, a worldwide research body, "Of the 857 million civilian-held firearms estimated in 2017, 393 million are in the United States—more than those held by civilians in the other top 25 countries combined." Aaron Karp, *Estimating Global Civilian-Held Firearms Numbers,* Small Arms Survey, June 2018, https://www.smallarmssurvey.org/sites/default/files/resources /SAS-BP-Civilian-Firearms-Numbers.pdf.

180 *comes to us from a time:* This discussion draws on the research conducted for my own book on the subject. See Michael Waldman, *The Second Amendment: A Biography* (New York: Simon & Schuster, 2014).

180 *The Second Amendment:* U.S. Constitution, Amendment II.

180 *"To place any dependence upon Militia":* George Washington to the President of Congress, September 24, 1776, in John C. Fitzpatrick, ed., *The Writings of George Washington* (Washington, D.C.: Government Printing Office, 1932), 112.

181 *Twelve congressmen spoke:* Waldman, *The Second Amendment,* 55–56. See also H. Richard Uviller and William C. Merkel, *The Militia and the Right to Arms, or How the Second Amendment Fell Silent* (Durham, NC: Duke University Press, 2002), 102–3.

181 *Within months after the amendment was ratified:* The act required adult men to join a state militia, and continued, "Every citizen, so enrolled and

notified, shall, within six months thereafter, provide himself with a good musket or firelock, a sufficient bayonet and belt, two spare flints, and a knapsack, a pouch, with a box therein, to contain not less than twenty four cartridges, suited to the bore of his musket or firelock, each cartridge to contain a proper quantity of powder and ball; or with a good rifle, knapsack, shot-pouch, and powder-horn, twenty balls suited to the bore of his rifle, and a quarter of a pound of powder; and shall appear so armed, accoutred and provided, when called out to exercise." This provision—in effect, a universal draft and a requirement that all free white men buy guns—reflects a profound degree of governmental compulsion. Militia Act: 1 stat. 271 (Uniform Militia Act of 1792). Its full title was "An Act more effectually to provide for the National Defense by establishing an Uniform Militia throughout the United States." The act introduced a racial element: it required only white men to join the militia. Previously in much of the country Black men also had been expected to join. For an example of the obligation to register guns, known as a "return," see, e.g., "return" for 1804: March 22, 1804, Library of Congress. "A Century of Lawmaking for a New Nation: U.S. Congressional Documents and Debates," 1774–1875, American State Papers, 8th Cong., 1st Sess., Military Affairs: Vol. 1, http://lcweb2.loc.gov/cgi-bin/ampage?collId=llsp&fileName=016/llsp016.db&recNum=173. President Thomas Jefferson's efforts to use the return to learn the readiness of the militias is described in John K. Mahon, *History of the Militia and the National Guard* (New York: Macmillan, 1983), 64.

181 *The institution persisted largely in the form of slave patrols:* See Carol Anderson, *The Second: Race and Guns in a Fatally Unequal America* (New York: Bloomsbury, 2021), 34–35.

181 *At the time of the Second Amendment:* See Saul Cornell and Nathan Dedino, "A Well Regulated Right: The Early American Origins of Gun Control," *Fordham Law Review* 73 (2004): 506.

181 *Always, there were limits and even bans:* For the most comprehensive assessment of those laws, see, Patrick J. Charles, *Armed in America: A History of Gun Rights from Colonial Militias to Concealed Carry* (Amherst, NY: Prometheus Books, 2018).

181 *Restrictions were stricter:* Joseph Blocher and Darrell A. H. Miller, *The Positive Second Amendment: Rights, Regulation, and the Future of* Heller (New York: Cambridge University Press, 2018), 29–35.

182 *"keep or use weapons":* "Minutes of the Board of Visitors of the University of Virginia, [4 October 1824]," Founders Online, National Archives, https://founders.archives.gov/documents/Madison/04-03-02-0393.

182 *"The Carrying of Fire Arms Strictly Prohibited":* Adam Winkler, *Gun Fight: The Battle over the Right to Bear Arms in America* (New York: W. W. Norton, 2011), 165.

182 *When visitors arrived:* Matt Jancer, "Gun Control Is as Old as the Old West," *Smithsonian Magazine,* February 5, 2018, https://www.smithsonian mag.com/history/gun-control-old-west-180968013/.

182 *Courts generally did not assume:* Waldman, *The Second Amendment,* 211. The dominant "Arkansas doctrine" was spelled out by legal scholar John Forrest Dillon in the 1870s. Dillon found a strong judicial consensus that the constitutional protection extended only to weapons to be used in the militia. The right to self-defense, rooted in common law, was subject to restrictions such as a ban on carrying a concealed weapon. Saul Cornell, *A Well Regulated Militia: The Founding Fathers and the Origins of Gun Control in America* (New York: Oxford University Press, 2006), 186–89. On the other hand, for a survey of state constitutions, commentaries, and rulings in the 1800s that support an individualist interpretation, see David B. Kopel, "The Second Amendment in the 19th Century," *Brigham Young Law Review* 1998, no. 4 (1998): 1360, http://lawreview.byu.edu /archives/1998/4/kop.pdf.

182 *"A man in the pursuit":* Aymette v. State, 21 Tenn. 154 (1840) at 161.

182 *Sullivan Act:* 1911 N.Y. Laws ch. 195, §1, p. 443.

183 *"I have never believed":* U.S. Congress, Hearings Before the Committee on Ways and Means of the House of Representatives, 73rd Cong., 2nd Sess. (1934), 52.

183 *"some reasonable relationship":* United States v. Miller, 307 U.S. 174 (1939).

183 *This has been the subject":* Charlayne Hunter-Gault, Interview with Warren Burger, *The NewsHour with Jim Lehrer* (Alexandria, VA: PBS Video, 1991).

183 *the swing to the right in the 1970s:* Kevin M. Kruse and Julian Zelizer, *Fault Lines: A History of the United States Since 1974* (New York: W. W. Norton, 2019), 88–112.

184 *". . . the right of the people":* Waldman, *The Second Amendment,* 96.

184 *"The great object is":* Patrick Henry's speech at the Virginia Ratifying Convention was transcribed here: *Documentary History of the Ratification of the Constitution,* X, 1276. Also available at http://press-pubs.uchicago.edu /founders/print documents/a1815s13.html. It continues to be liberally misquoted. One example that packs a lot of symbolic punch into one honorific: The NRA endowed a "Patrick Henry Professorship" in the Second Amendment at Antonin Scalia Law School at George Mason University.

184 *"The NRA is the reason":* Evelyn Theiss, "Clinton Blames Losses on NRA," Cleveland *Plain Dealer,* January 14, 1995. Clinton estimated the fight over the assault weapons ban cost twenty Democrats their seats.

184 *Citizens came to believe:* According to a poll by *USA Today*/Gallup, 73 percent of the public believed the Constitution "guarantees the rights of Americans to own guns," and only 20 percent believed it "only guarantees members of state militias such as the National Guard units the right

to own guns." Jeffrey M. Jones, "Public Believes Americans Have Right to Own Guns," Gallup Poll, March 27, 2008, https://news.gallup.com/poll/105721/public-believes-americans-right-own-guns.aspx.

184   *The gun group was still so nervous*: Adam Winkler, *Gun Fight: The Battle over the Right to Bear Arms in America* (New York: W. W. Norton, 2011), 61; Tony Mauro, "Both Sides Fear Firing Blanks if D.C. Gun Case Reaches High Court," *Legal Times*, July 30, 2007, www.law.com/jsp/article.jsp?id=1185527215310&slreturn=20130613111444.

185   *"vindication of originalism"*: Marcia Coyle, *The Roberts Court: The Struggle for the Constitution* (New York: Simon & Schuster, 2013), 163.

185   *This interjection:* Kennedy's role remains the subject of speculation. Still, it is known as the "Kennedy paragraph." See, e.g., Nicholas J. Johnson, "The Power Side of the Second Amendment Question: Limited, Enumerated Powers and the Continuing Battle over the Legitimacy of the Individual Right to Arms," *Hastings Law Journal* 70 (April 2019): 717, 724.

185   *Scholars looked again:* Josh Blackman and James C. Phillips, "Corpus Linguistics and the Second Amendment," *Harvard Law Review Blog* (August 7, 2018); Dennis Baron, "Corpus Evidence Illuminates the Meaning of Bear Arms," *Hastings Constitutional Law Quarterly* 46 (2019): 509, 510–13; Alison L. LaCroix, "Historical Semantics and the Meaning of the Second Amendment," *The Panorama* (August 3, 2018). See also Dennis Baron, "Antonin Scalia Was Wrong About the Meaning of 'Bear Arms,'" *Washington Post*, May 21, 2018.

186   *This author conducted a similar search:* Waldman, *The Second Amendment*, 63. The database was http://founders.archives.gov/.

186   *Two years later with far less fanfare:* McDonald v. City of Chicago, 561 U.S. 742 (2010).

187   *the most comprehensive research on the cases:* Eric Ruben and Joseph Blocher, "From Theory to Doctrine: An Empirical Analysis of the Right to Keep and Bear Arms After Heller," *Duke Law Journal* 67 (2018): 1433, https://scholarship.law.duke.edu/dlj/vol67/iss7/3. Ruben is a Fellow at the Brennan Center for Justice.

187   *judges chose a level of scrutiny:* The First, Second, Third, Fourth, Fifth, Sixth, Seventh, Ninth, Tenth, Eleventh, and District of Columbia Circuits explicitly adopted an "intermediate scrutiny" framework. See *Worman v. Healey*, 922 F.3d 26, 33 (1st Cir. 2019), cert. denied, 141 S. Ct. 109 (2020); *Libertarian Party of Erie County v. Cuomo*, 970 F.3d 106, 127 (2d Cir. 2020), cert. denied, 2021 WL 2519117 (U.S. June 21, 2021); *New Jersey Rifle & Pistol Clubs Inc. v. Att'y Gen. New Jersey*, 974 F.3d 237, 242 (3d Cir. 2020); *Harley v. Wilkinson*, 988 F.3d 766, 769 (4th Cir. 2021); *NRA v. Bureau of Alcohol, Tobacco, Firearms, & Explosives*, 700 F.3d 185, 194, 206 (5th Cir. 2012); *United States v. Green*, 679 F.3d 510, 518 (6th Cir. 2012); *Kanter v. Barr*, 919 F.3d 437, 442 (7th Cir. 2019); *Young v. Hawaii*, 992

F.3d 765, 783 (9th Cir. 2021); *United States v. Reese*, 627 F.3d 792, 800–1 (10th Cir. 2010); *GeorgiaCarry.Org*, 687 F.3d at 10 1260, n. 34; *United States v. Class*, 930 F.3d 460, 463 (D.C. Cir. 2019). The Eighth Circuit also acknowledged but did not formally adopt the approach. See *United States v. Adams*, 914 F.3d 602 (8th Cir. 2019).

187   *"this Court's constitutional orphan":* No. 17-342, *Sivester v. Becerra*, 583 U.S. ____ (2018) (Thomas, J., dissenting from denial of certiorari) (slip op. at 13), https://www.supremecourt.gov/opinions/17pdf/17-342_4hd5.pdf.

187   *"massive resistance":* See, e.g., NRA-ILA, "Turning Their Back on the Supreme Court," May 2, 2017, https://www.nraila.org/articles/20170502/turning-their-back-on-the-supreme-court.

187   *In these years, crime continued to drop:* See James Lartey and Wuehua Li, *New FBI Data: Violent Crime Still Falling,* Marshall Project, September 30, 2019, https://www.themarshallproject.org/2019/09/30/new-fbi-data-violent-crime-still-falling.

187   *"We are still living through":* Patrick Sharkey, *Uneasy Peace: The Great Crime Decline, the Renewal of City Life, and the Next War on Violence* (New York: W. W. Norton, 2018), 13.

187   *the worst day of his presidency:* Jonathan Alter, *The Center Holds: Obama and His Enemies* (New York: Simon & Schuster, 2013), 373.

188   *Twenty-five states:* "NRA Achieves Historical Milestone as 25 States Recognize Constitutional Carry," NRA-ILA, April 1, 2022, https://www.nraila.org/articles/20220401/nra-achieves-historical-milestone-as-25-states-recognize-constitutional-carry#:~:text=Kemp%20signs%20this%20legislation%2C%20Georgia,allowing%20law%2Dabiding%20individuals%20to.

188   *At the Democratic convention:* Lois Beckett, "Hillary Clinton's Focus on Guns Is Politically Bold. Her Solutions Are Old School," *The Guardian,* July 28, 2016.

188   *It had spent:* In 2016 the NRA spent $50 million in support of Trump and six U.S. Senate candidates, five of whom won.

188   *New York State attorney general: New York v. NRA,* August 6, 2020, https://ag.ny.gov/sites/default/files/summons_and_complaint_1.pdf.

189   *"affront to democracy":* Alex Gangitano, "NRA's LaPierre Responds to NY lawsuit: 'Bring It on,'" *The Hill,* August 6, 2020, https://thehill.com/homenews/510938-nras-lapierre-responds-to-ny-lawsuit-bring-it-on/.

189   *one of the few federal judges:* In words very similar to those used a decade later in *Bruen,* Kavanaugh wrote, "In my view, *Heller* and *McDonald* leave little doubt that courts are to assess gun bans and regulations based on text, history, and tradition, not by a balancing test such as strict or intermediate scrutiny." *Heller v. District of Columbia,* 670 F.3rd 1244 (2011) (Kavanaugh, J., dissenting).

189   *a peculiar lawsuit: New York State Rifle & Pistol Association, Inc. v. City of New York,* 590 U.S. __, 140 S. Ct. 1525 (2020).

189   *A quarter of the briefs:* Will Van Sant, "As SCOTUS Mulled *Bruen,* the NRA

Lobbied in the Shadows," *The Trace*, August 5, 2022, https://www.the trace.org/2022/08/nra-foundation-grants-amicus-briefs/.

190 *"There are a lot of armed people": New York State Rifle & Pistol Association v. Bruen*, transcript of argument, November 3, 2021, https://www.supreme court.gov/oral_arguments/argument_transcripts/2021/20-843_8n5a. pdf.

190 *Essex County, New Jersey:* Richard Cowen, "Violent Crime Up Slightly in Newark This Year, While Arrests Are Down, Officials Say," nj.com, December 29, 2021, https://www.nj.com/essex/2021/12/violent-crime -up-slightly-in-newark-this-year-while-arrests-are-down-officials-say.html.

191 *Major crimes fell:* N.Y.C. Police Dep't, "CompStat Report Covering the Week 8/30/2021 Through 9/5/2021," https://www1.nyc.gov/assets /nypd/downloads/pdf/crime_statistics/cs-en-us-city.pdf, cited in *New York Rifle & Pistol Association v. Bruen*, "Brief of *Amicus Curiae* Citizens Crime Commission in Support of Respondents," www.pbwt.com/con tent/uploads/2021/09/20210921144032621_20-843-New-York-State -Rifle-v-Bruen-Amicus-Curiae-Brief-in-Support-of-Respondents.pdf.

192 *On Sunday morning May 22:* Matt Wirz, "Daniel Enriquez Thrived Through a Changing New York. He Died in a Subway Shooting," *Wall Street Journal*, June 5, 2022.

192 *Tucker Carlson:* See Nicholas Confessore, "How Tucker Carlson Stoked White Fear to Conquer Cable," *New York Times*, April 30, 2022.

192 *"they can be dealt with in time":* Philissa Cramer, Ron Kampeas, "Buffalo Shooter's Manifesto Includes Antisemitic Rhetoric Along with Racism," Jewish Telegraph Agency, May 15, 2022, https://forward.com/fast-for ward/502458/buffalo-shooters-manifesto-includes-antisemitic-rhetoric -along-with-racism/; "Buffalo Shooter's Manifesto Promotes 'Great Replacement' Theory, Antisemitism and Previous Mass Shooters," Anti-Defamation League, May 14, 2022, https://www.adl.org/resources/blog /buffalo-shooters-manifesto-promotes-great-replacement-theory-anti semitism-and-previous-mass-shooters.

192 *417 mass shootings:* Gun Violence Archive 2022, https://www.gunviolence archive.org/ (accessed July 3, 2022). See also Julia Ledur and Kate Rabinowitz, "There Have Been over 250 Mass Shootings so Far in 2022," *Washington Post*, June 8, 2022.

193 *For months he had told friends:* Investigative Committee on the Robb Elementary Shooting, Texas House of Representatives, Interim Report, 29-39 (July 17, 2022), https://house.texas.gov/_media/pdf/committees /reports/87interim/Robb-Elementary-Investigative-Committee-Report .pdf.

193 *"The only thing that stops a bad guy":* Transcript: NRA Statement from December 21 press conference, *Hartford Courant,* December 21, 2012.

193 *According to the Gallup Poll:* Megan Brenan, "Public Pressure for Gun Legis-

lation Up After Shootings," Gallup poll, June 1, 2022, https://news.gallup
.com/poll/394022/public-pressure-gun-legislation-shootings.aspx.

194 *The measure was due for a vote:* It would become the Bipartisan Safer
Communities Act, Pub. L. No. 117-159, 136 Stat. 1313, https://www.con
gress.gov/117/plaws/publ159/PLAW-117publ159.pdf.

194 *When it comes to carrying weapons:* Even a partial compendium of nineteenth-
and early-twentieth-century laws restricting or banning the carrying of
weapons fills three full pages in small type. Patrick J. Charles, "The Faces
of the Second Amendment Outside the Home, Take Two: How We Got
Here and Why It Matters," *Cleveland State Law Review* 64 (2016): 373,
https://engagedscholarship.csuohio.edu/clevstlrev/vol64/iss3/5.

195 *White southerners passed laws:* See Nicholas Johnson, *Negroes and the Gun:
The Black Tradition of Arms* (Amherst, NY: Prometheus Books, 2014).

195 *"The constitutional rights of all loyal and well-disposed":* Thomas says this
South Carolina order showed that concealed carrying of handguns was
allowed in South Carolina, a strange form of textualism. ("Of course,
even during Reconstruction the right to keep and bear arms had limits.
But those limits were consistent with a right of the public to peaceably
carry handguns for self-defense.")

195 *"We will not address":* New York State Rifle & Pistol Association v. Bruen, 2154 n.28.

196 *"In each instance":* Ibid., 2190 (Breyer, J., dissenting).

196 *"Put simply":* Ibid., 2134.

197 *"Despite the popularity of this two-step approach":* Ibid., 2127.

197 *But judges can discard:* As Thomas did in discussing the many colonial era
laws limiting or prohibiting carrying of weapons. "Respondents, their
amici, and the dissent all misunderstand these statutes." Says who?

197 *By the time Trump was defeated:* Ian Millhiser, "What Trump Has Done to
the Courts, Explained," *Vox,* September 29, 2020, https://www.vox.com
/policy-and-politics/2019/12/9/20962980/trump-supreme-court-federal
-judges.

197 *"How can we expect":* New York State Rifle & Pistol Association v. Bruen, 597
U.S. ___, 142 S. Ct. 2111, 2180 (2022) (Breyer, J., dissenting).

198 *The rate of homicides:* Justin Fox, "New York City Is a Lot Safer than Small-
Town America," Bloomberg, June 8, 2022.

198 *the idea famously articulated:* H. H. Gerth and C. Wright Mills (translated
and edited), *From Max Weber: Essays in Sociology* (New York: Oxford University Press, 1946), 77–128.

198 *Police cannot protect you:* A point made by Corey Robin, "The Self-Fulfilling
Prophecies of Clarence Thomas," *The New Yorker,* July 9, 2022, https://
www.newyorker.com/news/daily-comment/the-self-fulfilling-prophecies
-of-clarence-thomas.

201 *"The decision ignores":* "Transcript: Mayor Eric Adams Delivers Remarks
on Bruen Supreme Court Ruling," Office of the Mayor, New York City,

June 23, 2022, https://www1.nyc.gov/office-of-the-mayor/news/428-22/transcript-mayor-eric-adams-delivers-remarks-bruen-supreme-court-ruling.

201 *Quickly it established:* The Concealed Carry Improvement Act, S.51001/A.41001.

201 *The NRA called the whole law "obnoxious":* "As Court Slams Door on One Obnoxious Gun Law, NY Enacts Fresh Version," NRA-ILA, July 11, 2022, https://www.nraila.org/articles/20220711/as-court-slams-door-on-one-obnoxious-gun-law-ny-enacts-fresh-version.

201 *One judge in western New York: Antonyuk v. Hochul,* Case 1:22-cv-00986-GTS-CFH WL 5239895 (N.D.N.Y. Oct. 6, 2022)

201 *another upstate judge: Hardaway v. Nigrelli,* Case 1:22-cv-00771-JLS (October 20, 2022).

201 *"This Court is not a trained historian": United States v. Bullock,* Case 3:18-cr-00165-CWR-FKB (October 27, 2022).

202 *In California:* The publication *The Trace* tracks the state responses to *Bruen.* See Jennifer Mascia, "Tracking the Effects of the Supreme Court's Gun Ruling," *The Trace,* August 19, 2022, https://www.thetrace.org/2022/08/nysrpa-v-bruen-challenge-gun-regulations/.

202 *In Maryland:* Dylan Segelbaum, "How Is the Supreme Court's Ruling on Concealed Carry Playing Out in Maryland? Here's What You Need to Know," *Baltimore Banner,* July 25, 2022, https://www.thebaltimorebanner.com/community/criminal-justice/how-is-the-supreme-courts-ruling-on-concealed-carry-playing-out-in-maryland-heres-what-you-need-to-know-TLHF6V7UQZFYZLZGHZI63BCHBM/.

202 *In California, for example, an innovative statute:* Complaint, *Boland v. Bonta,* No. 8:22-cv-01421 (C.D. Cal. S.D. August 1, 2022), https://storage.courtlistener.com/recap/gov.uscourts.cacd.858747/gov.uscourts.cacd.858747.1.0.pdf.

202 *In Colorado a town: Rocky Mountain Gun Owners et al. v. Town of Superior,* Civil Action No. 22-cv-1685, filed July 7, 2022, https://rmgo.org/wp-content/uploads/2022/07/Complaint_RMGO_Superior_Lawsuit.pdf.

FOURTEEN: *DOBBS* (JUNE 24, 2022)

203 *It was the first explicit repeal:* Arguably, the "freedom of contract" right upheld by *Lochner* was wiped out by the Supreme Court in *West Coast Hotel* in 1937. The Court did not say it was overturning *Lochner,* though, but that the freedom to contract could not overcome public policy goals.

204 *cited liberal icon Laurence Tribe:* Laurence Tribe, "Foreword: Toward a Model of Roles in the Due Process of Life and Law," *Harvard Law Review* 87 (1973): 1.

204 *did not "end the debate on the issue": Dobbs v. Jackson Women's Health Organization,* 597 U.S. ___, 142 S. Ct. 2228, 2279 (2022).

205 *the opinion headed off: Dobbs v. Jackson Women's Health* at 2245.

205   *"Abortion bans"*: Reva B. Siegel, Serena Mayeri, and Melissa Murray, "Equal Protection in *Dobbs* and Beyond: How States Protect Life Inside and Outside of the Abortion Context," *Columbia Journal of Gender and Law* 43 (2023 forthcoming), https://law.yale.edu/sites/default/files/documents/pdf/ssrn_-_siegel-mayeri-murray-ep_abortion_dobbs_colum_jgl_5-19-22_sm.pdf.

205   *"an unargued sentence fragment"*: The fragment simply says the argument is "squarely foreclosed" by precedent. Reva B. Siegel, "Memory Games: Dobbs's Originalism as Anti-Democratic Living Constitutionalism—and Some Pathways for Resistance," *Texas Law Review* 101 (2023 forthcoming).

205   *"The dissent has much to say"*: *Dobbs v. Jackson Women's Health* at 2261.

205   *"no half-measures"*: *Dobbs v. Jackson Women's Health Organization*, Brief for Respondents, at 50, https://www.supremecourt.gov/DocketPDF/19/19-1392/192267/20210913143126849_19-1392bs.pdf.

206   *"returned to the people and their elected representatives"*: *Dobbs v. Jackson Women's Health*, 2279.

206   *"the question of firearm regulation"*: *New York State Rifle & Pistol Association v. Bruen*, 597 U.S. ___, 142 S. Ct. 2111, 2167–68 (2022).

206   *This formulation comes from: Washington* v. *Glucksberg*, 521 U.S. 702, 721 (1997).

207   *"by their mutual matrimonial consent"*: Matthew Hale, *Hale's Pleas of the Crown*, vol. 1., 629, https://books.google.com/books?id=2KoDAAAAQAAJ&printsec=frontcover&source=gbs_ge_summary_r&cad=0#v=onepage&q&f=false. Alito mischievously cites an opinion from two years before referring to Hale as one of the "eminent common law authorities"—an opinion written by Elena Kagan. *Kahler v. Kansas*, 549 U.S. __, ___, 140 S. Ct. 1021, 1027 (2020).

207   *"great crime" and a "great misprision"*: *Dobbs v. Jackson Women's Health*, 2249 (quoting Pleas of the Crown 53 (P. Glazebrook ed. 1972); 1 History of the Pleas of the Crown 433 (1736) Hale), internal quotation marks omitted.

207   *As of 1800, no laws banned abortion*: "In 1800 no jurisdiction in the United States had enacted any statutes whatsoever on the subject of abortion; most forms of abortion were not illegal and those American women who wished to practice abortion did so. Yet by 1900 virtually every jurisdiction in the United States had laws upon its books that proscribed the practice sharply and declared most abortions to be criminal offenses." James C. Mohr, *Abortion in America: The Origins and Evolution of National Policy* (New York: Oxford University Press, 1978), vii. In the first third of the nineteenth century, mostly poorer women who had abortions sought to avoid the stigma of having an illegitimate child. By the middle of the century, wealthier and middle-class women were buying "Female Remedies" and going to midwives and using patent medicines, often married women who already had children. See Jessica Bruder, "The Future of Abortion in a Post-*Roe* America," *The Atlantic*, April 4, 2022, https://www.theatlantic.com/magazine/archive/2022/05/roe-v-wade-overturn-abortion-rights/629366/.

207   *part of a general crackdown:* See, e.g., Leslie J. Reagan, *When Abortion Was
      a Crime: Women, Medicine, and Law in the United States, 1867–1973,* rev. ed.
      (Berkeley: University of California Press, 2022), 90–112.
209   *"those that develop in cases involving property and contract rights":* Dobbs v.
      Jackson Women's Health* at 2238.
209   *"the effect of the abortion right":* Ibid. at 2239.
209   *It helpfully lists:* In one of the several passages listing cases that allegedly
      have nothing in common with *Roe,* the opinion explains:

> Nor does the right to obtain an abortion have a sound basis in
> precedent. *Casey* relied on cases involving the right to marry a
> person of a different race, *Loving v. Virginia,* 388 U.S. 1 (1967);
> the right to marry while in prison, *Turner v. Safley,* 482 U.S.
> 78 (1987); the right to obtain contraceptives, *Griswold v. Con-
> necticut,* 381 U.S. 479 (1965), *Eisenstadt v. Baird,* 405 U.S. 438
> (1972), *Carey v. Population Services Int'l,* 431 U.S. 678 (1977); the
> right to reside with relatives, *Moore v. East Cleveland,* 431 U.S.
> 494 (1977); the right to make decisions about the education
> of one's children, *Pierce v. Society of Sisters,* 268 U.S. 510 (1925),
> *Meyer v. Nebraska,* 262 U.S. 390 (1923); the right not to be steril-
> ized without consent, *Skinner v. Oklahoma ex rel. Williamson,* 316
> U.S. 535 (1942); and the right in certain circumstances not to
> undergo involuntary surgery, forced administration of drugs, or
> other substantially similar procedures, *Winston v. Lee,* 470 U.S.
> 753 (1985), *Washington v. Harper,* 494 U.S. 210 (1990), *Rochin v.
> California,* 342 U.S. 165 (1952). Respondents and the Solicitor
> General also rely on post-*Casey* decisions like *Lawrence v. Texas,*
> 539 U.S. 558 (2003) (right to engage in private, consensual sex-
> ual acts), and *Obergefell v. Hodges,* 576 U.S. 644 (2015) (right to
> marry a person of the same sex).

Again, not to worry: "These attempts to justify abortion through appeals
to a broader right to autonomy and to define one's 'concept of existence' prove too much."
209   *"fetal life":* Dobbs v. Jackson Women's Health,* 2265.
209   *"held that the abortion right, which is not mentioned":* Ibid. at 2245.
209   *"So one of two things must be true":* Ibid. at 2319 (Breyer, J., Sotomayor, J.,
      and Kagan, J., dissenting).
210   *Thomas's list of cases to be overturned:* Ibid. at 2301–2 (Thomas, J., concur-
      ring).
210   *Caustic observers noted:* Critics of originalism have long noted that it could
      not be used to justify *Loving.* Some defenders of originalism have essen-
      tially ignored the question. See, for example, Michael McConnell, an
      originalist scholar who became a federal judge, who made an originalist

argument for *Brown v. Board of Education* but did not try to do the same for *Loving*. See Michael W. McConnell, "Originalism and the Desegregation Decisions," *Virginia Law Review* 81 (1995): 947. Steven Calabresi, another originalist who cofounded the Federalist Society, did make an originalist argument for *Loving* as well as *Brown*. Steven G. Calabresi and Andrea Matthews, "Originalism and *Loving v. Virginia*," *2012 Brigham Young Law Review* (2012): 1393, https://digitalcommons.law.byu.edu /lawreview/vol2012/iss5/1.

210 *"Mr. Justice Thomas":* Andrew McDonald, a justice of the Connecticut Supreme Court, made the caustic comment. Dan Mangan, "Gay Connecticut Supreme Court Justice Calls Out U.S. Supreme Court Justice Clarence Thomas on Same-Sex Marriage Ruling Repeal Idea," CNBC, June 27, 2022, https://www.cnbc.com/2022/06/27/roe-v-wade-gay-connect icut-supreme-court-justice-calls-out-clarence-thomas.html.

210 *"If it is not necessary to decide more": Dobbs v. Jackson Women's Health* at 2310 (Roberts, C.J., concurring).

210 *"quest for a middle way":* Ibid. at 2283.

211 *Twenty-five states: Dobbs v. Jackson Women's Health Organization,* Brief for the States of Texas, Alabama, Alaska, Arizona, Arkansas, Florida, Georgia, Idaho, Indiana, Kansas, Kentucky, Louisiana, Missouri, Montana, Nebraska, North Dakota, Ohio, Oklahoma, South Carolina, South Dakota, Tennessee, Utah, West Virginia, and Wyoming in Support of Petitioners, July 2021, https://www.supremecourt.gov/DocketPDF/19/19-1392/185249 /20210729123524687_19-1392%20Amicus%20Brief.pdf. To those twenty -five states, Mississippi makes a twenty-fifth.

211 *"Whatever the exact scope":* Ibid. at 2318 (Breyer, J., Sotomayor, J., and Kagan, J., dissenting).

212 *"'intended to endure for ages to come'":* Ibid. at 2325 (Breyer, J., Sotomayor, J., and Kagan, J., dissenting) (quoting *McCulloch v. Maryland,* 4 Wheat. 316, 415 (1819)).

213 *"[A]pplications of liberty and equality":* ibid. at 2326 (Breyer, J., Sotomayor, J., and Kagan, J., dissenting).

213 *Stunned receptionists at health clinics:* "Inside Four Abortion Clinics the Day *Roe v. Wade* Ended," *The Daily* podcast, *New York Times,* June 27, 2022.

213 *twenty-two states:* Laura Deal, *State Laws Restricting or Prohibiting Abortion,* Congressional Research Service Legal Sidebar, updated November 17, 2022, https://crsreports.congress.gov/product/pdf/LSB/LSB10779; Elizabeth Nash and Lauren Cross, "26 States Are Certain or Likely to Ban Abortion Without Roe: Here's Which Ones and Why," Guttmacher Institute, October 28, 2021, https://www.guttmacher.org/article /2021/10/26-states-are-certain-or-likely-ban-abortion-without-roe-heres -which-ones-and-why.

213 *banned statewide for a few hours:* Jonathan Oosting and Robin Erb, "Michigan Abortion Ban Is—Then Isn't—In Effect After Two Court Rulings,"

Michigan Bridge, August 1, 2022, https://www.bridgemi.com/michigan-government/michigan-abortion-ban-then-isnt-effect-after-two-court-rulings.

213 *one in four abortion clinics:* R. Schroeder et al., "Trends in Abortion Care in the United States, 2017–2021," Advancing New Standards in Reproductive Health (ANSIRH), University of California, San Francisco, 2022.

214 *"I expected these horrifying, dystopian stories":* Laura Bassett, "Just 3 Weeks Post-*Roe*, the Stories Emerging Are Worse than Anyone Imagined," *Jezebel*, July 17, 2022, https://jezebel.com/just-3-weeks-post-roe-the-stories-emerging-are-worse-t-1849188588.

214 *Particularly agonizing was the story:* It was first reported by a local newspaper. Shari Rudavsky and Rachel Fradette, "Patients Head to Indiana for Abortion Services as Other States Restrict Care," *Indianapolis Star*, July 1, 2022.

214 *"She was forced to have to travel":* The White House, "Remarks by President Biden on Protecting Access to Reproductive Health Care Services," July 8, 2022.

214 *"fanciful tale":* Editorial, "An Abortion Story Too Good to Confirm," *Wall Street Journal*, July 13, 2022.

214 *"a fictive abortion and a fictive rape":* Michael Brendan Dougherty, Twitter, July 8, 2022, 3:49 p.m., https://twitter.com/michaelbd/status/1545495203590594572.

214 *"Every day that goes by":* *Jesse Watters Primetime*, Fox News, July 11, 2022, "Ohio Attorney General on Lack of Investigation into Alleged Child Rapist: 'Not a Whisper,'" https://www.foxnews.com/video/6309391986112; Laura Bischoff, "Ohio AG Dave Yost Cast Doubt on 10-Year-Old Rape Victim Case, Now 'Rejoices' at Arrest," *Columbus Dispatch*, July 13, 2022.

214 *police arrested a twenty-seven-year-old man:* Bethany Bruner, Monroe Trombly, and Tony Cook, "Arrest Made in Rape of Ohio Girl That Led to Indiana Abortion Drawing International Attention," *Columbus Dispatch*, July 13, 2022.

215 *"we would hope that she would understand":* Megan Messerly and Adam Wren, "National Right to Life Official: 10-Year-Old Should Have Had Baby," *Politico*, July 14, 2022, https://www.politico.com/news/2022/07/14/anti-abotion-10-year-old-ohio-00045843.

215 *"it was a little anticlimactic":* Christopher Wilson, "Top Democrats' Response to Abortion Ruling Sparks Frustration Within Party," Yahoo News, June 29, 2022, https://news.yahoo.com/top-democrats-response-to-abortion-ruling-sparks-frustration-within-party-190119831.html.

215 *After the leak:* S. 4132, U.S. Congress, Senate, "To protect a person's ability to determine whether to continue or end a pregnancy, and to protect a health care provider's ability to provide abortion services," S. 4132, 117th Cong., 2nd Sess., https://www.congress.gov/117

/bills/s4132/BILLS-117s4132pcs.pdf. The Senate failed to vote cloture for the measure on May 11, 2022, by a vote of 49–51.

215   *In September:* Department of Veterans Affairs, interim final rule, "Reproductive Health Services," 38 CFR Part 17 (September 1, 2022), https://www.womenshealth.va.gov/docs/AR57-IF-Reg-to-FR-Reproductive-Health-Services.pdf.

215   *Mitch McConnell mused:* David Jackson and Phillip M. Bailey, "McConnell Calls US Abortion Ban 'Possible,' Says He Won't Change Filibuster to Pass It," *USA Today*, May 6, 2022.

216   *"the opposite is true":* David S. Cohen, Greer Donley, and Rachel Rebouché, "The New Abortion Battleground," *Columbia Law Review* 123 (2023 forthcoming): 4.

216   *Already, in 2022, most pregnancies:* Rachel K. Jones, Elizabeth Nash, Lauren Cross, Jesse Philbin, and Marielle Kirstein, "February Policy Analysis: Medication Abortion Now Accounts for More than Half of All US Abortions," Guttmacher Institute, February 24, 2022, https://www.guttmacher.org/article/2022/02/medication-abortion-now-accounts-more-half-all-us-abortions.

216   *In December 2021, two weeks:* Pam Belluck, "F.D.A. Will Permanently Allow Abortion Pills by Mail," *New York Times*, December 16, 2021. The agency never issued a statement; rather, it updated its website (and contacted the two companies that manufacture the pills). https://www.fda.gov/drugs/postmarket-drug-safety-information-patients-and-providers/questions-and-answers-mifeprex.

216   *Americans have the right to travel:* The right to travel predates the Constitution and was protected in the Articles of Confederation. The Supreme Court ruled that there is a right to travel under the Privileges and Immunities Clause of the Fourteenth Amendment, among other provisions. The Court made clear, in 1999, "The word 'travel' is not found in the text of the Constitution. Yet the 'constitutional right to travel from one State to another' is firmly embedded in our jurisprudence." *Saenz v. Roe*, 526 U.S. 489 (1999). Most Supreme Court cases have addressed times when states prohibited others from entering, such as laws barring people from coming into a state to get access to public services.

217   *"Does that child":* Peter Sullivan, "GOP Senator Blocks Bill to Protect Interstate Travel for Abortion," *The Hill*, July 14, 2022, https://thehill.com/homenews/senate/3559360-gop-senator-blocks-bill-to-protect-interstate-travel-for-abortion/; United States Senate, 117th Cong., 2nd Sess., 168 *Congressional Record* 116: S3296.

217   *"Abortion travel will become":* Cohen, Donley, and Rebouché, "The New Abortion Battleground."

217   *"regardless of where an illegal abortion occurs":* National Right to Life Committee, Model Abortion Law, https://www.nrlc.org/wp-content/uploads/NRLC-Post-Roe-Model-AbortionLaw-FINAL-1.pdf.

217   *Meanwhile seventeen states:* "Abortion Policy in the Absence of Roe," Gutt-
      macher Institute, November 9, 2022, https://www.guttmacher.org/state
      -policy/explore/abortion-policy-absence-roe#:~:text=17%20states%20
      and%20the%20District,protect%20the%20right%20to%20abortion.

217   *California was expected to host:* Rachel Bluth, "California Makes Plans to Be
      the Nation's Abortion Provider in Post-Roe World," *Kaiser Health News*
      (November 15, 2021), https://www.latimes.com/california/story/2021
      -11-16/california-makes-plans-to-be-nations-abortion-provider.

217   *A first study:* "WeCount Study," Society of Family Planning, https://doi
      .org/10.46621/UKAI6324.

218   *The states that had already enacted:* Sonali Seth and Michael Li, "In Many
      States, Gerrymandering Blocks the Abortion Policy the Public Wants,"
      Brennan Center for Justice (2022), https://www.brennancenter.org
      /our-work/analysis-opinion/supreme-courts-abortion-ruling-shows
      -what-happens-when-democracy-thwarted.

FIFTEEN: *WEST VIRGINIA V. EPA* (JUNE 30, 2022)

221   *That was the year everything went wrong:* For an early vivisection of the "Con-
      stitution in Exile," see Cass R. Sunstein, *Radicals in Robes: Why Extreme
      Right-Wing Courts Are Wrong for America* (New York: Basic Books, 2005).
      Sunstein begins his book with a far-off dystopian vision of the future in
      which right-wing legal activists had prevailed: the right to privacy has been
      repealed by the Supreme Court, so states are free to ban abortion and
      contraception; regulatory agencies are curbed; "even modest gun control
      laws are invalid" because the Supreme Court for the first time would rec-
      ognize a right to gun ownership. Sunstein, *Radicals in Robes,* 1–3.

221   *Richard Nixon presented:* "Special Message to the Congress on Environ-
      mental Quality, February 10, 1970," *Public Papers of the Presidents of the
      United States: Richard Nixon: Containing the Public Messages, Speeches, and
      Statements of the President, 1970* (Washington, D.C: Government Printing
      Office, 1970), 95.

221   *Ralph Nader, who had exposed the dangers:* See Ralph Nader, *Unsafe at Any
      Speed: The Designed-in Dangers of the American Automobile* (New York: Gross-
      man Publishers, 1965).

221   *But in 1966:* U.S. Congress, Senate, "Federal Role in Traffic Safety, Hear-
      ings Before the Subcommittee on Executive Reorganization, Commit-
      tee on Government Operations," U.S. Senate, 89th Cong., 2nd Sess.,
      March 22, 1966, 1381; Jerry T. Baulch, "G.M.'s Head Apologizes to 'Ha-
      rassed' Car Critic," Associated Press, March 26, 1966.

221   *With money he won:* See Paul Sabin, *Public Citizens: The Attack on Big Gov-
      ernment and the Remaking of American Liberalism* (New York: W. W. Norton,
      2021).

222   *"The Neglected Opportunity in the Courts":* Lewis F. Powell Jr., "Confidential

Memorandum: Attack on American Free Enterprise System," August 23, 1971, 26, https://scholarlycommons.law.wlu.edu/powellmemo/1.

222 *"little noticed and little heeded":* Progressive strategist Mark Schmitt is skeptical of the memo's impact.

> Powell's note went unheeded and unnoticed when he sent it, but enjoyed a brief flurry of attention after journalist Jack Anderson discovered it after Powell had been named to the Court. It was then promptly forgotten for another thirty years—the memo goes unmentioned in almost all histories of the rise of conservatism published in the last third of the twentieth century—until about 2001, when it suddenly became the skeleton key for historians and advocates on the left seeking to explain conservative dominance.

Mark Schmitt, "The Myth of the Powell Memo," *Washington Monthly,* August 29, 2016.

222 *corporations already had begun to launch:* Conservative business agitation arose during the New Deal and the fight against the court packing plan. The Liberty League was formed to press for free market policies and against union organizing. See Kim Phillips-Fein, *Invisible Hands: The Businessmen's Crusade Against the New Deal* (New York: W. W. Norton, 2009).

222 *In 1977 and 1978, in a first major test:* See Jonathan Alter, *His Very Best: Jimmy Carter, A Life* (New York: Simon & Schuster, 2020), 348–50.

223 *"[T]he Great Depression and the determination of the Roosevelt Administration":* The speech was reprinted as Douglas H. Ginsburg, "On Constitutionalism," *Cato Supreme Court Review* 7 (2003).

223 *An influential 2005 article:* Jeffrey Rosen, "The Unregulated Offensive," *New York Times Magazine,* April 17, 2005.

223 *He chided the Court:* Richard A. Epstein, "Joe Biden's Constitutionalism," Defining Ideas, Hoover Institution, April 13, 2020, https://www.hoover.org/research/joe-bidens-constitutionalism; Richard A. Epstein, "Valuation Blunders in the Law of Eminent Domain," *Notre Dame Law Review* 96 (2021): 1441, https://scholarship.law.nd.edu/cgi/viewcontent.cgi?article=4959&context=ndlr.

223 *Joe Biden theatrically waved a copy: Nomination of Judge Clarence Thomas to Be Associate Justice of the Supreme Court of the United States: Hearing Before the S. Comm. on the Judiciary,* 102nd Cong., 1st Sess, 113–15, 127, 397 (1991) (statements of Sen. Joseph R. Biden Jr., Chairman, S. Comm. on the Judiciary). See Rosen, "The Unregulated Offensive."

223 *The Supreme Court rarely bought the idea:* It did start to edge closer to an aggressive notion of what constitutes a taking. In 2021, in *Cedar Point Nursery v. Hassid,* 594 U.S. ___, 141 S. Ct. 2063 (2021), in a six-to-three ruling written by Roberts, the Court said that a California law designed

to allow farmworker union organizers access to the workplace consti-
tuted a "physical taking." Breyer, Sotomayor, and Kagan dissented.

224   *"may be exercised to its utmost extent":* Gibbons v. Ogden, 22 U.S. 1 (1824).

224   *as part of their headlong retreat:* In 1941 the Court ruled that a lumber company still was engaged in interstate commerce. *U.S. v. Darby,* 312 U.S.
100 (1941). That overturned *Hammer v. Dagenhart,* 247 U.S. 251 (1918),
which had blocked federal laws prohibiting child labor.

224   *"If the government can order you to buy health insurance":* Matthew DeLuca,
"Did Scalia Parrot Fox News During Health-Care Arguments?," *Daily
Beast,* April 5, 2012, https://www.thedailybeast.com/did-scalia-parrot-fox
-news-during-health-care-arguments.

224   *"Everybody has to buy food":* Department of Health and Human Services v. Florida, transcript of argument, March 27, 2012, https://www.supremecourt
.gov/oral_arguments/argument_transcripts/2011/11-398-Tuesday.pdf.

224   *Scalia and three other conservatives:* They sought to distinguish this from
Wickard v. Filburn, 317 U.S. 111 (1942), which ruled that a farmer who
grew wheat for his own consumption was "affecting commerce" and thus
faced regulation.

225   *"Chevron deference":* Chevron, U.S.A., Inc. v. NRDC, 467 U.S. 837 (1984).
Its key passage read:

> If . . . the court determines that Congress has not directly ad-
> dressed the precise question at issue, the court does not simply
> impose its own construction on the statute, as would be neces-
> sary in the absence of an administrative interpretation. Rather,
> if the statute is silent or ambiguous with respect to the specific
> issue, the question for the court is whether the agency's answer
> is based on a permissible construction of the statute.

225   *The Supreme Court has applied it:* Kristin E. Hickman and Aaron L. Niel-
son, "Narrowing *Chevron's* Domain," *Duke Law Journal* 70, no. 5 (2021):
931.

225   *It has been the basis of thousands of legal decisions:* According to one analysis,
the Supreme Court has cited *Chevron* more than any case issued in the
past half century (it is fifteenth on the list overall). Frank B. Cross and
James F. Spriggs II, "The Most Important (and Best) Supreme Court
Opinions and Justices," *Emory Law Journal* 60 (2010): 407. *Chevron* was a
unanimous decision, authored by Stevens and joined by Brennan. Stevens's opinion—which overturned an opinion by Ruth Bader Ginsburg
as an appeals court judge—was a long and complex assessment. In the
decades that followed, lower courts (especially the D.C. Circuit Court of
Appeals) boiled it down to the two-step approach that became known
as *Chevron* deference. First, judges ask whether Congress's intent was
clear; then, if not, was the agency's interpretation reasonable and not

arbitrary. Scalia led this drive, often over objections from Stevens and Brennan, who disagreed with the simplification of the *Chevron* opinion and near-mechanical application of the two-step approach. See Thomas Merrill, *The Chevron Doctrine: Its Rise and Fall, and the Future of the Administrative State* (Cambridge: Harvard University Press, 2022).

225   *Antonin Scalia championed this permutation:* See, e.g., Antonin Scalia, "Judicial Deference to Administrative Interpretations of Law," *Duke Law Journal* 3 (1989): 511.

225   *Its administrator, Anne Gorsuch:* Her colorful life is described in Patricia Sullivan, "Anne Gorsuch Burford, 62, Dies," *Washington Post,* July 22, 2004. She remarried while EPA administrator and took the name of her husband, Robert Burford.

225   The New York Times *admonished:* "Mrs. Gorsuch Pollutes the EPA," editorial, *New York Times,* February 16, 1983.

225   *"A year in jail":* Leslie Maitland, "House Lawyer Says E.P.A. Erred in Destroying Documents," *New York Times,* February 12, 1983. Her bravado earned her the *Times* "Quote of the Day."

226   *"it's hard to lead a normal life":* Paula Schwed, "Anne Burford, Without Bitterness but Fighting Back Tears, Said . . . ," United Press International, March 10, 1983.

226   *"You raised me not to be a quitter":* Anne M. Burford with John Greenya, *Are You Tough Enough? An Insider's View of Washington Politics* (New York: McGraw Hill, 1986), 225.

226   *"nothingburger":* Alyssa Pereira, "Where Did the Term 'Nothing Burger' Actually Originate?," *SFGate,* July 12, 2017, https://www.sfgate.com /politics/article/Where-did-the-term-nothing-burger-actually-11283897.php.

226   *"too small to be a state":* "Burford Calls Appointment to Panel 'a Joke,'" Associated Press, July 29, 1984.

226   *"Nowhere in the Constitution": American Hospital Association v. Becerra,* "Brief of Amicus Curiae Americans for Prosperity Foundation in Support of Neither Party," September 10, 2021, https://www.supremecourt.gov /DocketPDF/20/20-1114/191972/20210910092618378_2021.09.10 .AFPF%20Amicus%20ISO%20Neither%20Party.AHA%20v.%20Bec erra.20%201114.pdf.

227   *The Court ruled unanimously: American Hospital Association v. Becerra,* 596 U.S. __, 142 S. Ct. 1896 (2022).

227   *"It's now or never":* António Guterres, "Secretary-General's Video Message on the Launch of the Third IPCC Report," United Nations, Apri 4, 2022, https://www.un.org/sg/en/content/sg/statement/2022-04-04/secretary -generals-video-message-the-launch-of-the-third-ipcc-report-scroll-down- for-languages; Intergovernmental Panel on Climate Change, "IPCC Sixth Assessment Report: Mitigation of Climate Change," April 4, 2022, https://www.ipcc.ch/report/ar6/wg3/.

227   *the world was suffering:* "2021 one of the seven warmest years on

record, WMO consolidated data shows," World Meteorological Organization, January 19, 2022, https://public.wmo.int/en/media/press
-release/2021-one-of-seven-warmest-years-record-wmo-consolidated-data
-shows. The seven warmest years on record were in the last decade. U.S.
Global Change Research Program, Fourth National Climate Assessment, vol. 1, (2017), 10.

227 *only in the United States:* Conservative political parties around the world
recognize the crisis of climate change (while having different views of
how to respond than more progressive parties). Dana Nuccitelli, "The
Republican Party Stands Alone in Climate Denial," *The Guardian,* October 5, 2015. See Sondre Båtstrand, "More than Markets: A Comparative
Survey of Nine Conservative Parties on Climate Change," *Politics & Policy*
43, no. 4 (August 2015).

227 *Fewer than one in three Republicans:* Lydia Saad, "Global Warming Attitudes
Frozen Since 2016," Gallup Poll (April 5, 2021), https://news.gallup
.com/poll/343025/global-warming-attitudes-frozen-2016.aspx.

227 *"the moment when the rise of the oceans":* Barack Obama, "Remarks in St. Paul,
Minnesota Claiming the Democratic Presidential Nomination Following
the Montana and South Dakota Primaries," *The American Presidency Project,*
June 3, 2008, https://www.presidency.ucsb.edu/node/277836. Obama's
remarks were mocked for their grandiosity by conservatives including
George F. Will, "As the Oceans Rise," *Newsweek,* June 7, 2008.

227 *Trump, who called climate change a "hoax":* "The concept of global warming
was created by and for the Chinese in order to make U.S. manufacturing
non-competitive." Donald Trump, Twitter, 2:15 p.m., November 6, 2012,
https://twitter.com/realdonaldtrump/status/265895292191248385
?lang=en. After cold weather, Trump demanded, "Is our country still
spending money on the GLOBAL WARMING HOAX?," Donald Trump,
Twitter, 6:48 p.m., January 25, 2014, https://twitter.com/realDonald
Trump/status/427226424987385856?. Trump often made the charge in
tweets which for a time were no longer available on the internet because
his account was suspended due to his lies about the 2020 election.

228 *It had been decades since Congress passed:* The Clean Air Act Amendments of
1990, Public Law 101-549. The Inflation Reduction Act, described below,
does not advance its climate change goals through regulation (as previous environmental laws had) but through investment.

228 *Elena Kagan's long scholarly article:* Kagan's principal point was that Congress did not pass legislation to preclude presidents from wielding that
authority. Elena Kagan, "Presidential Administration," *Harvard Law Review* 114 (2000–2001): 2245.

228 *Republican presidents tended to argue for:* For a thorough survey of how presidents exerted authority, at times coming into conflict with the judiciary,
see Ken Gormley, ed., *The Presidents and the Constitution: A Living History*
(New York: New York University Press, 2016).

228 *Trump melded both archetypes:* The Supreme Court responded accordingly. In the litigation around Trump's effort to ban visitors and immigrants from majority Muslim countries, the Court at first ruled that his officials had not properly followed the Adminisrative Procedures Act and other rules designed to bring procedural regularity to domestic agencies. When the Court finally upheld his actions, though, it relied on his foreign policy power.

228 *Coal companies staged protests:* Daniel J. Weiss, "Anatomy of a Senate Climate Bill Death," Center for American Progress, October 12, 2010, https://www.americanprogress.org/article/anatomy-of-a-senate-climate -bill-death/.

228 *"I've got a pen":* The White House, "Remarks by the President Before Cabinet Meeting," January 14, 2014, https://obamawhitehouse.archives .gov/the-press-office/2014/01/14/remarks-president-cabinet-meeting.

228 *He would use executive orders:* Obama ordered the EPA to find ways to address climate change, focusing on the electric utilities. "Presidential Memorandum—Power Sector Carbon Pollution Standards (June 25, 2013)," https://bit.ly/3EVALHA; 80 Fed. Reg. 64,662 (October 23, 2015). Obama's efforts were decried as a "war on coal." Some scholars argue that Obama's effort, far from radical, was actually a response to a design flaw in the original Clean Air Act. See Richard L. Revesz and Jack Lienke, *Struggling for Air: Power Plants and the "War on Coal"* (New York: Oxford University Press, 2016), 2–5, 150–57.

228 *The EPA launched a Clean Power Plan:* "Carbon Pollution Emission Guidelines for Existing Stationary Sources: Electric Utility Generating Units," 80 Fed. Reg. 64,662 (October 23, 2015).

228 *By 2030 the plan would produce:* "Fact Sheet: Overview of the Clean Power Plan," U.S. Environmental Protection Agency, accessed October 30, 2022, https://archive.epa.gov/epa/cleanpowerplan/fact-sheet-overview-clean -power-plan.html.

229 *appointed an EPA administrator who had denied:* Oliver Milman, "EPA Head Scott Pruitt Denies That Carbon Dioxide Causes Global Warming," *The Guardian,* March 9, 2017.

229 *West Virginia produced only 13 percent:* U.S. Energy Information Administration, West Virginia State Energy Profile, August 18, 2022, https://www .eia.gov/state/print.php?sid=WV#:~:text=In%202020%2C%20West%20 Virginia%20was,nation%2C%20after%20Wyoming%20and%20Illinois.

229 *the Supreme Court had already confirmed that the agency: Massachusetts v. Environmental Protection Agency,* 549 U.S. 497 (2007).

229 *"best system":* 84 Stat. 1683, 42 U.S.C. §§7411(a)(1 (b)(1), (d). For existing plants, the states then implemented that requirement by issuing rules restricting emissions from sources within their borders.

229 *It did not, in the end, address the* Chevron *doctrine:* In effect, "major questions" is an exception to *Chevron,* a "carve-out." Cass Sunstein, the former

Obama administration regulatory chief, called this the "weak" version of
"major questions." It does not imply that all agency action is unconstitutional. Cass R. Sunstein, "There Are Two 'Major Questions' Doctrines,"
Administrative Law Review 73, no. 3 (2021): 475.

230   *the most important environmental ruling in over a decade:* Richard L. Revesz,
"SCOTUS Ruling in *West Virginia v. EPA* Threatens All Regulation,"
Bloomberg, July 8, 2022, https://news.bloomberglaw.com/environment
-and-energy/scotus-ruling-in-west-virginia-v-epa-threatens-all-regulation.

231   *the decision about what health and safety measures:* The Court claimed it was
merely following the reasoning of a case from two decades before, a
case that followed the Food and Drug Administration's declaration that
nicotine was a drug, and thus it could regulate cigarettes. *FDA v. Brown
& Williamson Tobacco Corp.*, 529 U.S. 120, 159 (2000). In that case, the
Court said, the FDA would have had to *ban* cigarettes outright if it were
to follow the letter of the law. It was, in short, a ruling to avoid an absurd
result rather than a robust articulation of a new doctrine.

231   *Wilson became a target:* See, e.g., Jonah Goldberg, *Liberal Fascism: The Secret
History of the American Left, from Mussolini to the Politics of Change* (New
York: Broadway Books, 2009), 78–120.

232   *"I know it when I see it":* An analogy used by Revesz, "SCOTUS Ruling in
West Virginia v. EPA Threatens All Regulation." That is one of the more
famous quotes from an earlier Supreme Court opinion. In a 1964 case,
Potter Stewart and colleagues overturned the conviction of a film dis-
tributor arrested for distributing obscene material. He could not easily
define hard-core pornography, Stewart wrote, "But I know it when I see
it, and the motion picture involved in this case is not that." *Jacobellis v.
Ohio*, 378 U.S. 184 (1964).

232   *very first time that any Supreme Court governing opinion used the phrase:* It had
been floating around before, but never articulated, perhaps because it
was so radical. Earlier in the term, the Court used similar arguments
when it struck down the CDC's moratorium on evictions. "Even if the
text were ambiguous, the sheer scope of the CDC's claimed authority . . .
would counsel against the Government's interpretation. We expect Congress to speak clearly when authorizing an agency to exercise powers of
vast economic and political significance." Eight years before, Scalia had
written in another case involving air pollution regulation, "We expect
Congress to speak clearly if it wishes to assign to an agency decisions of
vast 'economic and political significance.'" *Utility Air Regulatory Group v.
EPA*, 573 U.S. 302 (2014).

232   *even comic strips:* In Garry Trudeau's *Doonesbury*, widely syndicated, a de-
spondent EPA bureaucrat sat on a ledge outside Burford's office, con-
templating his fate.

232   *a well-regarded book:* Neil M. Gorsuch, *The Future of Assisted Suicide and Eu-
thanasia* (Princeton: Princeton University Press, 2006).

233   *A fluffy* Washington Post *article:* Kimberly Kindy, Sari Horwitz, and William Wan, "Simply Stated, Gorsuch Is Steadfast and Surprising," *Washington Post,* February 18, 2017.

233   *In his first fifteen cases:* Oliver Roeder and Harry Enten, "Neil Gorsuch Is Paying Off for Trump So Far," *FiveThirtyEight,* June 28, 2017, https://fivethirtyeight.com/features/neil-gorsuch-is-paying-off-for-trump-so-far/.

233   *"It's not just about you":* Kevin Daley, "Chief Justice Appears to Take Shot Across Gorsuch's Bow," *Daily Caller,* July 7, 2017, https://dailycaller.com/2017/07/07/chief-justice-appears-to-take-shot-across-gorsuchs-bow/.

233   *Black and white people used marijuana:* "The War on Marijuana in Black and White," ACLU (2013). "[O]n average, a Black person is 3.73 times more likely to be arrested for marijuana possession than a white person, even though Blacks and whites use marijuana at similar rates." https://www.aclu.org/sites/default/files/field_document/1114413-mj-report-rfs-rel1.pdf. In Brooklyn and Manhattan, that ratio was nine to one. With marijuana law reform, these numbers have declined.

234   *In rulings and dissents:* Amy Howe, "Gorsuch and the Fourth Amendment," *SCOTUSblog,* March 17, 2017, 1:35 p.m., https://www.scotusblog.com/2017/03/gorsuch-fourth-amendment/.

234   *"We live in a world":* Lange v. California, transcript of argument, February 24, 2021, 52.

234   *he and the other justices ruled unanimously:* Lange v. California, 594 U.S. ___, 141 S. Ct. 2011 (2021).

234   *devotion to textualism:* For an explication of the approach, see Antonin Scalia and Bryan A. Garner, *Reading Law: The Interpretation of Legal Texts* (Minneapolis: West Publishing, 2012).

234   *"If Congress passes energy legislation":* Robert A. Katzmann, *Judging Statutes* (New York: Oxford University Press, 2014), 26. Katzmann was the first political scientist ever to serve as a federal judge.

235   *Gorsuch had "bungled textualism:":* Carrie Severino, Twitter, 10:32 a.m., June 15, 2020, https://twitter.com/JCNSeverino/status/1272537436791484416?s=20&t=rEqESWePJCo6y2jD7QTYCw. She was only slightly more measured in Carrie Campbell Severino, "The Court's Literal Assault on Textualism," *National Review,* June 16, 2020, https://www.nationalreview.com/bench-memos/the-courts-literal-assault-on-textualism/.

235   *has not struck down a statute on nondelegation:* The cases were *Panama Refining Co. v. Ryan,* 293 U.S. 388 (1935), *Carter v. Carter Coal Co.,* 298 U.S. 238 (1936), and *A. L. A. Schechter Poultry Corporation v. United States,* 295 U.S. 495 (1935), the legendary "sick chicken" case which struck down the National Industrial Recovery Act.

235   *Gorsuch launched a flare:* Gundy v. United States, 588 U.S. ___, 139 S. Ct. 2116, 2134 (2019) (Gorsuch, J., dissenting).

236   *Buried in the budget bill:* Lisa Friedman, "Democrats Designed the Climate

Law to Be a Game Changer. Here's How," *New York Times*, August 22, 2022.

236 *It did not:* See Kate Aronoff, "No, the Inflation Reduction Act Did Not 'Overturn' *West Virginia v. EPA*," *The New Republic*, August 24, 2022, https://newrepublic.com/article/167520/inflation-reduction-act-over turn-west-virginia-epa; Patrick Parenteau, "The Inflation Reduction Act Doesn't Get Around the Supreme Court's Climate Ruling in West Virginia v. EPA, but It Does Strengthen EPA's Future Abilities," *The Conversation*, August 24, 2022, https://theconversation.com/the-inflation-reduction -act-doesnt-get-around-the-supreme-courts-climate-ruling-in-west-virginia -v-epa-but-it-does-strengthen-epas-future-abilities-189279.

237 *"More gloom than doom":* David Wallace-Wells, "The Supreme Court's E.P.A. Decision Is More Gloom than Doom," *New York Times,* July 1, 2022.

237 *"a long-overdue step":* Jonathan Lesser, "New York's Climate Virtue-Signaling Will Condemn Millions to Energy Poverty," *National Review,* July 11, 2022, https://www.nationalreview.com/2022/07/new-yorks-climate-virtue -signaling-will-condemn-millions-to-energy-poverty/.

237 *"The contours of the major questions doctrine":* Revesz, "SCOTUS Ruling in *West Virginia v. EPA* Threatens All Regulation."

237 *Throughout the term the Court issued a mixed set of rulings:* On barring federal vaccine mandates for private sector employees, see *NFIB v. OSHA*, 595 U.S. ___, 142 S. Ct. 661 (2022). Gorsuch, Thomas, and Alito concurred and said that the mask mandate was barred by, among other things, the "nondelegation doctrine," the "major questions" doctrine, and *Chevron*. "If the statutory subsection the agency cites really did endow OSHA with the power it asserts, that law would likely constitute an unconstitutional delegation of legislative authority." Ibid. at 669. Dissenters Kagan, Breyer, and Sotomayor objected, noting that employees were required to work in person and put at risk by Covid spread in the workplace; this was a basic prophylactic step. For that position, which once would have easily commanded a majority, there were now three votes. Government's ability to require vaccinations to protect public health dates back to *Jacobson v. Massachusetts*, 197 U.S. 11 (1905). On the shadow docket, the Supreme Court let Maine require vaccinations for health care workers, following that precedent. *Does v. Mills*, 595 U.S. ___, 142 S. Ct. 17 (2021). It was the first vaccination case in a century to come before the Court. Gorsuch, Thomas, and Alito dissented. See Richard Hughes IV, "The Supreme Court and the Future of State Vaccine Requirements," *Health Affairs*, July 7, 2022, healthaffairs.org/do/10.1377/forefront.20220705.879853. The CDC's eviction moratorium was voided in *Alabama Association of Realtors v. HHS*, 594 U.S. ___, 141 S. Ct. 2485 (2021).

238 *graduate of Covenant College:* The school explains on its website that it is "Distinctly Christian: Our motto, 'In all things, Christ preeminent,' says

it all: We exist to glorify and make known the name of Jesus Christ." www
.covenant.edu.

238 *In 2022 she struck down:* Health Freedom Defense Fund, Inc. v. Biden, No
8:21-cv-1693-KKM-AEP, 2022 WL 1134138 (M.D. Fla., April 18, 2022).

238 *"It seems to me that mandatory masking":* Ilya Somin, "Federal Court Rules
Against CDC Transportation Mask Mandate," *Volokh Conspiracy,* April 19,
2022, https://reason.com/volokh/2022/04/19/federal-court-rules-against
-cdc-transportation-mask-mandate/.

238 *Amelia Bedelia:* Fabio Bertoni, "Samuel Alito's 'Amelia Bedelia' Reading
of the Constitution," *The New Yorker,* May 13, 2022, https://www.new
yorker.com/news/daily-comment/abortion-supreme-court-leak-samuel
-alito-originalism-amelia-bedelia.

239 *many years ahead of them:* According to public health data, a thirty-five-
year-old woman on average will live another forty-seven years. Social
Security Administration, *Actuarial Life Table,* https://www.sa.gov/oact
/STATS/table4c6.html.

239 *Due to an unresolved issue:* An examination of these injunctions, their history, and the uncertain standards that govern them is Zyan Siddique,
"Nationwide Injunctions," *Columbia Law Review* 117 (2017): 2095, https://
columbialawreview.org/content/nationwide-injunctions/.

239 *Perhaps the most unnerving: Jarkesy v. Securities and Exchange Commission,* 34
F.4th 446 (U.S. 5th Cir. 2022).

239 *More or less out of nowhere:* For a good summary and also a sense of the as-
tonishment brought on by the ruling, see Blake Emerson, "The 5th Circuit's Ambush Against the SEC Is Unprecedented and Shocking," *Slate,*
May 20, 2022, https://slate.com/news-and-politics/2022/05/5th-circuit
-sec-securities-fraud-civil-service.html.

240 *Under the Dodd-Frank law:* Dodd-Frank Wall Street Reform and Consumer
Protection Act, Pub. Law No. 111-203, § 929P, 124 Stat. 1376, 1862–64
(2010) (codified at 15 U.S.C. §§ 77h-1(g), 78u-2(a)(2), 80a-9(d), and 80b-3(i).

240 *"Administrative adjudication is a key":* Emerson, "The 5th Circuit's
Ambush."

240 *Active in the Federalist Society:* As a federal judge she served as a member of
the Board of Advisors for the Federalist Society's *Harvard Journal of Law
& Public Policy.*

240 *Elrod earlier had upheld:* See *Whole Woman's Health v. Cole,* 790 F.3d 563
(5th Cir. 2015).

241 *It even blames the whole thing on Woodrow Wilson:* Franklin Roosevelt, not
Woodrow Wilson, created the SEC. During World War I, Congress did
pass a law to scrutinize sales of securities over $100,000 to see if they
were in the "national interest." Wilson urged Congress to pass a federal
law "to prevent the fraudulent methods of promotion by which our people are annually fleeced of many millions of hard earned money." Such

proposals failed until 1933. See the authoritative history of the SEC: Joel Seligman, *The Transformation of Wall Street: A History of the Securities and Exchange Commission and Modern Corporate Finance*, 3rd ed. (New York: Aspen Publishers, 2003), 49.

241 *It cites a book promoted by Glenn Beck:* R. J. Walters, "Fox News Host Glenn Beck Puts Hillsdale College Professor Ronald J. Pestritto on the Map," *Michigan Live*, October 21, 2010, https://www.mlive.com/news/jackson /2010/10/fox_news_host_puts_hillsdale_c.html. Pestritto is a dean at conservative Hillsdale College. He has argued that "the ideas that gave rise to what is today called 'the administrative state' are fundamentally at odds with those that gave rise to our Constitution." Ronald Pestritto, "The Birth of the Administrative State: Where It Came from and What It Means for Limited Government," Heritage Foundation, November 20, 2007, https://www.heritage.org/political-process/report/the-birth-the -administrative-state-where-it-came-and-what-it-means-limited.

SIXTEEN: RACE AND DEMOCRACY

245 *"I'm not talking about":* Elena Kagan, Remarks at Ninth Circuit Judicial Conference, July 21, 2022.

246 *with a perfect winning record:* Dahlia Lithwick and Mark Joseph Stern, "Alito's Speech Mocking Foreign Leaders Has a Deeper, Darker Message," *Slate*, July 29, 2022, https://slate.com/news-and-politics/2022/07/alito -rome-religious-liberty-foreign-leaders-secularism.html. Other speakers included Cornel West and the director of the Vatican Museums.

246 *"This is a man":* Stephanie Barclay became director of the initiative in 2020. Then she served as a clerk for Gorsuch in the 2021–22 term. "One ND Law Professor and One Graduate Are Clerking at the U.S. Supreme Court This Term," press release, Notre Dame Law School, October 12, 2021, https://law.nd.edu/news-events/news/stephanie-barclay-alexa-baltes -supreme-court/. Barclay is a well-known advocate for religious liberty and has argued before the Court. She serves on the executive committee of the Federalist Society's Religious Liberties Practice Group.

247 *"I had the honor this term":* British prime minister Boris Johnson called *Dobbs* "a big step backwards." A few weeks before Alito spoke, conflict and scheming among his ministers forced the disheveled Johnson to announce his resignation. Macron had called abortion a fundamental right and said the Supreme Court had "compromised" women's freedoms. Trudeau called the ruling "horrific." "U.S. Supreme Court Justice Alito Mocks Foreign Critics of Abortion Ruling," Reuters, July 29, 2022.

247 *A Marquette University poll:* "New Marquette Law School Poll National Survey Finds Approval of the Supreme Court at New Lows, with Strong Partisan Differences over Abortion and Gun Rights," Marquette University,

July 20, 2022, https://www.marquette.edu/news-center/2022/new-mar
quette-law-poll-national-survey-finds-approval-of-supreme-court-at-new
-lows.php.

248   *Later in the summer:* Chuck Todd, Mark Murray, Ben Kamisar, Bridget
Bowman, and Alexandra Marquez, "Public's Opinion of Supreme
Court Plummets After Abortion Decision," NBC News, August 26, 2022,
https://www.nbcnews.com/meet-the-press/first-read/publics-opinion
-supreme-court-plummets-abortion-decision-rcna44962. The Court's approval rating had sunk to 35 percent positive and 42 percent negative
among registered voters. "And a combined 37% of voters say they have
very little or no confidence in the nation's highest court, versus 27% who
have great or quite a bit of confidence in the institution."

248   *voters in Kansas:* The "Kansas No State Constitutional Right to Abortion
and Legislative Power to Regulate Abortion Amendment" ballot measure read, "Because Kansans value both women and children, the constitution of the state of Kansas does not require government funding
of abortion and does not create or secure a right to abortion. To the
extent permitted by the constitution of the United States, the people,
through their elected state representatives and state senators, may pass
laws regarding abortion, including, but not limited to, laws that account for circumstances of pregnancy resulting from rape or incest, or
circumstances of necessity to save the life of the mother." https://sos
.ks.gov/elections/22elec/2022-Primary-Election-Constitutional-Amend
ment-HCR-5003.pdf.

248   *A 2019 state supreme court ruling had found:* The Kansas Supreme Court
had ruled six to one that the state constitution protected a right to an
abortion as part of a "right to autonomy." *Hodes & Nauser, MDs, P.A. v.
Schmidt,* 440 P.3d 461, 466 (Kan. 2019) (upholding a trial court order
granting a preliminary injunction to prevent enforcement of the Kansas Unborn Child Protection from Dismemberment Abortion Act, KAN.
STAT. ANN. §§ 65-6741 to 66-6749 (West 2018), which prohibits the di-
lation and evacuation abortion procedure).

248   *"wolf in sheep's clothing":* Memorandum from James Bopp Jr. and Court-
ney Milbank to David O'Steen and Mike Fichter, July 24, 2022, https://
d1ps7ys6589pid.cloudfront.net/wp-content/uploads/2022/07/BLF
-Legal-Memo-on-SB-1-1.pdf.

249   *be hard "to attract":* Kate Gibson, "Eli Lilly Pushes Back Against Indiana's
New Abortion Law," *CBS Moneywatch,* August 8, 2022, https://www.cbs
news.com/news/abortion-indiana-eli-lilly-cummins-roche/.

249   *Rev. Rob Schenck:* "'Operation Higher Court': Inside the Religious Right's
Efforts to Wine and Dine Supreme Court Justices," *Politico,* July 8,
2022, https://www.politico.com/news/2022/07/08/religious-right-supreme
-court-00044739; Kara Voght and Tim Dickinson, "SCOTUS Justices

'Prayed With' Her—Then Cited Her Bosses to End Roe," *Rolling Stone*, July 6, 2022, https://www.rollingstone.com/politics/politics-features/roe-supreme-court-justices-1378046/.

249   *In 2022 he wrote to John Roberts:* Jodi Kantor and Jo Becker, "Former Anti-Abortion Leader Alleges Another Supreme Court Breach," *New York Times*, November 19, 2022.

249   *A single donor:* Andrew Perez, Andy Kroll, and Justin Elliott, "How a Secretive Billionaire Handed His Fortune to the Architect of the Right-Wing Takeover of the Courts," *The Lever/Pro Publica*, August 22, 2022, https://www.propublica.org/article/dark-money-leonard-leo-barre-seid; Kenneth Vogel and Shane Goldmacher, "An Unusual $1.6 Billion Donation Bolsters Conservatives," *New York Times*, August 22, 2022.

249   *Marble Freedom Trust:* Chris McGreal, "Leonard Leo: The Secretive Rightwinger Using Billions to Reshape America," *The Guardian*, September 4, 2022.

250   *Even before* Brown: For a description of the Supreme Court's increasing willingness to rule for racial equality in the years before *Brown*, see Michael J. Klarman, *From Jim Crow to Civil Rights: The Supreme Court and the Struggle for Racial Equality* (New York: Oxford University Press, 2004), 171–235. Klarman identifies World War II as the catalyst, due to both the industrial and social upheavals caused by full-scale mobilization, and also the greater ideological opposition to racism expressed in the fight against the Third Reich. "The ideology of the war was antifascist and prodemocratic."

250   *The marquee cases:* The two cases were now known as *Students for Fair Admissions v. President and Fellows of Harvard* and *Students for Fair Admissions v. University of North Carolina.*

250   *In 1978, in* Bakke: *Regents of the University of California v. Bakke*, 438 U.S. 265 (1978). This was the first time that "diversity" as a legal rationale was embraced by the Court. See Goodwin Liu, "Affirmative Action in Higher Education: The Diversity Rationale and the Compelling Interest Test," *Harvard Civil Rights and Civil Liberties Law Review* 33 (1998): 381.

250   *In 2003, a white applicant challenged:* Grutter v. Bollinger, 539 U.S. 306 (2003).

251   *"a highly qualified, racially diverse":* Grutter v. Bollinger, Consolidated Brief of Lt. Gen. Julius W. Becton, Jr., Admiral Dennis Blair, Major General Charles Bolden, Hon. James M. Cannon, Lieutenant General Daniel W. Christman, General Wesley K. Clark, Sen. Max Cleland, Admiral Archie Clemins, Hon. William Cohen, Admiral William Crowe, General Ronald R. Fogelman, Lieutenant General Howard D. Graves, General Joseph P. Hoar, Sen. Robert J. Kerrety, et al. as *Amici Curiae* in Support of Respondents, February 19, 2003, https://www.armfor.uscourts.gov/new caaf/ConfHandout/2016ConfHandout/2016JPSchnapperCasterasGrutter VBollingerAmiciCuriaeBrief.pdf. On Gerald Ford's role, see University of

Michigan, "A Look Back at Grutter v. Bollinger," April 22, 2013, https://fordschool.umich.edu/news/2013/look-back-grutter-v-bollinger.

251   *a sharp drop in minority attendance:* Evan Thomas, *First: Sandra Day O'Connor* (New York: Random House, 2019), 351–52.

251   *" 'What I ask for the negro' ": Grutter v. Bollinger,* 539 U.S. 306 (2003) (Thomas, J., dissenting).

251   *The country has changed:* William H. Frey, "New 2020 Census Results Show Increased Diversity Countering Decade-Long Declines in America's White and Youth Populations," Brookings Institution, August 13, 2021, https://www.brookings.edu/research/new-2020-census-results-show -increased-diversity-countering-decade-long-declines-in-americas-white -and-youth-populations/. See also William H. Frey, *Diversity Explosion: How New Racial Demographics Are Remaking America* (Washington, D.C.: Brookings Institution Press, 2018).

252   *Yet the share of Black students:* That was especially acute in schools where voters had ended affirmative action. In 2006, Michigan voters passed Proposition Two, which prohibited state universities "discriminat[ing] against, or grant[ing] preferential treatment to, any individual or group on the basis of race, sex, color, ethnicity, or national origin in the operation of . . . public education." Mich. Const. art. I, §26(1). According to the University of Michigan, in a brief filed in the case challenging Harvard's plans, Black and Native American enrollment fell from 7 percent in 2003 to 4 percent in 2021. *Students for Fair Admissions v. President and Fellows of Harvard College,* "Brief for the University of Michigan in Support of Respondents," August 1, 2022, https://www.supremecourt.gov /DocketPDF/20/20-1199/232447/20220801155455154_Nos.%2020 -1199%2021-707%20U-M%20amicus%20ISO%20resps..pdf. The University of California at Berkeley showed a similar drop. Other briefs argued that inclusion of students identifying as more than one race showed no drop-off of diversity after Oklahoma banned affirmative action in 2012, for example. *Students for Fair Admissions v. President and Fellows of Harvard College,* "Brief of Oklahoma and Thirteen Other States in Support of Petitioner," March 31, 2022, https://www.supremecourt.gov /DocketPDF/20/20-1199/173604/20210331161510903_2021.03.31%20 Amicus%20of%20OK%20et%20al..pdf.

254   *"That's not a race-neutral": Merrill v. Milligan,* transcript of argument, October 4, 2022, 58–59, https://www.supremecourt.gov/oral_arguments /argument_transcripts/2022/21-1086_f204.pdf.

255   *"The Times, Places and Manner":* U.S. Constitution, Article I, Section 4, Clause 1.

255   *"it was impossible to foresee": Notes of Debates in the Federal Convention of 1787,* reported by James Madison (Athens: Ohio University Press, 1985) (August 9, 1787), 423–24.

255   *The framers knew:* Indeed, the drafting of these written state

constitutions—which in many cases supplanted earlier systems with
more power for the legislature—was a major achievement for the new
country. See Rosemarie Zagarri, "The Historian's Case Against the Independent State Legislature Theory," *Boston College Law Review* (March
2023) (forthcoming).

255 *Donald Trump and his legal team first floated the idea:* In *Bush v. Gore*, Chief
Justice William Rehnquist hinted at the theory in a concurrence. "Isolated sections of the code may well admit of more than one interpretation, but the general coherence of the legislative scheme may not be
altered by judicial interpretation so as to wholly change the statutorily
provided apportionment of responsibility among these various bodies."
Bush v. Gore, 531 U.S. 98, 114 (2000). However, Rehnquist was principally
talking about the Electors Clause, which assigns to the legislature the
ability to choose the manner of designating electors.

255 *Four of the sitting justices:* See, e.g., *Wise v. Circosta*, No. 20A71, 2020 WL
6305035, at *1 (U.S. October 28, 2020) (Justices Thomas, Alito, and
Gorsuch would have granted an application to enjoin the North Carolina State Board of Elections' extension of the state's absentee ballot receipt deadline, which was challenged based on the claim that the board
is not the "legislature" under the Elections and Electors Clauses); *Democratic National Committee. v. Wisconsin State Legislature*, No. 20A66, 2020
WL 6275871, at *2–*3 (U.S. October 26, 2020) (in denying an application to stay a Seventh Circuit decision—which stayed the district court's
order to extend the ballot receipt deadline—Justice Gorsuch, concurring, wrote that state legislatures, not judges or other state officials, bear
primary responsibility for setting election rules, and Justice Kavanaugh
agreed that designing electoral procedures is a "legislative task"); *Republican Party of Pa. v. Boockvar*, No. 20A54, 2020 WL 6128193, at *1 (U.S.
October 19, 2020) (Justices Thomas, Alito, Gorsuch, and Kavanaugh
would have granted an application to stay the Pennsylvania Supreme
Court's ruling to extend the mail ballot receipt deadline, which was
challenged based on the claim that the state court is not the "legislature" under the Elections and Electors Clauses). See Joshua A. Douglas,
"Undue Deference to States in the 2020 Election Litigation," *William and
Mary Bill of Rights Journal* 30 (2021): 59.

255 *In 2015 the chief justice dissented: Arizona State Legislature v. Arizona Independent Redistricting Commission*, 576 U.S. 787 (2015) (Roberts, C.J.,
dissenting).

256 *state courts under state constitutions could do so*: *Rucho v. Common Cause*, 588
U.S. ___, 139 S. Ct. 2484 (2019).

256 *There could be administrative chaos:* See *The Independent State Legislature
Theory and Its Potential to Disrupt Our Democracy, Before the Committee on Administration, U.S. House of Representatives*, 117th Cong., 2nd Sess. (2022)
(statement of Eliza Sweren-Becker), https://docs.house.gov/meetings

/HA/HA00/20220728/115042/HHRG-117-HA00-Wstate-Sweren-Becker
E-20220728.pdf.

256   *Federal judges would be called on to referee:* On the new role for federal judges, see Leah M. Litman and Katherine Shaw, "Textualism, Judicial Supremacy, and the Independent State Legislature Theory," *Wisconsin Law Review*, No. 5 (2022): 1236.

256   *Luttig calls the ISLT claim:* J. Michael Luttig, "Opinion: The Republican Blueprint to Steal the 2024 Election," CNN.com, April 27, 2022, https://www.cnn.com/2022/04/27/opinions/gop-blueprint-to-steal-the-2024-election-luttig/index.html.

257   *"the most important case":* J. Michael Luttig, "There Is Absolutely Nothing to Support the 'Independent State Legislature' Theory," *The Atlantic*, October 3, 2022, https://www.theatlantic.com/ideas/archive/2022/10/moore-v-harper-independent-legislature-theory-supreme-court/671625/.

257   *a Colorado artist: 303 Creative LLC v. Elenis*, No. 19-1413 (10th Cir. July 26, 2021).

257   *Section 230:* The case being appealed is *Gonzalez v. Google LLC*, 2 F.4th 871 (9th Cir. 2021). Section 230 is part of the Communications Act of 1934, 47 U.S.C. § 230. This reflects changes made in the Communications Decency Act, Pub. L. No. 104-104, Tit. V, 110 Stat. 133 (1996), early in the internet era.

CONCLUSION: WE THE PEOPLE

260   *National exit polls:* William Saletan, "The Data Have Spoken: Abortion Was a Decisive Issue in the 2022 Midterms," *The Bulwark*, November 11, 2022, https://www.thebulwark.com/the-data-have-spoken-abortion-was-a-decisive-issue-in-the-2022-midterms/.

260   *Lilly Ledbetter: Ledbetter v. Goodyear Tire & Rubber Co.*, 550 U.S. 618 (2007) was undone by the Lilly Ledbetter Fair Pay Act of 2009 (Pub.L. 111–2, S. 181).

260   *Such legislative responses:* Matthew R. Christiansen and William N. Eskridge Jr., "Congressional Overrides of Supreme Court Statutory Interpretation Decisions, 1967–2011," *Texas Law Review* 92 (2014): 1317.

261   *Spending and tax powers:* The Spending Clause (U.S. Constitution, Article I, Section 8, Clause 1) broadly authorizes spending for the "general Welfare." The Necessary and Proper Clause (U.S. Constitution, Article I, Section 8, Clause 18) gives Congress power to condition receipt of the funds. These provisions provoked an early debate among the Founders. Madison later claimed that the "general welfare" language merely referred to other enumerated powers in the Constitution; Hamilton argued that "the clause confers a power separate and distinct from those later enumerated."

261 *Every state constitution but one:* Joshua A. Douglas, "The Right to Vote Under State Constitutions," *Vanderbilt Law Review* 67 (2019): 89, https://schol arship.law.vanderbilt.edu/vlr/vol67/iss1/1. That one state is Rhode Island.

261 *state courts in Alaska:* Cases include those in Ohio (*League of Women Voters of Ohio v. Ohio Redistricting Comm'n,* Nos. 2021-1193,—— N.E.3d——, 2022 WL 110261 (Ohio Jan. 12, 2022) (legislative); *Adams v. DeWine,* No. 2021-1428,—— N.E.3d——, 2022 WL 129092 (Ohio January 14, 2022) (congressional)), New York (*Harkenrider v. Hochul,* No. 60,—— N.E.3d——, 2022 WL 1236822 (N.Y. April 27, 2022) (congressional and state senate)), North Carolina: *Harper v. Hall,* 868 S.E.2d 499 (N.C. 2022) (legislative and congressional), Maryland: *Szeliga v. Lamone,* No. C-02-CV-21-001816 (Md. Cir. Ct. December 23, 2021) (congressional), and Alaska (*In re 2021 Redistricting Cases,* No. S-18332 (Alaska March 25, 2022) (legislative)).

262 *amendments come in clusters:* Ten amendments were ratified in 1791, of course. The three Civil War amendments were ratified over five years from 1865 to 1870. Three were ratified between 1913 and 1919. Four were ratified in the decade between 1961 (giving the District of Columbia presidential electors) and 1971 (lowering the voting age to eighteen nationwide). The only one since then, addressing congressional pay, actually had largely been approved along with the rest of the Bill of Rights, but did not achieve final ratification until 1992.

262 *Often these have overturned:* The Eleventh Amendment in 1795 overturned *Chisholm v. Georgia,* 2 U.S. 419 (1793), which had allowed citizens of one state to sue another state in federal court. As described in Chapter Three, the Thirteenth and Fourteenth Amendments (and arguably the Fifteenth) overturned *Dred Scott v. Sandford.* The Seventeenth Amendment authorizing an income tax overturned *Pollock v. Farmers' Loan and Trust Co.,* 157 U.S. 429 (1895), described in Chapter Four of this book. The Nineteenth Amendment, which guaranteed women the right to vote, effectively overturned *Minor v. Happersett,* 88 U.S. 162 (1875). The Twenty-fourth Amendment, which ended the poll tax levied on voters, overturned *Breedlove v. Suttles,* 302 U.S. 277 (1937). The Twenty-sixth Amendment, establishing that eighteen-year-old citizens could vote in state as well as federal elections, responded to *Oregon v. Mitchell,* 400 U.S. 112 (1970), which had limited that change only to federal elections. The comprehensive account of how amendments have been added to the Constitution is John F. Kowal and Wilfred U. Codrington III, *The People's Constitution: 200 Years, 27 Amendments, and the Promise of a More Perfect Union* (New York: The New Press, 2021).

262 *"the tragedies of the civil rights movement":* Obama made this point in an interview, available at missrnc08, "2001 Obama WBEZ Interview Redistribution Wealth Warren Court," YouTube video, www.youtube.com/watch ?v=OkpdNtTgQNM. During the 2008 presidential campaign his thoughtful point was distorted into proof of his radicalism. Senator

John McCain's campaign had charged the interview proved then Senator Obama wanted to redistribute wealth through the courts. The tape
and transcript showed Obama was actually making the opposite point.

262   *One in four women:* Rachel Jones and Jenna Jerman, "Population Group
      Abortion Rates and Lifetime Incidence of Abortion: United States,
      2008–2014," *American Journal of Public Health* 112 (September 2022): 9,
      https://doi.org/10.2105/AJPH.2017.304042.

262   *Three quarters happen:* Usha Ranji, Karen Diep, and Alina Salganicoff,
      "Key Facts on Abortion in the United States," Kaiser Family Foundation,
      July 12, 2022, https://www.kff.org/womens-health-policy/report/key-facts
      -on-abortion-in-the-united-states/.

262   *"a common but unrecognized problem":* Jamal Greene, *How Rights Went
      Wrong: Why Our Obsession with Rights Is Tearing America Apart* (New York:
      Houghton Mifflin Harcourt, 2021), ix.

263   *the popular vote loser:* Al Gore won 547,398 more votes than George W.
      Bush (48.4 to 47.9 percent), and Hillary Clinton won 2.9 million more
      votes than Donald Trump (48.2 to 46.1 percent). In 2004, Bush won 3.3
      million more votes than John Kerry (50.7 to 48.3 percent). But if 60,000
      votes in Ohio had switched out of the more than 5.6 million cast, Kerry
      would have been elected president.

263   *the only major constitutional democracy:* "Among the world's democracies, at
      least 27 have term limits for their constitutional courts. And those that do
      not have term limits, such as the Supreme Court of the United Kingdom,
      typically impose age limits." Presidential Commission on the Supreme
      Court of the United States, *Final Report,* December, 2021, 112, https://
      www.whitehouse.gov/pcscotus/final-report/.

263   *With younger nominees:* Until the 1960s, justices typically served fifteen
      years; now they average twenty-six years. Ibid., 18. According to one of
      the founders of the Federalist Society, Steven Calabresi, during the pe-
      riod between 1941 and 1970, justices left the Court after an average of
      twelve years. Steven G. Calabresi and James Lindgren, "Term Limits for
      the Supreme Court: Life Tenure Reconsidered," in Roger C. Cramton
      and Paul D. Carrington, eds., *Reforming the Court: Term Limits for Supreme
      Court Justices* (Durham, NC: Carolina Academic Press, 2006), 23.

264   *Many argue:* See, for example, "H.R.8500 - To amend title 28, United
      States Code, to provide for the duration of active service of justices of
      the Supreme Court, and for other purposes," 117th Cong., 2d Sess., in-
      troduced in House, July 26, 2022.

264   *past cases have suggested: Booth v. United States,* 291 U.S. 339 (1934).

264   *Most plans would limit:* See Alicia Bannon, "An Overlooked Idea for
      Fixing the Supreme Court," Brennan Center for Justice (March 12,
      2021), https://www.brennancenter.org/our-work/analysis-opinion/over
      looked-idea-fixing-supreme-court; Daniel Hemel, "Can Structural Changes
      Fix the Supreme Court," *Journal of Economic Perspectives* 35, no. 1 (Winter

2021): 119; and Frederick A. O. Schwarz, "Saving the Supreme Court," *Democracy*, Fall 2019, https://democracyjournal.org/magazine/54/saving
-the-supreme-court/.

264   *In a May 2022 Quinnipiac poll, 69 percent:* Quinnipiac University Poll,
      "Nearly 7 in 10 Favor a Limit on How Long SCOTUS Justices Can Serve,
      Quinnipiac University National Poll Finds; 85 Percent of Americans
      Expect Economic Recession in Next Year," news release, May 18, 2022,
      https://poll.qu.edu/poll-release?releaseid=3846. The wording of the question
      was straightforward: "Do you support or oppose limiting the number of
      years a Supreme Court Justice can serve on the Supreme Court?"

264   *An annual survey conducted by professors:* Stephen Jessee, Neil Malhotra, and
      Maya Sen, "SCOTUSPoll 2021," Supreme Court Public Opinion Project
      (2021), https://projects.iq.harvard.edu/scotus-poll. See also Maya Sen,
      "Written Testimony: Maya Sen Professor of Public Policy John F. Ken-
      nedy School of Government Harvard University," Presidential Commis-
      sion on the Supreme Court of the United States, June 30, 2021, https://
      scholar.harvard.edu/files/msen/files/sen-testimony-scotuscomission.pdf.

264   *"considerable, bipartisan support":* Presidential Commission on the Su-
      preme Court, *Final Report*, 111.

264   *the National Constitution Center had asked:* Robert P. George, Michael W.
      McConnell, Colleen A. Sheehan, and Ilan Wurman, *The Conservative Con-
      stitution*, National Constitution Center (2020), and Caroline Fredrickson,
      Jamal Greene, and Melissa Murray, *The Progressive Constitution*, National
      Constitution Center (2020). Both are available at The Constitution Draft-
      ing Project, National Constitution Center (2020), https://constitution
      center.org/debate/special-projects/constitution-drafting-project.

265   *Authoritarians around the world:* Presidential Commission on the Supreme
      Court, *Final Report*, 81.

265   *the idea is truly unpopular:* See, for example, a Marist/*PBS NewsHour* poll
      conducted just after the *Dobbs* decision. Despite wide opposition to that
      ruling, only 34 percent of adults surveyed supported court expansion,
      and 54 percent opposed. (The question: "Given the majority decision
      to overturn Roe versus Wade, do you favor or oppose adding justices
      to expand the U.S. Supreme Court?") NPR/*PBS NewsHour*/Marist Na-
      tional Poll, "The Overturning of *Roe v. Wade*, June 2022," June 27, 2022,
      https://maristpoll.marist.edu/polls/npr-pbs-newshour-marist-national
      -poll-the-overturning-of-roe-v-wade-june-2022/.

265   *"not the cause, but the catalyst":* Jeff Shesol, *Supreme Power: Franklin Roosevelt
      v. the Supreme Court* (New York: W. W. Norton, 2010), 525.

266   *The Judicial Conference of the United States:* "Judiciary Seeks New Judgeships,
      Reaffirms Need for Enhanced Security," Judicial Conference of the
      United States, press release, March 16, 2021, https://www.uscourts.gov
      /news/2021/03/16/judiciary-seeks-new-judgeships-reaffirms-need-en

hanced-security. The Judicial Conference is the policymaking body for the federal judiciary.

266 *the first fully American dictionary:* None other than Noah Webster himself declared that "very attempt to make perpetual constitutions, is the assumption of a right to control the opinions of future generations; and to legislate for those over whom we have as little authority as we have over a nation in Asia." Noah Webster (writing as Giles Hickory), "On Bills of Rights," *American Magazine* 1 (December 1787): 13, 14, cited in Michael W. McConnell, "Textualism and the Dead Hand of the Past," *George Washington Law Review* 66 (1997): 1127.

266 *its flaws are on full display:* Many of these contradictions and flaws are well described in a compact book by the law school dean at Berkeley, Erwin Chemerinsky, *Worse Than Nothing: The Dangerous Fallacy of Originalism* (New Haven: Yale University Press, 2022).

266 *Just four years after:* Anonymously, James Madison wrote "A Candid State of Parties." "For the *National Gazette*, 22 September 1792," Founders Online, National Archives, https://founders.archives.gov/documents /Madison/01-14-02-0334. Original source: *The Papers of James Madison, vol. 14, 6 April 1791 16 March 1793,* ed. Robert A. Rutland and Thomas A. Mason (Charlottesville: University Press of Virginia, 1983), pp. 370–372.

266 *In fact, the Founders delegated plenty:* See Julian Davis Mortenson and Nicholas Bagley, "Delegation at the Founding," *Columbia Law Review* 121, no. 2 (2021): 277. *Slate* lauded this essay as "one of the most important and topical scholarly articles in recent memory." That fact is itself a sign of the distortions brought on by the arrival of originalism. Mark Joseph Stern, "Neil Gorsuch Supports an Originalist Theory That Would Destroy Modern Governance," *Slate*, March 19, 2021, https://slate.com/news-and-politics/2021/03/neil-gorsuch-nondelegation -bagley-mortenson.html.

267 *a form of living constitutionalism:* See Michael Waldman, *The Second Amendment: A Biography* (New York: Simon & Schuster, 2014), 130; and Reva B. Siegel, "Memory Games: Dobbs's Originalism as Anti-Democratic Living Constitutionalism—and Some Pathways for Resistance," *Texas Law Review* 101 (2023 forthcoming).

267 *"The Constitution of the United States":* Franklin D. Roosevelt, "Address on Constitution Day," September 17, 1937, Washington, D.C., https://www .presidency.ucsb.edu/node/208747.

267 *Such moments create:* See Bruce Ackerman, *We the People*, vols. 1–3 (Cambridge: Belknap Press, 1991, 2000, 2018), for a sweeping description of such "constitutional moments."

267 *And what happened after that?:* Some of the liberal justices intermittently pushed this approach. Stephen Breyer in effect wrote a response to *Heller* in a case five years later, looking at whether a commissioner on the

National Labor Relations Board could be named by a president through a "recess appointment" without Senate confirmation. Breyer's ruling answered Scalia. Yes, Breyer wrote, the original public meaning of the constitutional provision matters. That was in 1787. Breyer then traced the development of the law in the more than two centuries after that. He began to find a way to make the full history of the development of our system and country matter. *NLRB v. Noel Canning*, 573 U.S. 513 (2014). Ruth Bader Ginsburg did the same in a 2015 ruling on the Elections Clause.

268 *a charter for a thriving and equal democracy:* Stephen Breyer argued for this view—that above all, the Constitution is "centrally focused" on "the right of individuals to participate in democratic self-government," in a book, *Active Liberty.* Stephen Breyer, *Active Liberty: Interpreting Our Democratic Constitution* (New York: Alfred A. Knopf, 2005), 21.

268 *For a short time:* A point made by Ian Millhiser, "The Uncomfortable Problem with Roe v. Wade," *Vox*, August 2, 2022, https://www.vox.com /policy-and-politics/23219138/supreme-court-roe-wade-substantive-due -process-samuel-alito.

268 *Public support for same sex marriage:* Justin McCarthy, "Same-Sex Marriage Support Inches Up to New High of 71%," Gallup, June 1, 2022, https:// news.gallup.com/poll/393197/same-sex-marriage-support-inches-new -high.aspx.

269 *Until recently:* On July 1, 2015, Gallup reported, 76 percent of Democrats approved of the way the Supreme Court "is handling its job," versus 18 percent of Republicans and 49 percent of independents. Mohamed Younis, "Democrats' Approval of Supreme Court at Record-Low 13%," Gallup, August 2, 2022, https://news.gallup.com/poll/395387/democrats -approval-supreme-court-record-low.aspx.

269 *"As absurd as it was": The Contemporary Debate over Supreme Court Reform: Origins and Perspectives,* written statement of Nikolas Bowie, Presidential Commission on the Supreme Court of the United States, June 30, 2021, https://www.whitehouse.gov/wp-content/uploads/2021/06/Bowie-SCOTUS -Testimony.pdf.

269 *"We are not final": Brown v. Allen*, 344 U.S. 443 (1953), at 540 (Jackson, J., concurring).

Index

Warren Court (*cont.*)
Brown and, 4, 51–54, 250
Plessy overturned by, 130
as reluctant to strike down laws passed by Congress, 58
Washington, George, 10, 12, 180, 186, 263
Washington administration, 14
Washington v. Glucksberg, 147–48, 206
Watergate scandal, 65, 71, 164
Weber, Max, 198
Webster, Daniel, 19
Webster, Noah, 266, 363
Wellspring Committee, 76
West Coast Hotel v. Parrish, 46, 338
West Virginia, 229
abortion laws in, 213
West Virginia v. EPA, 220, 229–32, 235, 236, 239
What's the Matter with Kansas (Frank), 248
Whigs, 20
white supremacists, 192
Whitmer, Gretchen, 213
Whole Women's Health, 117
Wicker, Roger, 140
Will, George F., 166
Williams, Juan, 153–54
Wills, Garry, 64
Wilson, James, 9–10, 14
Wilson, Woodrow, 39, 69, 231, 275, 353
Supreme Court nominations by, 69, 300
Wisconsin, 25, 188, 260
abortion laws in, 213
women, 4, 36, 42, 188, 207–8, 218, 219, 267, 328
abortion and, *see* abortion; abortion laws; abortion rights
activism of, 5, 35
Black, 118, 206
citizenship denied to, 208
domestic disputes and, 199
Equal Rights Amendment and, 262
on federal courts, 85–86
gender gap and, 141
political activism of, 35
on Supreme Court, *see also specific justices*
U.S. population of, 141
voting rights for, 31, 39, 360
Women's March (2017), 91
women's movement, 56
women's rights, 36, 56, 62
Woodward, Bob, 64
Works Progress Administration (WPA), 42
World War I, 59
World War II, 49, 51
writ of habeas corpus, 26

Yale Law School, 153, 169
Yale University, 132–33
Yates, Robert, 13
Year of the Woman (1992), 156
Yost, Dave, 24
YouTube, ISIS recruitment videos on, 257

Ziegler, Mary, 85